S0-BYC-517

桂　　正　和

Masakazu Katsura

I still mostly play dance music while I work, but it's been a year now since I started writing *I"s*, and right now I'm really into the Village People. In volume 2, I wrote that I liked '80s Euro-beat, but now I've gone back ten more years. I really loved the song "Macho Man" when I was a kid. I recorded it off the radio and listened to it all the time. Even now, whenever I hear "Go West," I still get a little teary-eyed. The lyrics are great.

When Masakazu Katsura was a high school student, he entered a story he had drawn into a manga contest in hopes of winning money to buy a stereo. He won the contest and was soon published in the immensely popular weekly manga anthology magazine *WEEKLY SHONEN JUMP*. Katsura was quickly propelled into manga-artist stardom, and his subsequent comic series, *WINGMAN*, *VIDEO GIRL AI*, *DNA²*, and *SHADOW LADY* are perennial fan favorites. *I"s*, which began publication in 1997, also inspired an original video series. Katsura lives in Tokyo and possesses an extensive collection of Batman memorabilia.

I"s

VOL. 5: BURNT PAST
The SHONEN JUMP ADVANCED Graphic Novel Edition

STORY AND ART BY
MASAKAZU KATSURA

English Adaptation/Lance Caselman
Translation/Joe Yamazaki
Touch-up Art & Lettering/Freeman Wong
Design/Hidemi Sahara
Editor/Nancy Thistlethwaite

Managing Editor/Elizabeth Kawasaki
Director of Production/Noboru Watanabe
Vice President of Publishing/Alvin Lu
Vice President & Editor in Chief/Yumi Hoashi
Sr. Director of Acquisitions/Rika Inouye
Vice President of Sales & Marketing/Liza Coppola
Publisher/Hyoe Narita

I"S © 1997 by Masakazu Katsura. All rights reserved.
First published in Japan in 1997 by SHUEISHA Inc., Tokyo. English translation rights in the
United States of America and Canada arranged by SHUEISHA Inc.
Some scenes containing nudity and sexual situations have been modified
from the original Japanese edition. The stories, characters and incidents mentioned
in this publication are entirely fictional.

No portion of this book may be reproduced or transmitted in any form or by any means without
written permission from the copyright holders.

Printed in the U.S.A.

Published by VIZ Media, LLC
P.O. Box 77010
San Francisco, CA 94107

SHONEN JUMP ADVANCED Graphic Novel Edition
10 9 8 7 6 5 4 3 2 1
First printing, December 2005

PARENTAL ADVISORY
I"S is rated T+ for Older Teen and is recommended
for ages 16 and up. This volume contains harsh
language and sexual situations.

www.viz.com

THE WORLD'S MOST
CUTTING-EDGE MANGA

SHONEN JUMP ADVANCED

www.shonenjump.com

SHONEN JUMP ADVANCED GRAPHIC NOVEL

Vol. 5
BURNT PAST

STORY & ART BY
MASAKAZU KATSURA

Vol. 5

CONTENTS

Chapter 36 Three Gates 5

Chapter 37 A Crumbling Memory 25

Chapter 38 Opened Recollection 43

Chapter 39 The First Problem 61

Chapter 40 Words From a Dream......... 78

Chapter 41 One Answer..................... 96

Chapter 42 Stop Wavering! 115

Chapter 43 Children's Conversation 135

Chapter 44 Self-Doubt 154

Chapter 45 Unknown World 172

I"s

アイズ

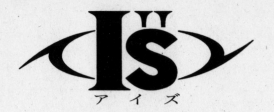

Chapter 36: Three Gates

I̋s

READ THIS WAY

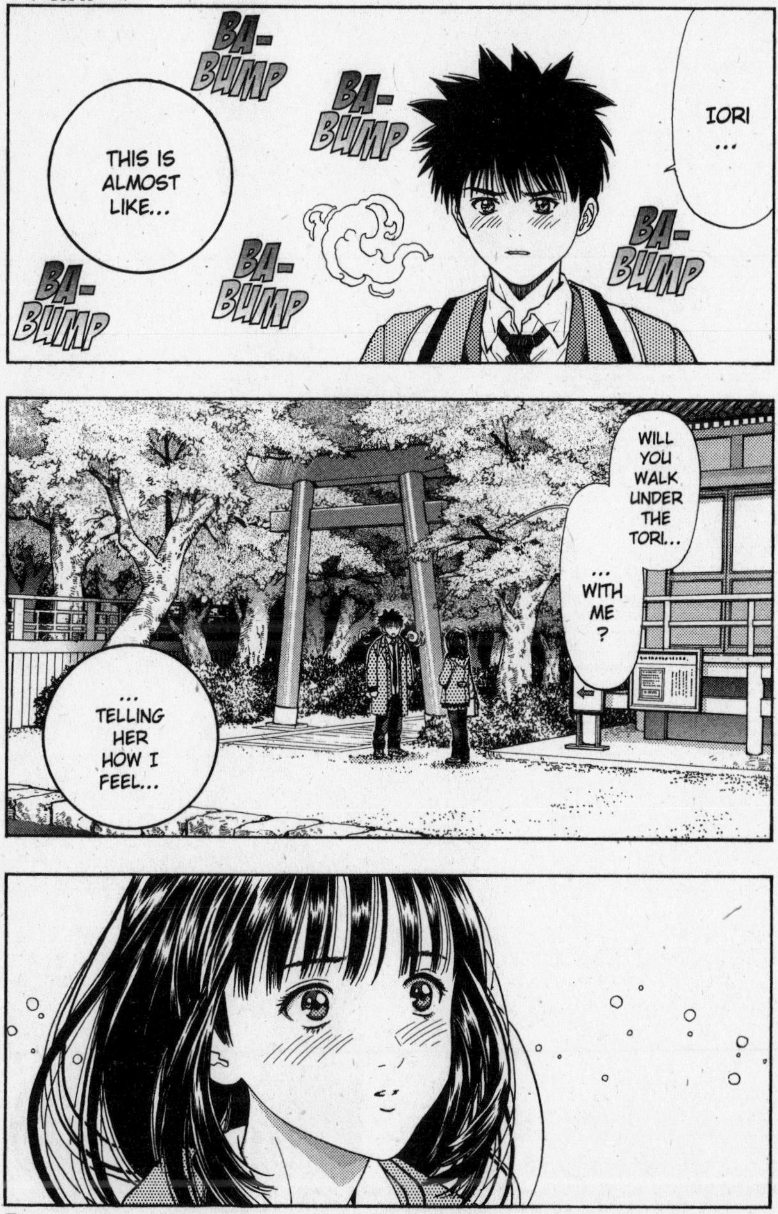
IORI ...
BA-BUMP
BA-BUMP
BA-BUMP
THIS IS ALMOST LIKE...
BA-BUMP
BA-BUMP
WILL YOU WALK UNDER THE TORI...
... WITH ME ?
... TELLING HER HOW I FEEL...

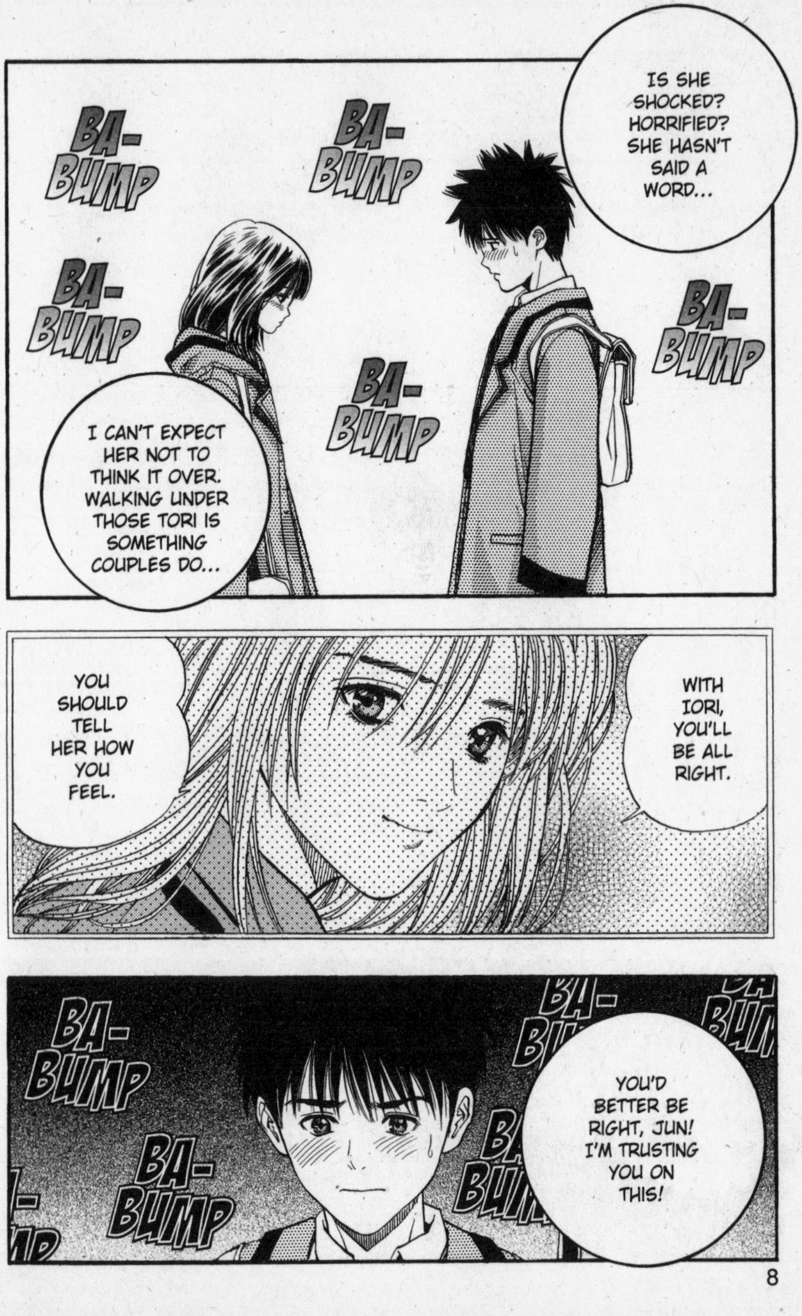
IS SHE SHOCKED? HORRIFIED? SHE HASN'T SAID A WORD...
BA-BUMP
BA-BUMP
BA-BUMP
BA-BUMP
BA-BUMP
I CAN'T EXPECT HER NOT TO THINK IT OVER. WALKING UNDER THOSE TORI IS SOMETHING COUPLES DO...
WITH IORI, YOU'LL BE ALL RIGHT.
YOU SHOULD TELL HER HOW YOU FEEL.
YOU'D BETTER BE RIGHT, JUN! I'M TRUSTING YOU ON THIS!
BA-BUMP
BA-BUMP
BA-BUMP

READ THIS WAY

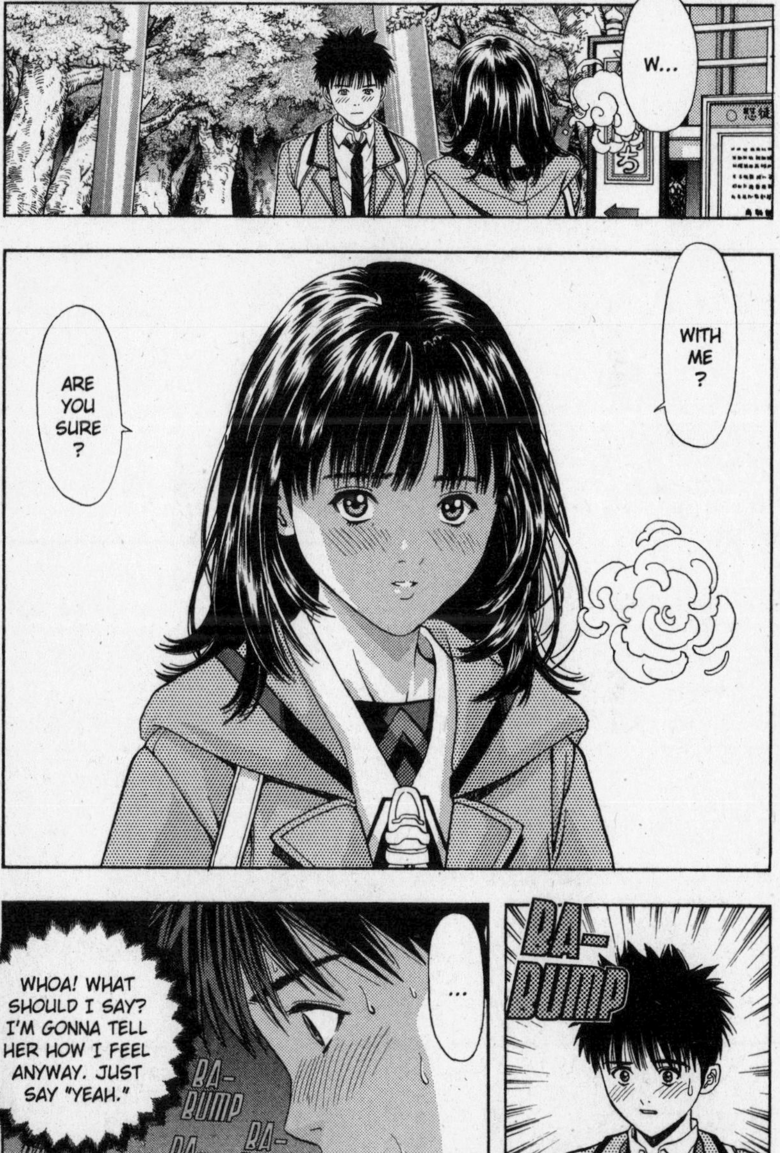
W...
WITH ME?
ARE YOU SURE?
BA-BUMP
...
WHOA! WHAT SHOULD I SAY? I'M GONNA TELL HER HOW I FEEL ANYWAY. JUST SAY "YEAH."
BA-BUMP
BA-BUMP
BA-BUMP
BA-BUMP

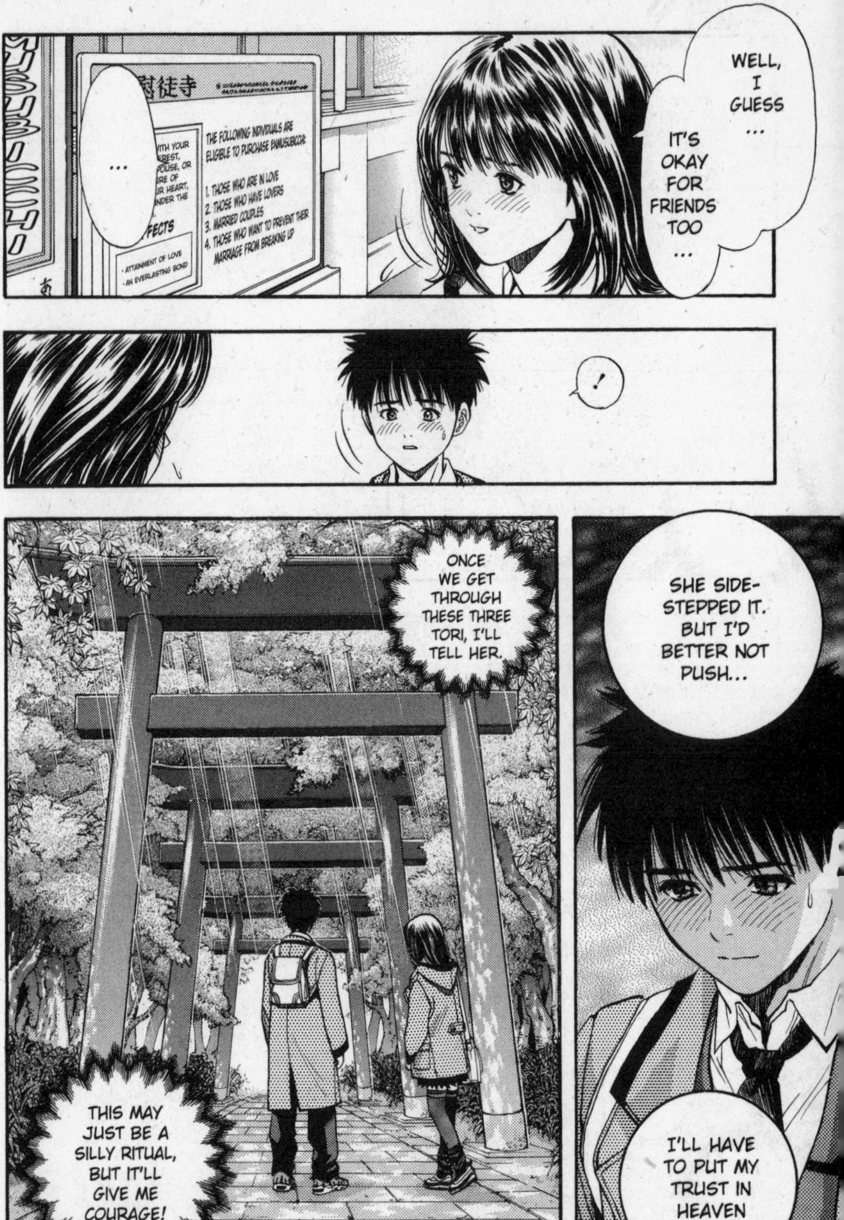

WELL, I GUESS...
IT'S OKAY FOR FRIENDS TOO...
...
THE FOLLOWING INDIVIDUALS ARE ELIGIBLE TO PURCHASE ENMUSUBICCHI:
1. THOSE WHO ARE IN LOVE
2. THOSE WHO HAVE LOVERS
3. MARRIED COUPLES
4. THOSE WHO WANT TO PREVENT THEIR MARRIAGE FROM BREAKING UP
· ATTAINMENT OF LOVE
· AN EVERLASTING BOND
!
SHE SIDE-STEPPED IT. BUT I'D BETTER NOT PUSH...
I'LL HAVE TO PUT MY TRUST IN HEAVEN HERE...
ONCE WE GET THROUGH THESE THREE TORI, I'LL TELL HER.
THIS MAY JUST BE A SILLY RITUAL, BUT IT'LL GIVE ME COURAGE!

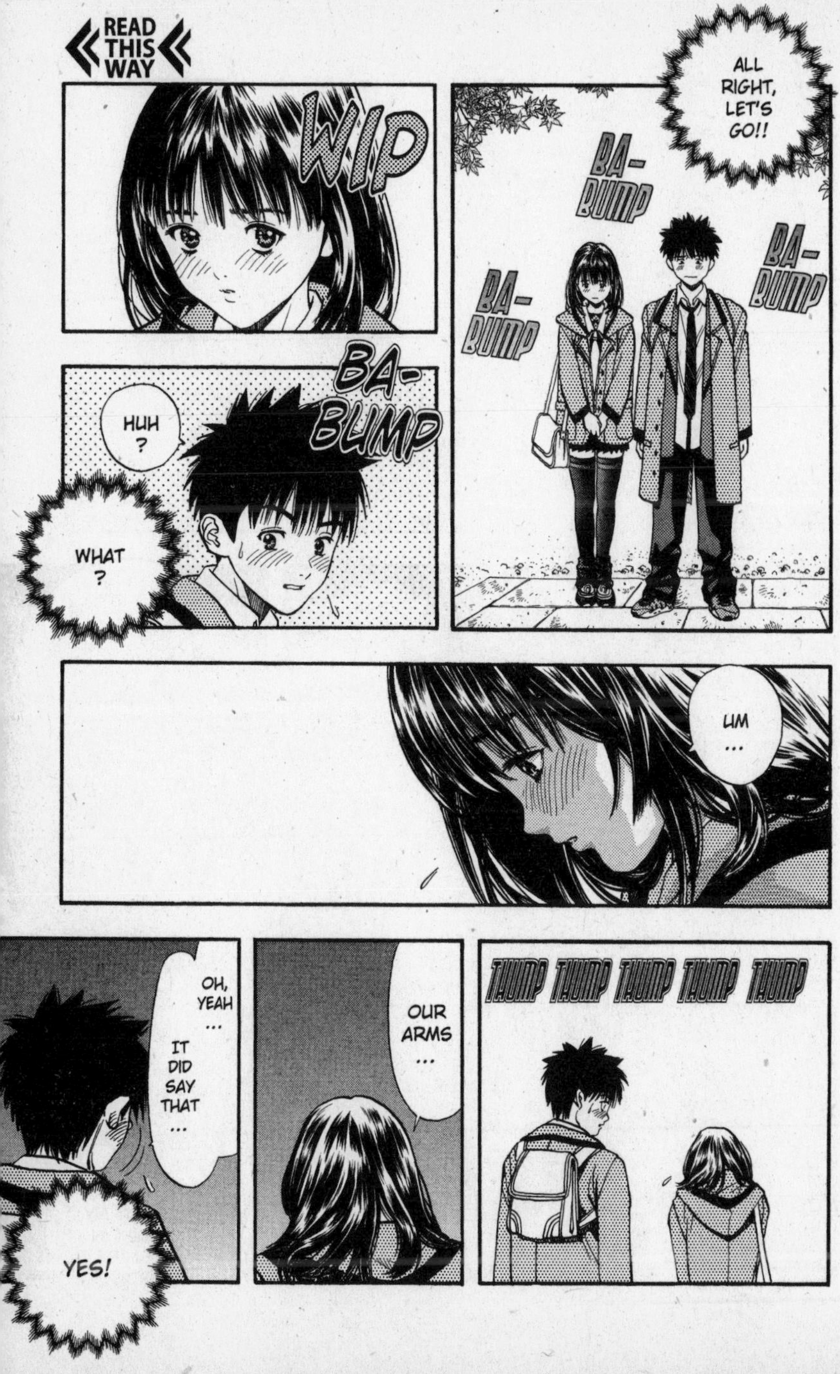
READ THIS WAY
ALL RIGHT, LET'S GO!!
BA-BUMP
BA-BUMP
BA-BUMP
WIP
BA-BUMP
HUH?
WHAT?
UM...
THUMP THUMP THUMP THUMP THUMP
OUR ARMS...
OH, YEAH...
IT DID SAY THAT...
YES!

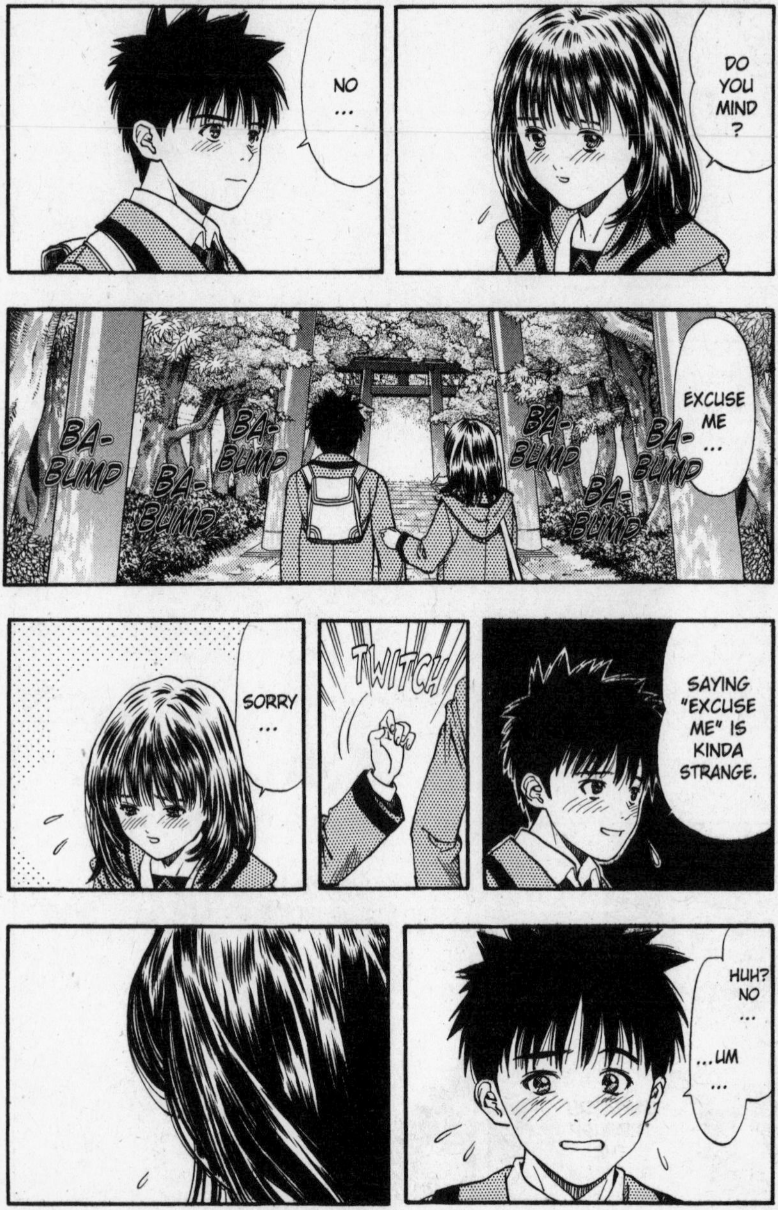
DO YOU MIND ?
NO ...
EXCUSE ME ...
BA-BUMP
BA-BUMP
BA-BUMP
BA-BUMP
BA-BUMP
BA-BUMP
SAYING "EXCUSE ME" IS KINDA STRANGE.
TWITCH
SORRY ...
HUH? NO ...
...UM ...

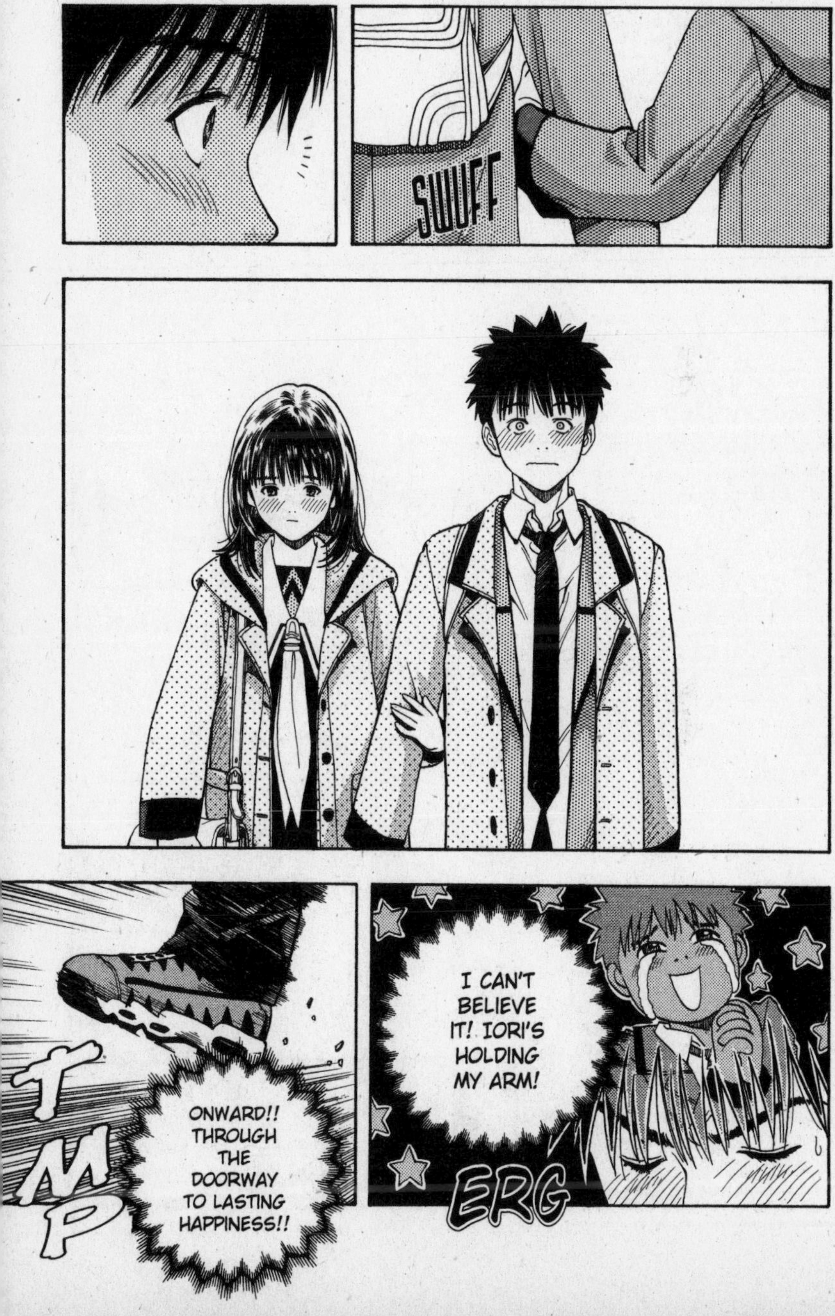
SWUFF
I CAN'T BELIEVE IT! IORI'S HOLDING MY ARM!
ERG
TMP
ONWARD!! THROUGH THE DOORWAY TO LASTING HAPPINESS!!

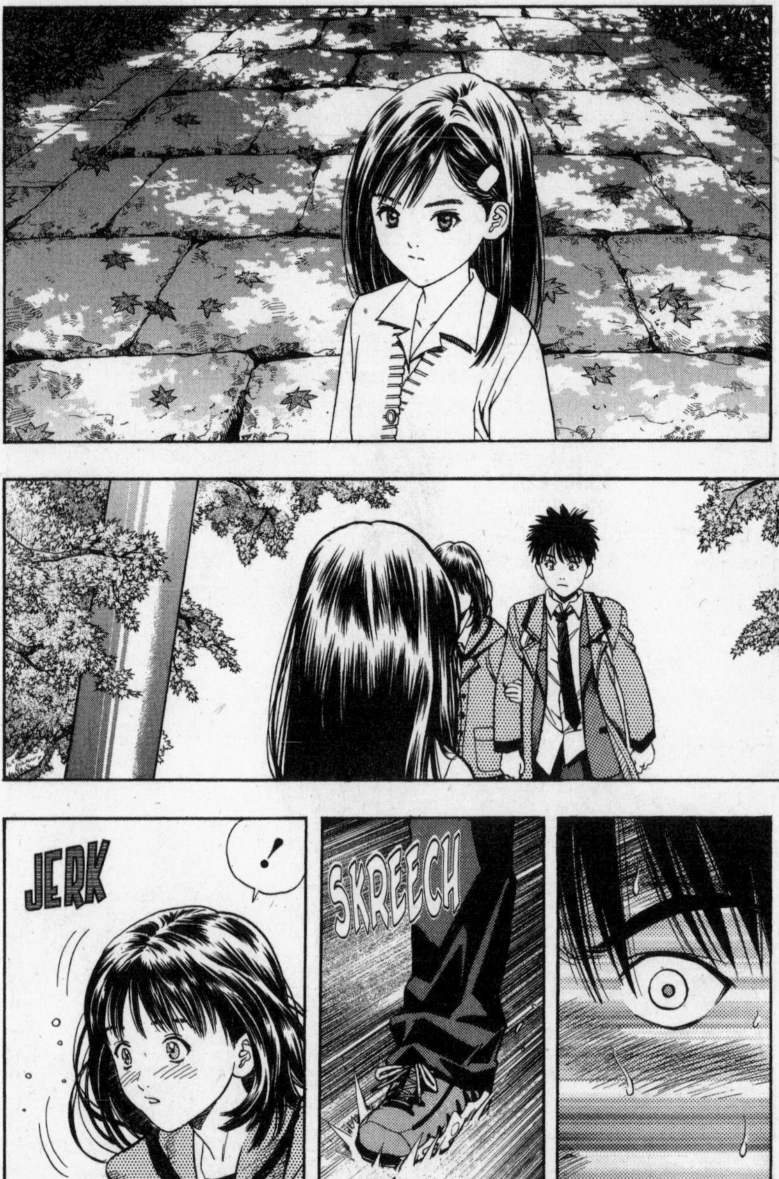
SKREECH
JERK
!

READ THIS WAY

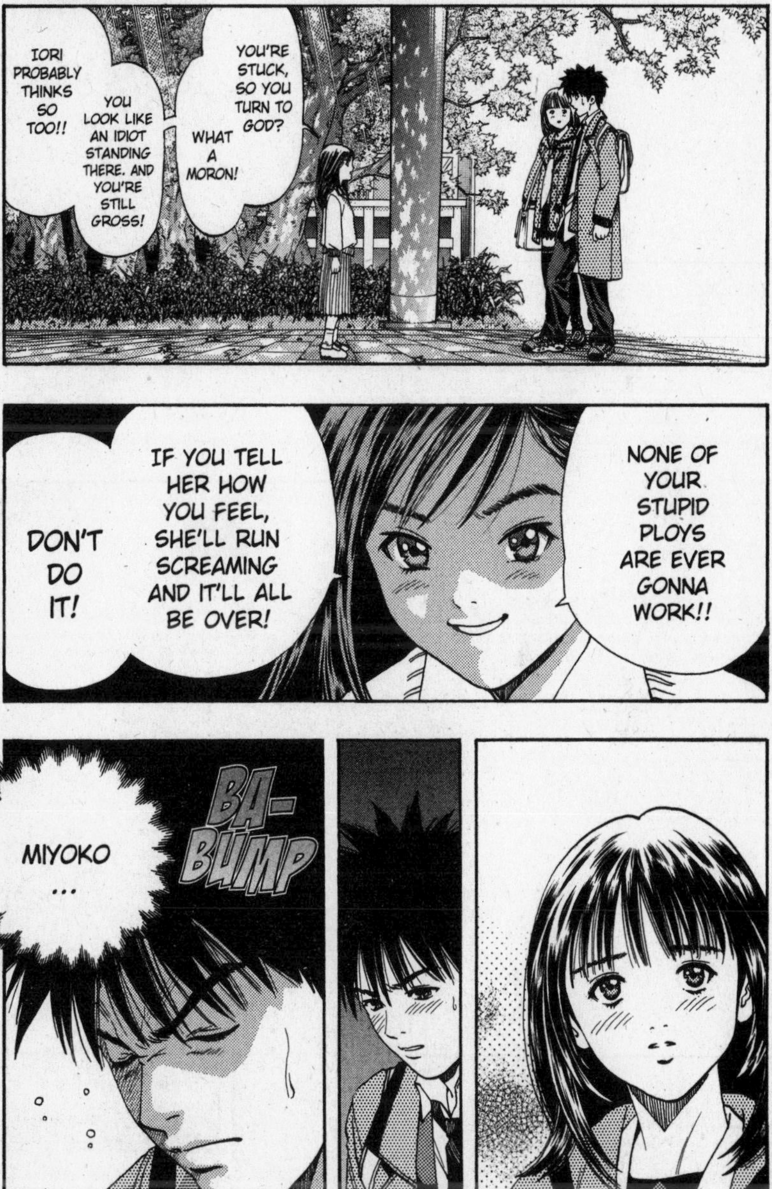

YOU'RE STUCK, SO YOU TURN TO GOD?
WHAT A MORON!
YOU LOOK LIKE AN IDIOT STANDING THERE. AND YOU'RE STILL GROSS!
IORI PROBABLY THINKS SO TOO!!
NONE OF YOUR STUPID PLOYS ARE EVER GONNA WORK!!
IF YOU TELL HER HOW YOU FEEL, SHE'LL RUN SCREAMING AND IT'LL ALL BE OVER!
DON'T DO IT!
BA-BUMP
MIYOKO ...

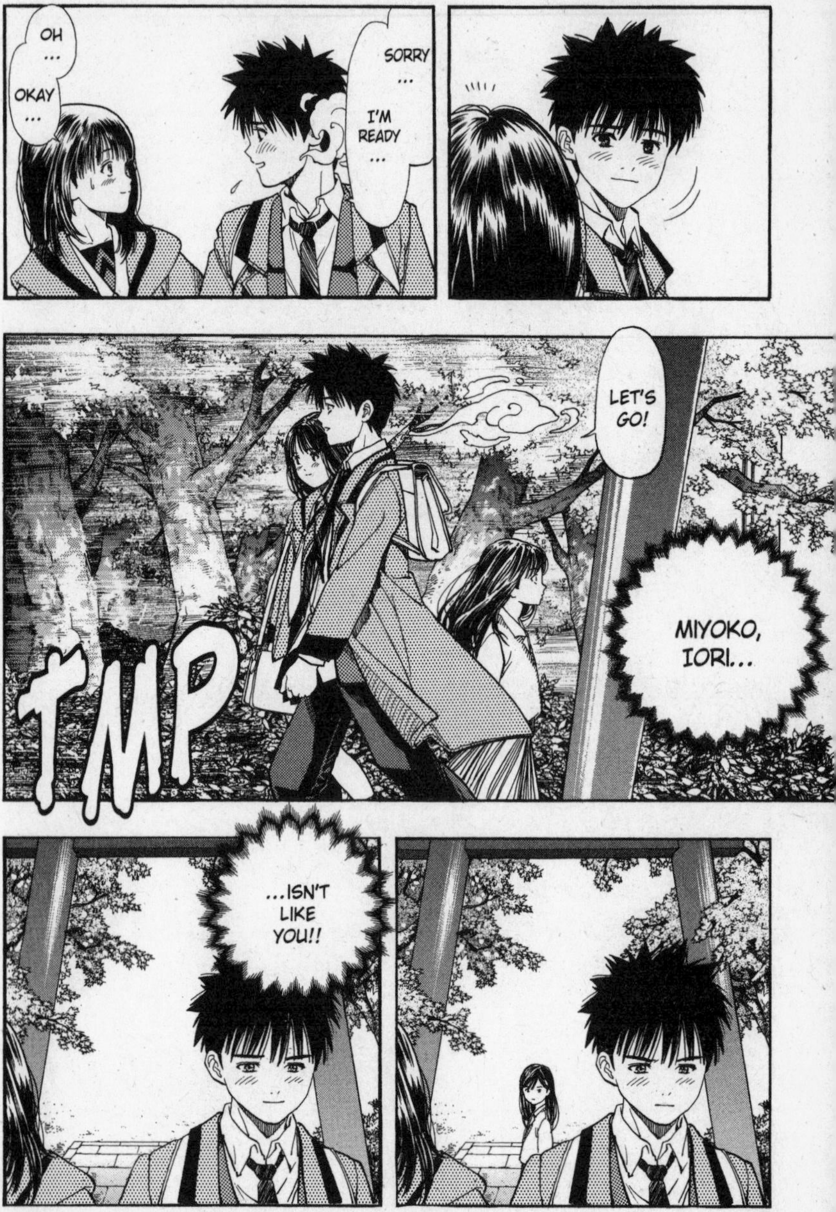
SORRY ... I'M READY ...
OH ... OKAY ...
LET'S GO!
MIYOKO, IORI...
TMP
...ISN'T LIKE YOU!!

READ THIS WAY

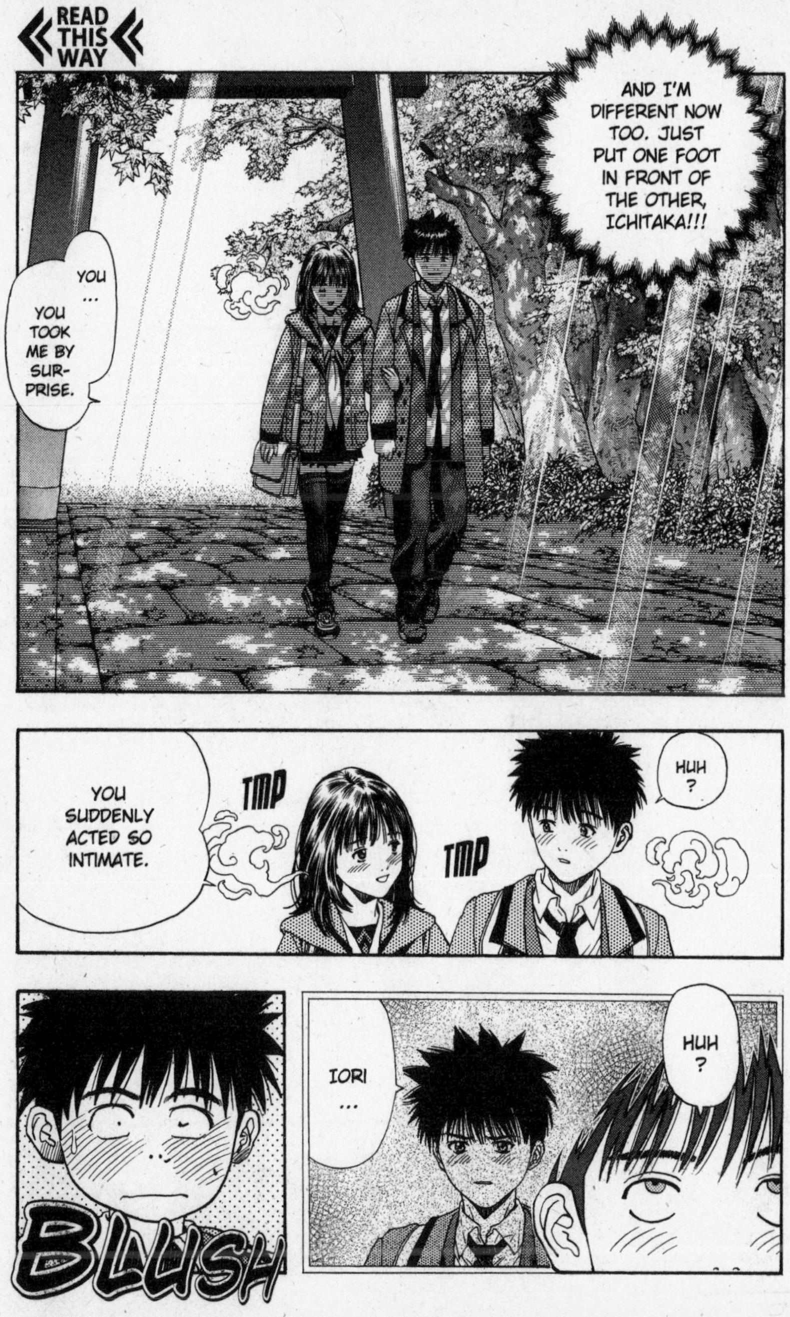
AND I'M DIFFERENT NOW TOO. JUST PUT ONE FOOT IN FRONT OF THE OTHER, ICHITAKA!!!
YOU ... YOU TOOK ME BY SUR-PRISE.
HUH?
TMP
TMP
YOU SUDDENLY ACTED SO INTIMATE.
HUH?
IORI ...
BLUSH

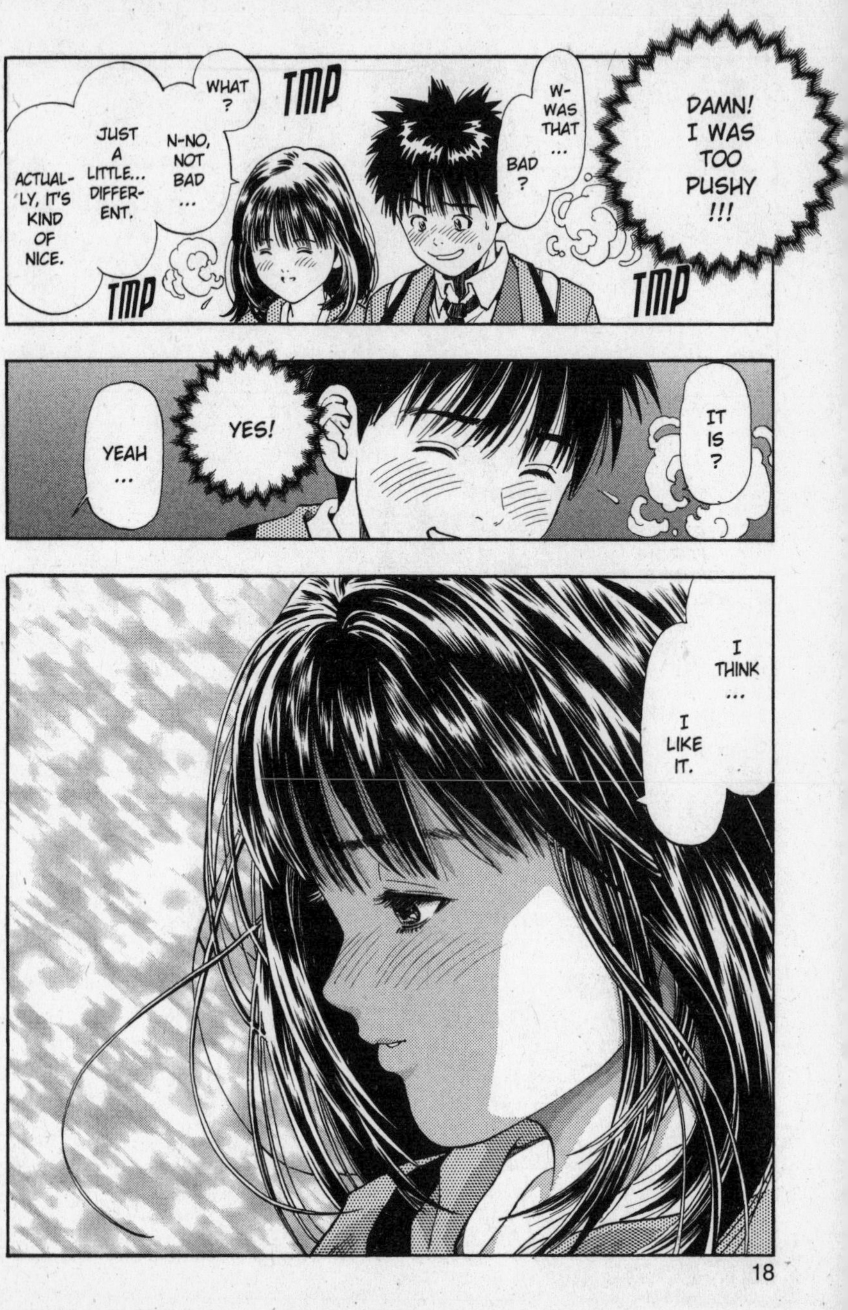
DAMN! I WAS TOO PUSHY!!!
TMP
W-WAS THAT... BAD?
TMP
WHAT?
N-NO, NOT BAD...
JUST A LITTLE... DIFFERENT.
ACTUAL-LY, IT'S KIND OF NICE.
TMP
IT IS?
YES!
YEAH...
I THINK... I LIKE IT.

READ THIS WAY

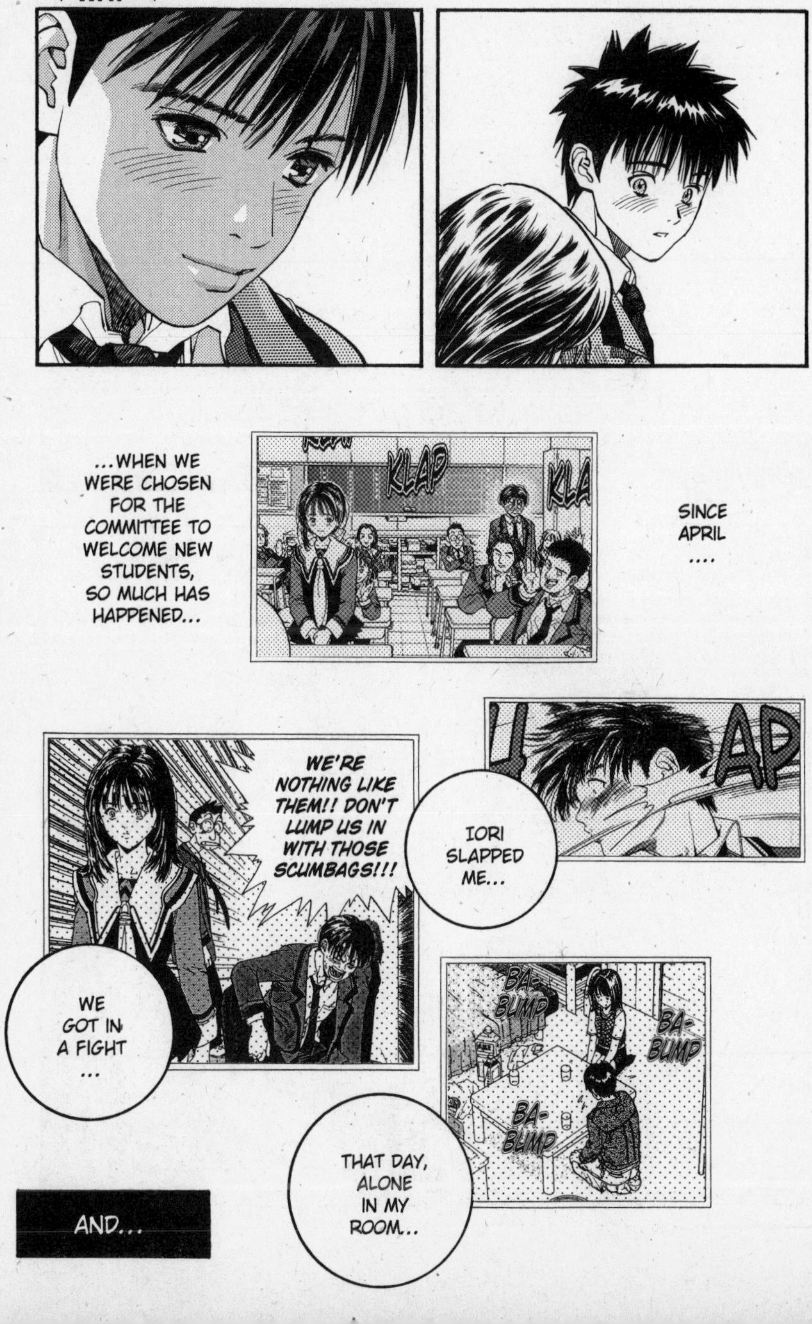
SINCE APRIL ....
KLA
KLAP
...WHEN WE WERE CHOSEN FOR THE COMMITTEE TO WELCOME NEW STUDENTS, SO MUCH HAS HAPPENED...
AP
IORI SLAPPED ME...
WE'RE NOTHING LIKE THEM!! DON'T LUMP US IN WITH THOSE SCUMBAGS!!!
WE GOT IN A FIGHT ...
BA-BUMP
BA-BUMP
BA-BUMP
THAT DAY, ALONE IN MY ROOM...
AND...

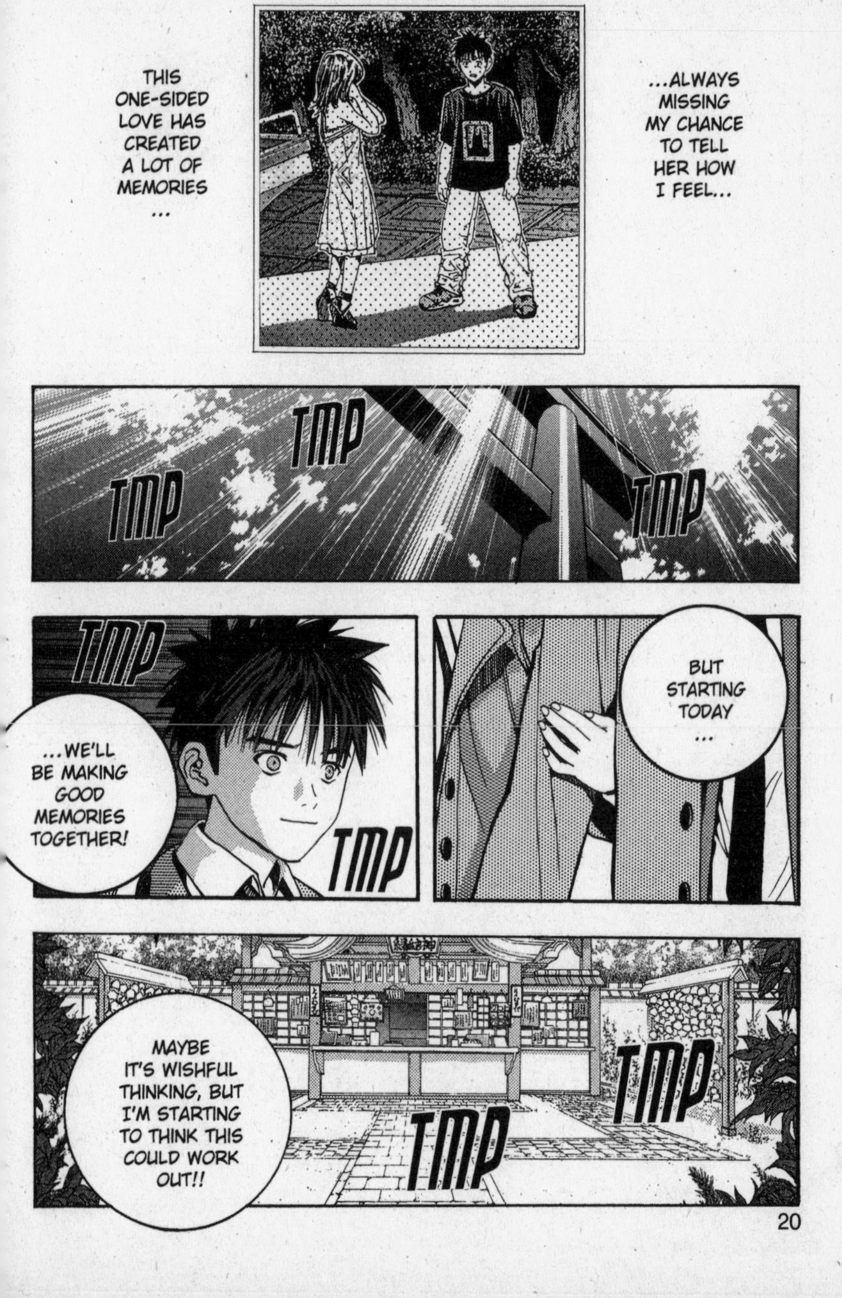
...ALWAYS MISSING MY CHANCE TO TELL HER HOW I FEEL...
THIS ONE-SIDED LOVE HAS CREATED A LOT OF MEMORIES ...
TMP
TMP
TMP
BUT STARTING TODAY ...
TMP
...WE'LL BE MAKING GOOD MEMORIES TOGETHER!
TMP
TMP
TMP
MAYBE IT'S WISHFUL THINKING, BUT I'M STARTING TO THINK THIS COULD WORK OUT!!

READ THIS WAY

GATE SIGN: ENMUSUBICCHI

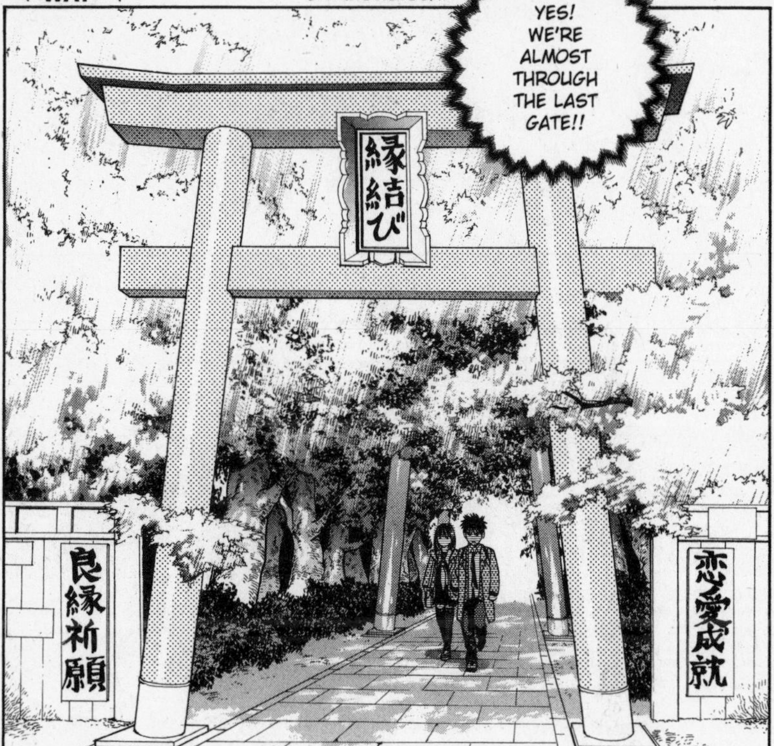
YES! WE'RE ALMOST THROUGH THE LAST GATE!!
縁結び
恋愛成就
良縁祈願

SIGN (LEFT): GOOD MATCH PRAYER

SIGN (RIGHT): ATTAIN LOVE

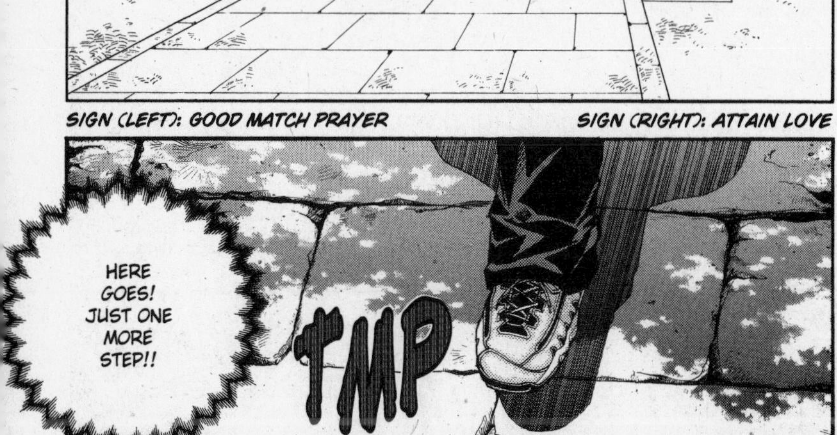
HERE GOES! JUST ONE MORE STEP!!
TMP

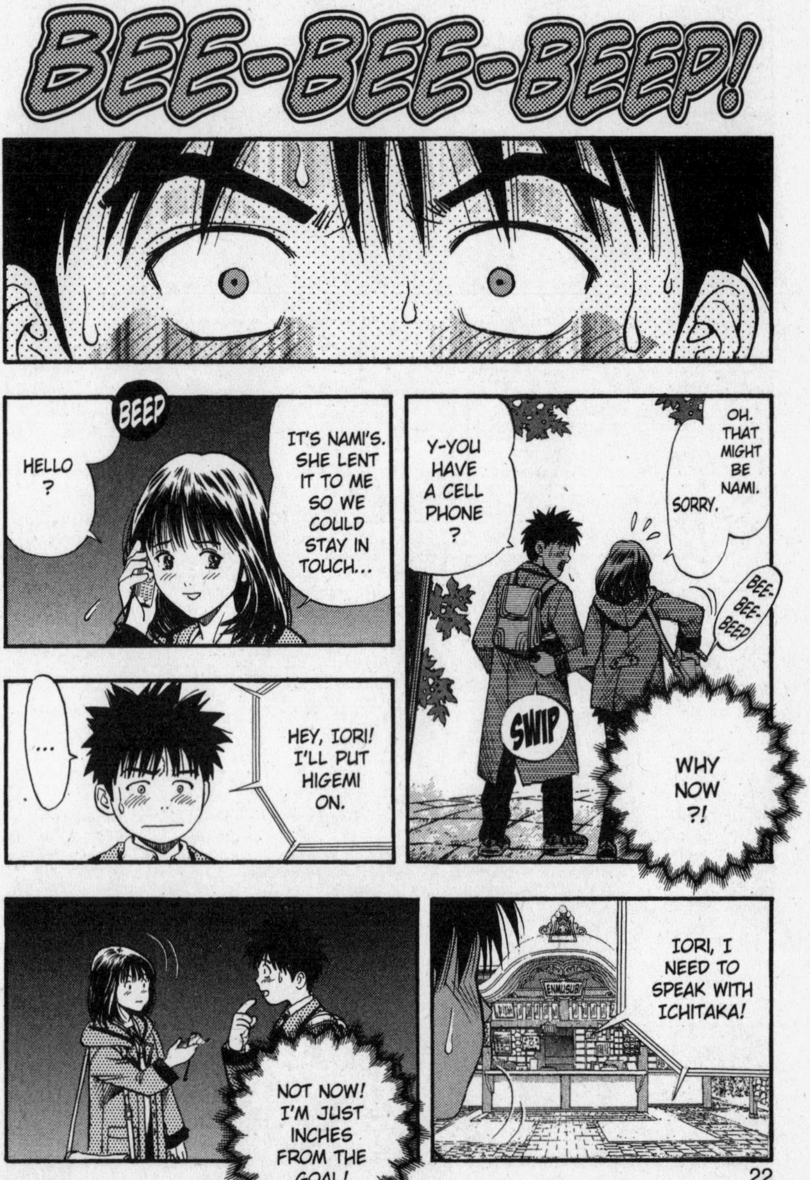
BEE-BEE-BEEP!
OH. THAT MIGHT BE NAMI.
SORRY.
Y-YOU HAVE A CELL PHONE?
BEE-BEE-BEEP
SWIP
WHY NOW?!
IT'S NAMI'S. SHE LENT IT TO ME SO WE COULD STAY IN TOUCH...
BEEP
HELLO?
HEY, IORI! I'LL PUT HIGEMI ON.
...
IORI, I NEED TO SPEAK WITH ICHITAKA!
ENMUSUBI
NOT NOW! I'M JUST INCHES FROM THE GOAL!

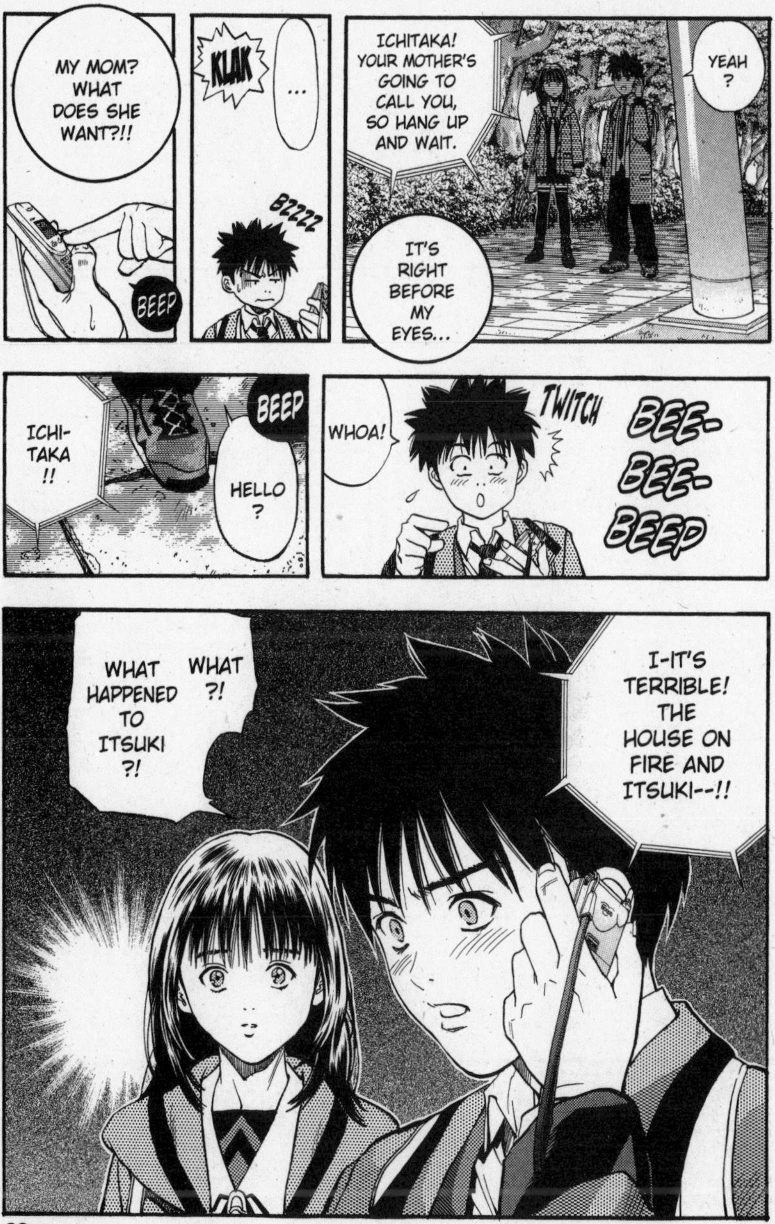
YEAH ?
ICHITAKA! YOUR MOTHER'S GOING TO CALL YOU, SO HANG UP AND WAIT.
IT'S RIGHT BEFORE MY EYES...
...
KLAK
BZZZZ
MY MOM? WHAT DOES SHE WANT?!!
BEEP
BEE-BEE-BEEP
TWITCH
WHOA!
BEEP
HELLO ?
ICHI-TAKA !!
I-IT'S TERRIBLE! THE HOUSE ON FIRE AND ITSUKI--!!
WHAT ?!
WHAT HAPPENED TO ITSUKI ?!

Chapter 37:
A Crumbling Memory

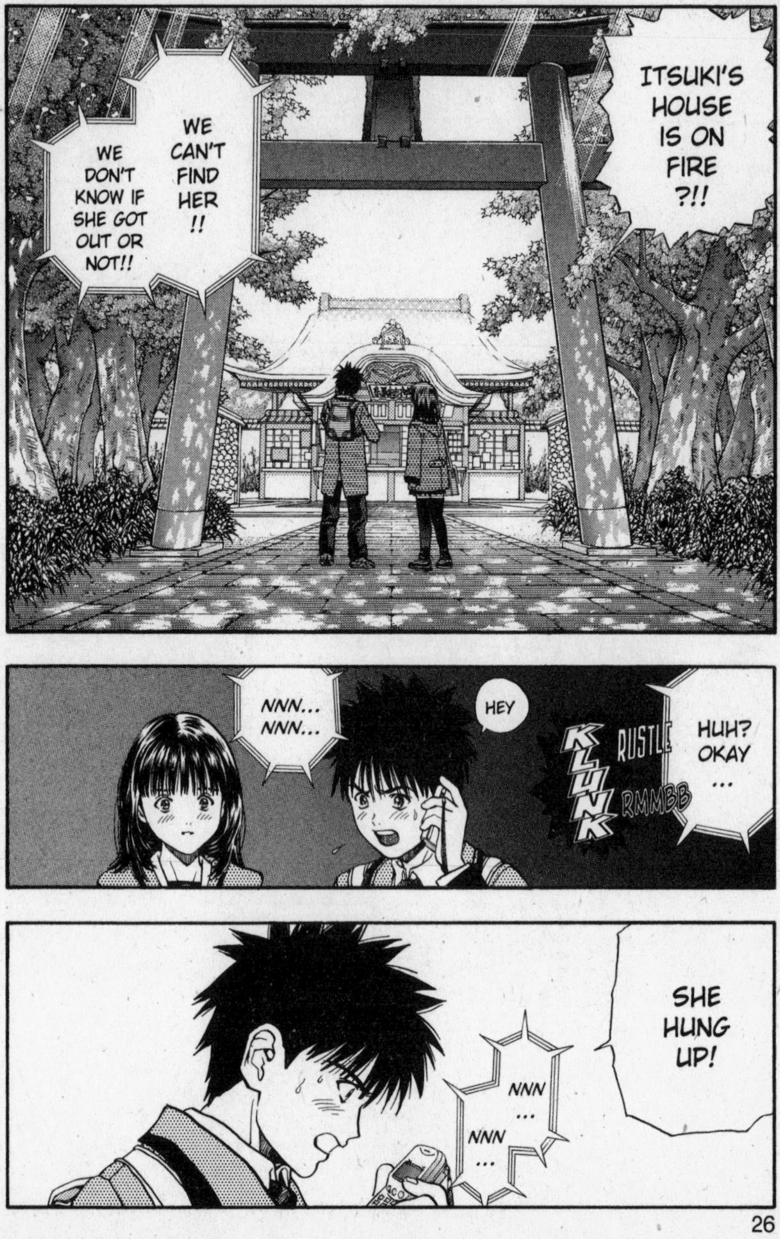
ITSUKI'S HOUSE IS ON FIRE ?!!
WE CAN'T FIND HER !!
WE DON'T KNOW IF SHE GOT OUT OR NOT!!
HUH? OKAY ...
RUSTLE
KLUNK
RMMBB
HEY
NNN... NNN...
SHE HUNG UP!
NNN ... NNN ...

READ THIS WAY

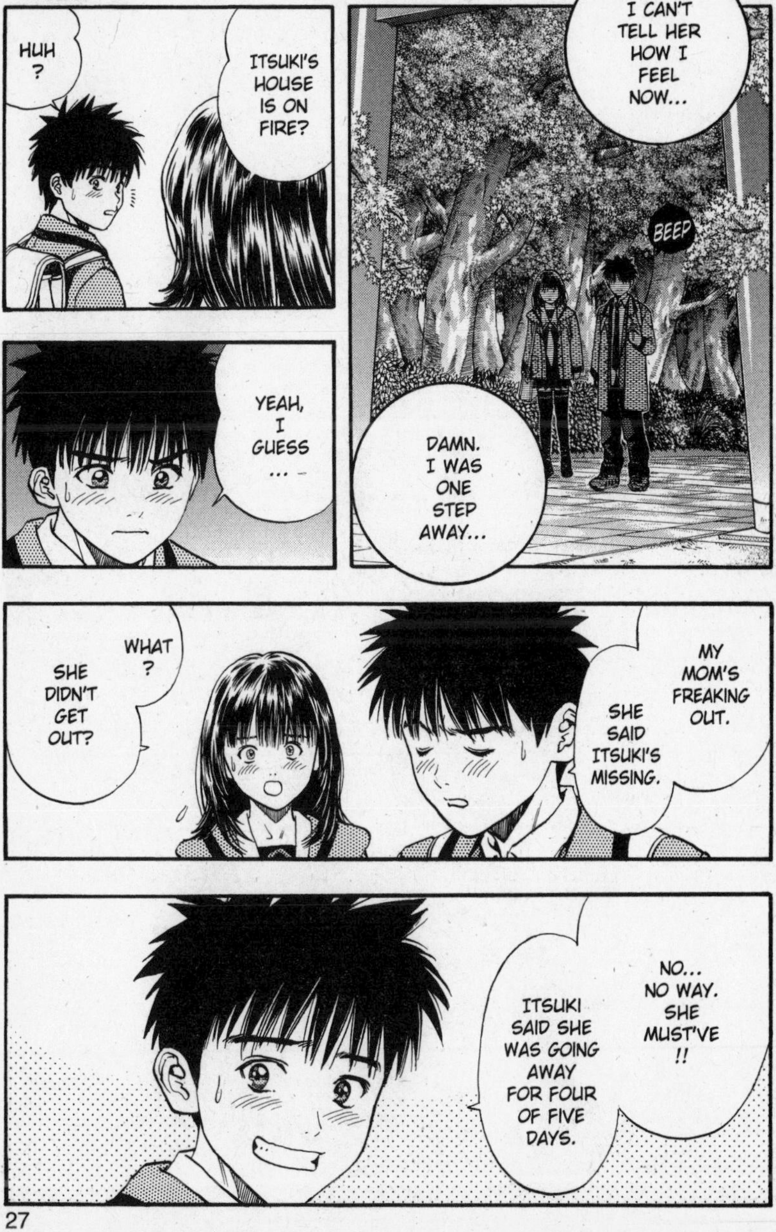
I CAN'T TELL HER HOW I FEEL NOW...
BEEP
DAMN. I WAS ONE STEP AWAY...
ITSUKI'S HOUSE IS ON FIRE?
HUH?
YEAH, I GUESS ...
MY MOM'S FREAKING OUT.
SHE SAID ITSUKI'S MISSING.
WHAT?
SHE DIDN'T GET OUT?
NO... NO WAY. SHE MUST'VE!!
ITSUKI SAID SHE WAS GOING AWAY FOR FOUR OF FIVE DAYS.

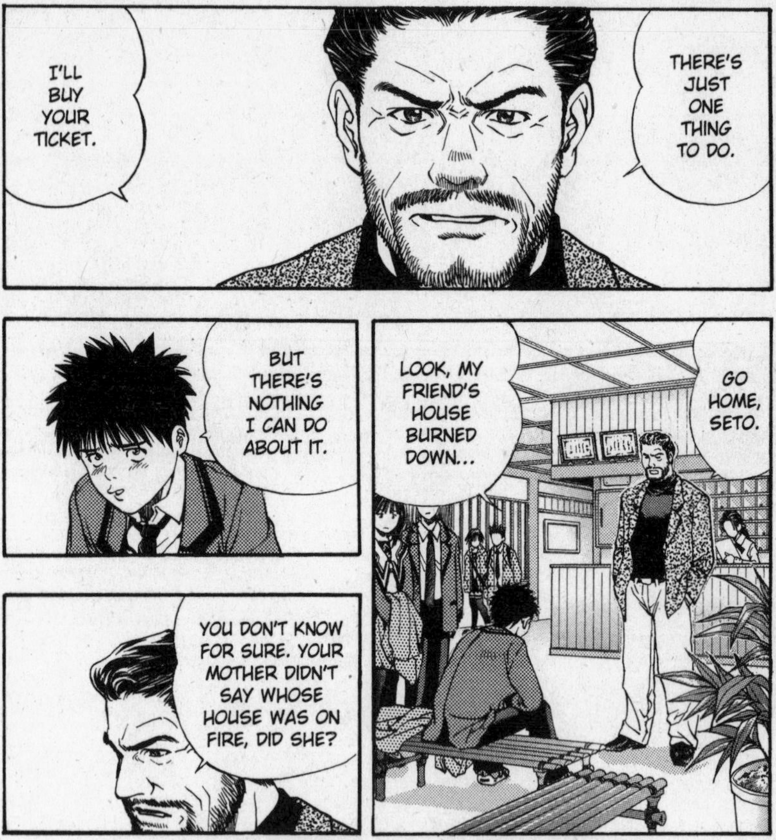
THERE'S JUST ONE THING TO DO.
I'LL BUY YOUR TICKET.
GO HOME, SETO.
LOOK, MY FRIEND'S HOUSE BURNED DOWN...
BUT THERE'S NOTHING I CAN DO ABOUT IT.
YOU DON'T KNOW FOR SURE. YOUR MOTHER DIDN'T SAY WHOSE HOUSE WAS ON FIRE, DID SHE?

SIGN: HAPPY CRANE LODGE

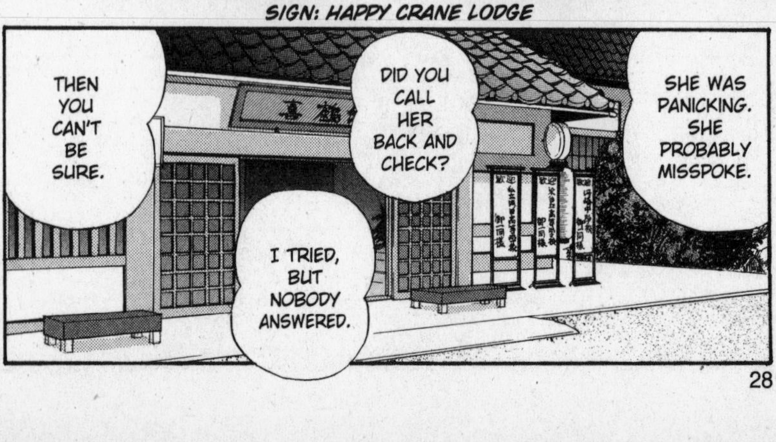
SHE WAS PANICKING. SHE PROBABLY MISSPOKE.
DID YOU CALL HER BACK AND CHECK?
I TRIED, BUT NOBODY ANSWERED.
THEN YOU CAN'T BE SURE.

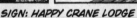

READ THIS WAY

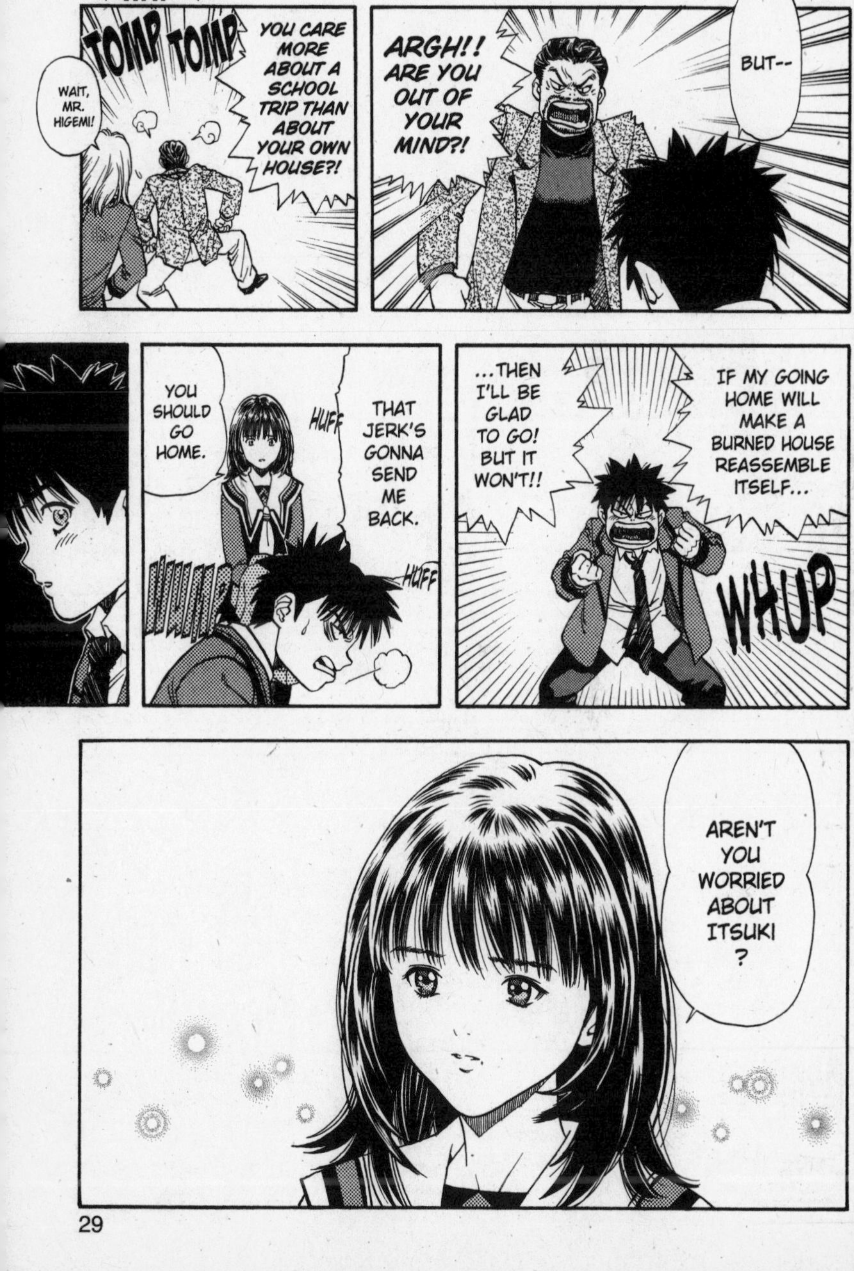
BUT--
ARGH!! ARE YOU OUT OF YOUR MIND?!
YOU CARE MORE ABOUT A SCHOOL TRIP THAN ABOUT YOUR OWN HOUSE?!
TOMP TOMP
WAIT, MR. HIGEMI!
IF MY GOING HOME WILL MAKE A BURNED HOUSE REASSEMBLE ITSELF...
...THEN I'LL BE GLAD TO GO! BUT IT WON'T!!
WHUP
THAT JERK'S GONNA SEND ME BACK.
HUFF
YOU SHOULD GO HOME.
HUFF
AREN'T YOU WORRIED ABOUT ITSUKI?

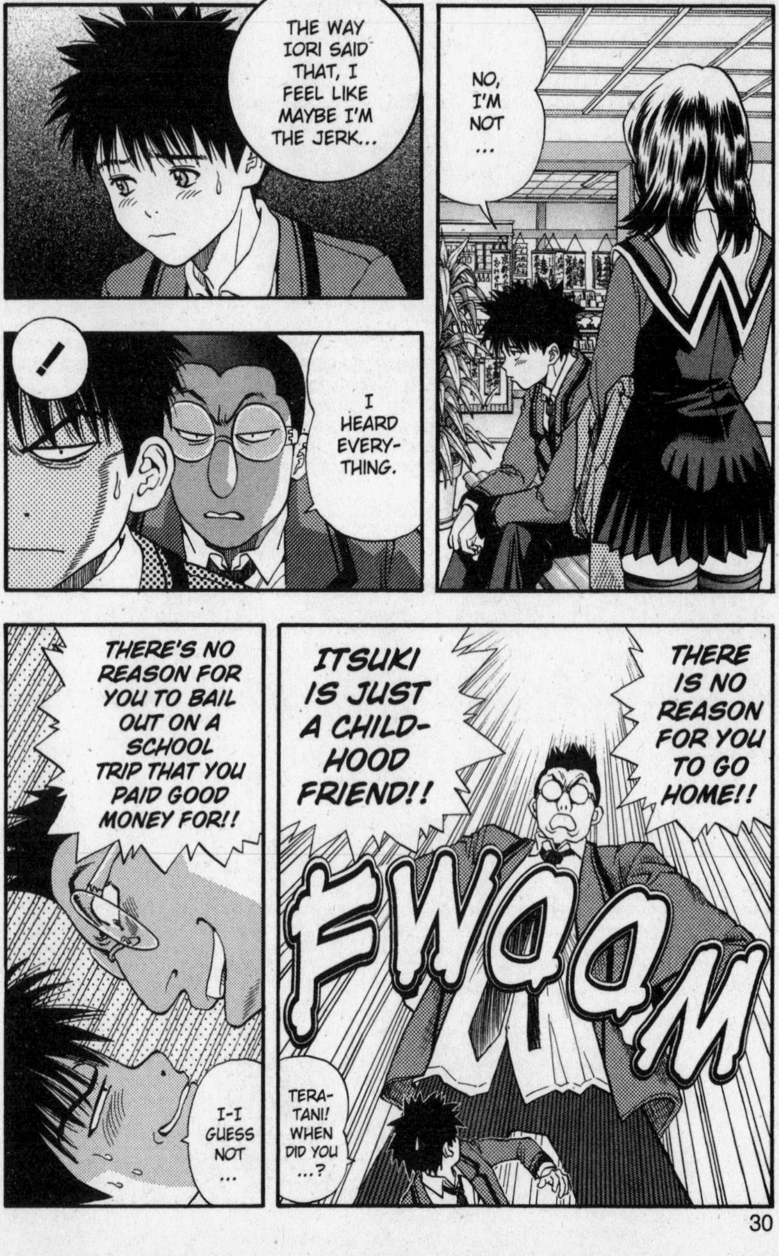
NO, I'M NOT ...
THE WAY IORI SAID THAT, I FEEL LIKE MAYBE I'M THE JERK...
!
I HEARD EVERY-THING.
THERE IS NO REASON FOR YOU TO GO HOME!!
ITSUKI IS JUST A CHILD-HOOD FRIEND!!
FWOOM
TERA-TANI! WHEN DID YOU ...?
THERE'S NO REASON FOR YOU TO BAIL OUT ON A SCHOOL TRIP THAT YOU PAID GOOD MONEY FOR!!
I-I GUESS NOT ...

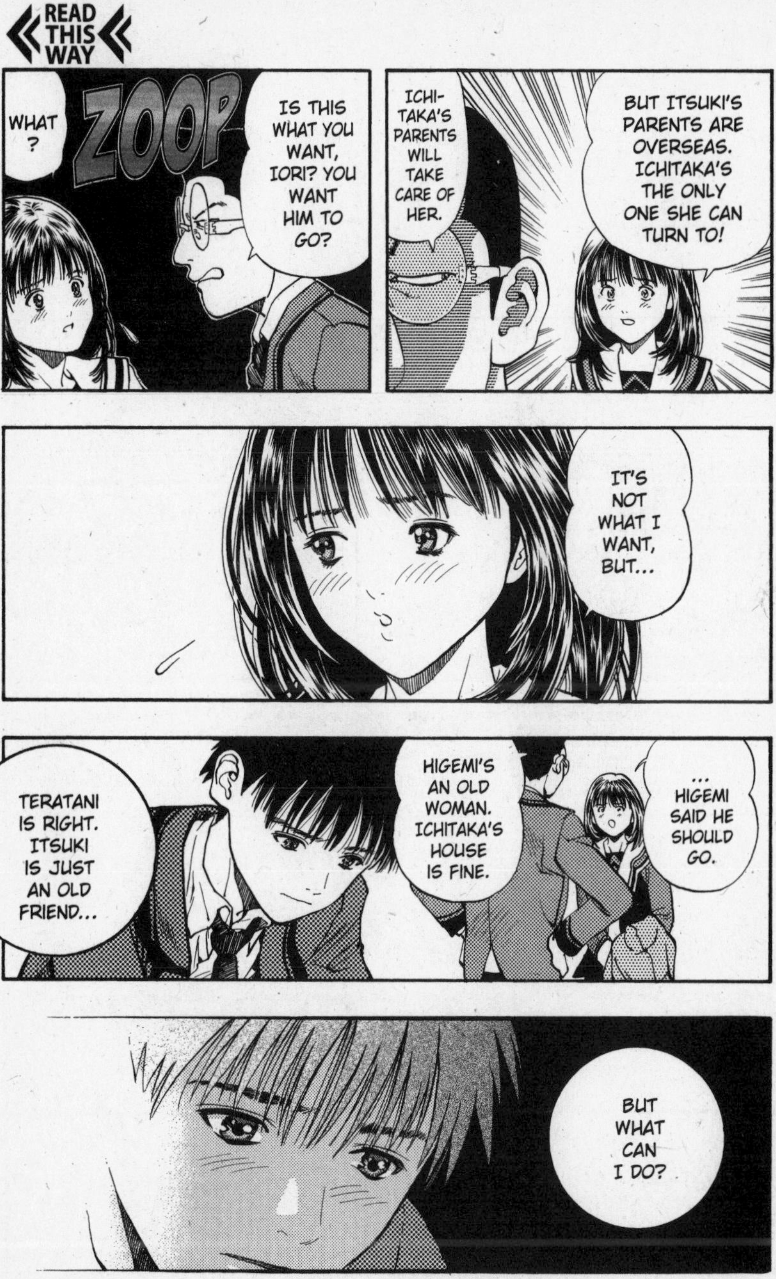
READ THIS WAY
BUT ITSUKI'S PARENTS ARE OVERSEAS. ICHITAKA'S THE ONLY ONE SHE CAN TURN TO!
ICHI-TAKA'S PARENTS WILL TAKE CARE OF HER.
IS THIS WHAT YOU WANT, IORI? YOU WANT HIM TO GO?
ZOOP
WHAT ?
IT'S NOT WHAT I WANT, BUT...
... HIGEMI SAID HE SHOULD GO.
HIGEMI'S AN OLD WOMAN. ICHITAKA'S HOUSE IS FINE.
TERATANI IS RIGHT. ITSUKI IS JUST AN OLD FRIEND...
BUT WHAT CAN I DO?

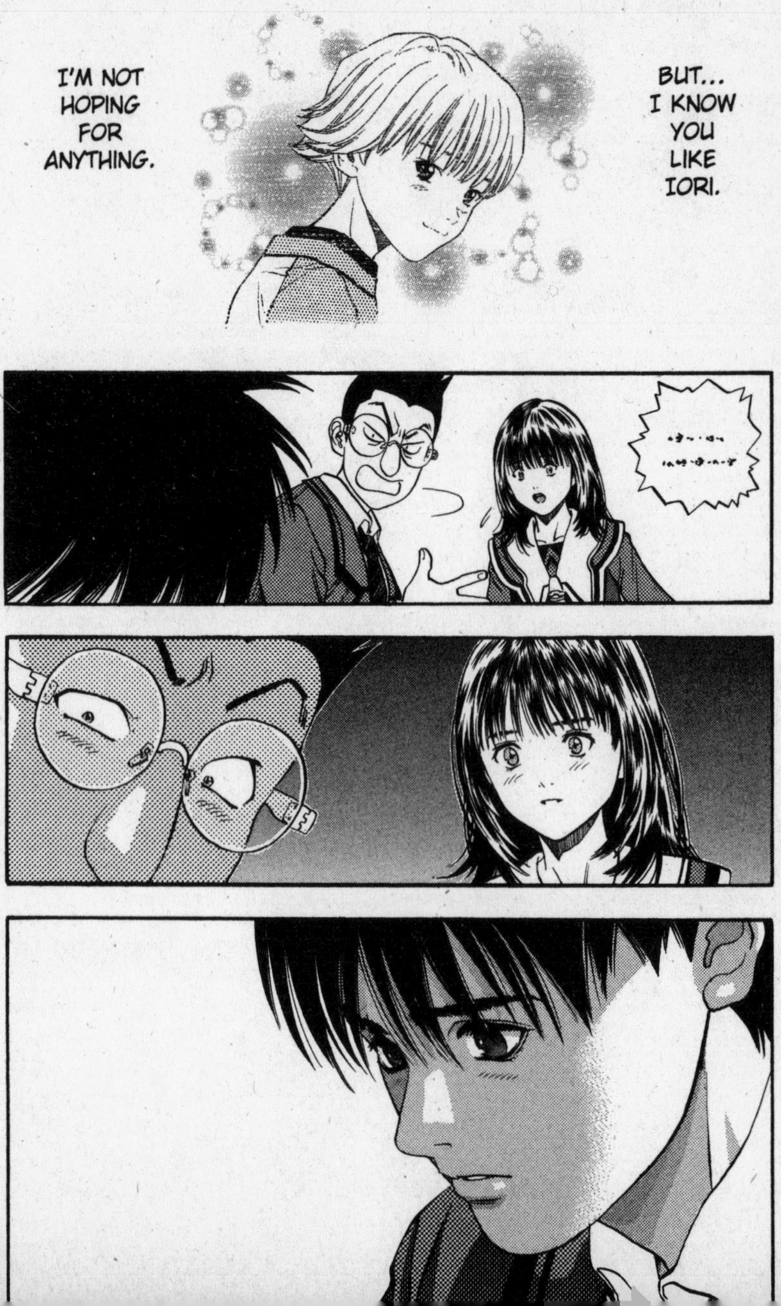
I'M NOT HOPING FOR ANYTHING.
BUT... I KNOW YOU LIKE IORI.

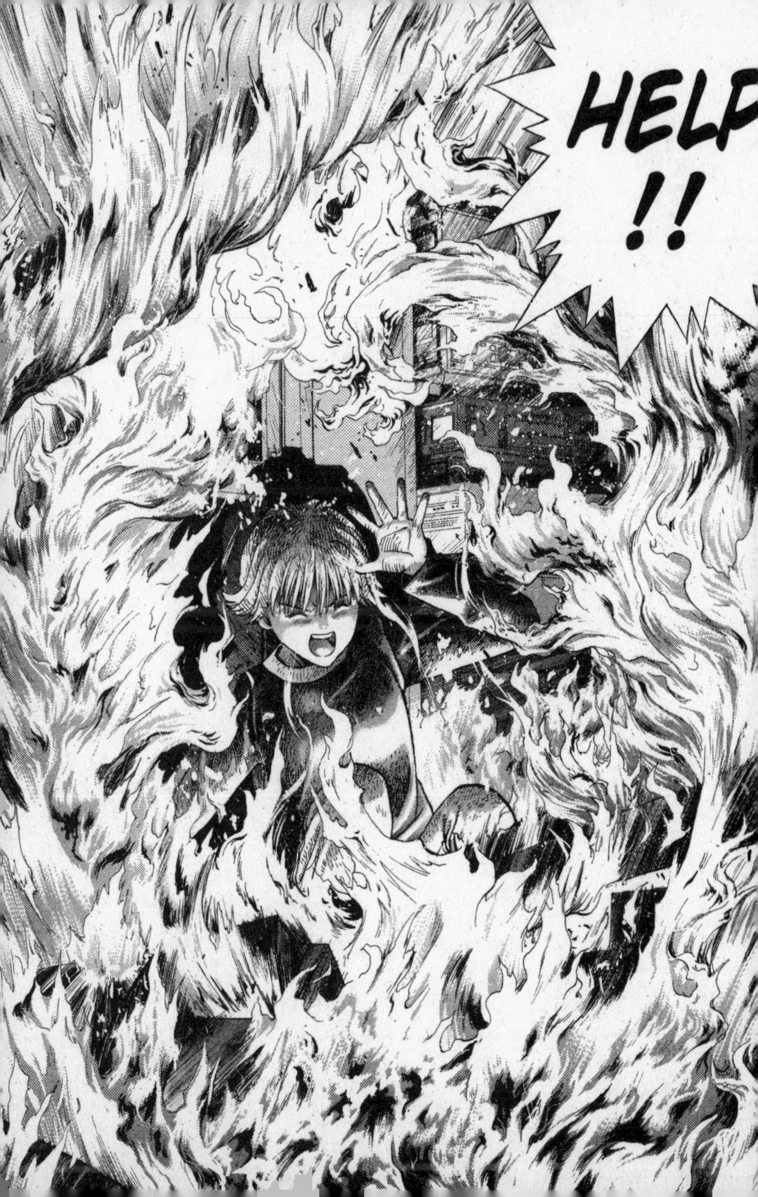
HELP!!

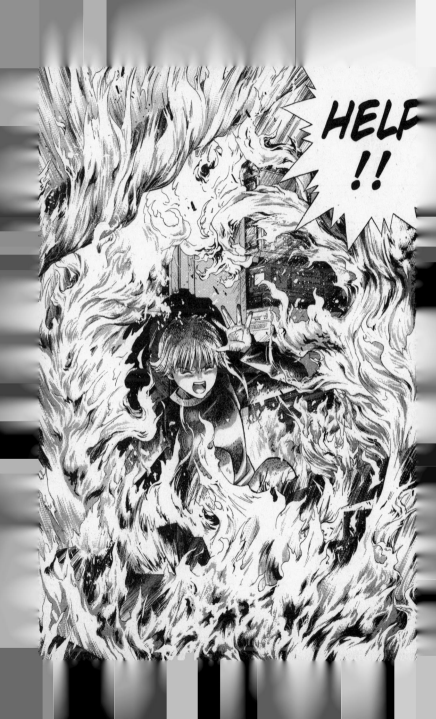

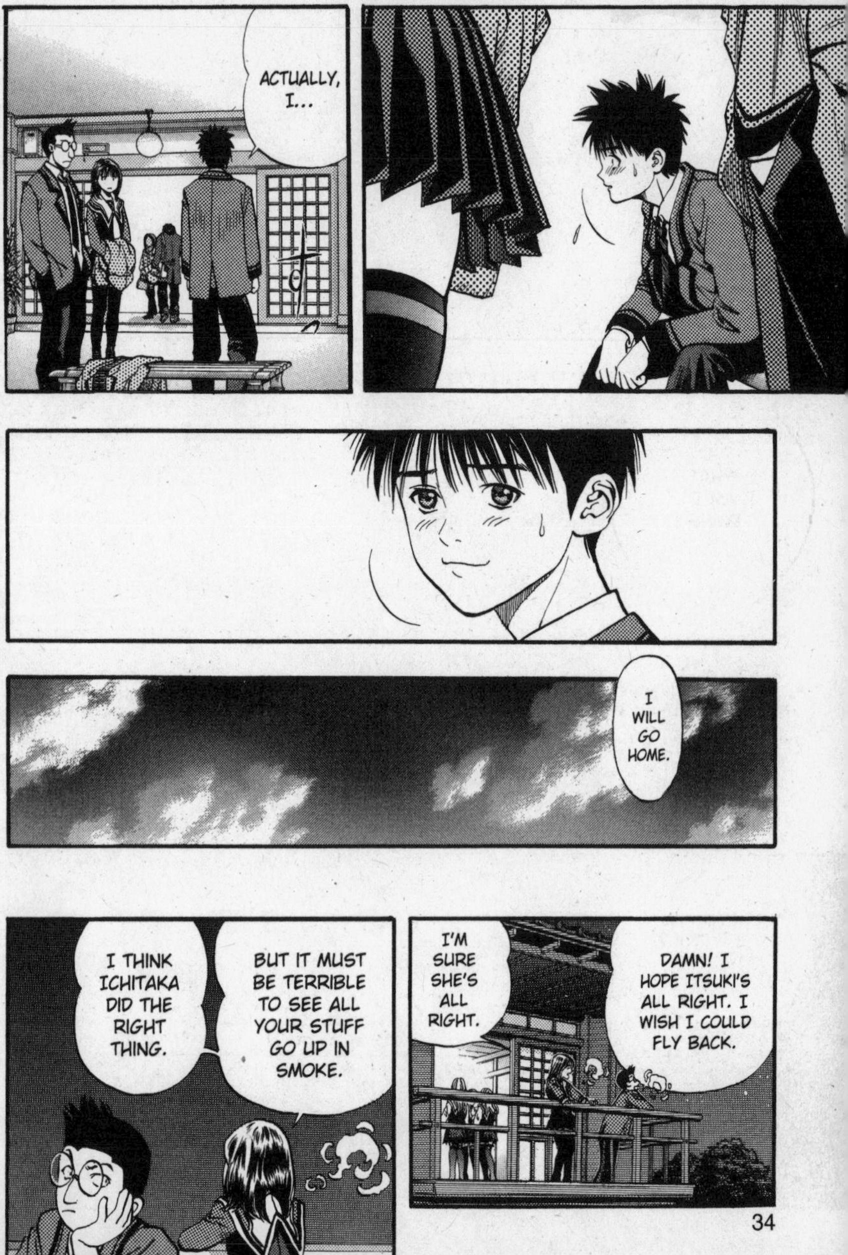
ACTUALLY, I...
I WILL GO HOME.
DAMN! I HOPE ITSUKI'S ALL RIGHT. I WISH I COULD FLY BACK.
I'M SURE SHE'S ALL RIGHT.
BUT IT MUST BE TERRIBLE TO SEE ALL YOUR STUFF GO UP IN SMOKE.
I THINK ICHITAKA DID THE RIGHT THING.

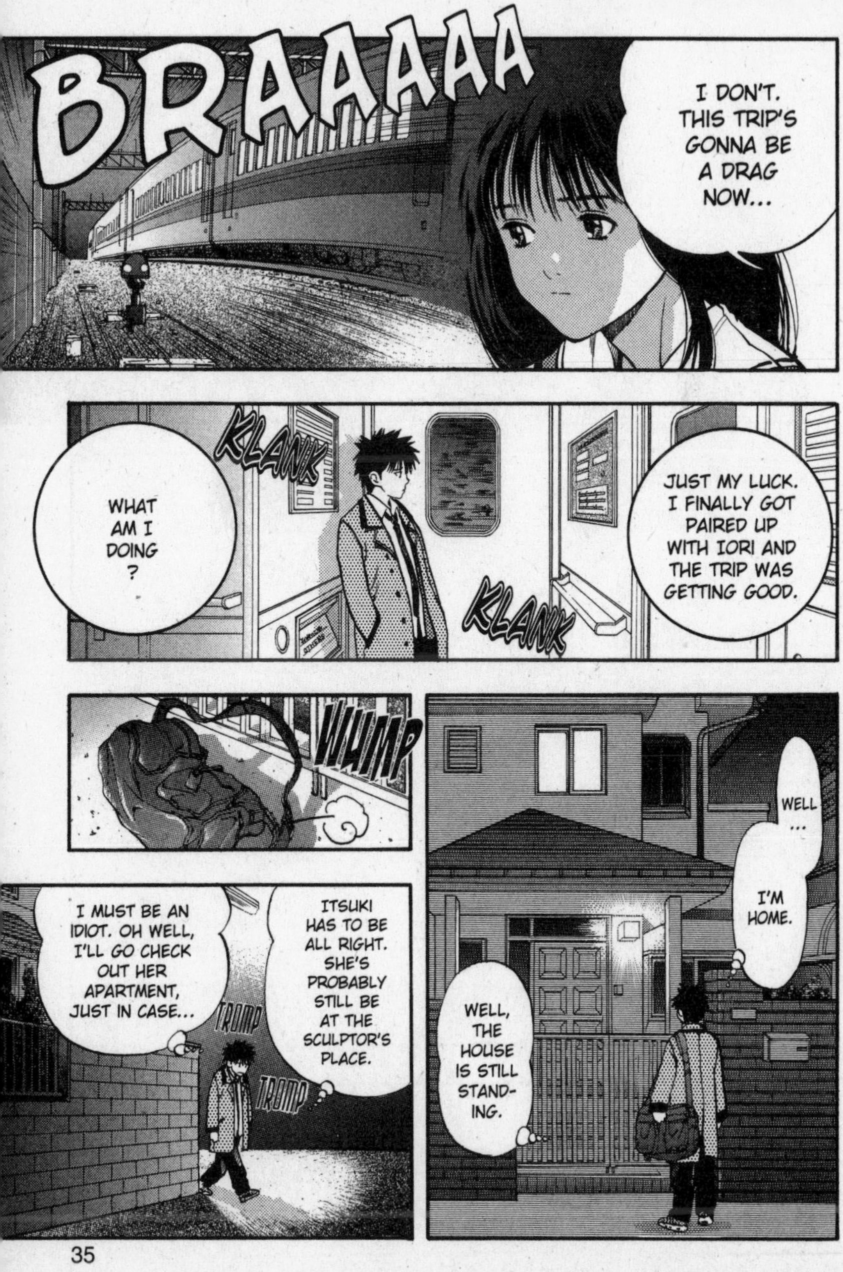
I DON'T. THIS TRIP'S GONNA BE A DRAG NOW...
BRAAAAA
JUST MY LUCK. I FINALLY GOT PAIRED UP WITH IORI AND THE TRIP WAS GETTING GOOD.
KLANK
KLANK
WHAT AM I DOING?
WELL...
I'M HOME.
WELL, THE HOUSE IS STILL STANDING.
WHUMP
ITSUKI HAS TO BE ALL RIGHT. SHE'S PROBABLY STILL BE AT THE SCULPTOR'S PLACE.
TRAMP
TRAMP
I MUST BE AN IDIOT. OH WELL, I'LL GO CHECK OUT HER APARTMENT, JUST IN CASE...

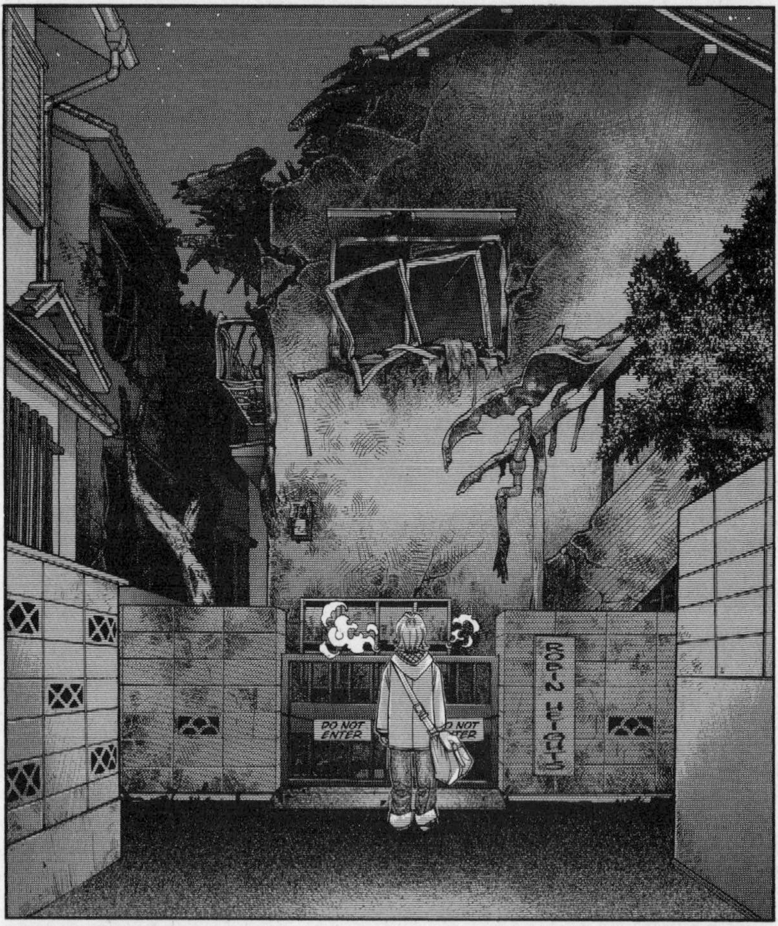
DO NOT ENTER
ROBIN HEIGHTS

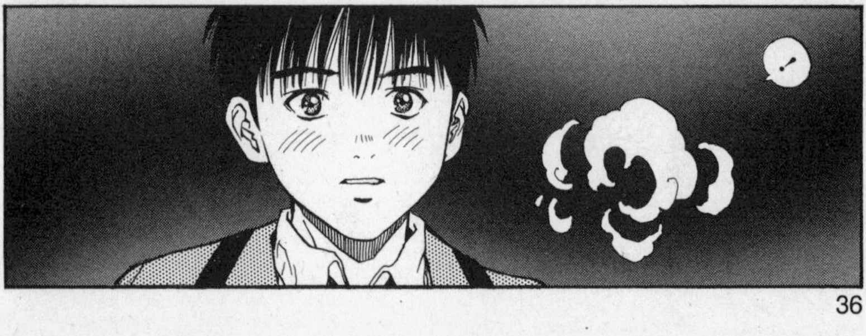
!

READ THIS WAY

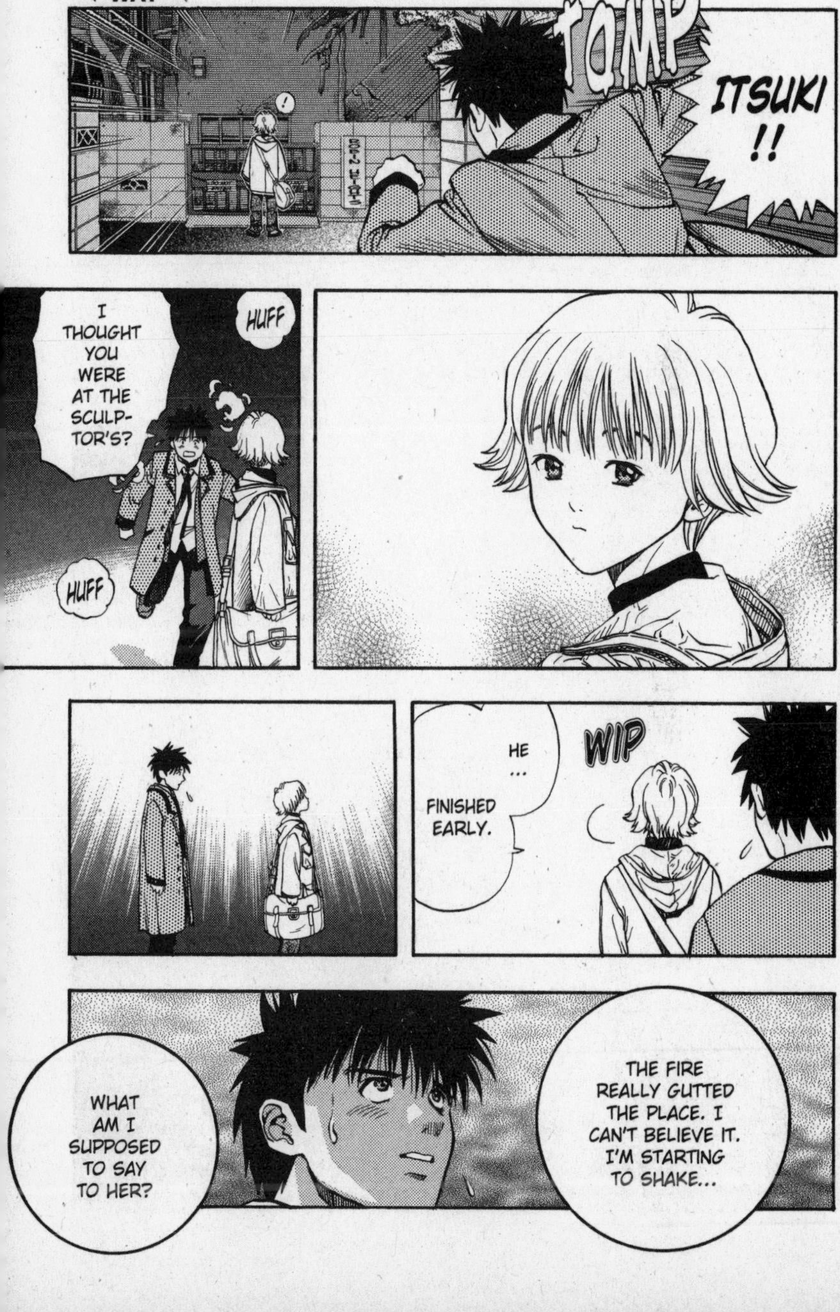
TOMP
ITSUKI !!
!
I THOUGHT YOU WERE AT THE SCULPTOR'S?
HUFF
HUFF
WIP
HE ... FINISHED EARLY.
THE FIRE REALLY GUTTED THE PLACE. I CAN'T BELIEVE IT. I'M STARTING TO SHAKE...
WHAT AM I SUPPOSED TO SAY TO HER?

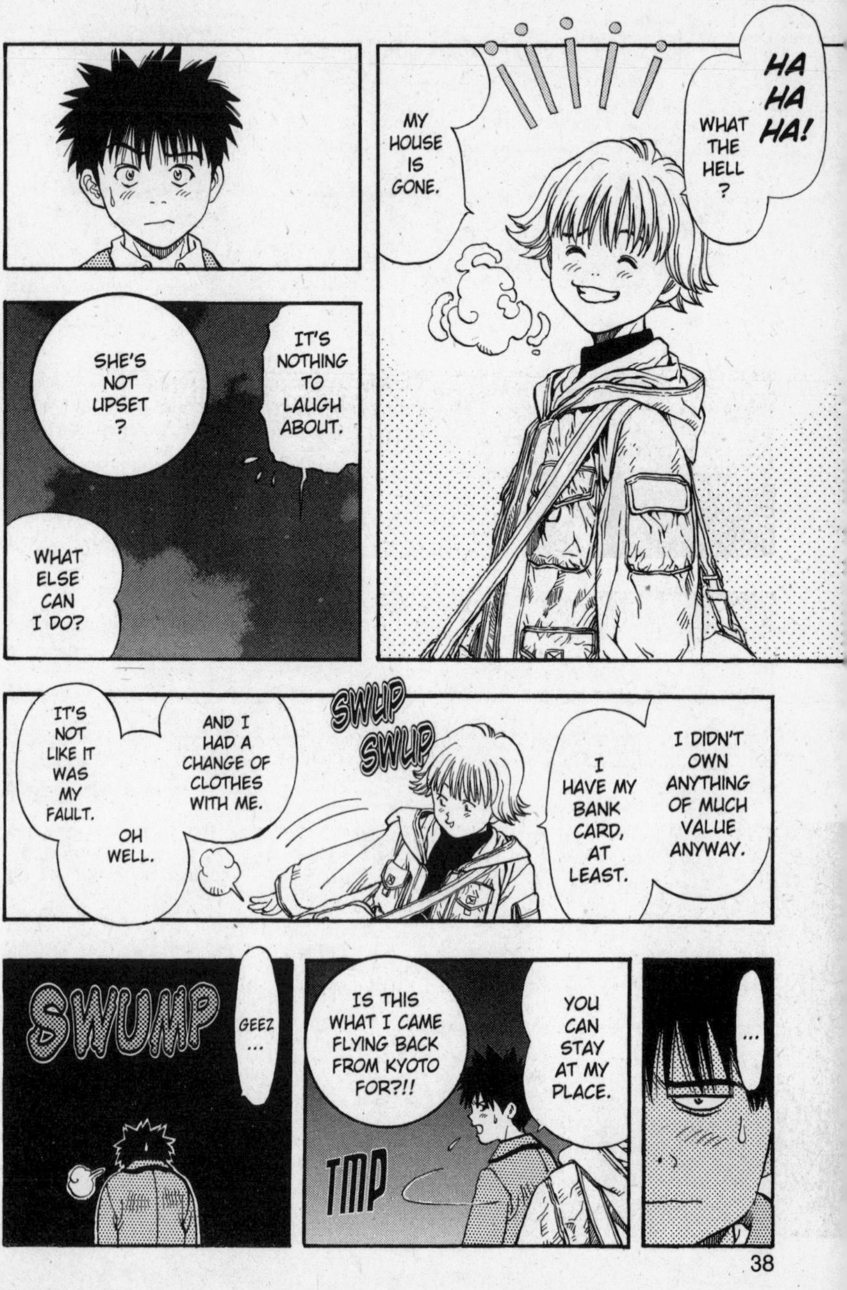
HA HA HA!
WHAT THE HELL ?
MY HOUSE IS GONE.
IT'S NOTHING TO LAUGH ABOUT.
SHE'S NOT UPSET ?
WHAT ELSE CAN I DO?
I DIDN'T OWN ANYTHING OF MUCH VALUE ANYWAY.
I HAVE MY BANK CARD, AT LEAST.
SWUP SWUP
AND I HAD A CHANGE OF CLOTHES WITH ME.
IT'S NOT LIKE IT WAS MY FAULT.
OH WELL.
...
YOU CAN STAY AT MY PLACE.
IS THIS WHAT I CAME FLYING BACK FROM KYOTO FOR?!!
TMP
GEEZ ...
SWUMP

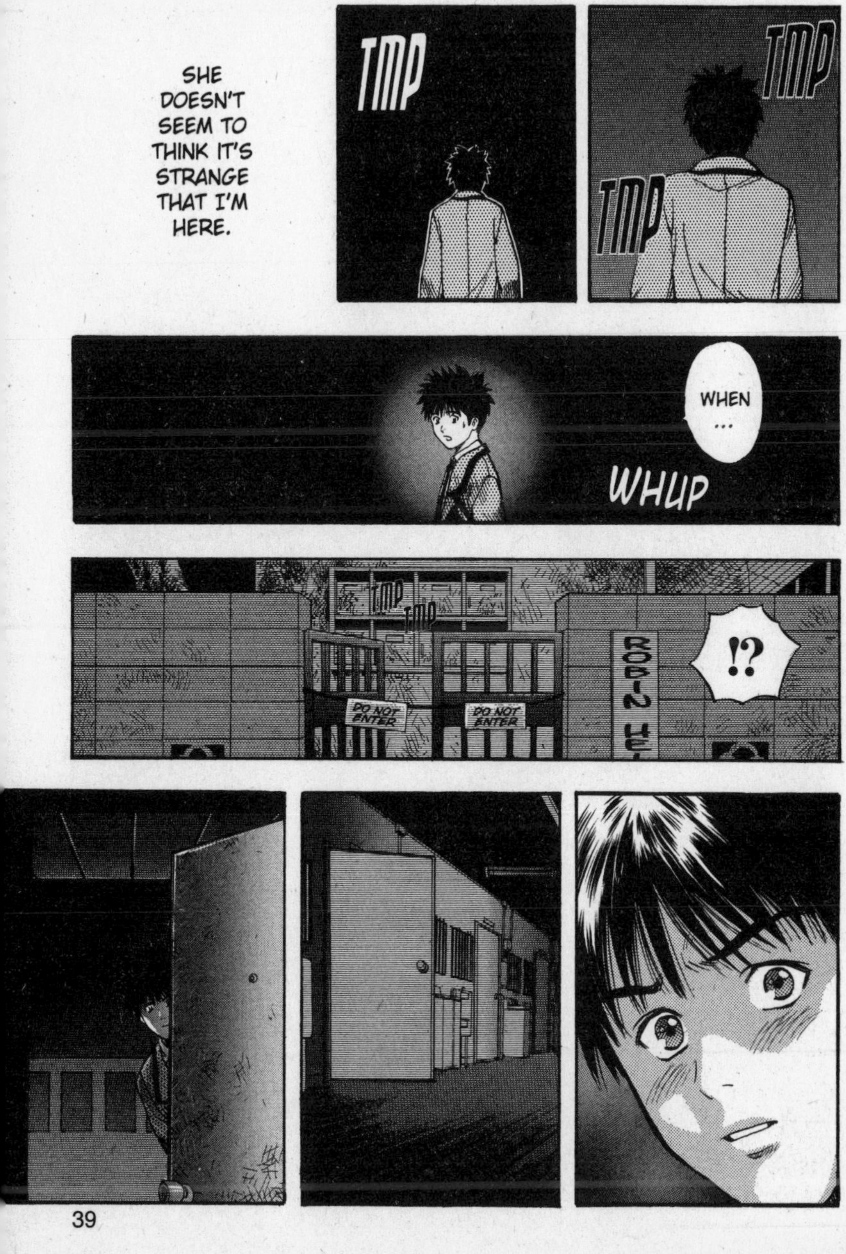
TMP
TMP
TMP
SHE DOESN'T SEEM TO THINK IT'S STRANGE THAT I'M HERE.
WHEN ...
WHUP
!?
ROBIN HE
DO NOT ENTER
TMP
TMP
DO NOT ENTER

!!

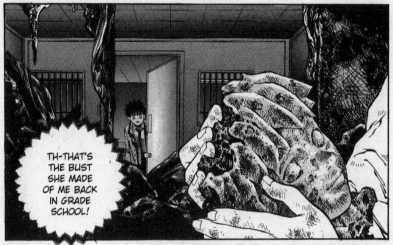

TH-THAT'S THE BUST SHE MADE OF ME BACK IN GRADE SCHOOL!

I TREASURED IT....

FOR SO LONG...

40

READ THIS WAY

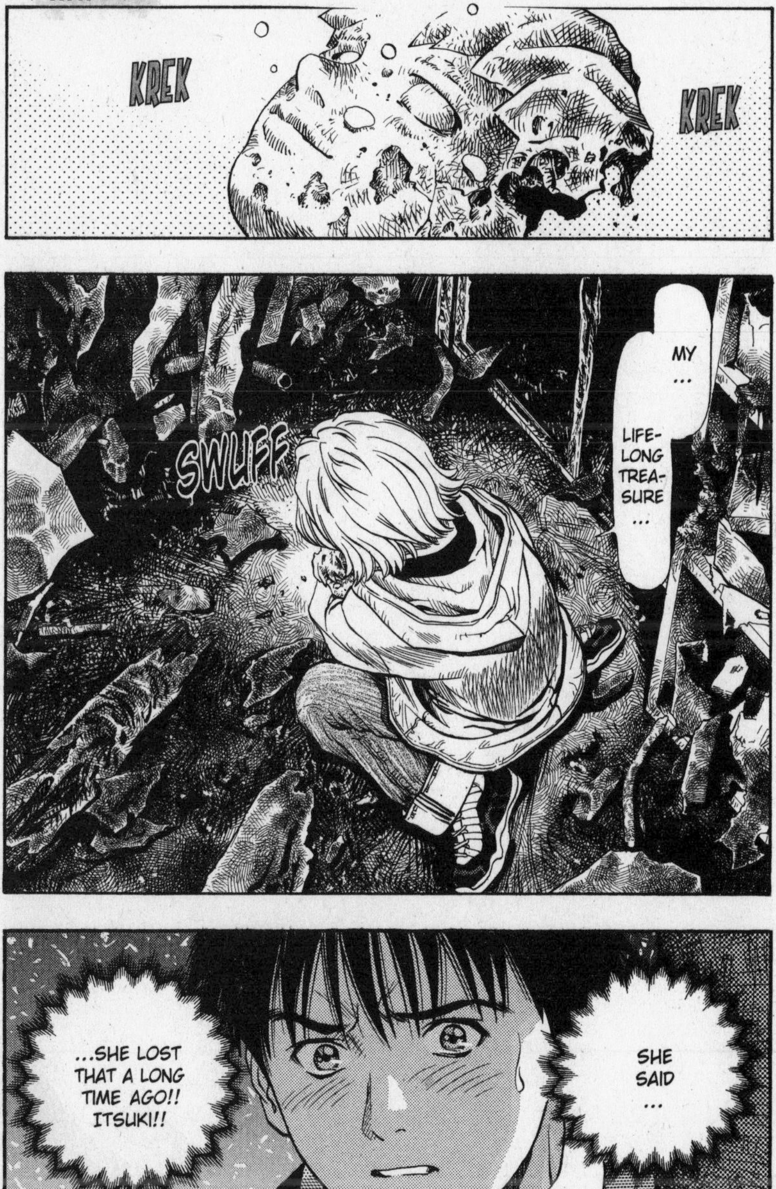
KREK
KREK
MY ... LIFE-LONG TREASURE ...
SWUFF
SHE SAID ...
...SHE LOST THAT A LONG TIME AGO!! ITSUKI!!

アイズ

Chapter 38:
Opened Recollection

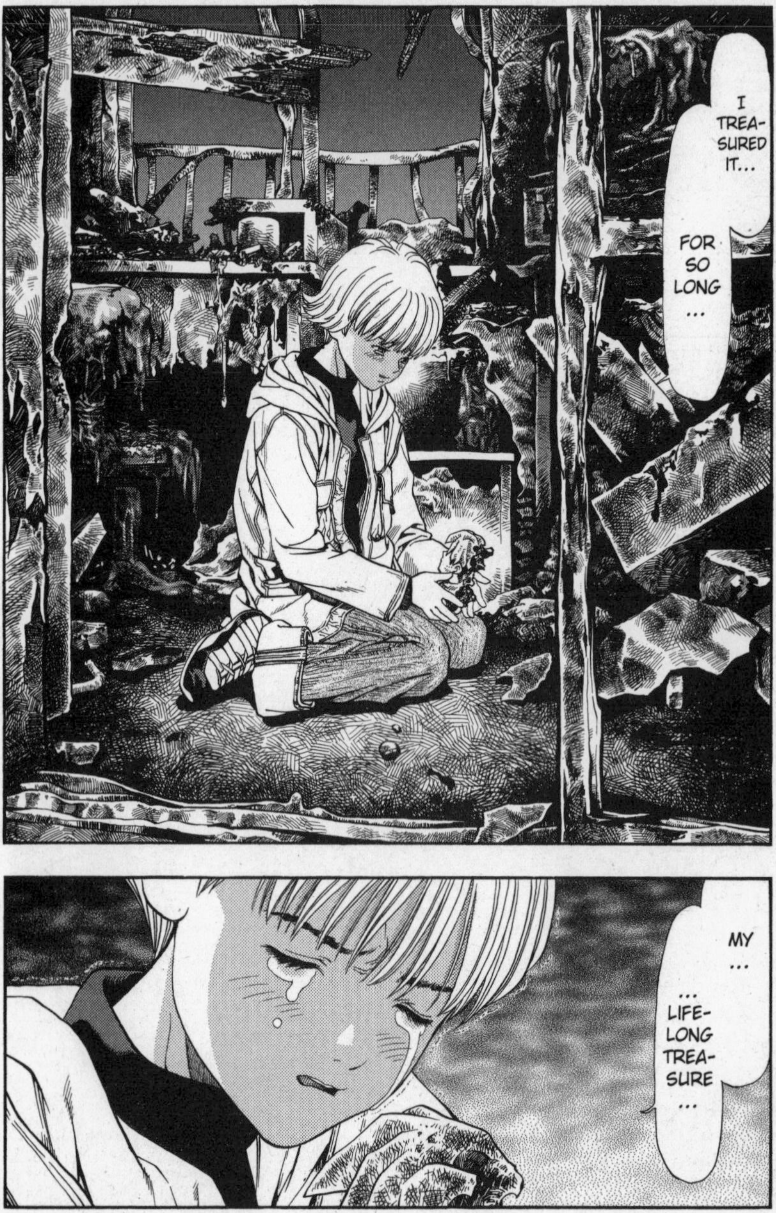
I TREA-SURED IT...
FOR SO LONG ...
MY ...
... LIFE-LONG TREA-SURE ...

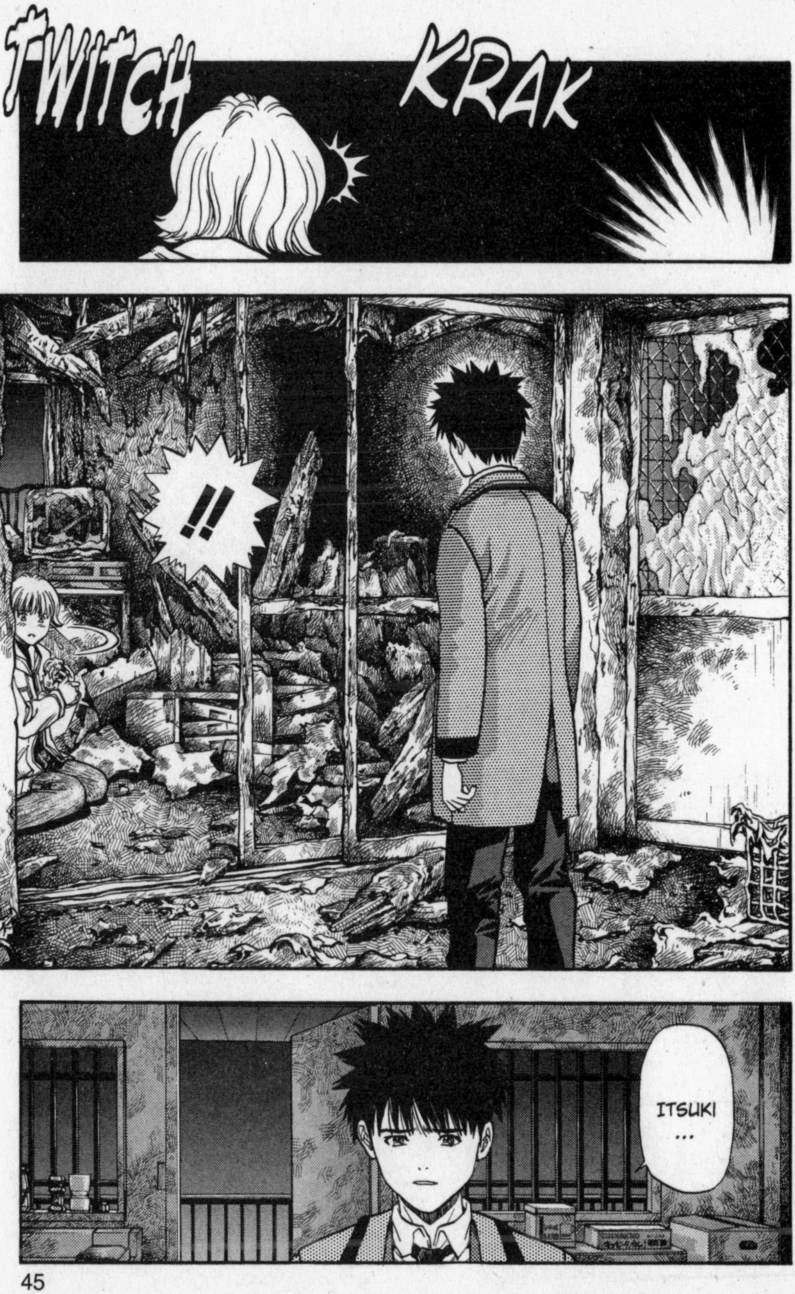
KRAK
TWITCH
!!
ITSUKI ...

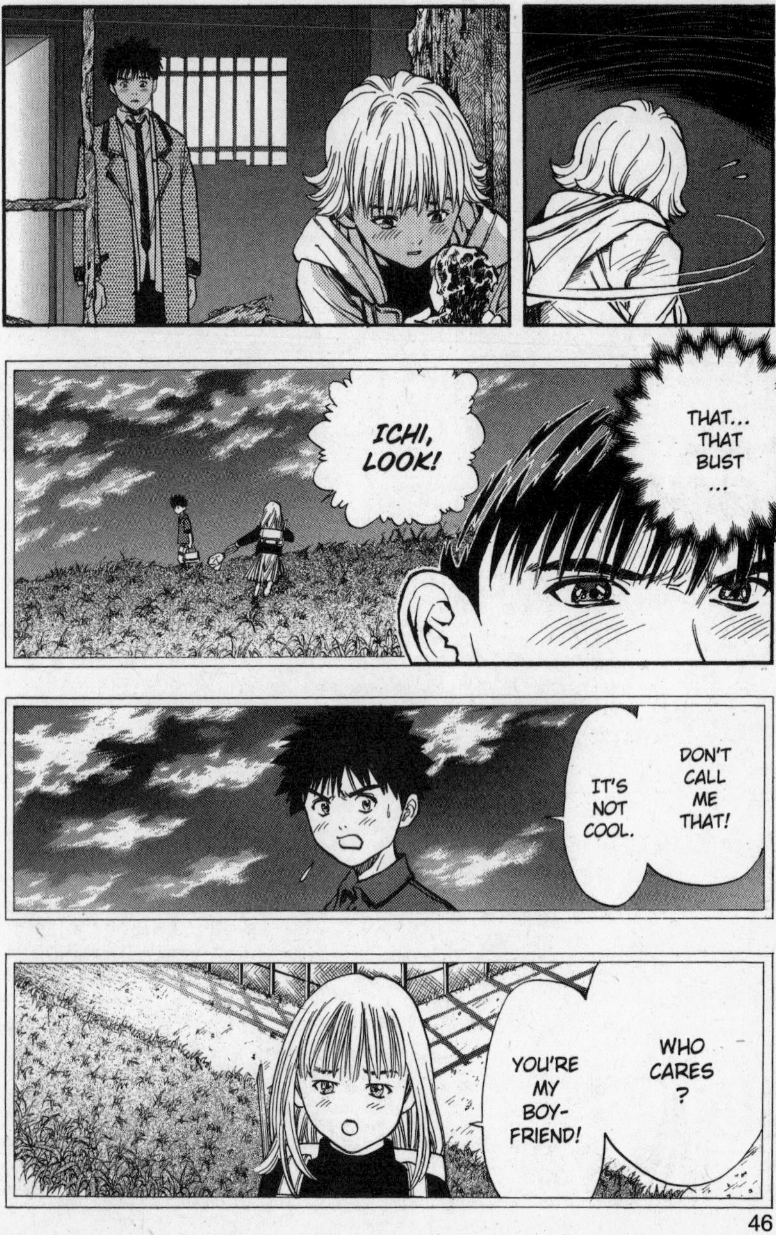
THAT... THAT BUST ...
ICHI, LOOK!
DON'T CALL ME THAT!
IT'S NOT COOL.
WHO CARES?
YOU'RE MY BOY-FRIEND!

READ THIS WAY

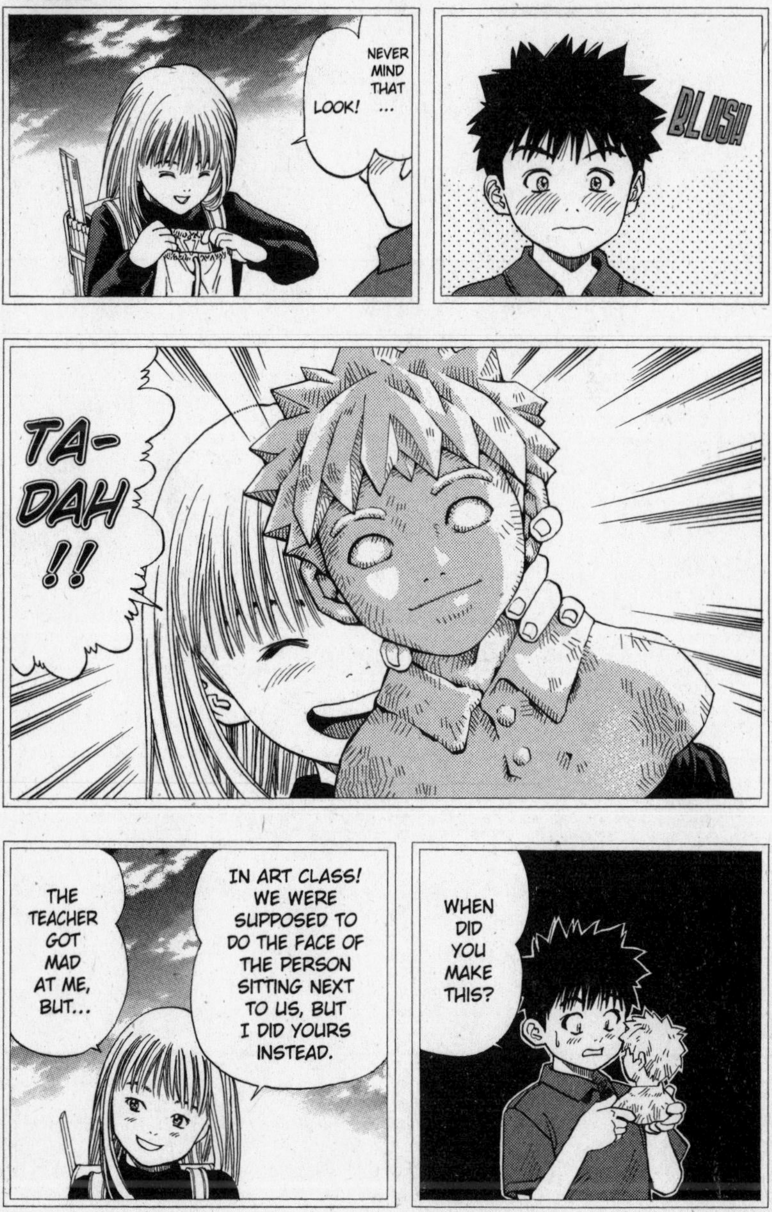

BLUSH
NEVER MIND THAT ...
LOOK!
TA-DAH!!
WHEN DID YOU MAKE THIS?
IN ART CLASS! WE WERE SUPPOSED TO DO THE FACE OF THE PERSON SITTING NEXT TO US, BUT I DID YOURS INSTEAD.
THE TEACHER GOT MAD AT ME, BUT...

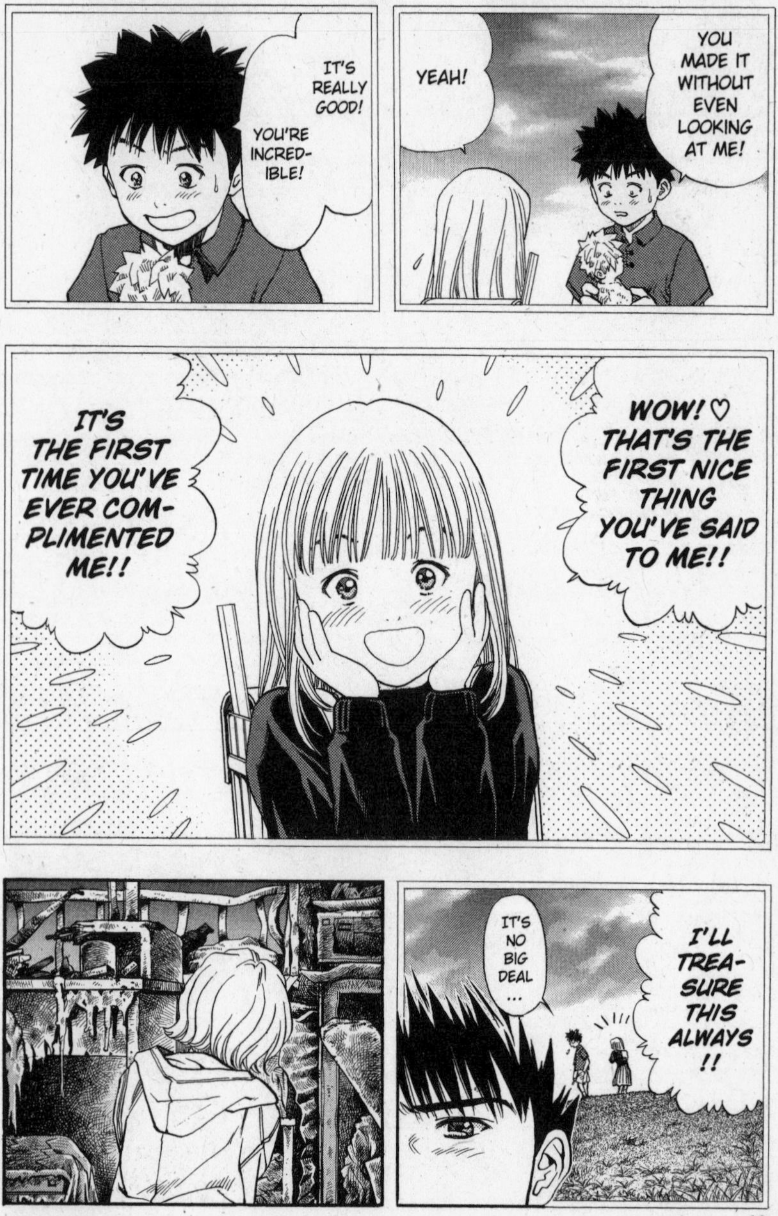
YOU MADE IT WITHOUT EVEN LOOKING AT ME!
YEAH!
IT'S REALLY GOOD!
YOU'RE INCREDIBLE!
WOW! ♡ THAT'S THE FIRST NICE THING YOU'VE SAID TO ME!!
IT'S THE FIRST TIME YOU'VE EVER COMPLIMENTED ME!!
I'LL TREASURE THIS ALWAYS!!
IT'S NO BIG DEAL...

READ THIS WAY

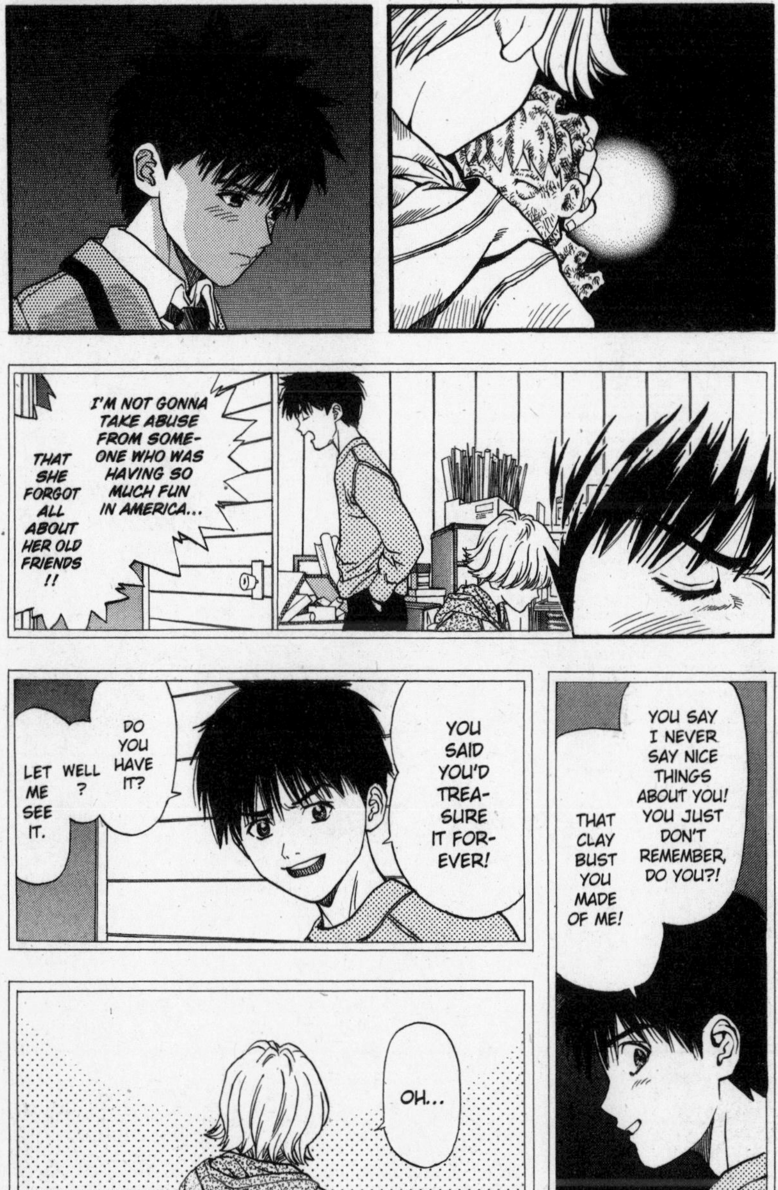

I'M NOT GONNA TAKE ABUSE FROM SOME-ONE WHO WAS HAVING SO MUCH FUN IN AMERICA...
THAT SHE FORGOT ALL ABOUT HER OLD FRIENDS !!
YOU SAY I NEVER SAY NICE THINGS ABOUT YOU! YOU JUST DON'T REMEMBER, DO YOU?!
THAT CLAY BUST YOU MADE OF ME!
YOU SAID YOU'D TREA-SURE IT FOR-EVER!
DO YOU HAVE IT?
WELL ?
LET ME SEE IT.
OH...

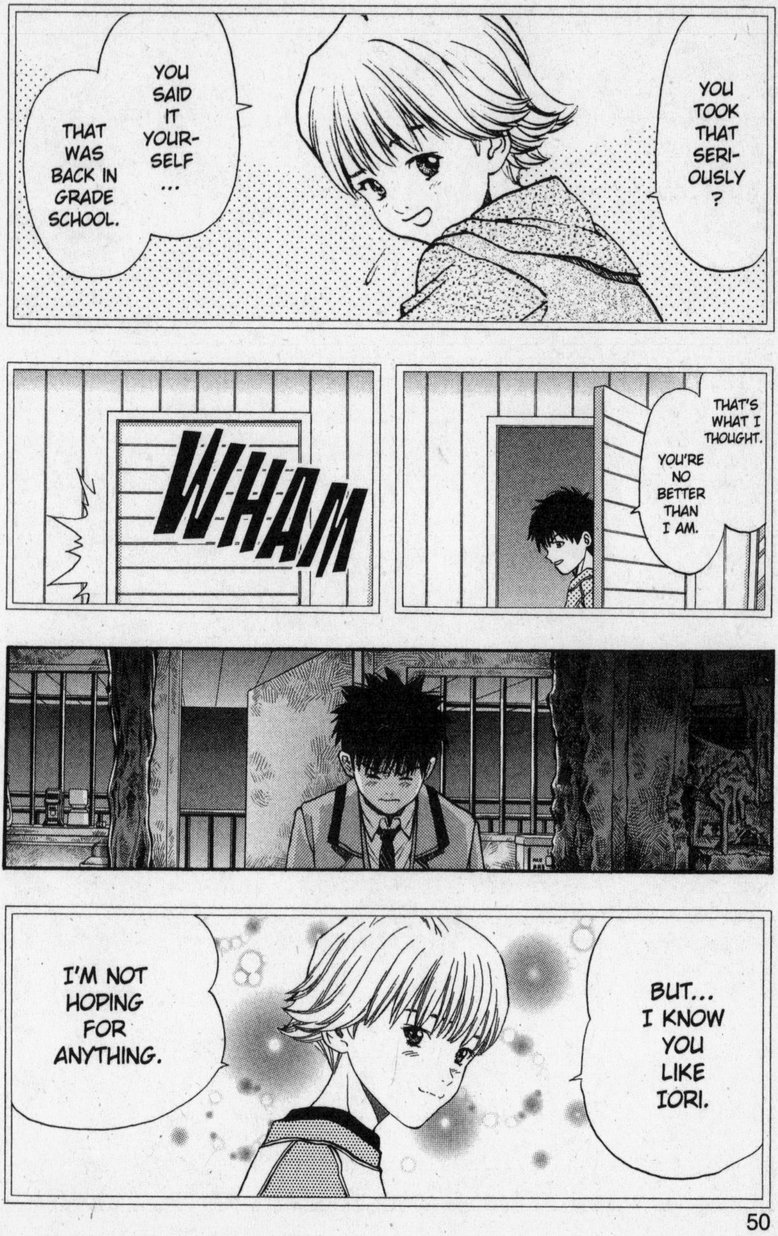
YOU TOOK THAT SERIOUSLY?
YOU SAID IT YOURSELF...
THAT WAS BACK IN GRADE SCHOOL.
THAT'S WHAT I THOUGHT.
YOU'RE NO BETTER THAN I AM.
WHAM
BUT... I KNOW YOU LIKE IORI.
I'M NOT HOPING FOR ANYTHING.

READ THIS WAY

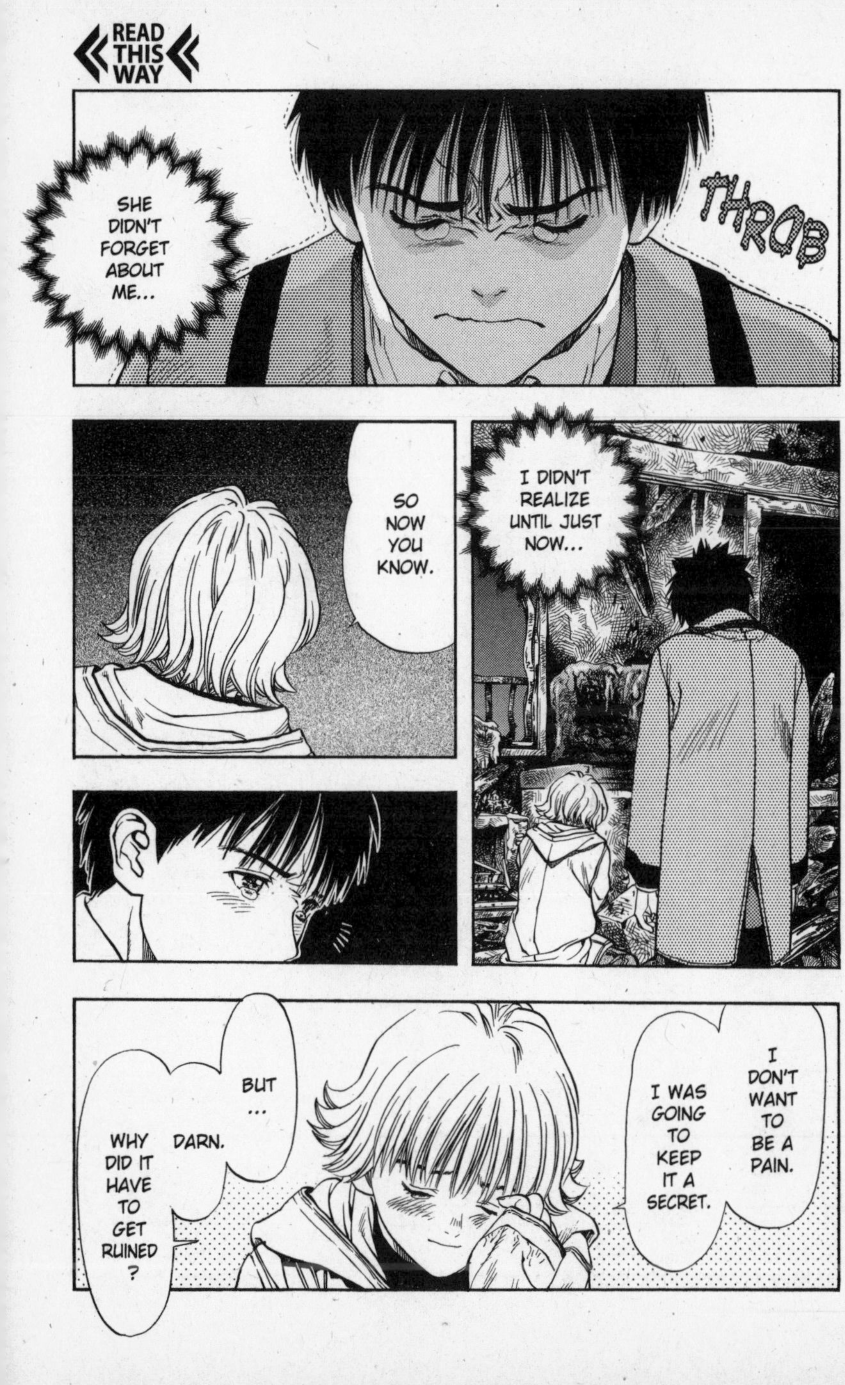
THROB
SHE DIDN'T FORGET ABOUT ME...
I DIDN'T REALIZE UNTIL JUST NOW...
SO NOW YOU KNOW.
I DON'T WANT TO BE A PAIN.
I WAS GOING TO KEEP IT A SECRET.
BUT ...
DARN.
WHY DID IT HAVE TO GET RUINED?

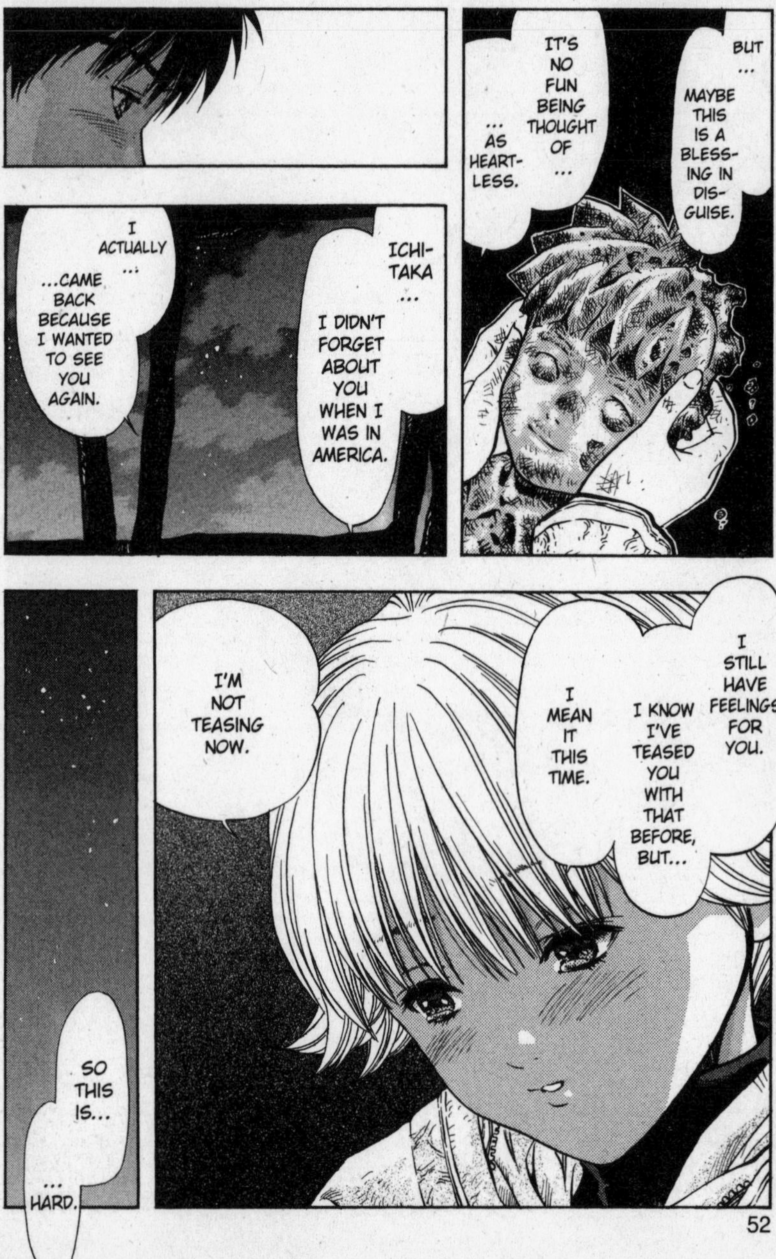
BUT... MAYBE THIS IS A BLESSING IN DISGUISE.
IT'S NO FUN BEING THOUGHT OF...
...AS HEARTLESS.
ICHITAKA... I DIDN'T FORGET ABOUT YOU WHEN I WAS IN AMERICA.
I ACTUALLY...
...CAME BACK BECAUSE I WANTED TO SEE YOU AGAIN.
I STILL HAVE FEELINGS FOR YOU.
I KNOW I'VE TEASED YOU WITH THAT BEFORE, BUT...
I MEAN IT THIS TIME.
I'M NOT TEASING NOW.
SO THIS IS...
...HARD.

READ THIS WAY

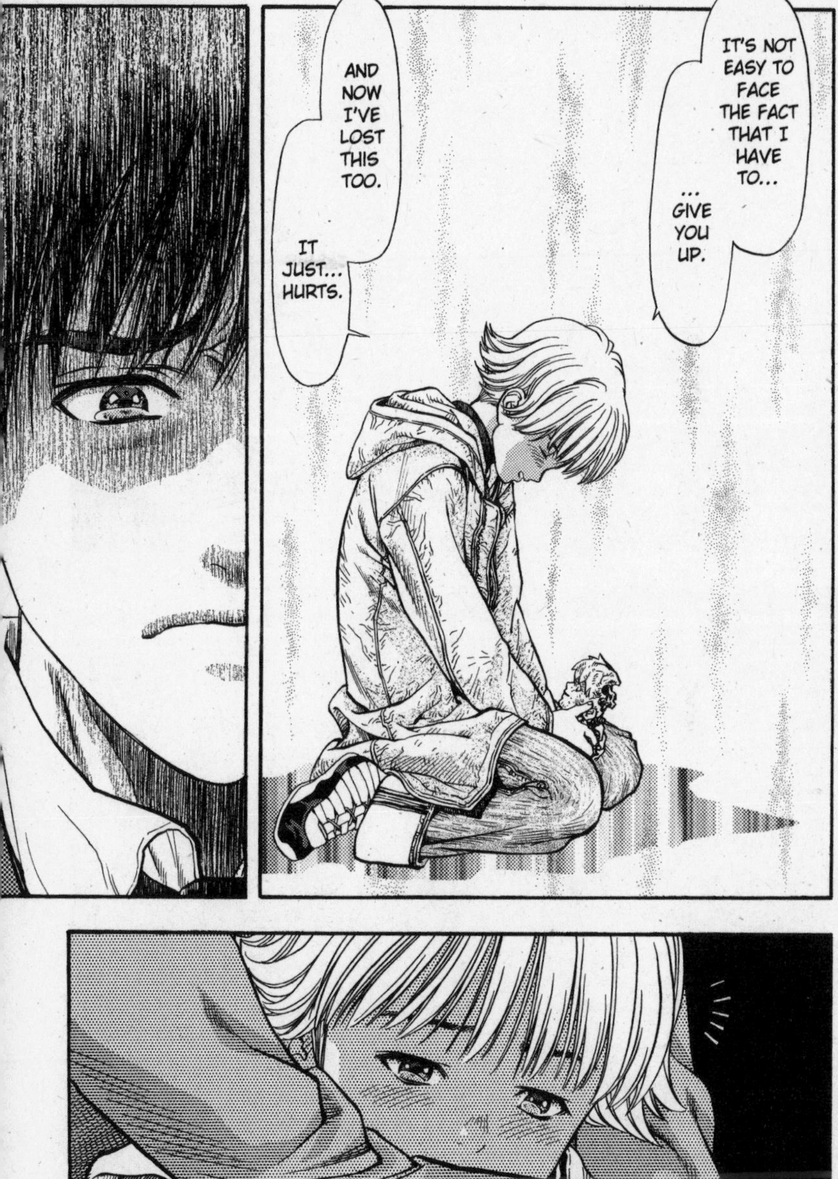
IT'S NOT EASY TO FACE THE FACT THAT I HAVE TO...
... GIVE YOU UP.
AND NOW I'VE LOST THIS TOO.
IT JUST... HURTS.

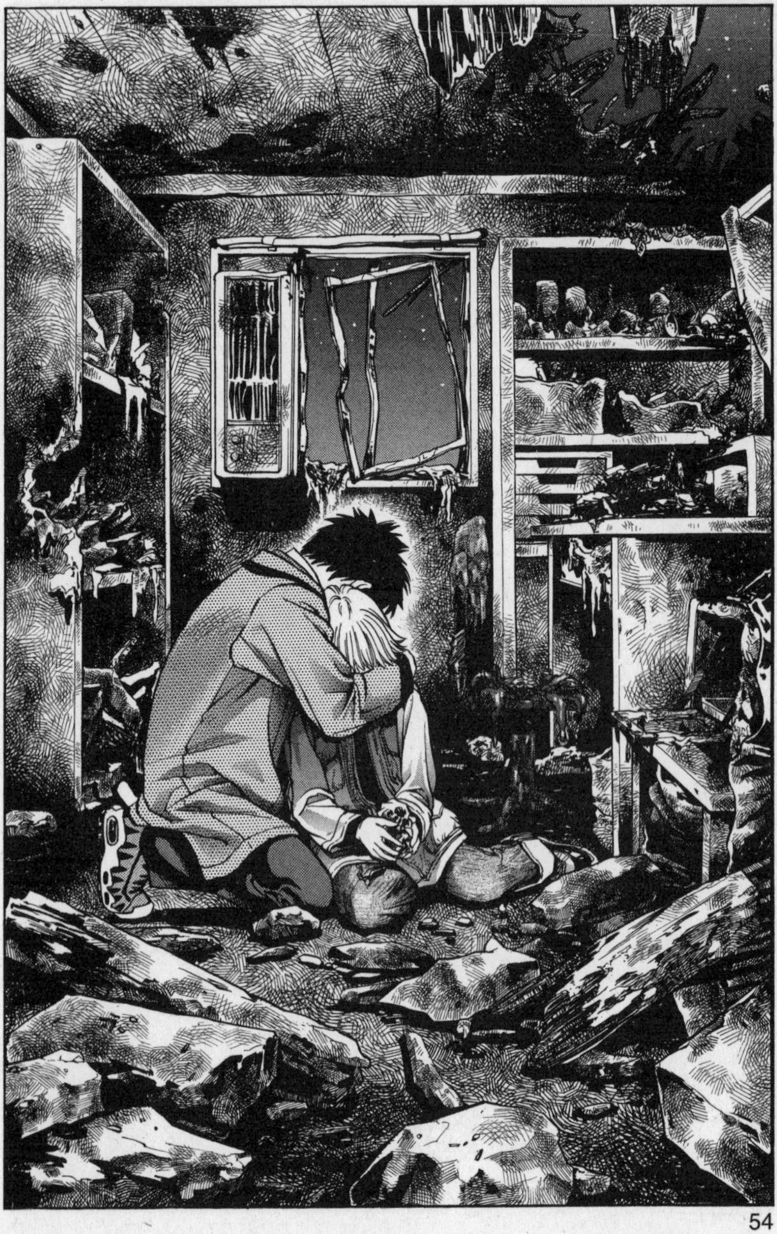

READ THIS WAY

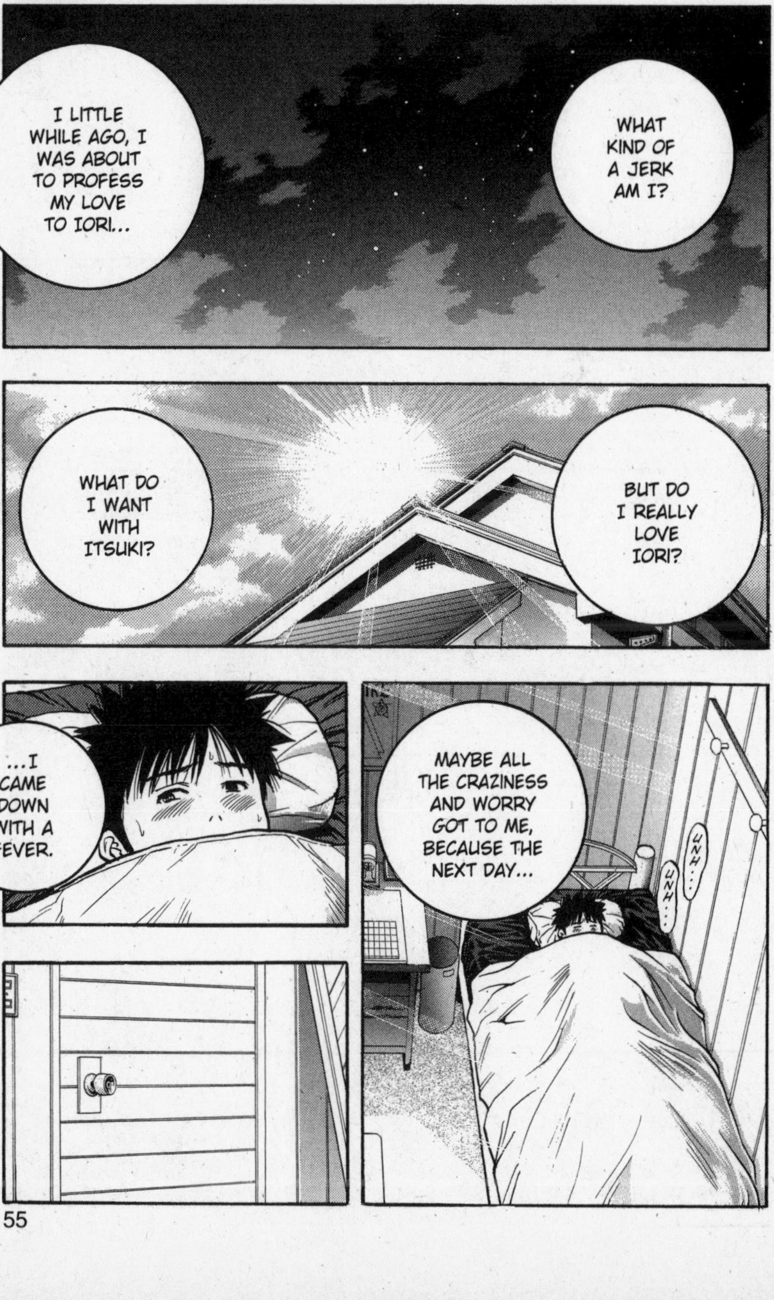

WHAT KIND OF A JERK AM I?
I LITTLE WHILE AGO, I WAS ABOUT TO PROFESS MY LOVE TO IORI...
BUT DO I REALLY LOVE IORI?
WHAT DO I WANT WITH ITSUKI?
MAYBE ALL THE CRAZINESS AND WORRY GOT TO ME, BECAUSE THE NEXT DAY...
UNH...
UNH...
...I CAME DOWN WITH A FEVER.

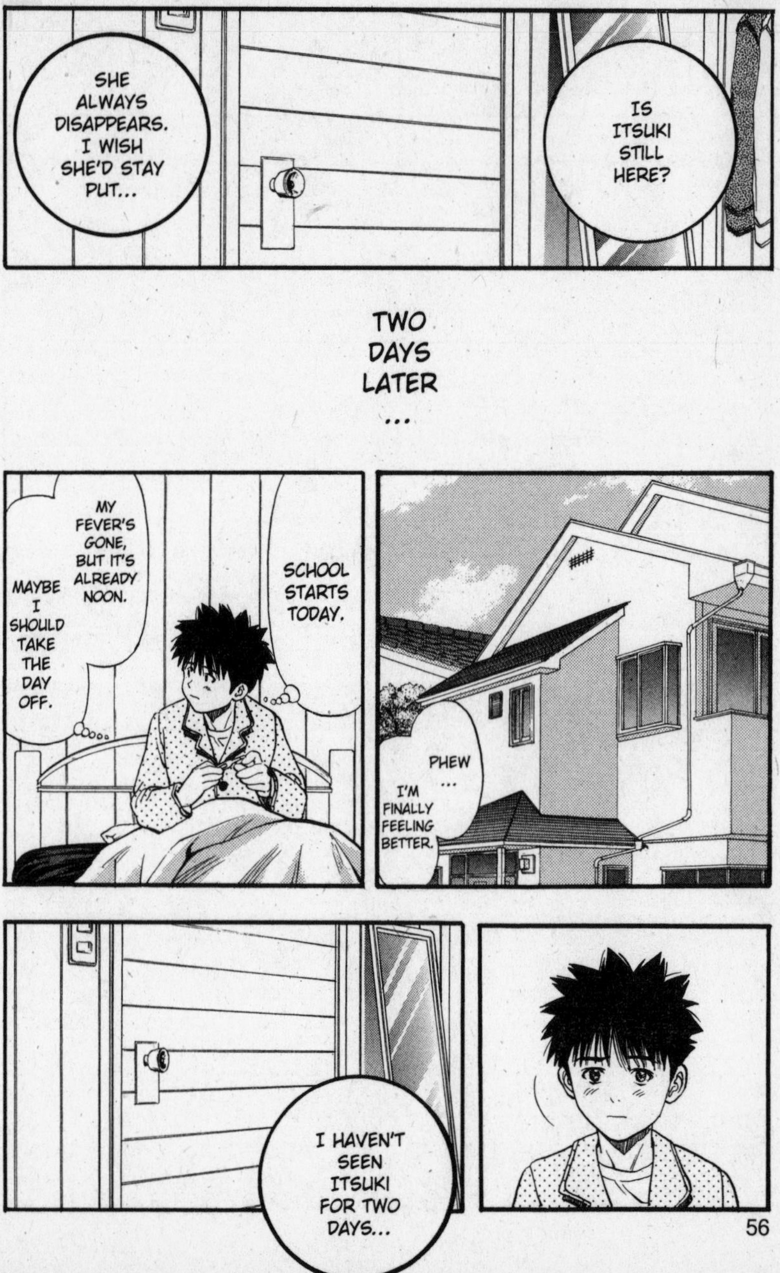
IS ITSUKI STILL HERE?
SHE ALWAYS DISAPPEARS. I WISH SHE'D STAY PUT...
TWO DAYS LATER...
PHEW... I'M FINALLY FEELING BETTER.
SCHOOL STARTS TODAY.
MY FEVER'S GONE, BUT IT'S ALREADY NOON.
MAYBE I SHOULD TAKE THE DAY OFF.
I HAVEN'T SEEN ITSUKI FOR TWO DAYS...

READ THIS WAY

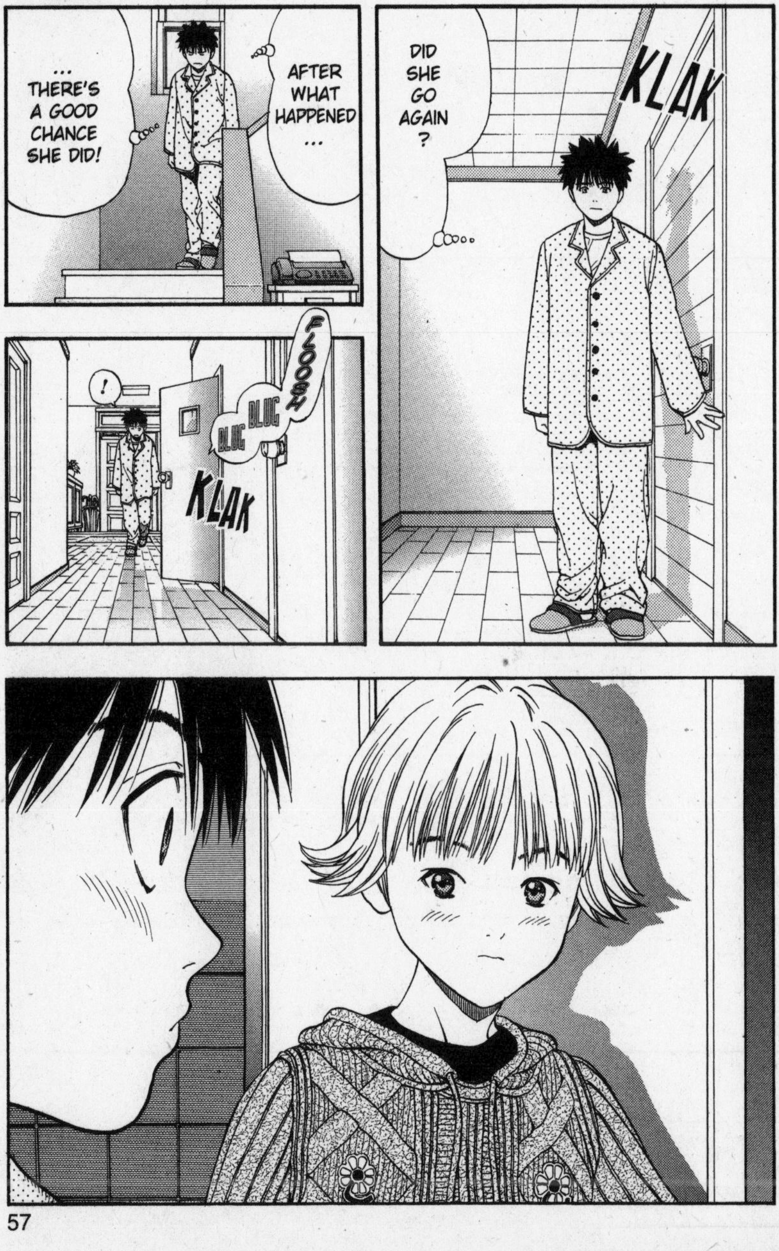

DID SHE GO AGAIN?
KLAK
AFTER WHAT HAPPENED...
...THERE'S A GOOD CHANCE SHE DID!
FLOOSH
BLUG BLUG
!
KLAK

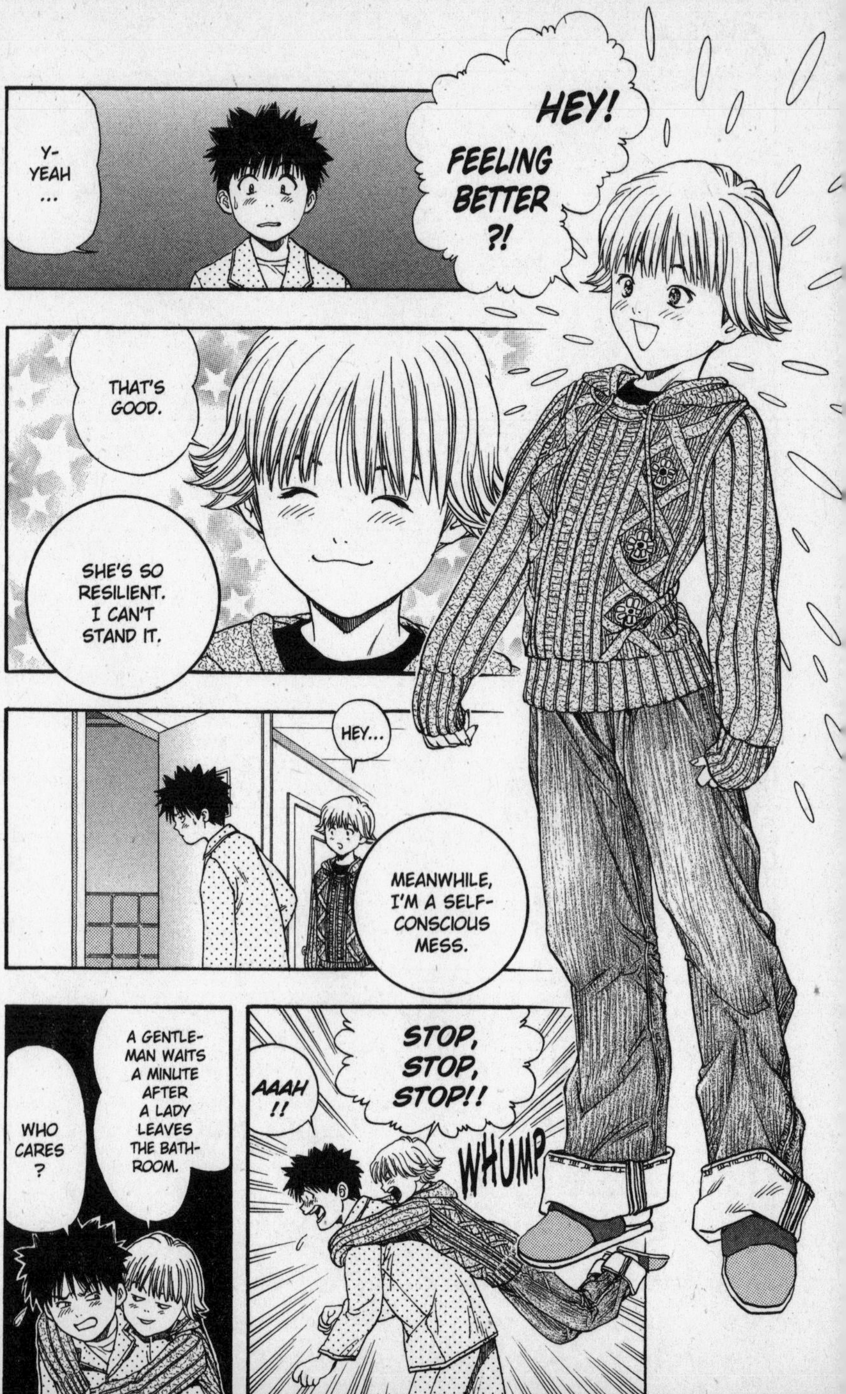
HEY! FEELING BETTER ?!
Y-YEAH ...
THAT'S GOOD.
SHE'S SO RESILIENT. I CAN'T STAND IT.
HEY...
MEANWHILE, I'M A SELF-CONSCIOUS MESS.
STOP, STOP, STOP!!
AAAH !!
WHUMP
A GENTLE-MAN WAITS A MINUTE AFTER A LADY LEAVES THE BATH-ROOM.
WHO CARES ?

READ THIS WAY

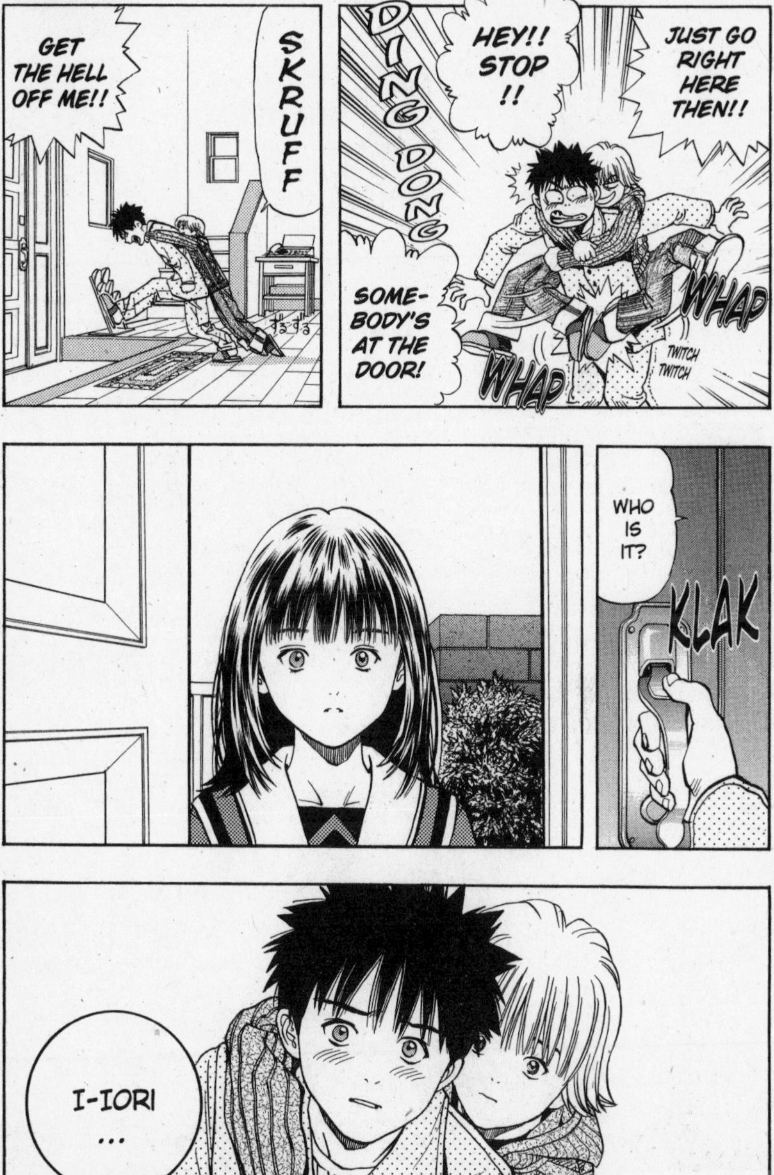
JUST GO RIGHT HERE THEN!!
HEY!! STOP !!
DING DONG
SOMEBODY'S AT THE DOOR!
WHAP
WHAP
TWITCH TWITCH
SKRUFF
GET THE HELL OFF ME!!
ずるずる
WHO IS IT?
KLAK
I-IORI ...

Chapter 39:
The First Problem

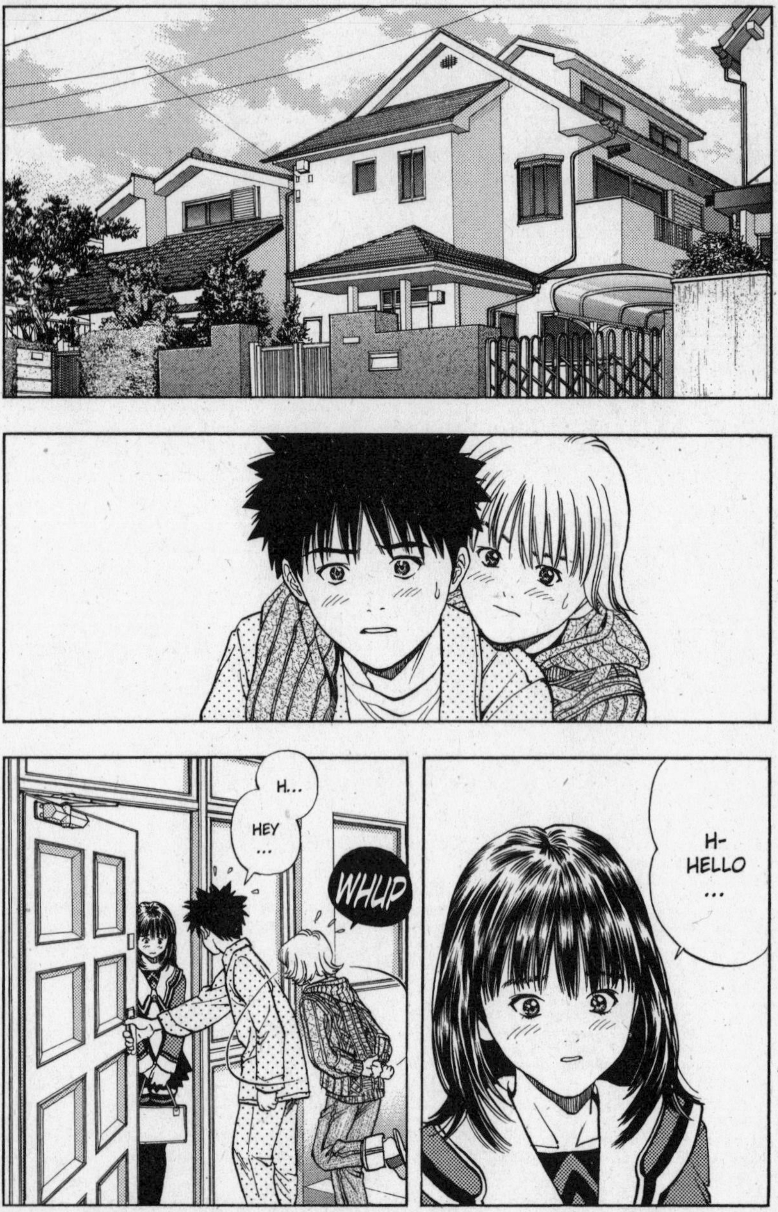
H- HELLO ...
H... HEY ...
WHUP

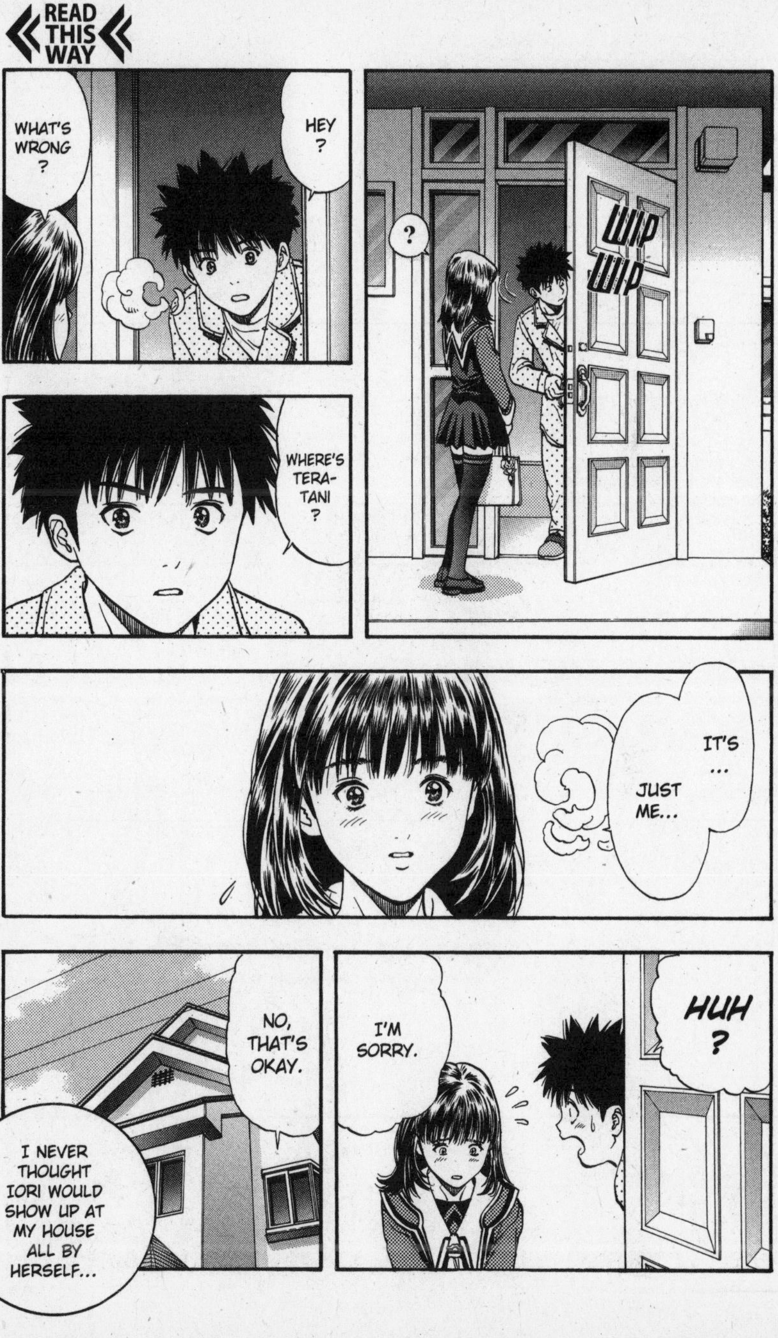
READ THIS WAY
WIP WIP
?
HEY ?
WHAT'S WRONG ?
WHERE'S TERA-TANI ?
IT'S ...
JUST ME...
HUH ?
I'M SORRY.
NO, THAT'S OKAY.
I NEVER THOUGHT IORI WOULD SHOW UP AT MY HOUSE ALL BY HERSELF...

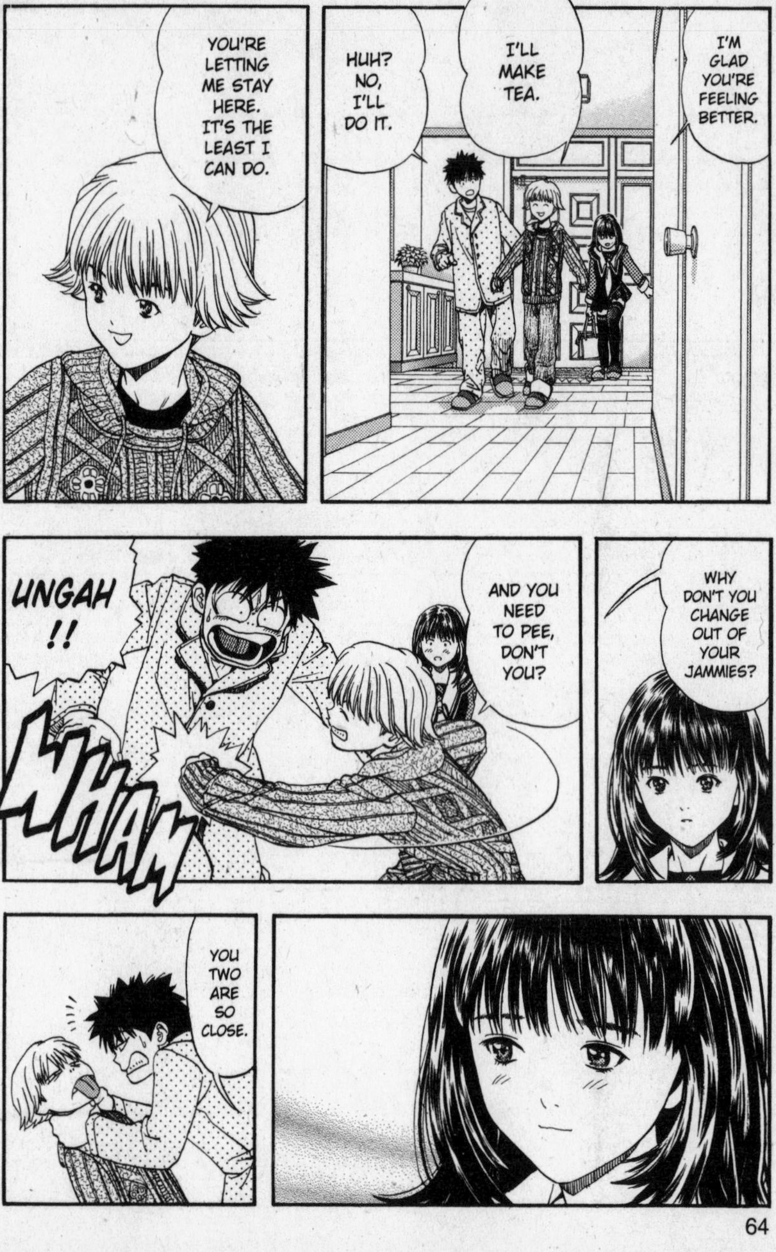
I'M GLAD YOU'RE FEELING BETTER.
I'LL MAKE TEA.
HUH? NO, I'LL DO IT.
YOU'RE LETTING ME STAY HERE. IT'S THE LEAST I CAN DO.
WHY DON'T YOU CHANGE OUT OF YOUR JAMMIES?
AND YOU NEED TO PEE, DON'T YOU?
UNGAH !!
WHAM
YOU TWO ARE SO CLOSE.

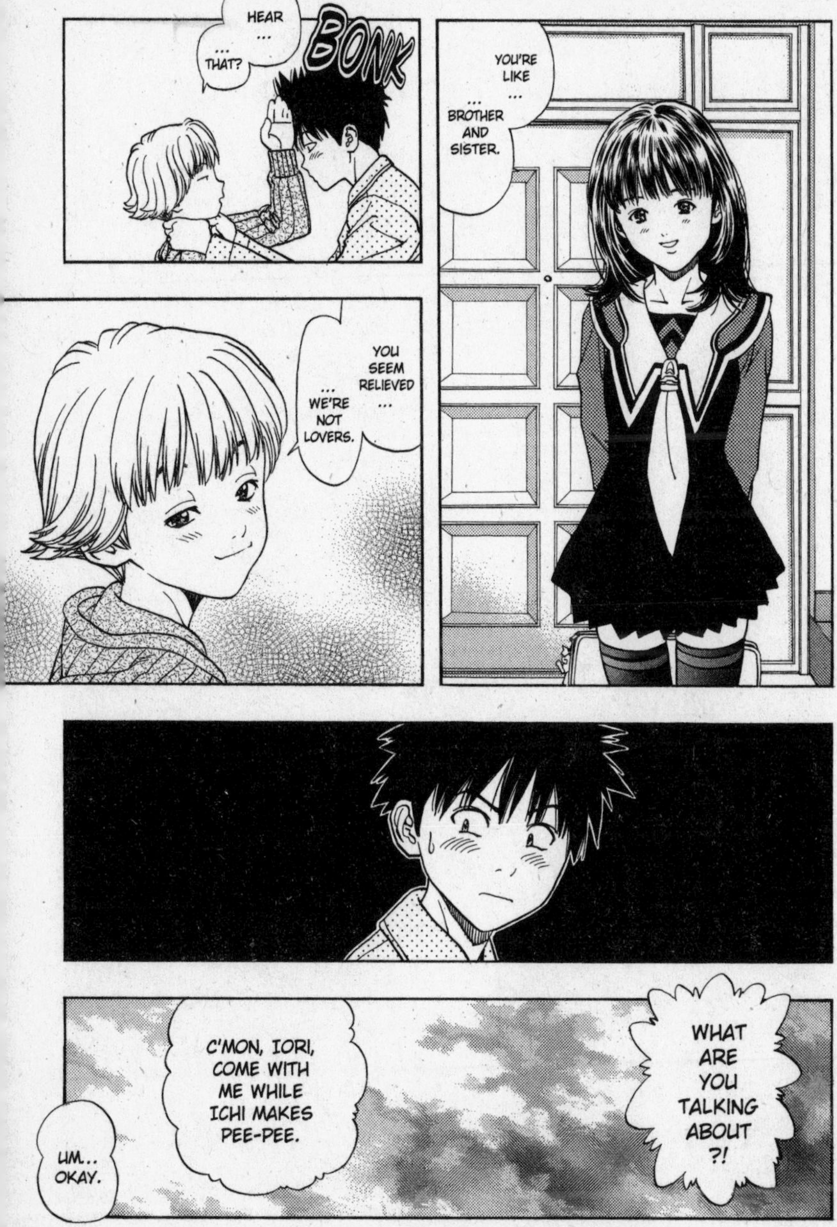
YOU'RE LIKE ... BROTHER AND SISTER.
HEAR ... THAT?
BONK
YOU SEEM RELIEVED ... WE'RE NOT LOVERS.
WHAT ARE YOU TALKING ABOUT ?!
C'MON, IORI, COME WITH ME WHILE ICHI MAKES PEE-PEE.
UM... OKAY.

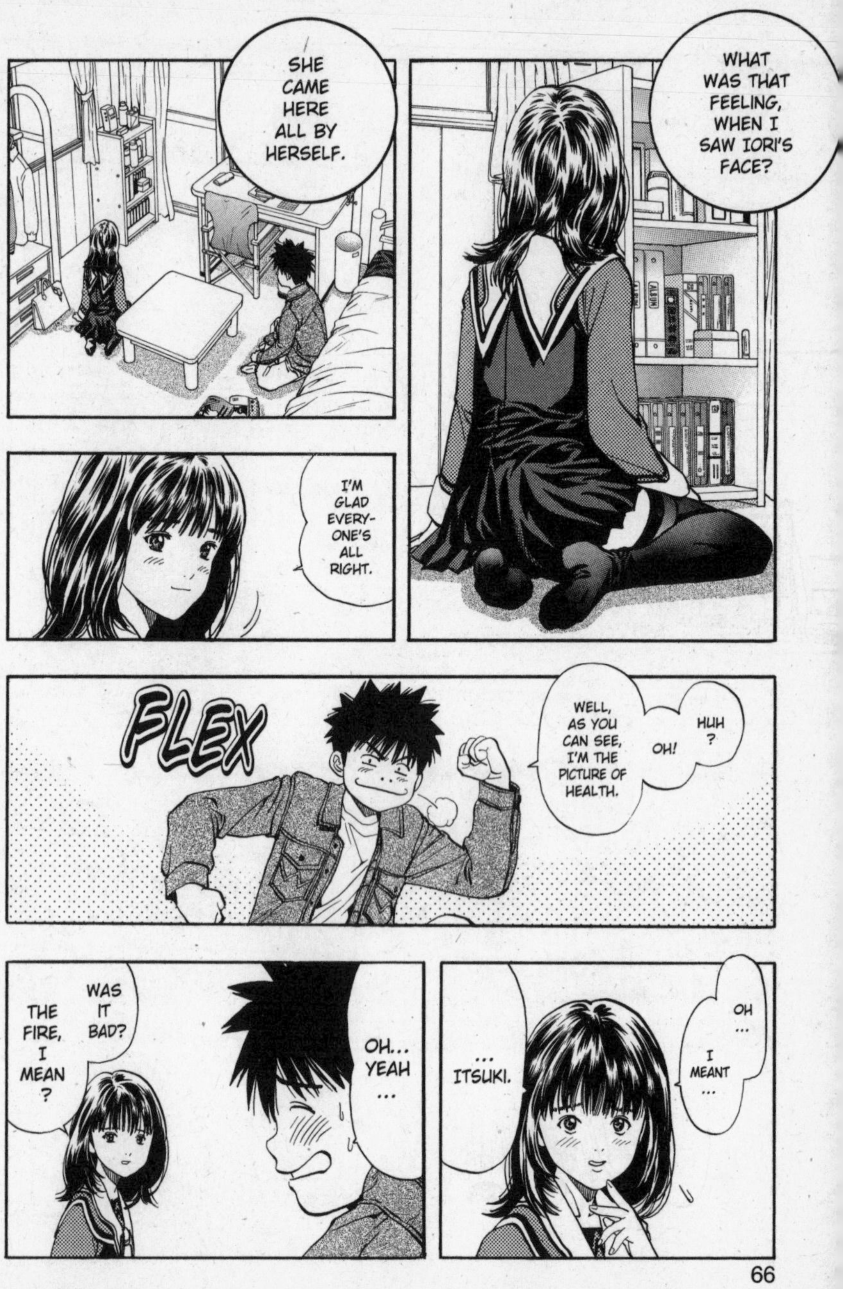
WHAT WAS THAT FEELING, WHEN I SAW IORI'S FACE?
SHE CAME HERE ALL BY HERSELF.
I'M GLAD EVERY-ONE'S ALL RIGHT.
HUH?
OH!
WELL, AS YOU CAN SEE, I'M THE PICTURE OF HEALTH.
FLEX
OH... I MEANT...
...ITSUKI.
OH... YEAH...
WAS IT BAD?
THE FIRE, I MEAN?

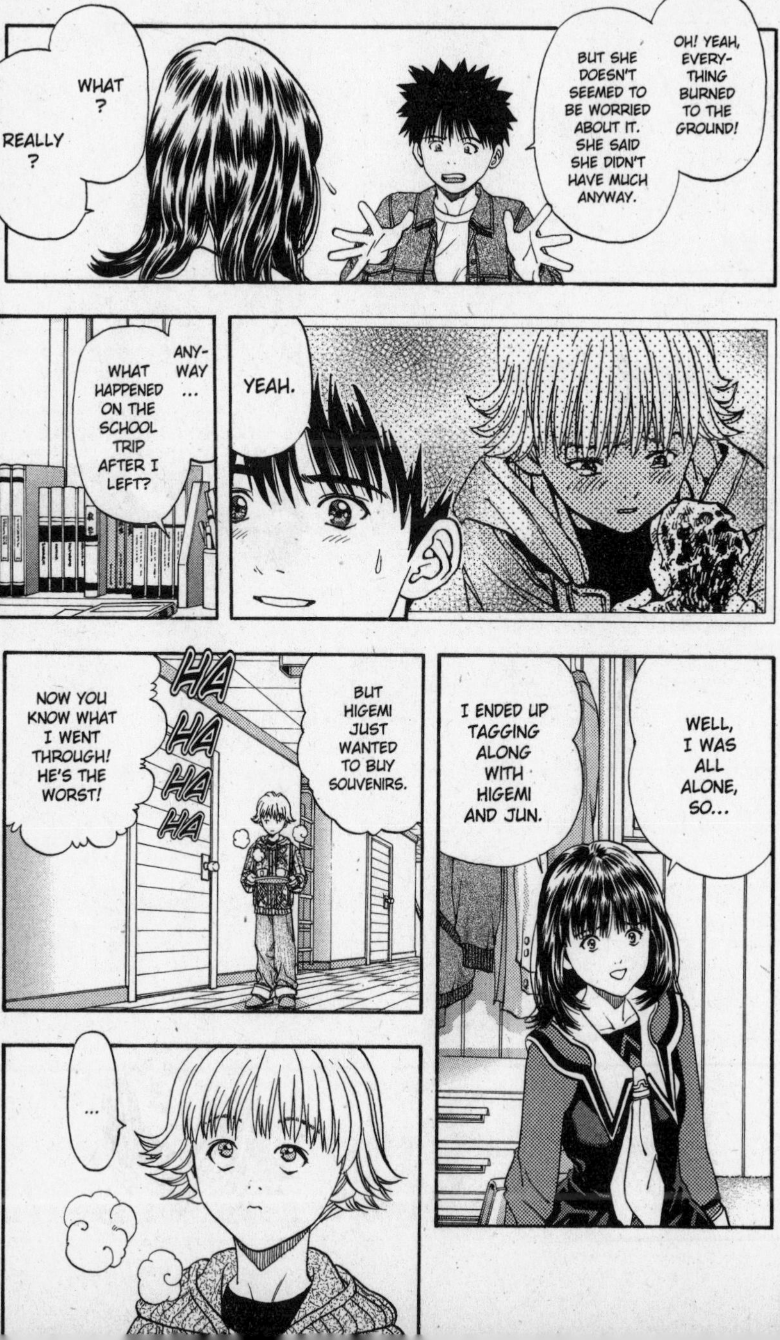
OH! YEAH, EVERYTHING BURNED TO THE GROUND!
BUT SHE DOESN'T SEEMED TO BE WORRIED ABOUT IT. SHE SAID SHE DIDN'T HAVE MUCH ANYWAY.
WHAT? REALLY?
YEAH.
ANYWAY...
WHAT HAPPENED ON THE SCHOOL TRIP AFTER I LEFT?
WELL, I WAS ALL ALONE, SO...
I ENDED UP TAGGING ALONG WITH HIGEMI AND JUN.
BUT HIGEMI JUST WANTED TO BUY SOUVENIRS.
HA HA HA HA
NOW YOU KNOW WHAT I WENT THROUGH! HE'S THE WORST!
...

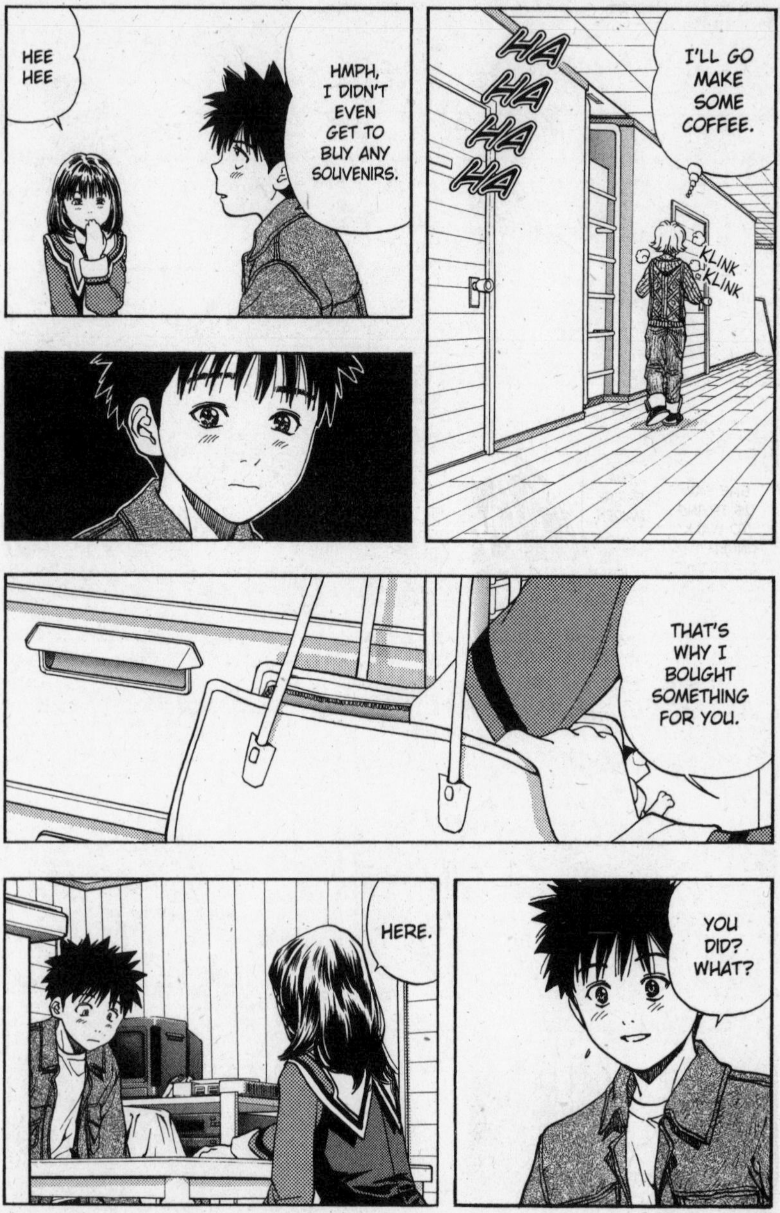
I'LL GO MAKE SOME COFFEE.
HA HA HA HA
KLINK KLINK
HMPH, I DIDN'T EVEN GET TO BUY ANY SOUVENIRS.
HEE HEE
THAT'S WHY I BOUGHT SOMETHING FOR YOU.
YOU DID? WHAT?
HERE.

READ THIS WAY

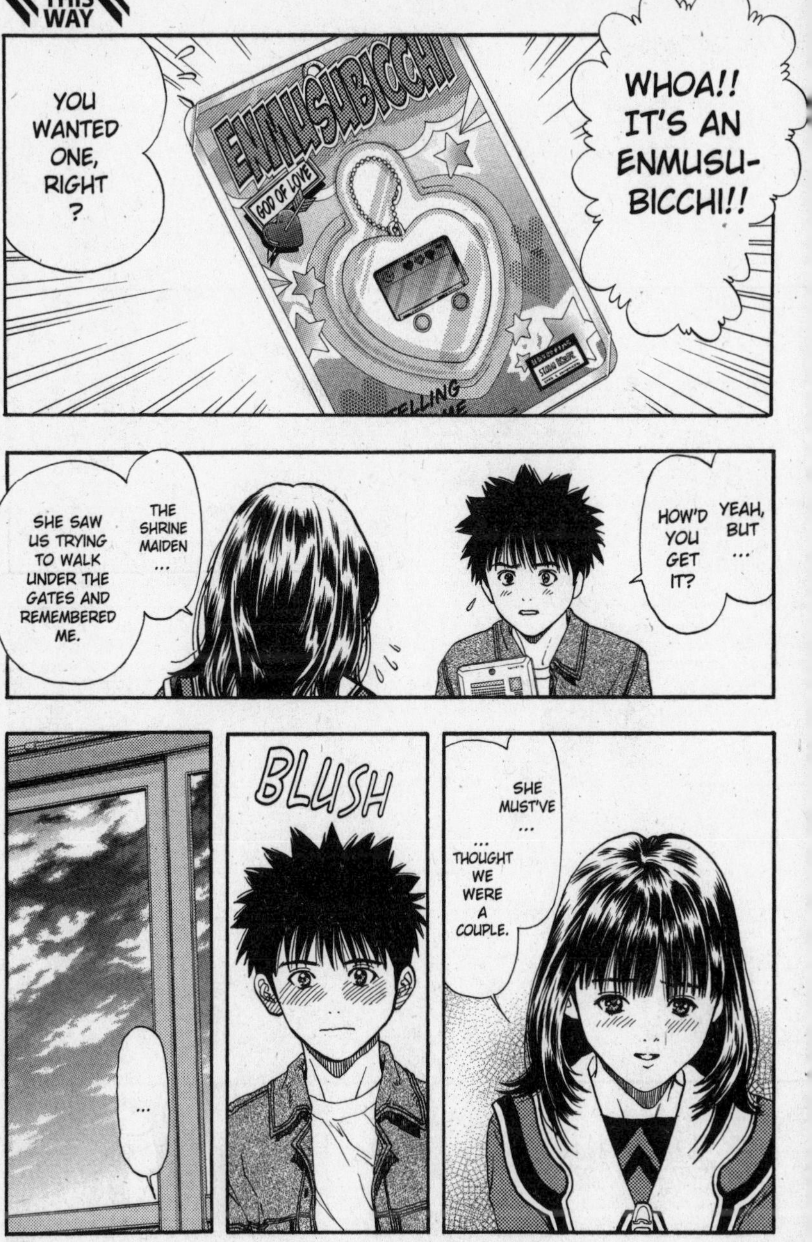
WHOA!! IT'S AN ENMUSU-BICCHI!!
ENMUSUBICCHI
GOD OF LOVE
YOU WANTED ONE, RIGHT?
YEAH, BUT ...
HOW'D YOU GET IT?
THE SHRINE MAIDEN ...
SHE SAW US TRYING TO WALK UNDER THE GATES AND REMEMBERED ME.
SHE MUST'VE ...
... THOUGHT WE WERE A COUPLE.
BLUSH
...

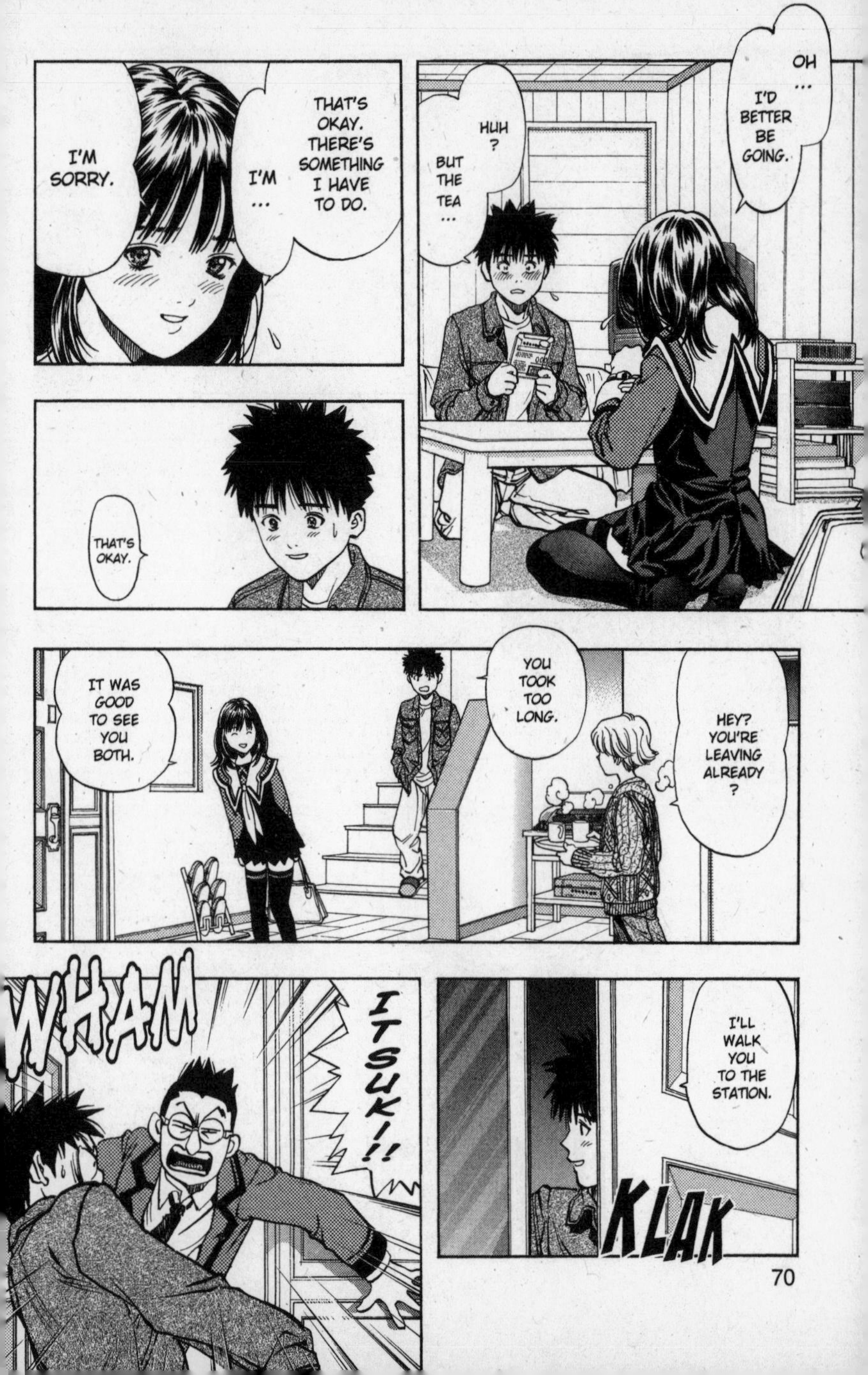
OH ... I'D BETTER BE GOING.
HUH ? BUT THE TEA ...
THAT'S OKAY. THERE'S SOMETHING I HAVE TO DO.
I'M ...
I'M SORRY.
THAT'S OKAY.
HEY? YOU'RE LEAVING ALREADY ?
YOU TOOK TOO LONG.
IT WAS GOOD TO SEE YOU BOTH.
I'LL WALK YOU TO THE STATION.
KLAK
ITSUKI!!
WHAM

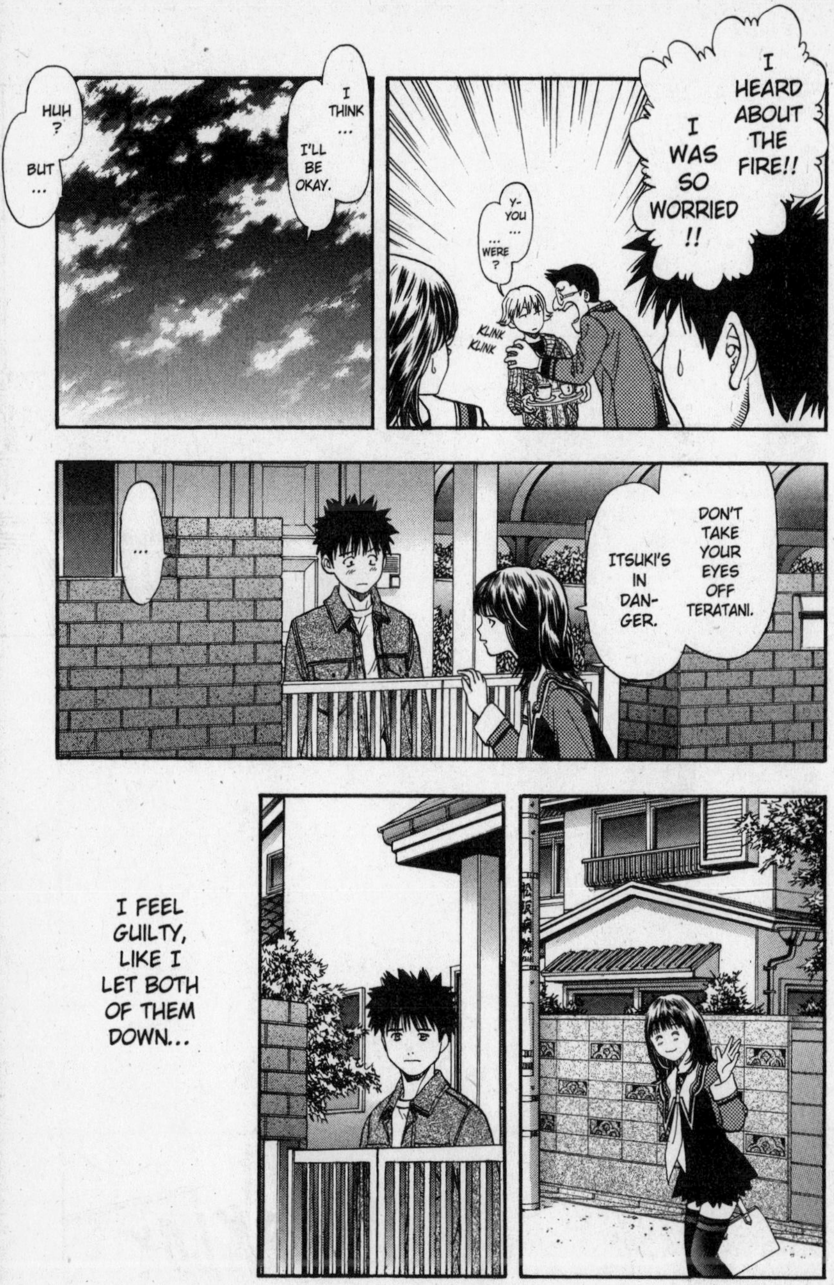
I HEARD ABOUT THE FIRE!!
I WAS SO WORRIED!!
Y-YOU... ...WERE?
KLINK KLINK
I THINK... I'LL BE OKAY.
HUH? BUT...
DON'T TAKE YOUR EYES OFF TERATANI.
ITSUKI'S IN DAN-GER.
...
I FEEL GUILTY, LIKE I LET BOTH OF THEM DOWN...

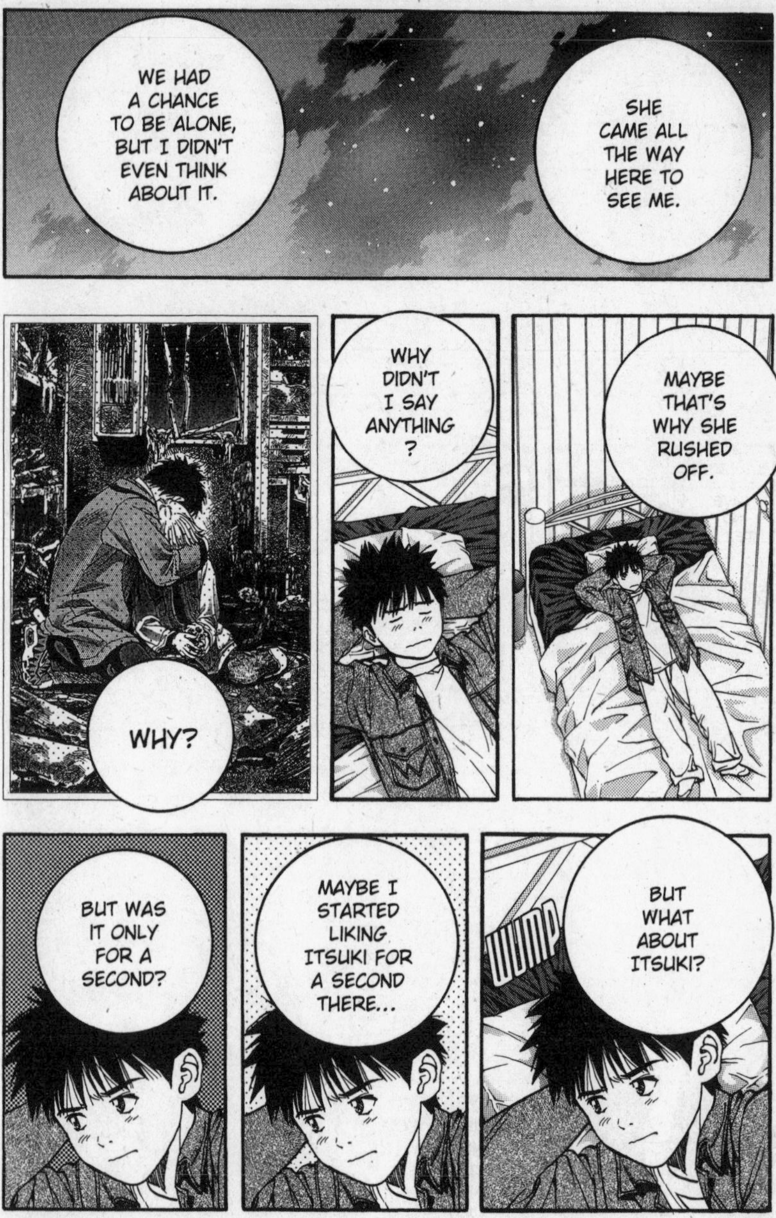
SHE CAME ALL THE WAY HERE TO SEE ME.
WE HAD A CHANCE TO BE ALONE, BUT I DIDN'T EVEN THINK ABOUT IT.
MAYBE THAT'S WHY SHE RUSHED OFF.
WHY DIDN'T I SAY ANYTHING?
WHY?
WUMP
BUT WHAT ABOUT ITSUKI?
MAYBE I STARTED LIKING ITSUKI FOR A SECOND THERE...
BUT WAS IT ONLY FOR A SECOND?

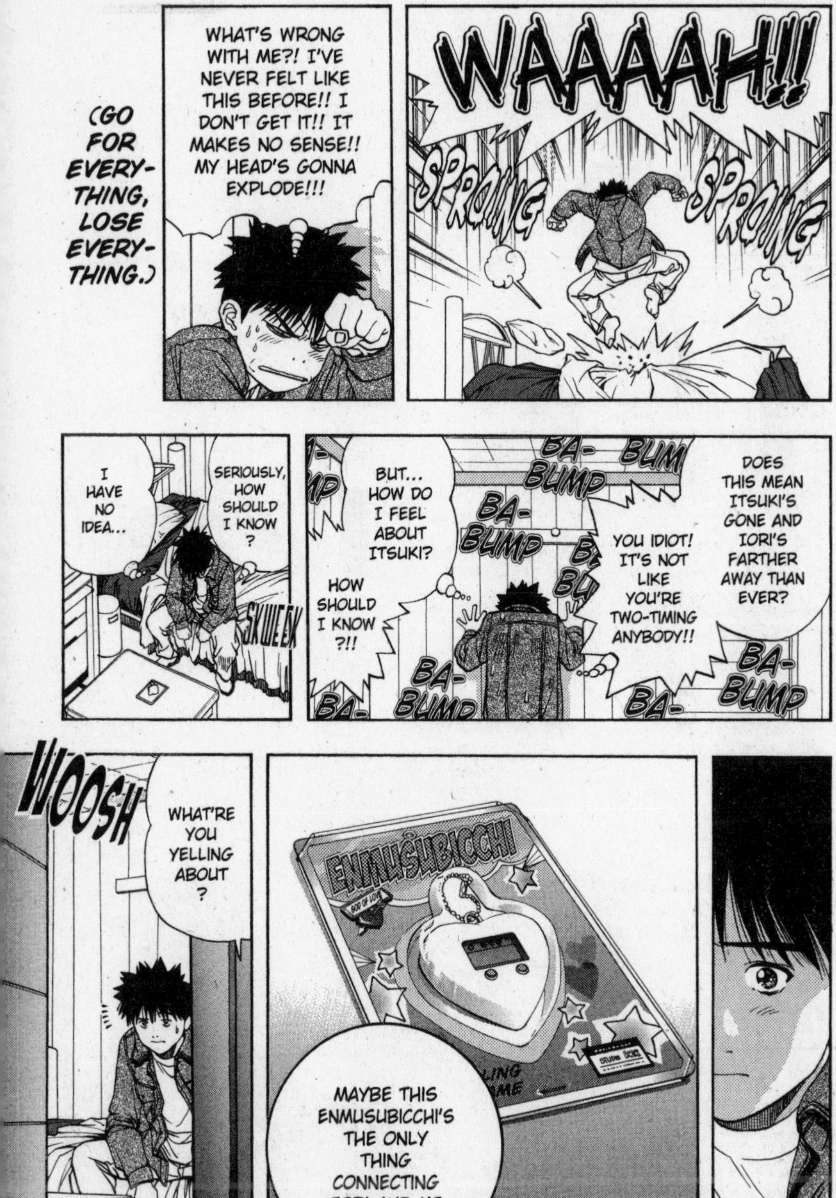
WAAAAH!!
SPROING
SPROING
WHAT'S WRONG WITH ME?! I'VE NEVER FELT LIKE THIS BEFORE!! I DON'T GET IT!! IT MAKES NO SENSE!! MY HEAD'S GONNA EXPLODE!!!
(GO FOR EVERYTHING, LOSE EVERYTHING.)
BA-BUMP
BUMP
DOES THIS MEAN ITSUKI'S GONE AND IORI'S FARTHER AWAY THAN EVER?
YOU IDIOT! IT'S NOT LIKE YOU'RE TWO-TIMING ANYBODY!!
BA-BUMP
BUT... HOW DO I FEEL ABOUT ITSUKI?
HOW SHOULD I KNOW?!!
BA-BUMP
BA-BUMP
SERIOUSLY, HOW SHOULD I KNOW?
I HAVE NO IDEA...
SKWEEK
ENMUSUBICCHI
GOD OF LOVE
MAYBE THIS ENMUSUBICCHI'S THE ONLY THING CONNECTING IORI AND ME.
WOOSH
WHAT'RE YOU YELLING ABOUT?

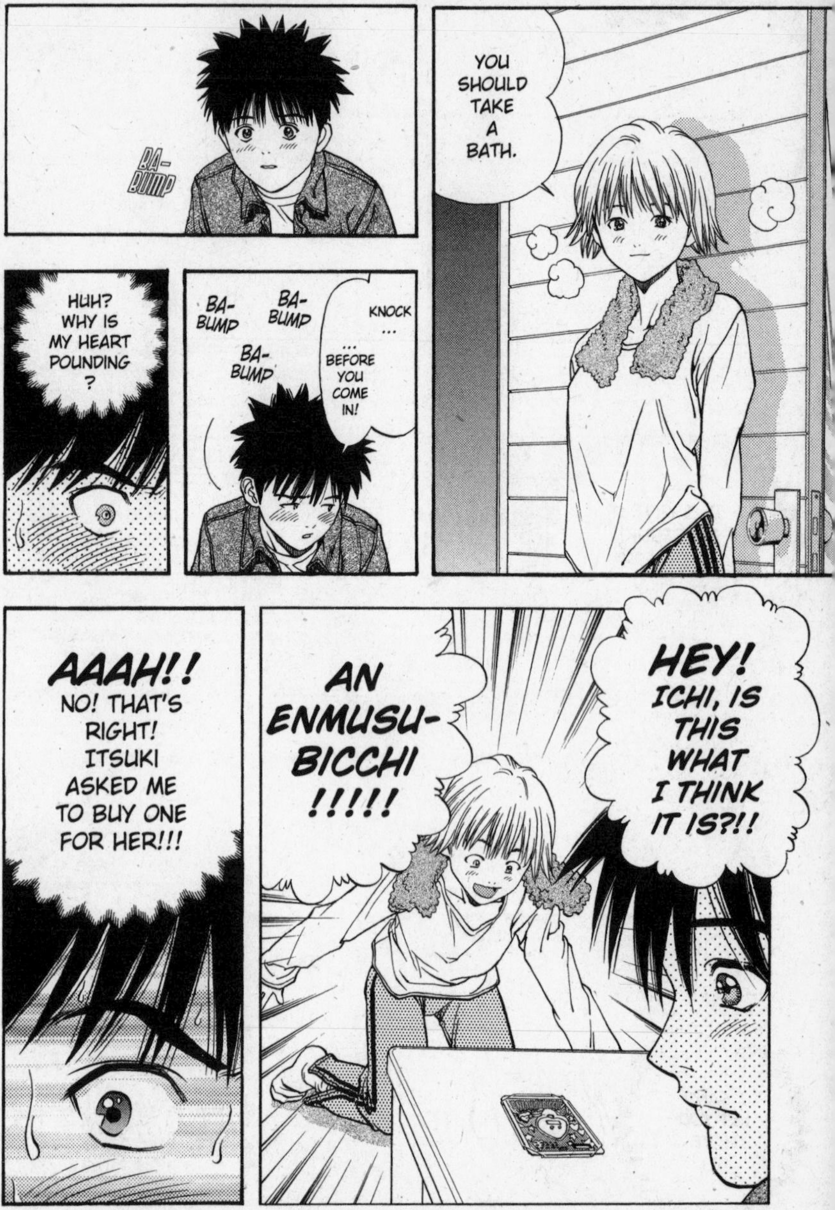
YOU SHOULD TAKE A BATH.
BA-BUMP
KNOCK ... ... BEFORE YOU COME IN!
BA-BUMP
BA-BUMP
BA-BUMP
HUH? WHY IS MY HEART POUNDING ?
HEY! ICHI, IS THIS WHAT I THINK IT IS?!!
AN ENMUSU-BICCHI !!!!!
AAAH!! NO! THAT'S RIGHT! ITSUKI ASKED ME TO BUY ONE FOR HER!!!

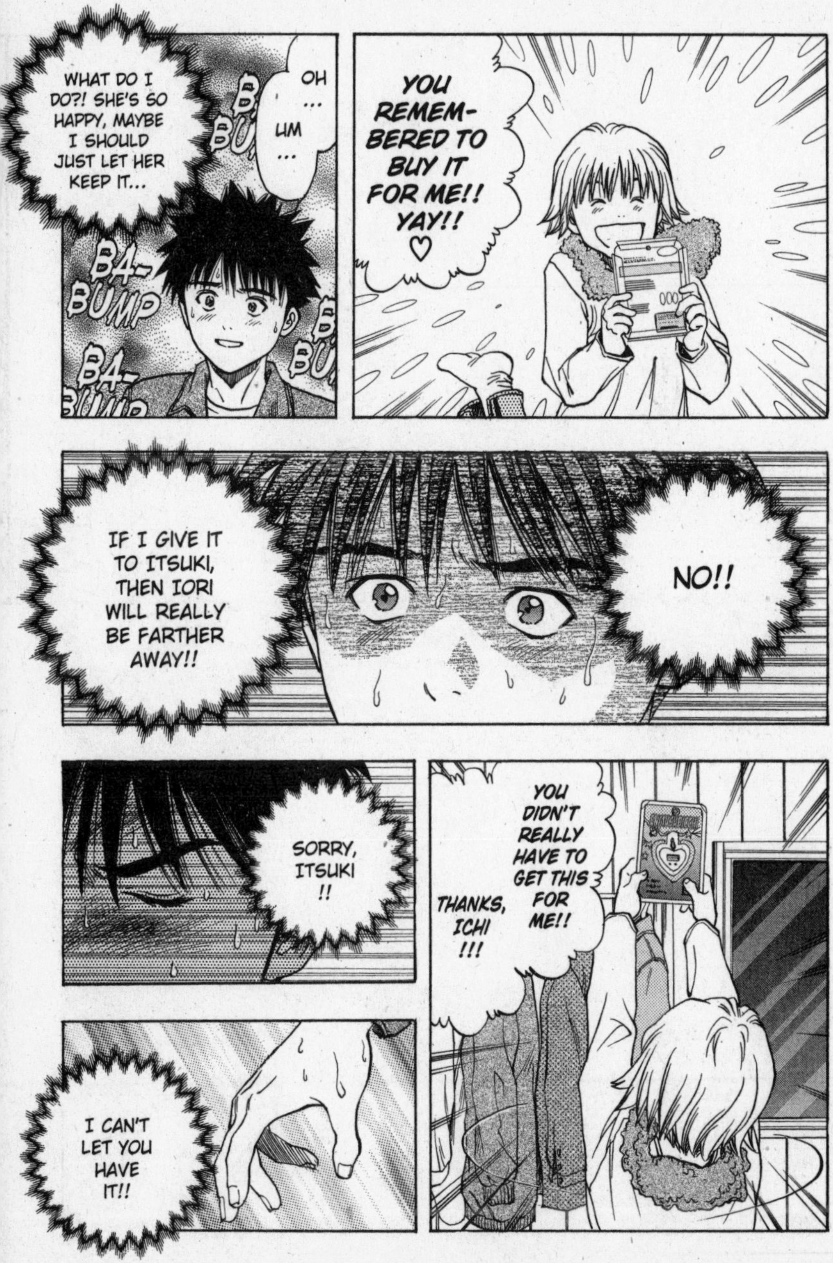

YOU REMEMBERED TO BUY IT FOR ME!! YAY!! ♡
OH ... UM ...
BA-BUMP
WHAT DO I DO?! SHE'S SO HAPPY, MAYBE I SHOULD JUST LET HER KEEP IT...
BA-BUMP
BA-BUMP
NO!!
IF I GIVE IT TO ITSUKI, THEN IORI WILL REALLY BE FARTHER AWAY!!
YOU DIDN'T REALLY HAVE TO GET THIS FOR ME!!
THANKS, ICHI !!!
SORRY, ITSUKI !!
I CAN'T LET YOU HAVE IT!!

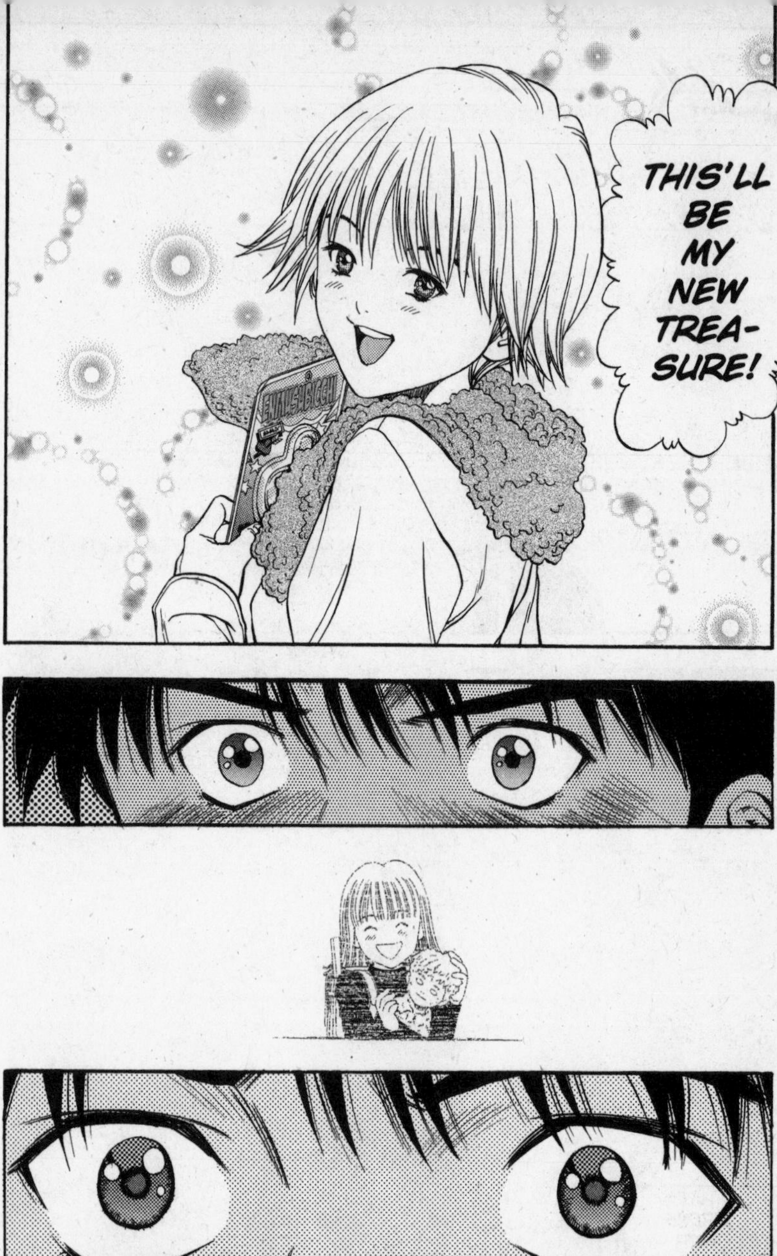
THIS'LL BE MY NEW TREA-SURE!

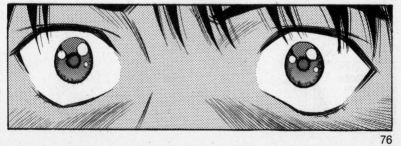

READ THIS WAY

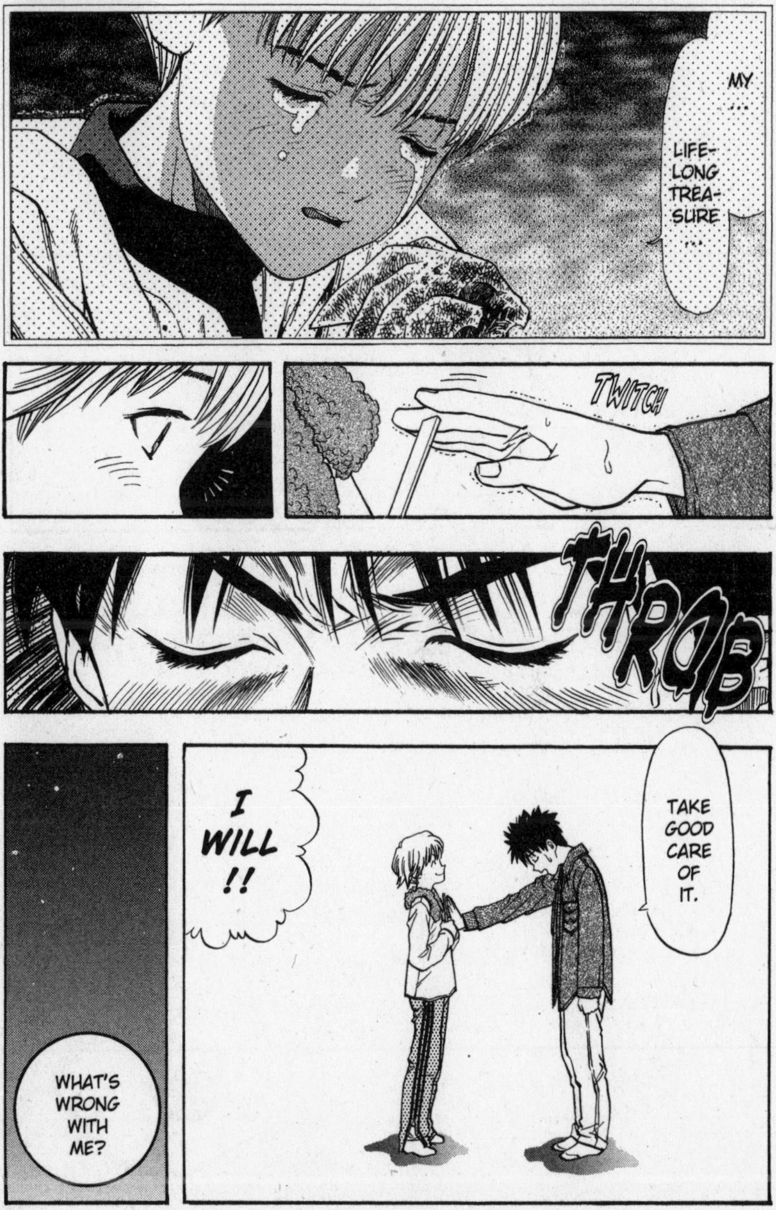
MY ... LIFE-LONG TREASURE ...
TWITCH
THROB
TAKE GOOD CARE OF IT.
I WILL !!
WHAT'S WRONG WITH ME?

Chapter 40:
Words From a Dream

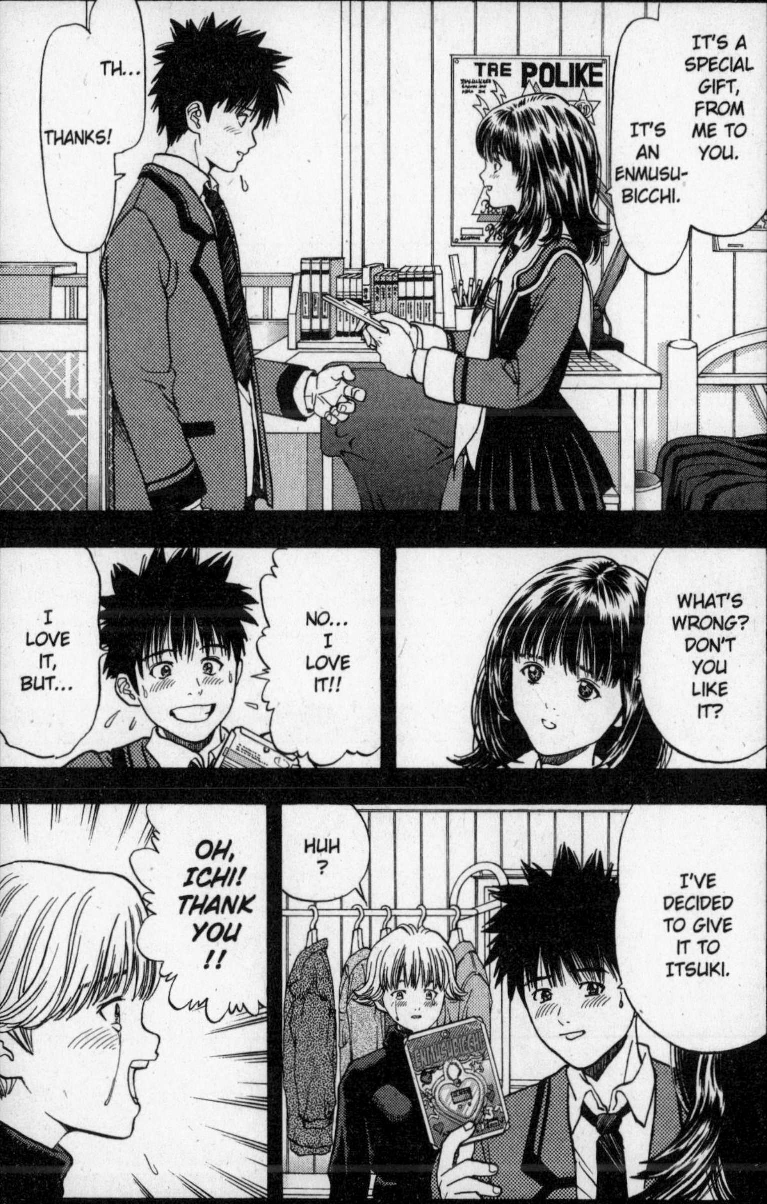
IT'S A SPECIAL GIFT, FROM ME TO YOU.
IT'S AN ENMUSU-BICCHI.
TH... THANKS!
WHAT'S WRONG? DON'T YOU LIKE IT?
NO... I LOVE IT!!
I LOVE IT, BUT...
I'VE DECIDED TO GIVE IT TO ITSUKI.
HUH?
OH, ICHI! THANK YOU!!

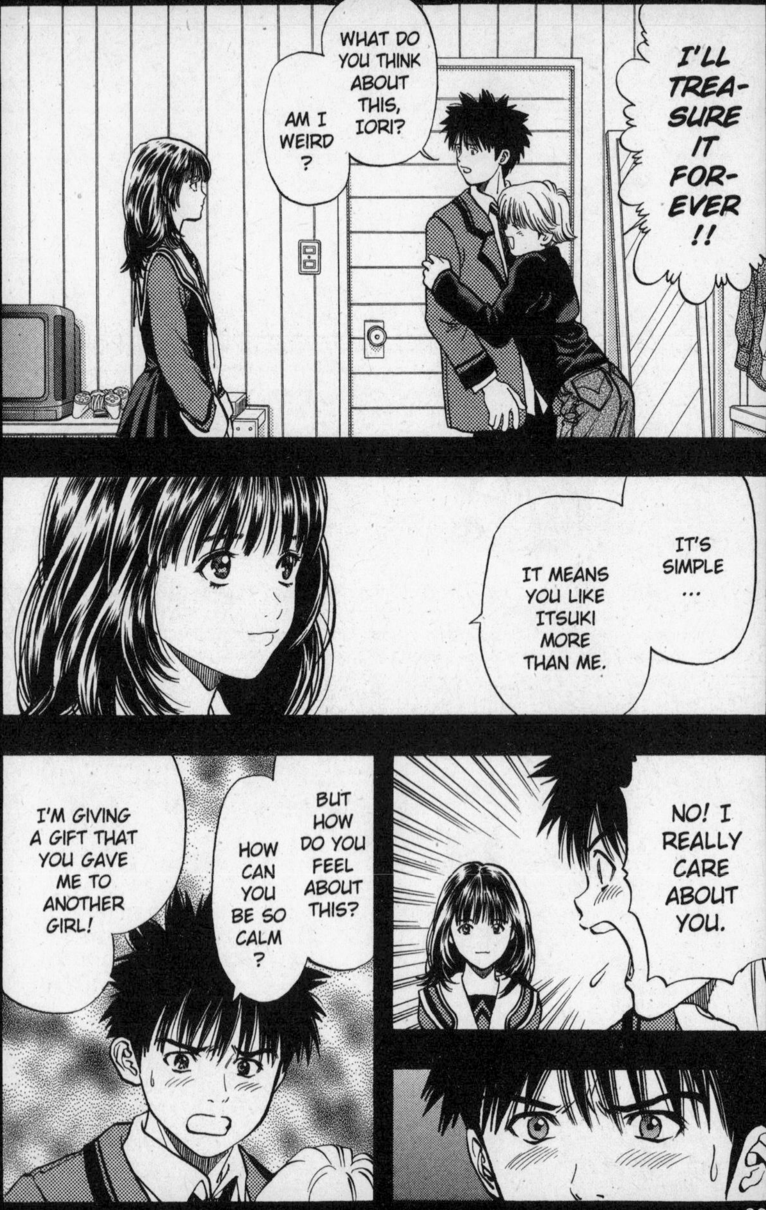
I'LL TREASURE IT FOREVER!!
WHAT DO YOU THINK ABOUT THIS, IORI?
AM I WEIRD ?
IT'S SIMPLE ...
IT MEANS YOU LIKE ITSUKI MORE THAN ME.
NO! I REALLY CARE ABOUT YOU.
BUT HOW DO YOU FEEL ABOUT THIS?
HOW CAN YOU BE SO CALM ?
I'M GIVING A GIFT THAT YOU GAVE ME TO ANOTHER GIRL!

READ THIS WAY

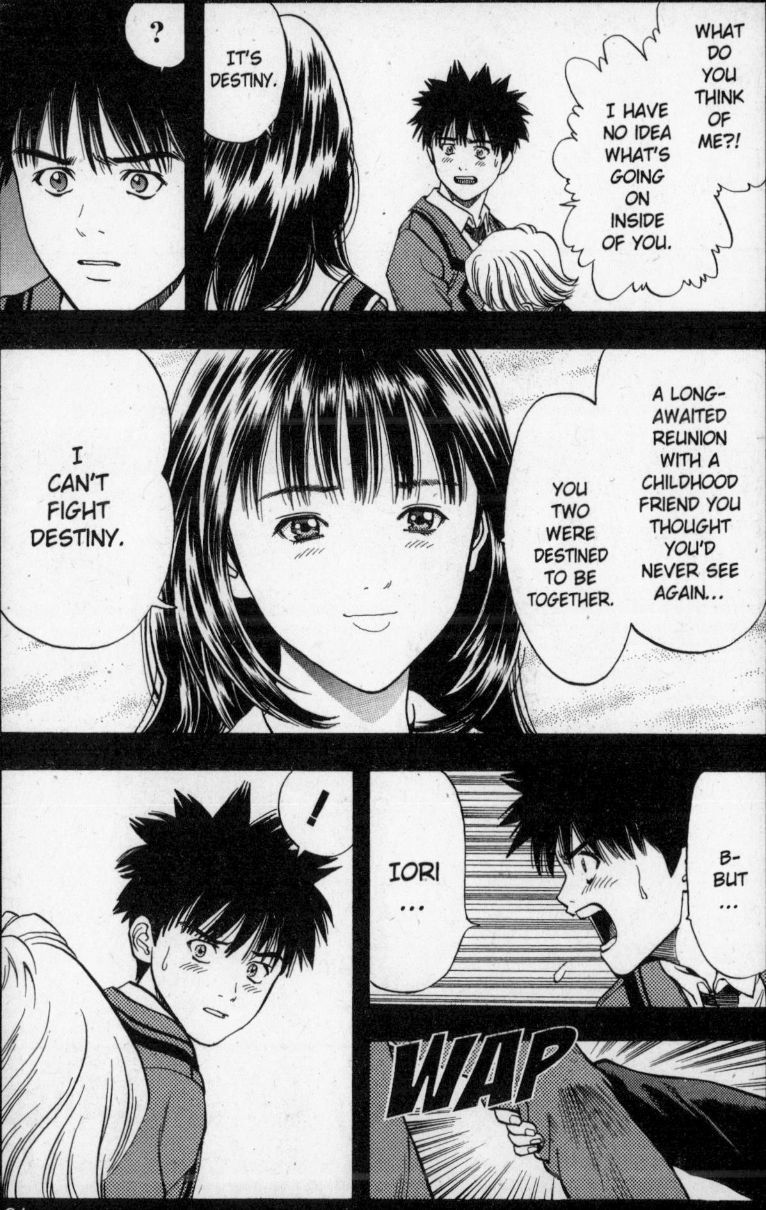

WHAT DO YOU THINK OF ME?!
I HAVE NO IDEA WHAT'S GOING ON INSIDE OF YOU.
IT'S DESTINY.
?
A LONG-AWAITED REUNION WITH A CHILDHOOD FRIEND YOU THOUGHT YOU'D NEVER SEE AGAIN...
YOU TWO WERE DESTINED TO BE TOGETHER.
I CAN'T FIGHT DESTINY.
B-BUT...
IORI...
WAP
!

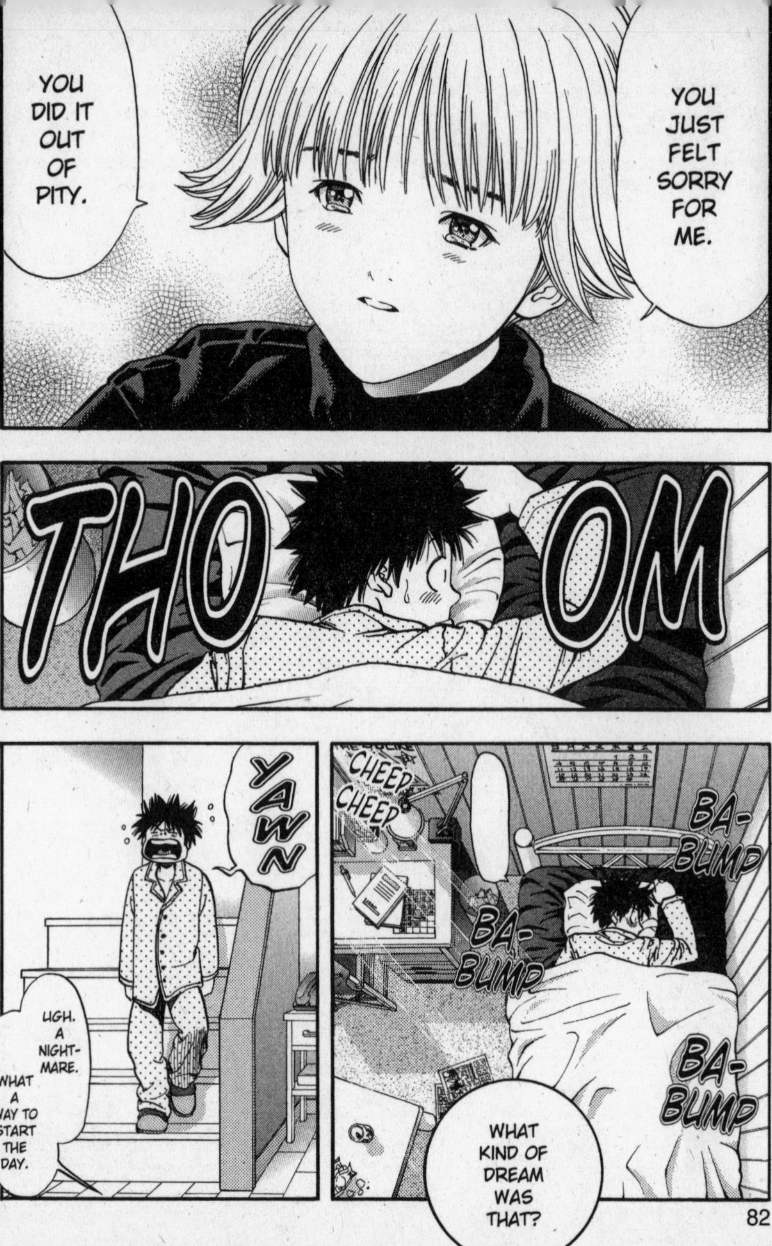
YOU JUST FELT SORRY FOR ME.
YOU DID IT OUT OF PITY.
THOOM
CHEEP CHEEP
BA-BUMP
BA-BUMP
BA-BUMP
WHAT KIND OF DREAM WAS THAT?
YAWN
UGH. A NIGHT-MARE.
WHAT A WAY TO START THE DAY.

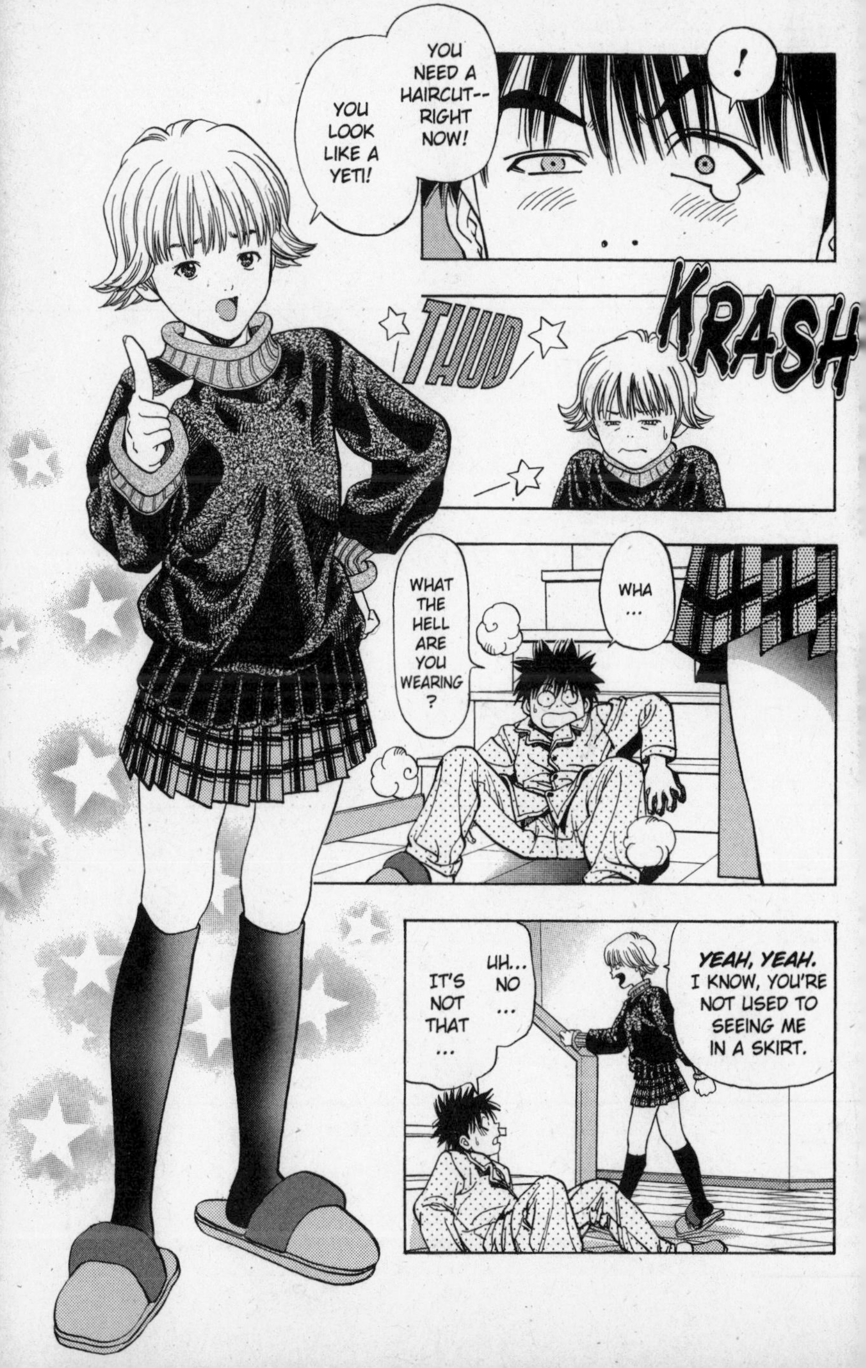
!
KRASH
THUD
WHA...
WHAT THE HELL ARE YOU WEARING?
YEAH, YEAH. I KNOW, YOU'RE NOT USED TO SEEING ME IN A SKIRT.
UH... NO...
IT'S NOT THAT...
YOU NEED A HAIRCUT--RIGHT NOW!
YOU LOOK LIKE A YETI!

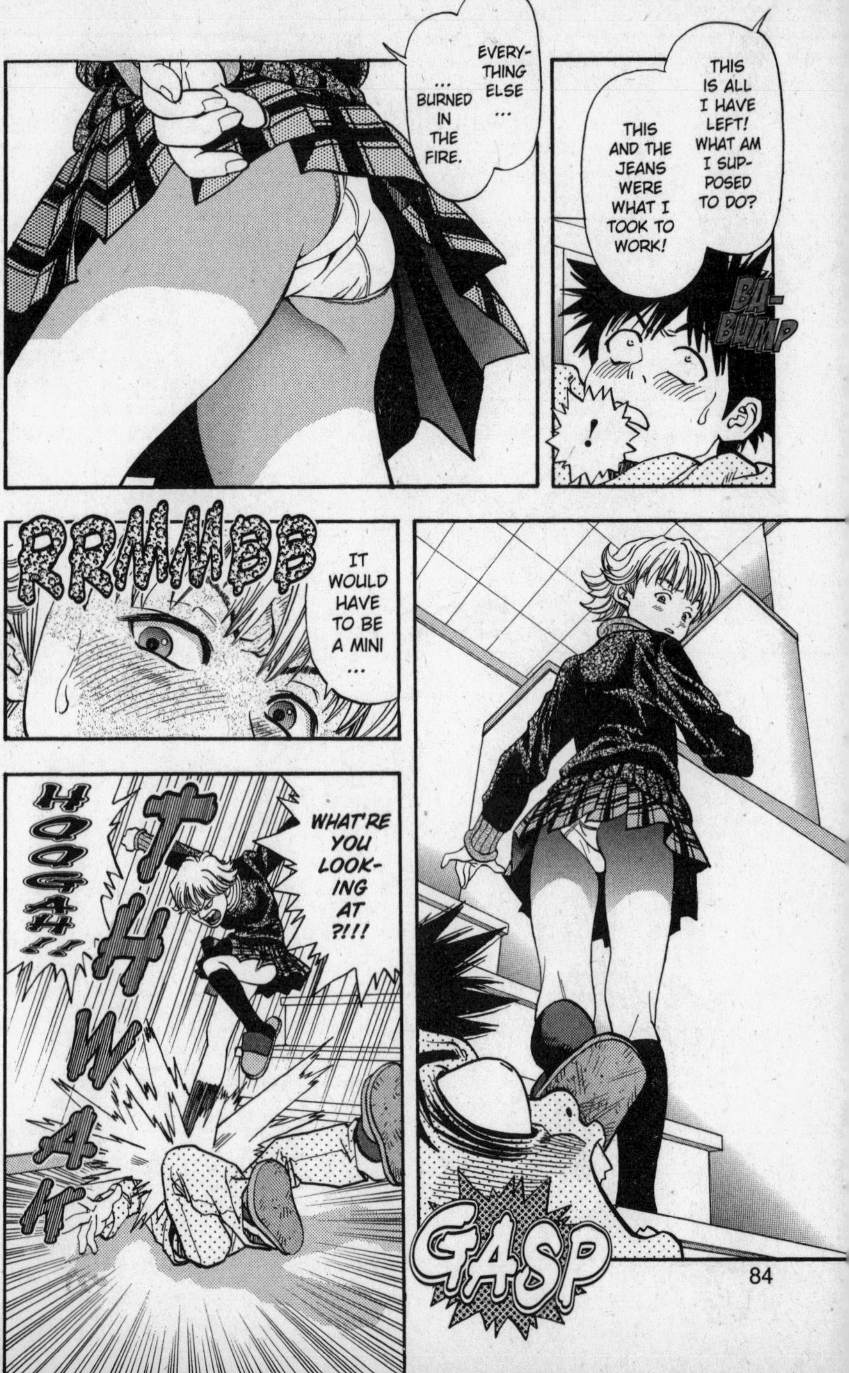
THIS IS ALL I HAVE LEFT! WHAT AM I SUPPOSED TO DO?
THIS AND THE JEANS WERE WHAT I TOOK TO WORK!
BA-BUMP
!
EVERYTHING ELSE ...
... BURNED IN THE FIRE.
GASP
RRMMBB
IT WOULD HAVE TO BE A MINI ...
WHAT'RE YOU LOOKING AT?!!!
THWAK
HOOGAH!!

READ THIS WAY

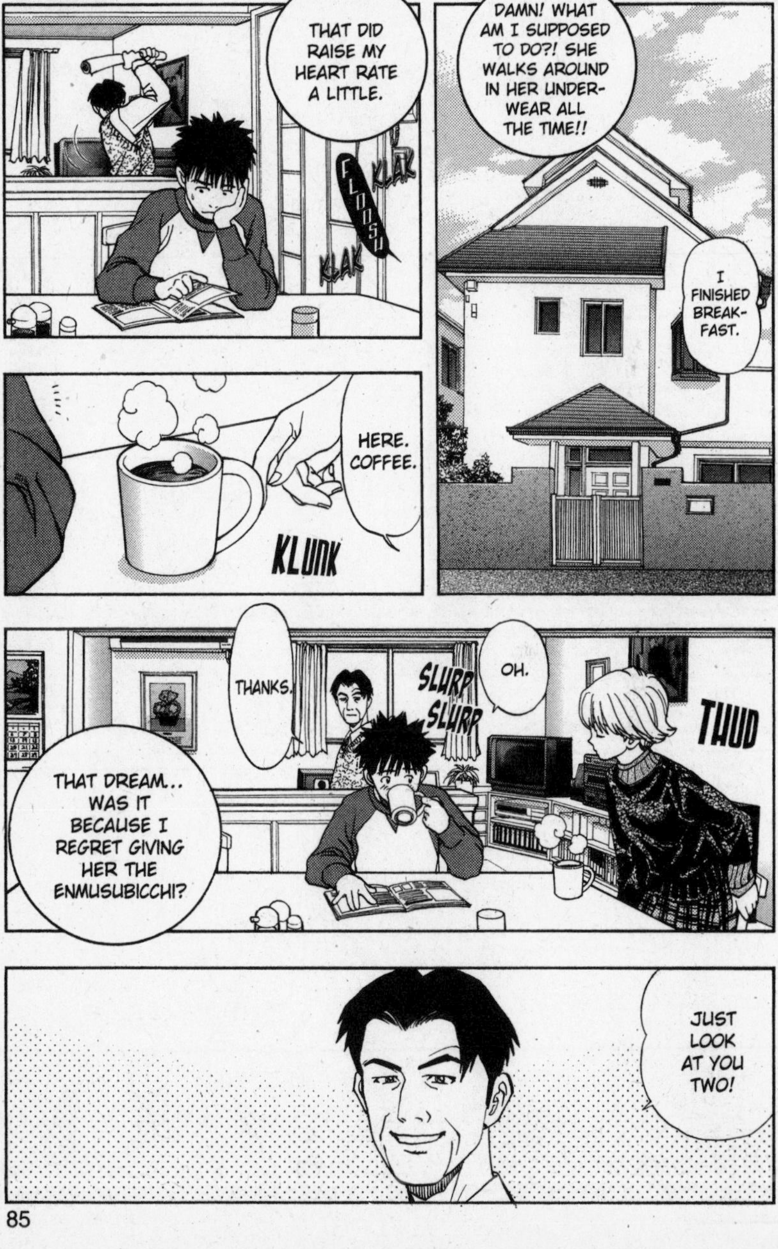
DAMN! WHAT AM I SUPPOSED TO DO?! SHE WALKS AROUND IN HER UNDER-WEAR ALL THE TIME!!
I FINISHED BREAK-FAST.
THAT DID RAISE MY HEART RATE A LITTLE.
KLAK
FLOOSH
KLAK
HERE. COFFEE.
KLUNK
THUD
OH.
SLURP SLURP
THANKS.
THAT DREAM... WAS IT BECAUSE I REGRET GIVING HER THE ENMUSUBICCHI?
JUST LOOK AT YOU TWO!

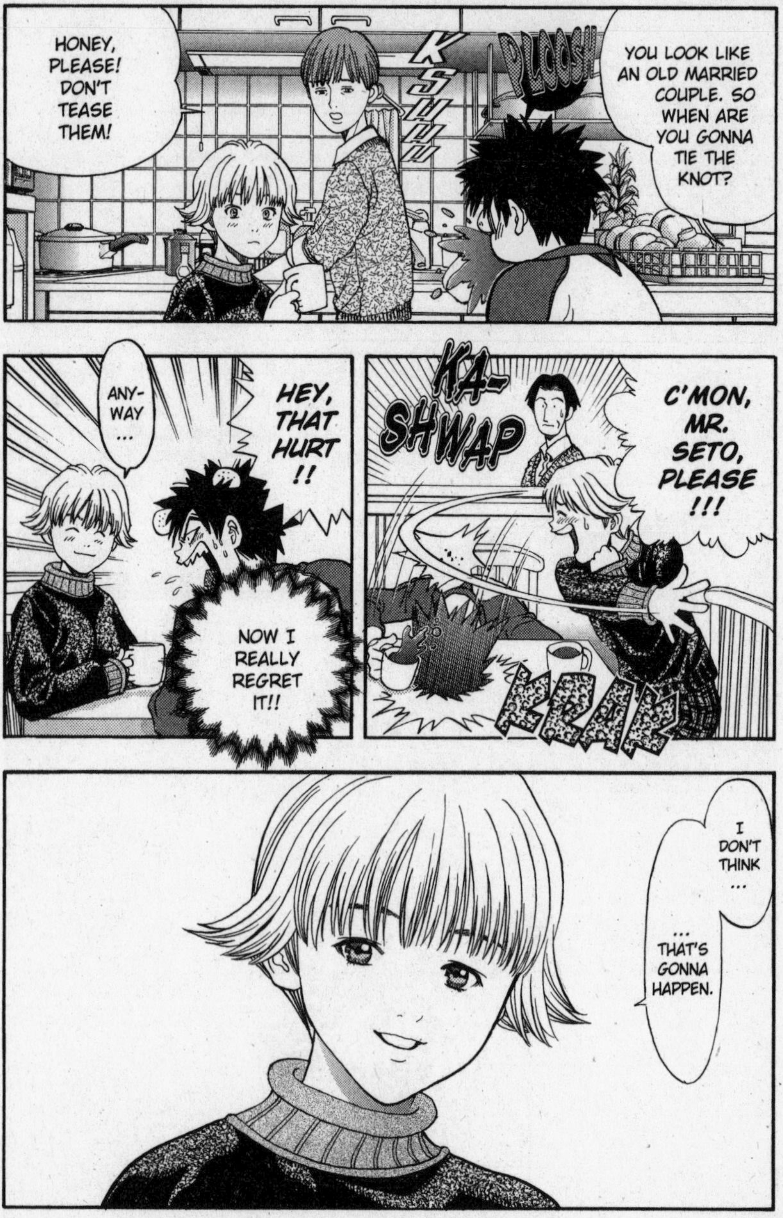
YOU LOOK LIKE AN OLD MARRIED COUPLE. SO WHEN ARE YOU GONNA TIE THE KNOT?
PLOOSH
HONEY, PLEASE! DON'T TEASE THEM!
C'MON, MR. SETO, PLEASE!!!
KA-SHWAP
KRAK
HEY, THAT HURT!!
NOW I REALLY REGRET IT!!
ANY-WAY...
I DON'T THINK...
...THAT'S GONNA HAPPEN.

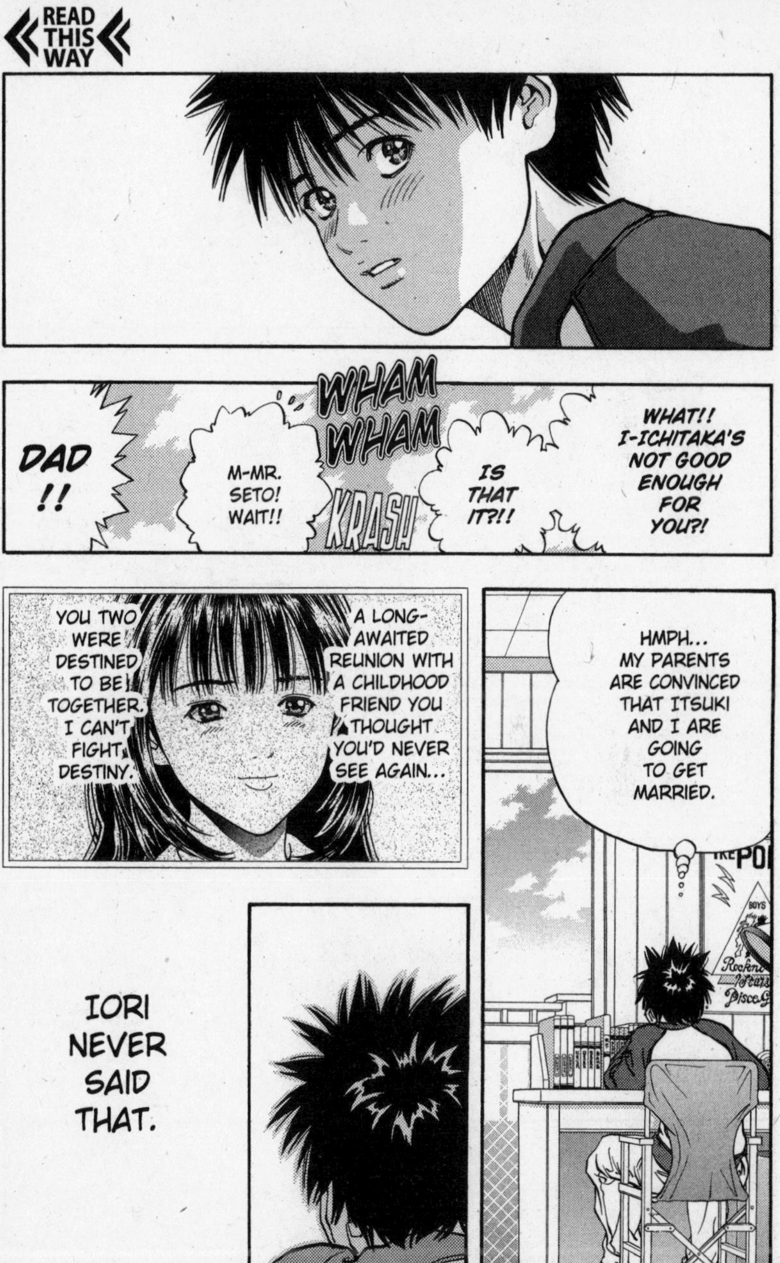
READ THIS WAY
WHAT!! I-ICHITAKA'S NOT GOOD ENOUGH FOR YOU?!
IS THAT IT?!!
WHAM WHAM
KRASH
M-MR. SETO! WAIT!!
DAD!!
HMPH... MY PARENTS ARE CONVINCED THAT ITSUKI AND I ARE GOING TO GET MARRIED.
A LONG-AWAITED REUNION WITH A CHILDHOOD FRIEND YOU THOUGHT YOU'D NEVER SEE AGAIN...
YOU TWO WERE DESTINED TO BE TOGETHER. I CAN'T FIGHT DESTINY.
IORI NEVER SAID THAT.

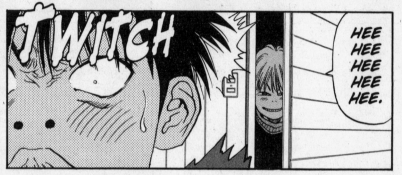

TWITCH

HEE
HEE
HEE
HEE
HEE.

KLAK

BY
THE
WAY
...

SORRY.

KNOCK,
DAMN
YOU!
KNOCK!!

TA-
DAH
!! ♥

READ THIS WAY

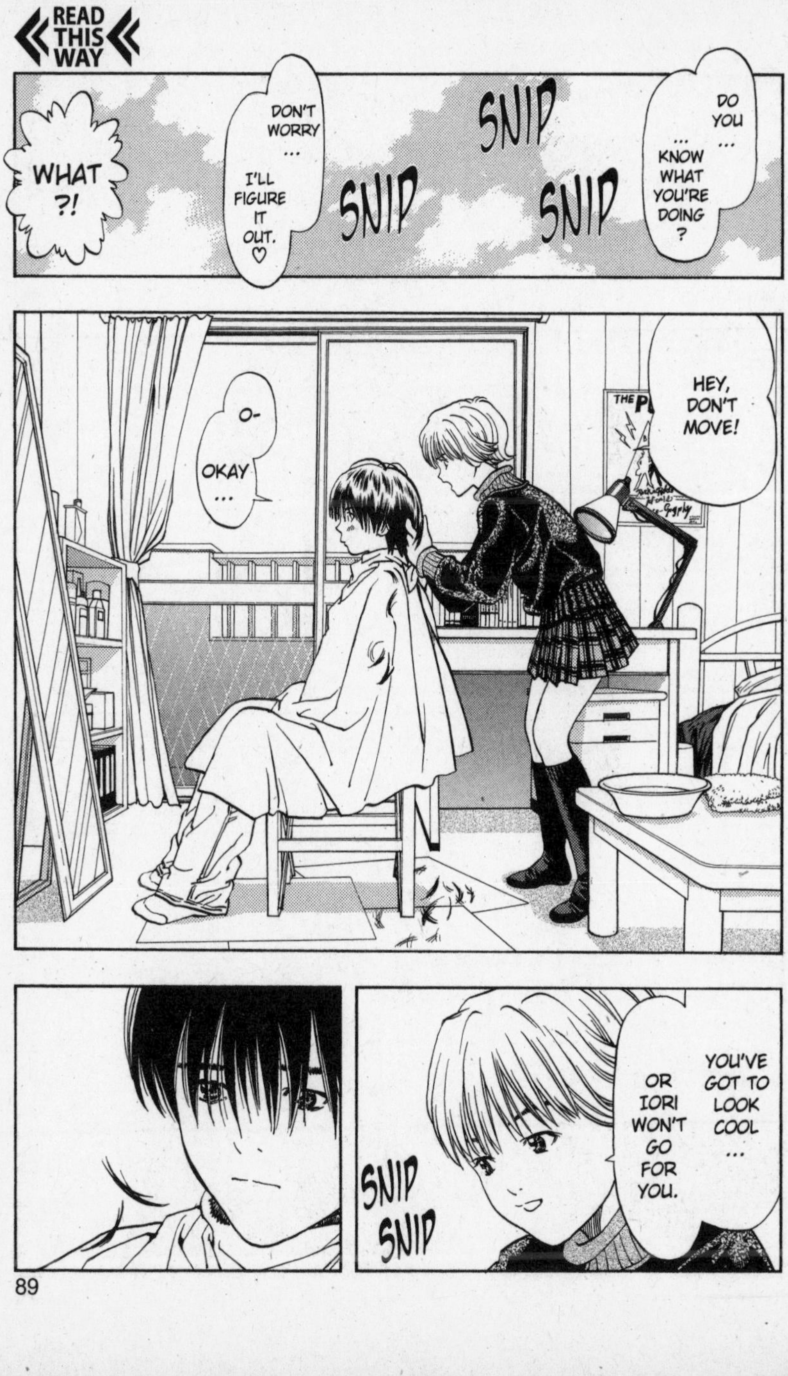

DO YOU ... KNOW WHAT YOU'RE DOING ?
SNIP
SNIP
SNIP
DON'T WORRY ... I'LL FIGURE IT OUT. ♡
WHAT ?!
HEY, DON'T MOVE!
O- OKAY ...
YOU'VE GOT TO LOOK COOL ...
OR IORI WON'T GO FOR YOU.
SNIP SNIP

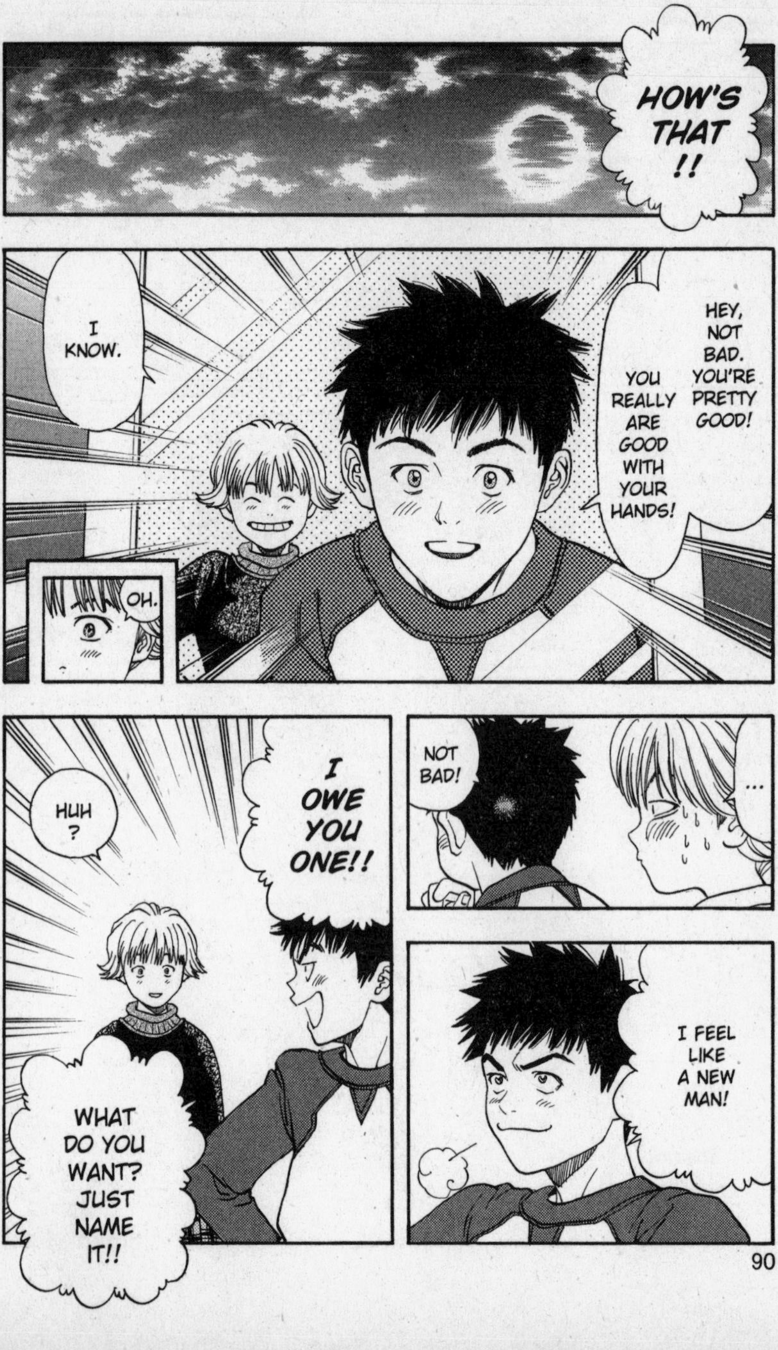
HOW'S THAT !!
HEY, NOT BAD. YOU'RE PRETTY GOOD!
YOU REALLY ARE GOOD WITH YOUR HANDS!
I KNOW.
OH.
NOT BAD!
...
I FEEL LIKE A NEW MAN!
I OWE YOU ONE!!
HUH?
WHAT DO YOU WANT? JUST NAME IT!!

READ THIS WAY

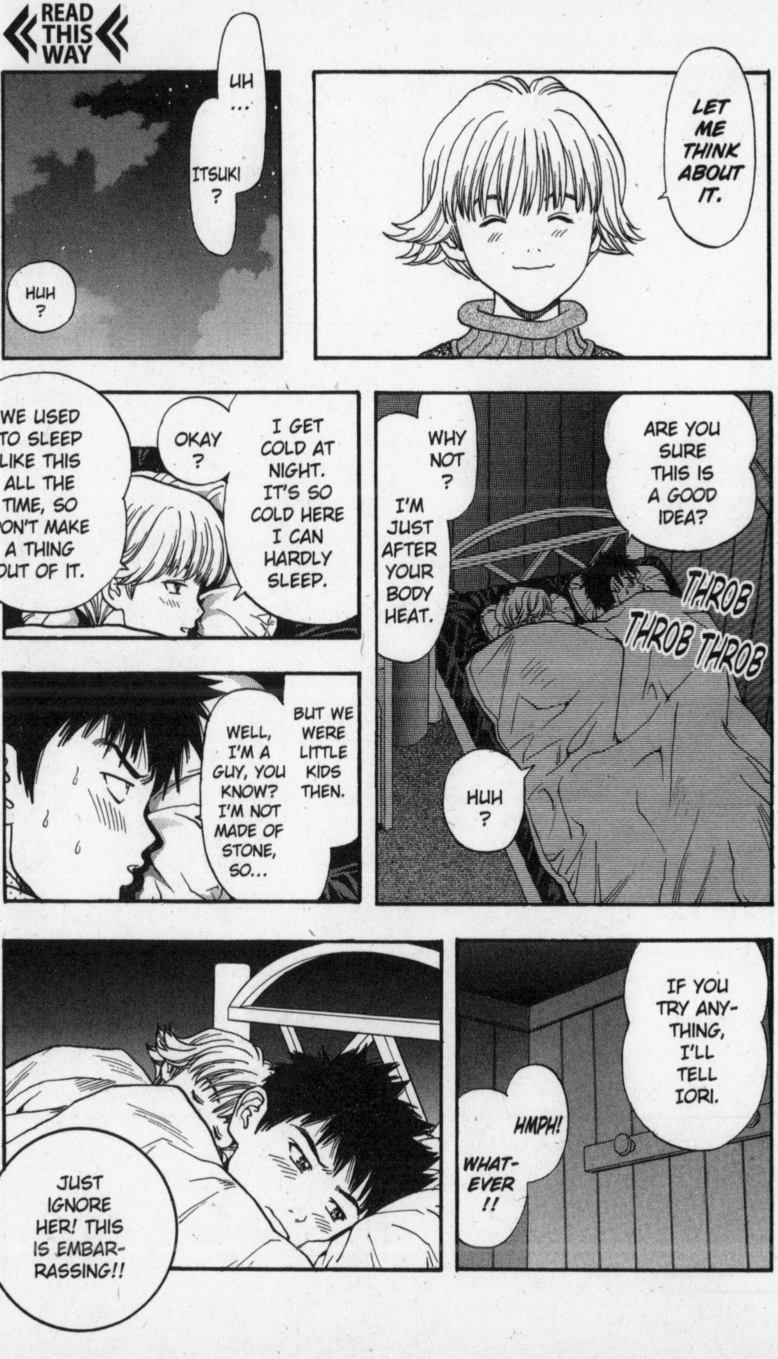

LET ME THINK ABOUT IT.
UH... ITSUKI?
HUH?
ARE YOU SURE THIS IS A GOOD IDEA?
THROB THROB THROB
WHY NOT? I'M JUST AFTER YOUR BODY HEAT.
HUH?
I GET COLD AT NIGHT. IT'S SO COLD HERE I CAN HARDLY SLEEP.
OKAY?
WE USED TO SLEEP LIKE THIS ALL THE TIME, SO DON'T MAKE A THING OUT OF IT.
BUT WE WERE LITTLE KIDS THEN.
WELL, I'M A GUY, YOU KNOW? I'M NOT MADE OF STONE, SO...
IF YOU TRY ANYTHING, I'LL TELL IORI.
HMPH! WHATEVER!!
JUST IGNORE HER! THIS IS EMBARRASSING!!

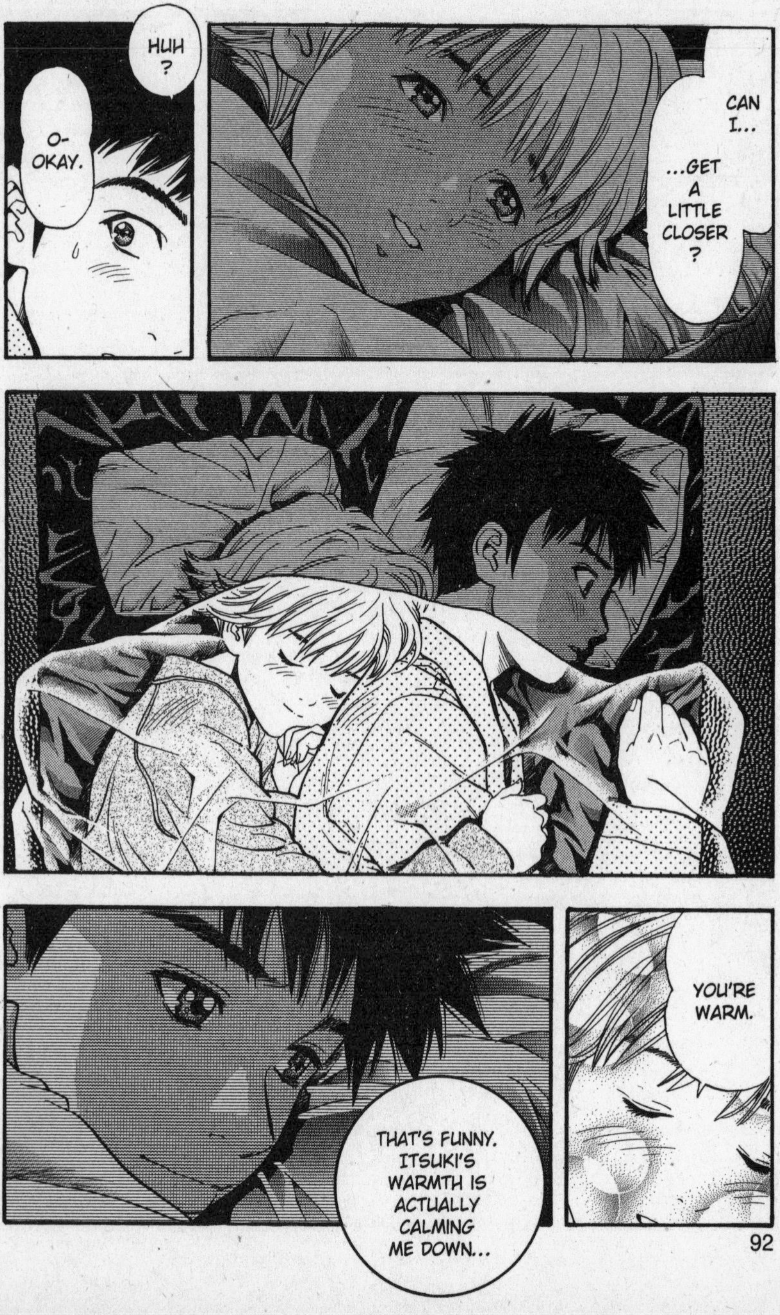
CAN I...
...GET A LITTLE CLOSER?
HUH?
O-OKAY.
YOU'RE WARM.
THAT'S FUNNY. ITSUKI'S WARMTH IS ACTUALLY CALMING ME DOWN...

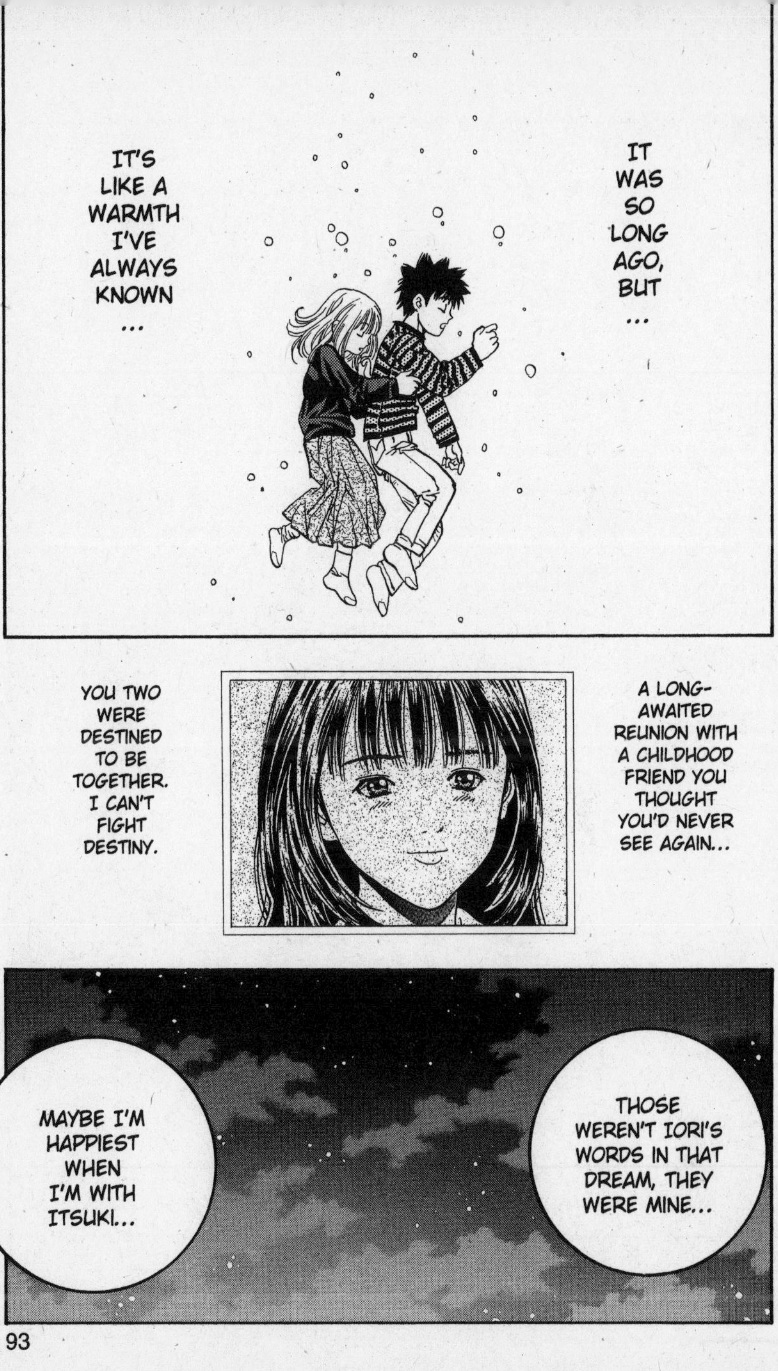
IT WAS SO LONG AGO, BUT...
IT'S LIKE A WARMTH I'VE ALWAYS KNOWN...
A LONG-AWAITED REUNION WITH A CHILDHOOD FRIEND YOU THOUGHT YOU'D NEVER SEE AGAIN...
YOU TWO WERE DESTINED TO BE TOGETHER. I CAN'T FIGHT DESTINY.
THOSE WEREN'T IORI'S WORDS IN THAT DREAM, THEY WERE MINE...
MAYBE I'M HAPPIEST WHEN I'M WITH ITSUKI...

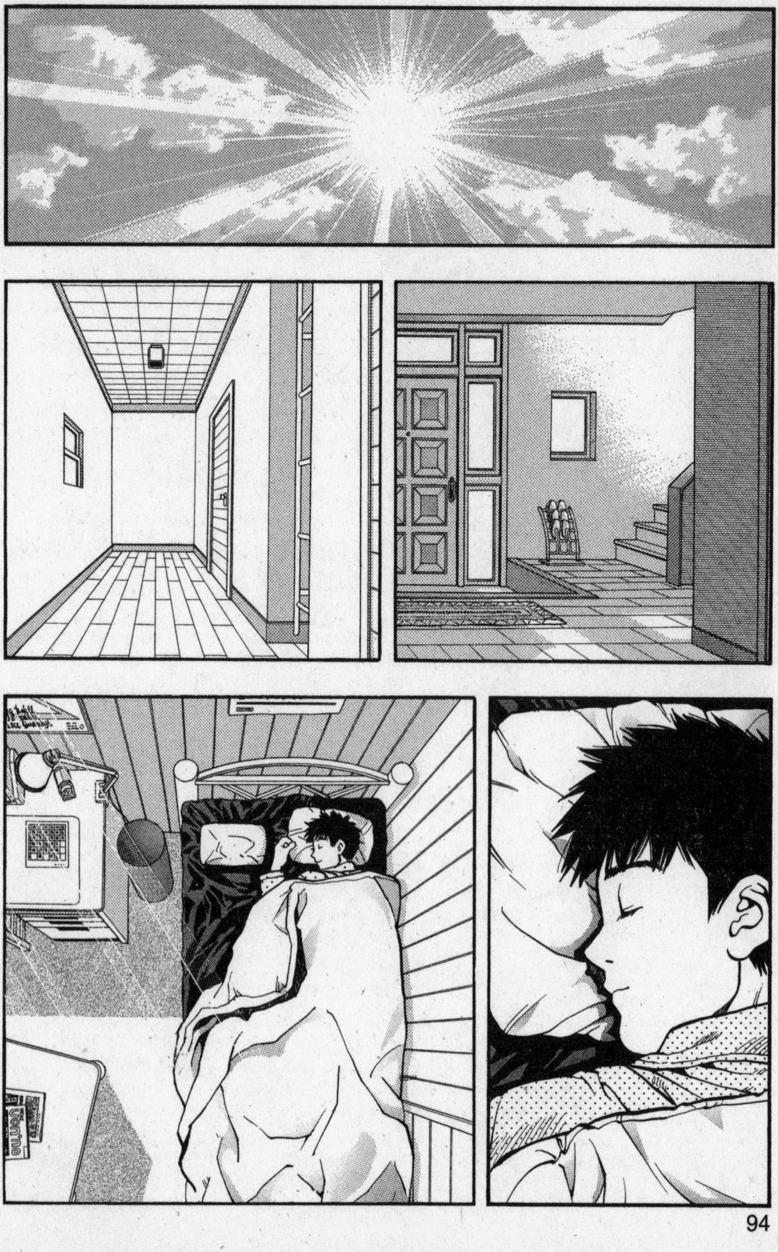

READ THIS WAY

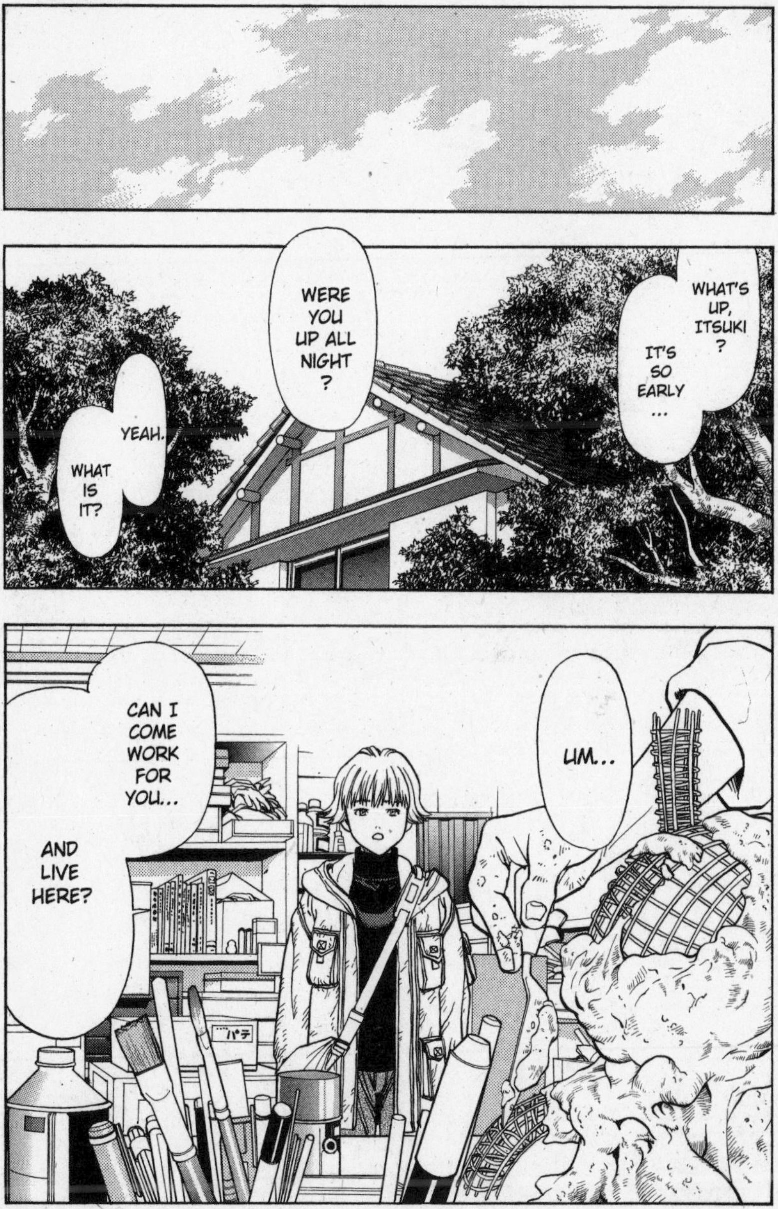
WHAT'S UP, ITSUKI?
IT'S SO EARLY...
WERE YOU UP ALL NIGHT?
YEAH.
WHAT IS IT?
UM...
CAN I COME WORK FOR YOU...
AND LIVE HERE?

I"s

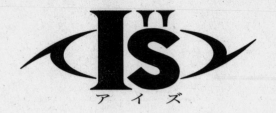

アイズ

Chapter 41: One Answer

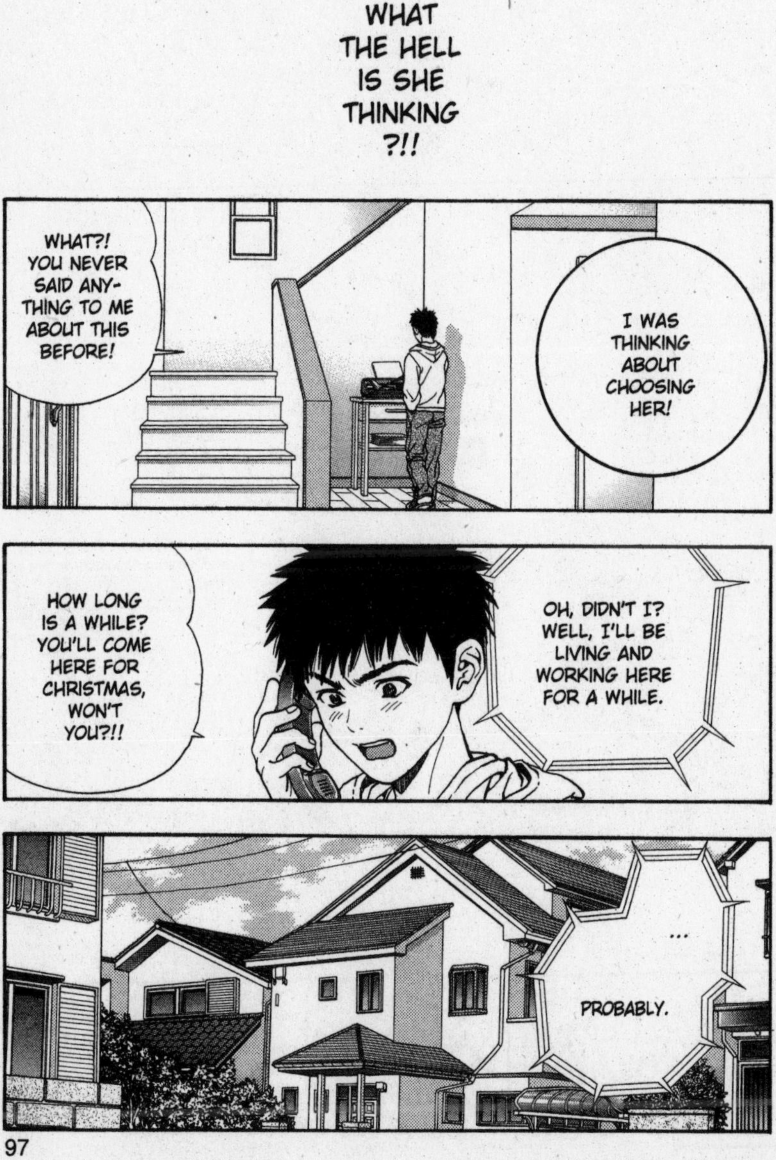
WHAT THE HELL IS SHE THINKING ?!!
I WAS THINKING ABOUT CHOOSING HER!
WHAT?! YOU NEVER SAID ANY-THING TO ME ABOUT THIS BEFORE!
OH, DIDN'T I? WELL, I'LL BE LIVING AND WORKING HERE FOR A WHILE.
HOW LONG IS A WHILE? YOU'LL COME HERE FOR CHRISTMAS, WON'T YOU?!!
...
PROBABLY.

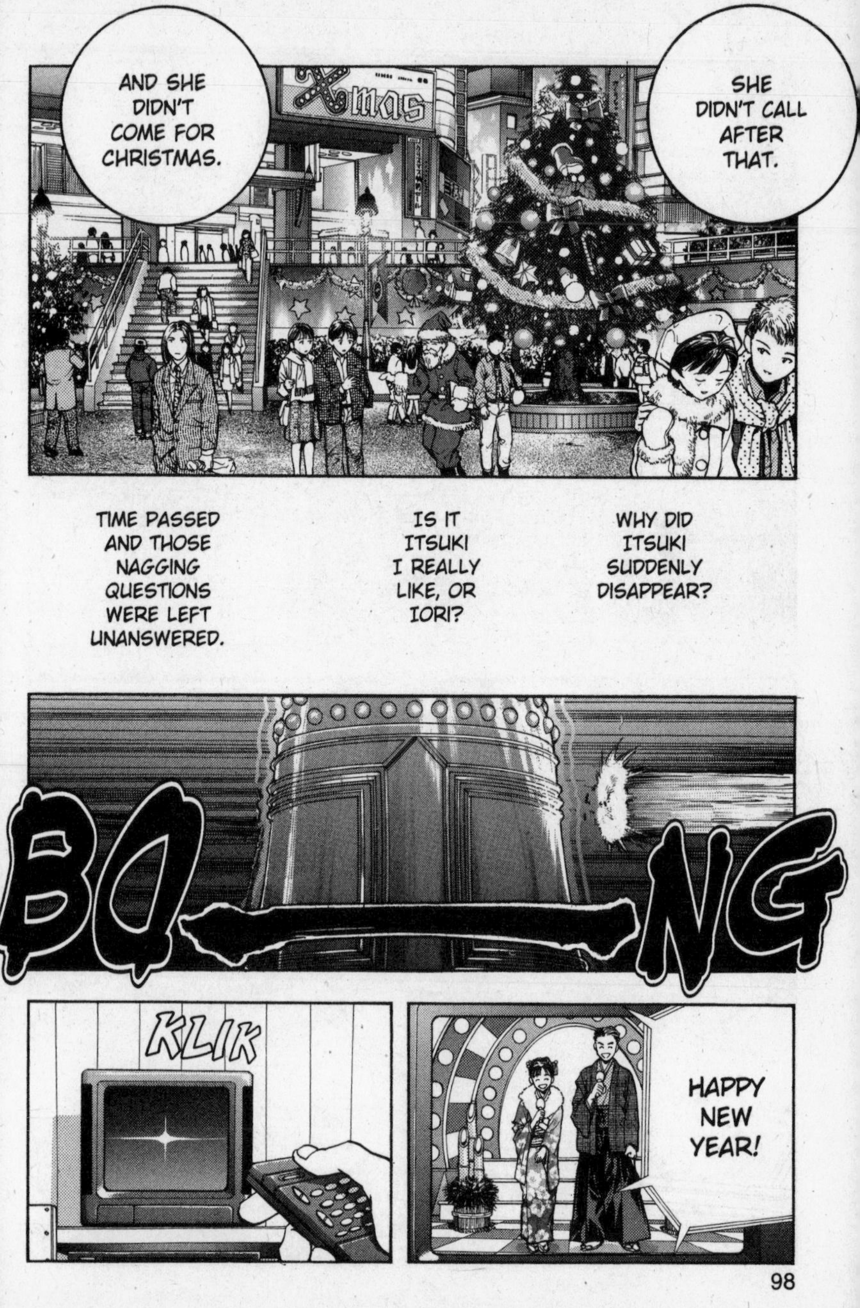
SHE DIDN'T CALL AFTER THAT.
AND SHE DIDN'T COME FOR CHRISTMAS.
WHY DID ITSUKI SUDDENLY DISAPPEAR?
IS IT ITSUKI I REALLY LIKE, OR IORI?
TIME PASSED AND THOSE NAGGING QUESTIONS WERE LEFT UNANSWERED.
BO——NG
HAPPY NEW YEAR!
KLIK

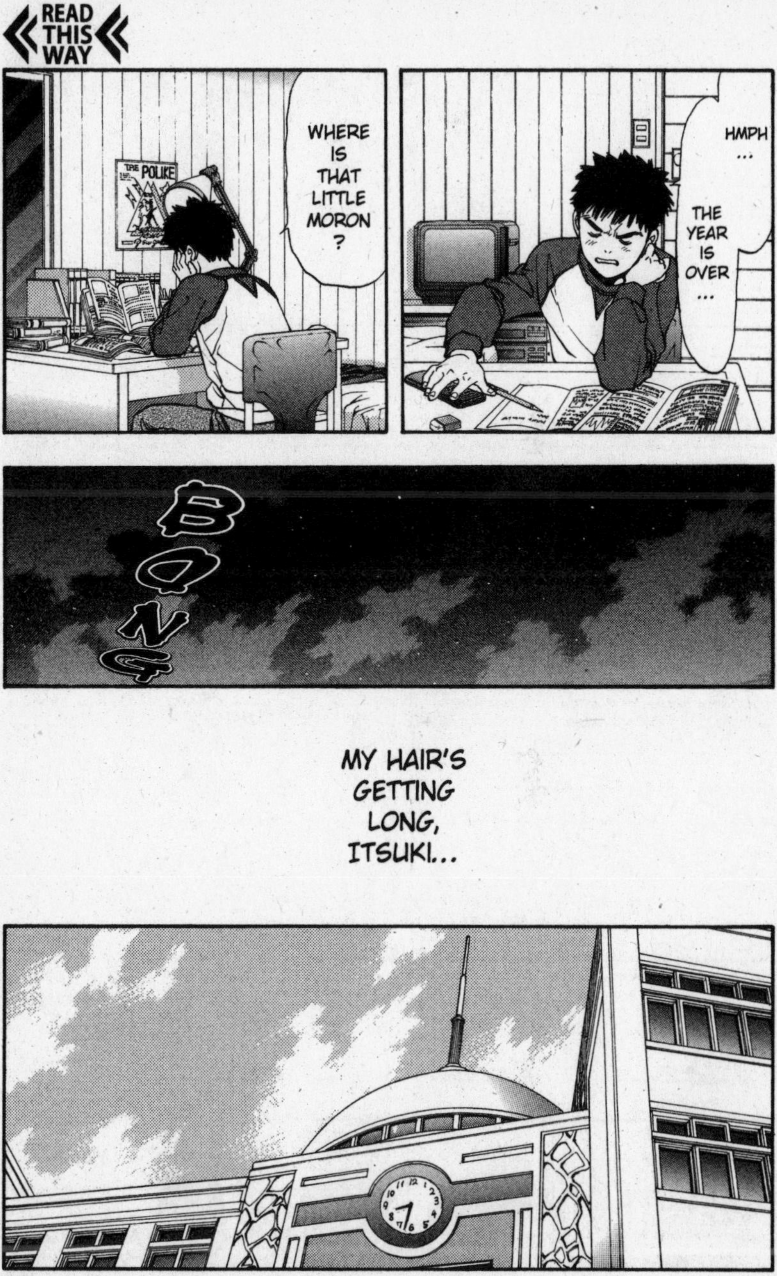
READ THIS WAY
HMPH... THE YEAR IS OVER...
WHERE IS THAT LITTLE MORON?
BONG
MY HAIR'S GETTING LONG, ITSUKI...

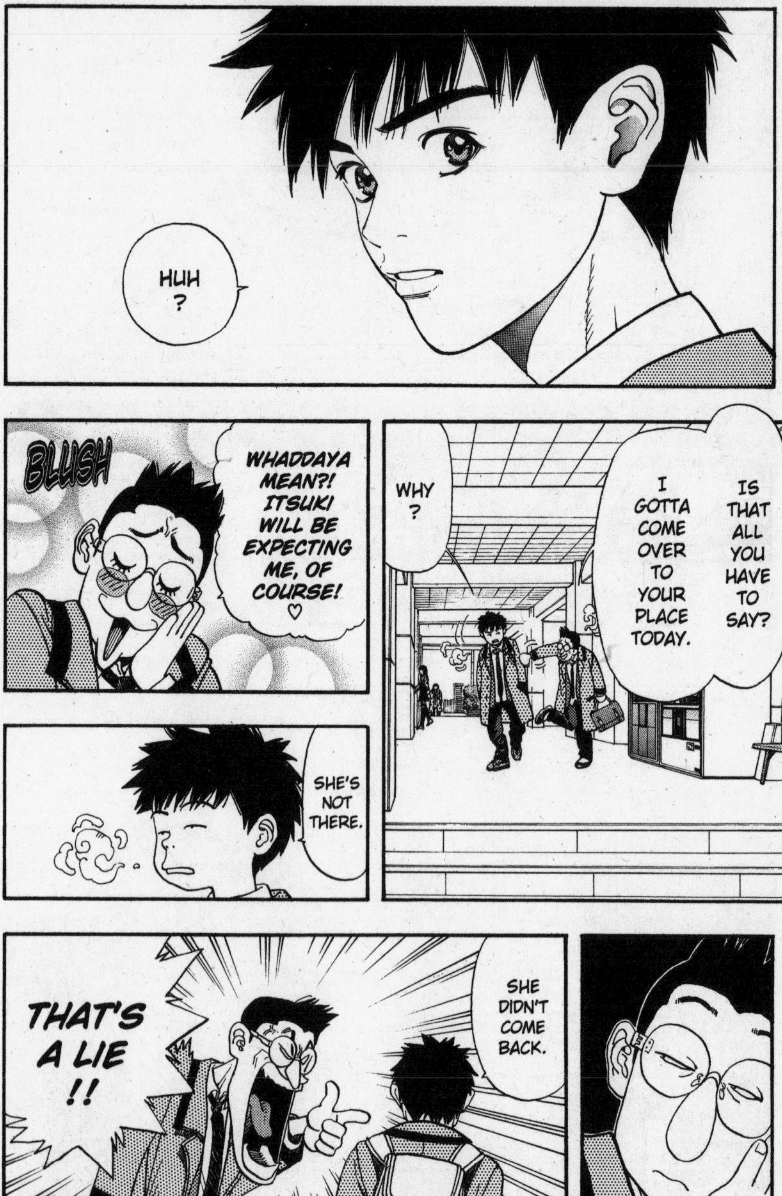
HUH ?
IS THAT ALL YOU HAVE TO SAY?
I GOTTA COME OVER TO YOUR PLACE TODAY.
WHY ?
BLUSH
WHADDAYA MEAN?! ITSUKI WILL BE EXPECTING ME, OF COURSE! ♡
SHE'S NOT THERE.
SHE DIDN'T COME BACK.
THAT'S A LIE !!

READ THIS WAY

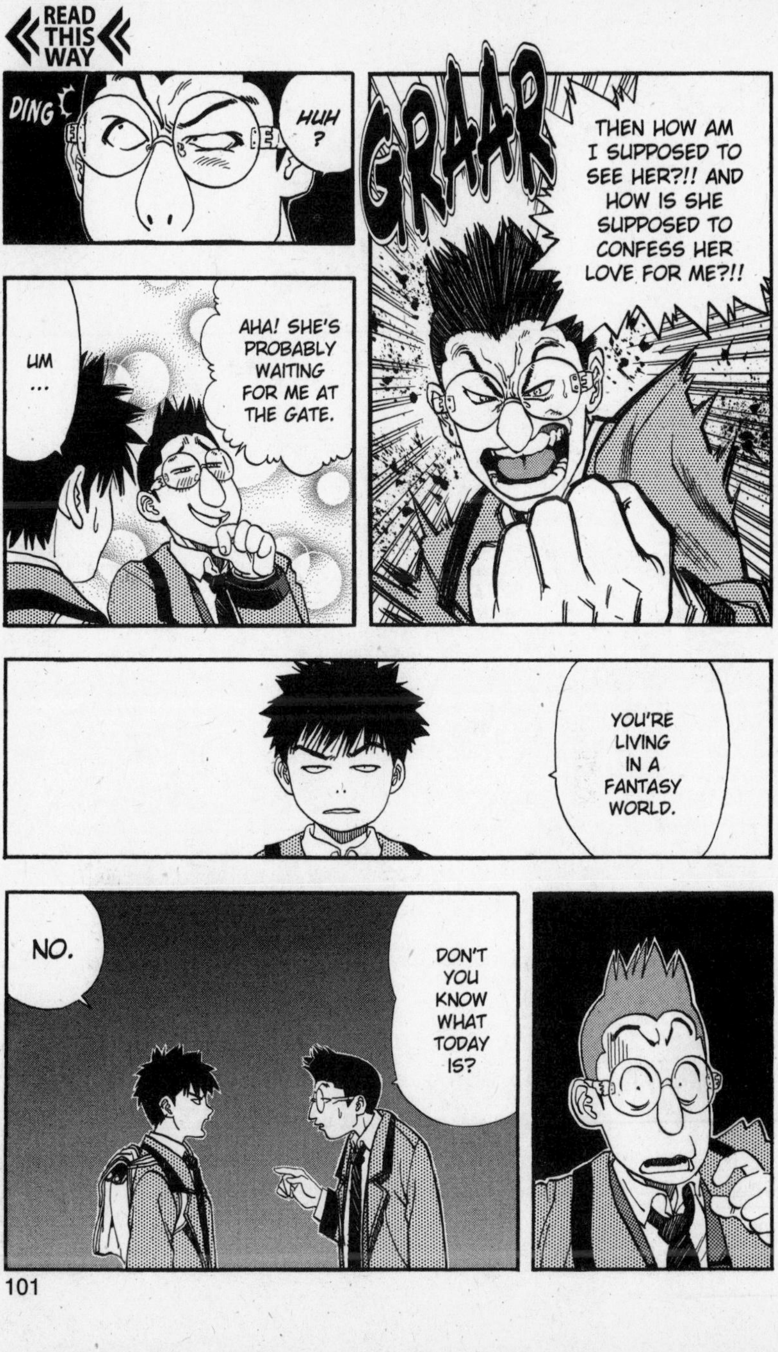
GRAAR
THEN HOW AM I SUPPOSED TO SEE HER?!! AND HOW IS SHE SUPPOSED TO CONFESS HER LOVE FOR ME?!!
DING
HUH?
AHA! SHE'S PROBABLY WAITING FOR ME AT THE GATE.
UM ...
YOU'RE LIVING IN A FANTASY WORLD.
DON'T YOU KNOW WHAT TODAY IS?
NO.

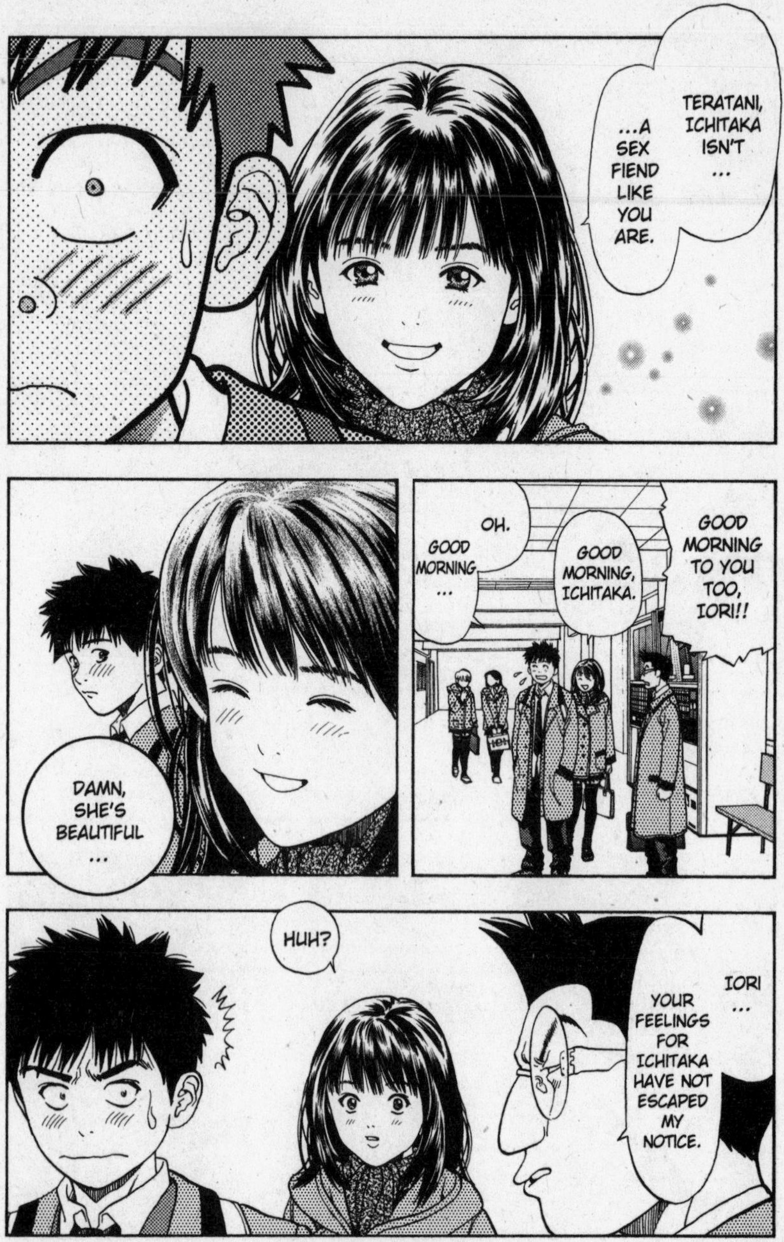
TERATANI, ICHITAKA ISN'T ...
...A SEX FIEND LIKE YOU ARE.
GOOD MORNING TO YOU TOO, IORI!!
GOOD MORNING, ICHITAKA.
OH.
GOOD MORNING ...
DAMN, SHE'S BEAUTIFUL ...
IORI ...
YOUR FEELINGS FOR ICHITAKA HAVE NOT ESCAPED MY NOTICE.
HUH?

READ THIS WAY

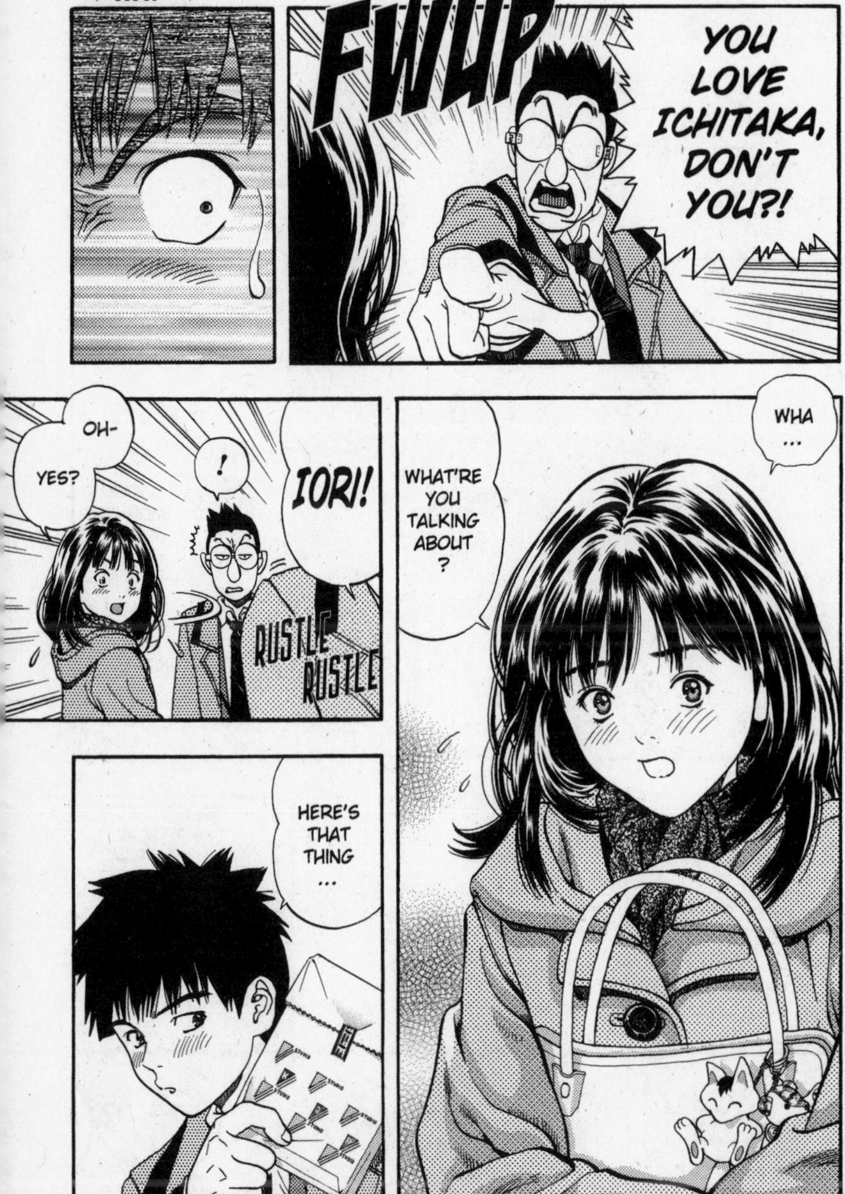
FWUP
YOU LOVE ICHITAKA, DON'T YOU?!
WHA ...
WHAT'RE YOU TALKING ABOUT ?
IORI!
!
OH- YES?
RUSTLE RUSTLE
HERE'S THAT THING ...

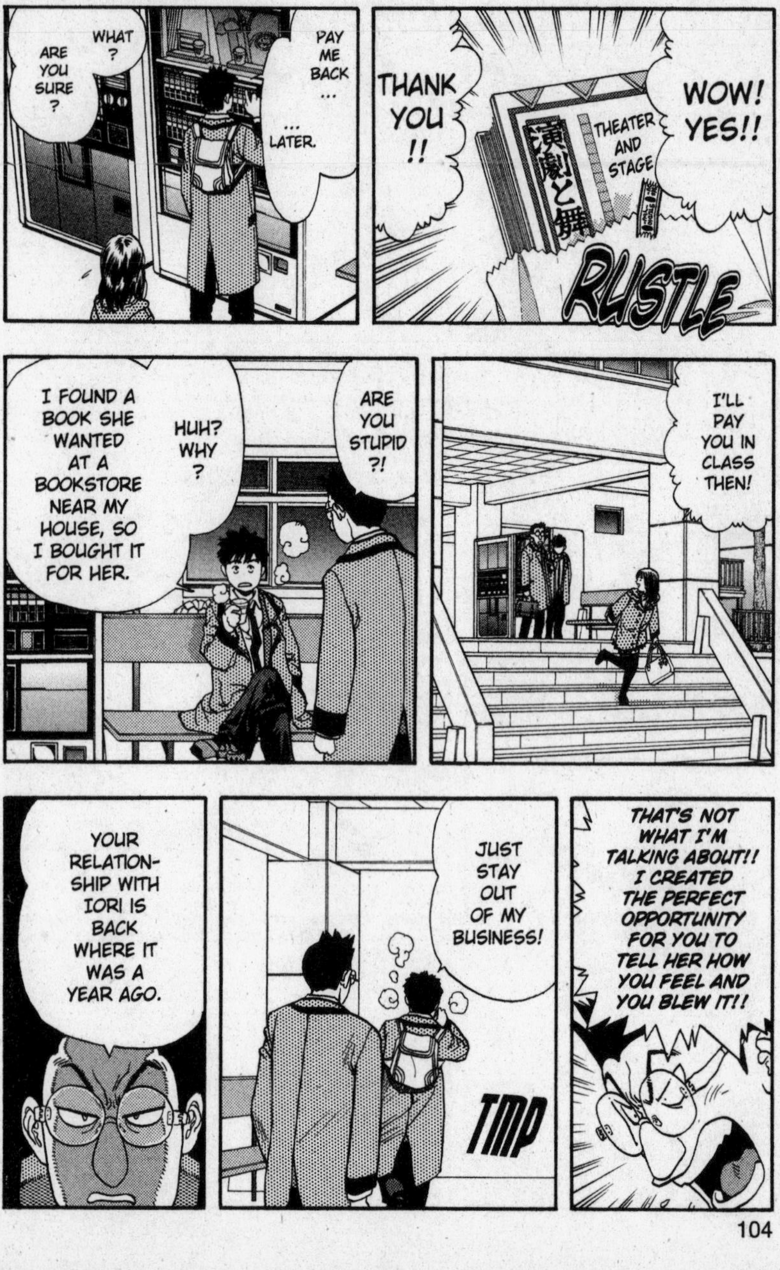
WOW! YES!!
THEATER AND STAGE
演劇と舞
THANK YOU !!
RUSTLE
PAY ME BACK ...
... LATER.
WHAT ?
ARE YOU SURE ?
I'LL PAY YOU IN CLASS THEN!
ARE YOU STUPID ?!
HUH? WHY ?
I FOUND A BOOK SHE WANTED AT A BOOKSTORE NEAR MY HOUSE, SO I BOUGHT IT FOR HER.
THAT'S NOT WHAT I'M TALKING ABOUT!! I CREATED THE PERFECT OPPORTUNITY FOR YOU TO TELL HER HOW YOU FEEL AND YOU BLEW IT!!
JUST STAY OUT OF MY BUSINESS!
TMP
YOUR RELATION-SHIP WITH IORI IS BACK WHERE IT WAS A YEAR AGO.

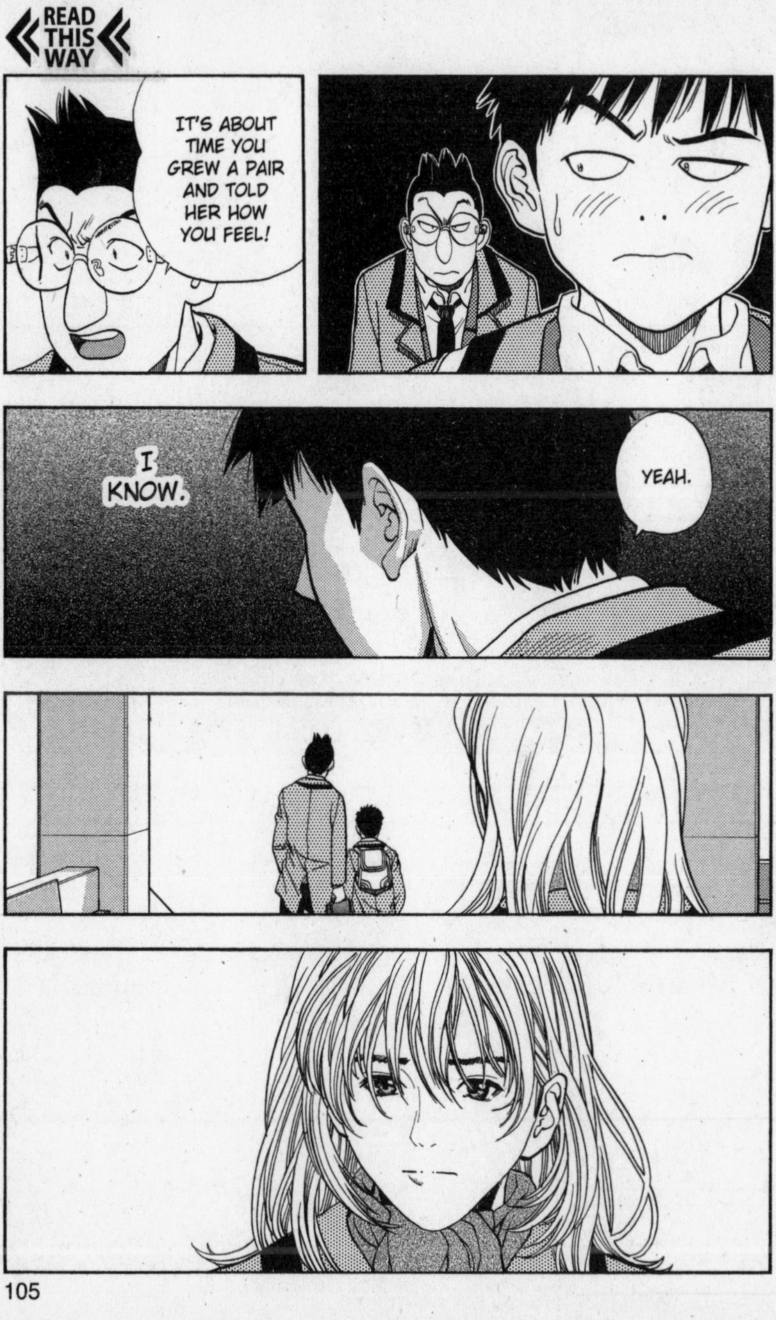
READ THIS WAY
IT'S ABOUT TIME YOU GREW A PAIR AND TOLD HER HOW YOU FEEL!
YEAH.
I KNOW.

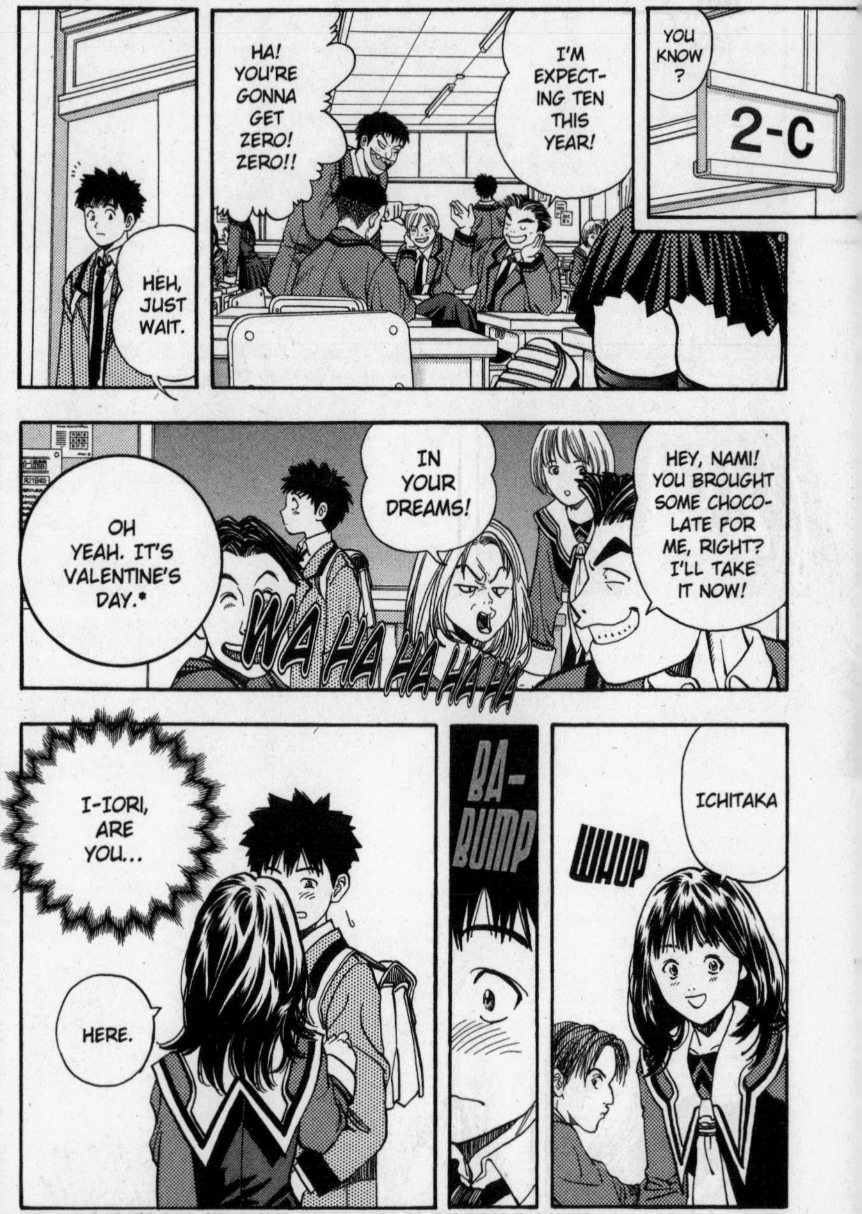
YOU KNOW ?
2-C
I'M EXPECT-ING TEN THIS YEAR!
HA! YOU'RE GONNA GET ZERO! ZERO!!
HEH, JUST WAIT.
HEY, NAMI! YOU BROUGHT SOME CHOCO-LATE FOR ME, RIGHT? I'LL TAKE IT NOW!
IN YOUR DREAMS!
WA HA HA HA HA HA
OH YEAH. IT'S VALENTINE'S DAY.*
ICHITAKA
WHUP
BA-BUMP
I-IORI, ARE YOU...
HERE.

*ON VALENTINE'S DAY, GIRLS GIVE CHOCOLATES TO THE BOYS THEY LIKE. THE BOYS RECIPROCATE ON WHITE DAY, MARCH 14.

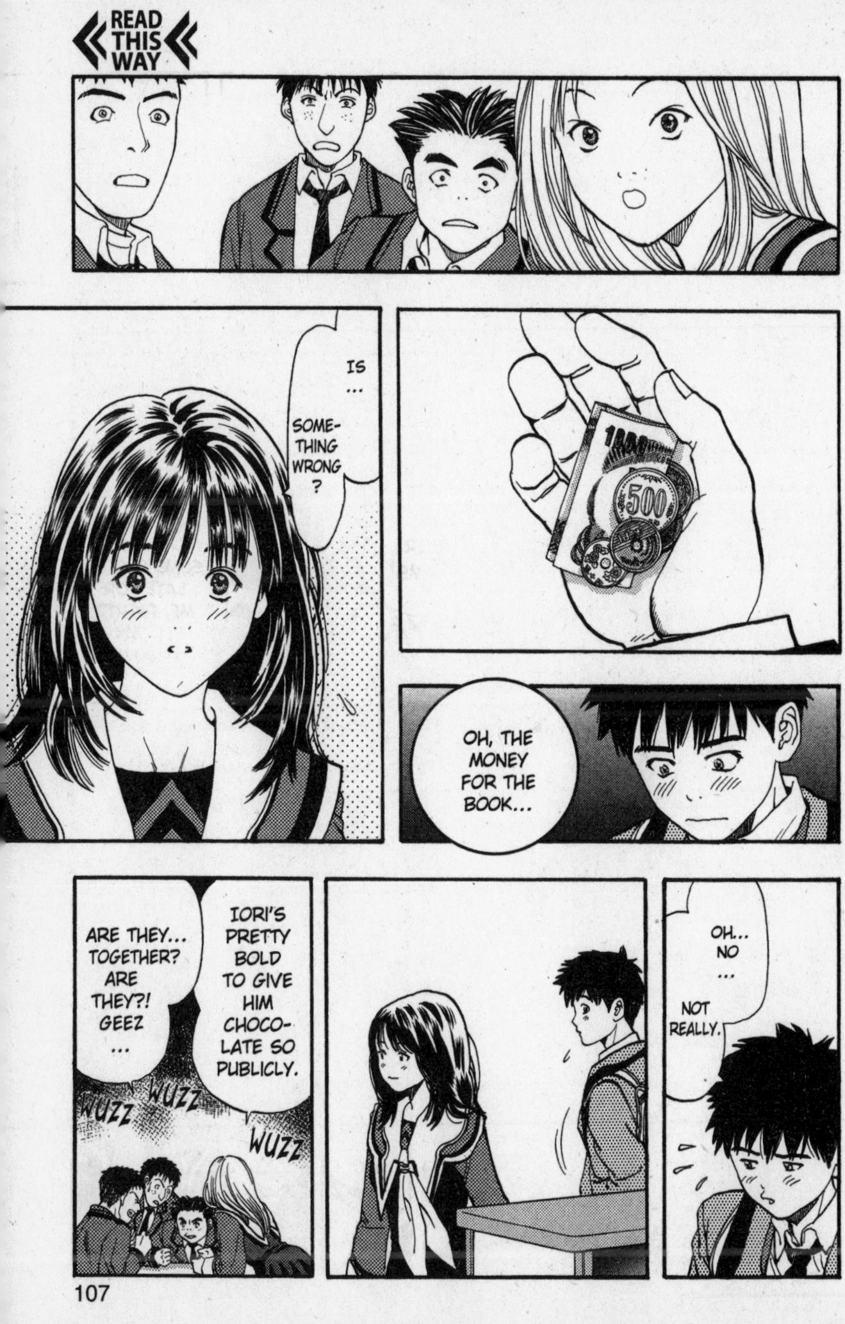
READ THIS WAY
OH, THE MONEY FOR THE BOOK...
IS... SOMETHING WRONG?
OH... NO... NOT REALLY.
IORI'S PRETTY BOLD TO GIVE HIM CHOCOLATE SO PUBLICLY.
ARE THEY... TOGETHER? ARE THEY?! GEEZ...
WUZZ
WUZZ
WUZZ

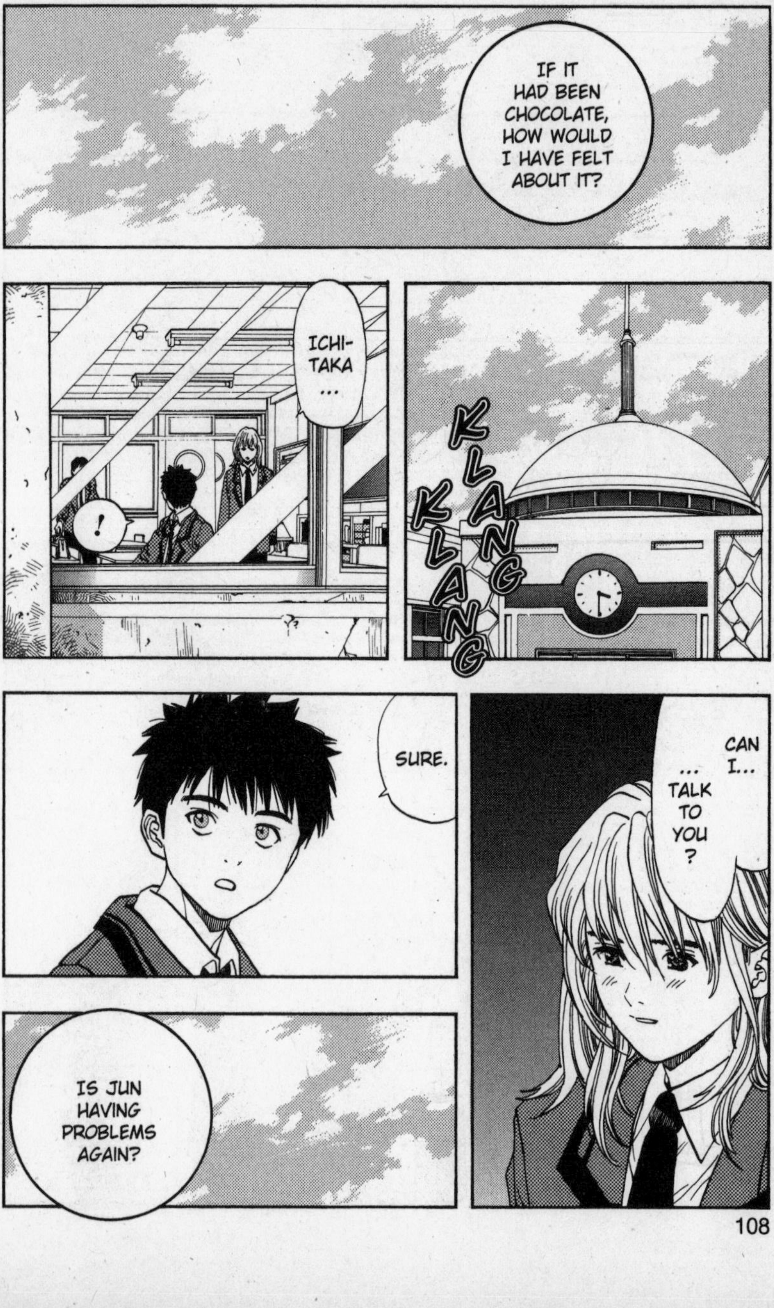
IF IT HAD BEEN CHOCOLATE, HOW WOULD I HAVE FELT ABOUT IT?
KLANG
KLANG
ICHI-TAKA ...
!
CAN I... ...TALK TO YOU?
SURE.
IS JUN HAVING PROBLEMS AGAIN?

READ THIS WAY

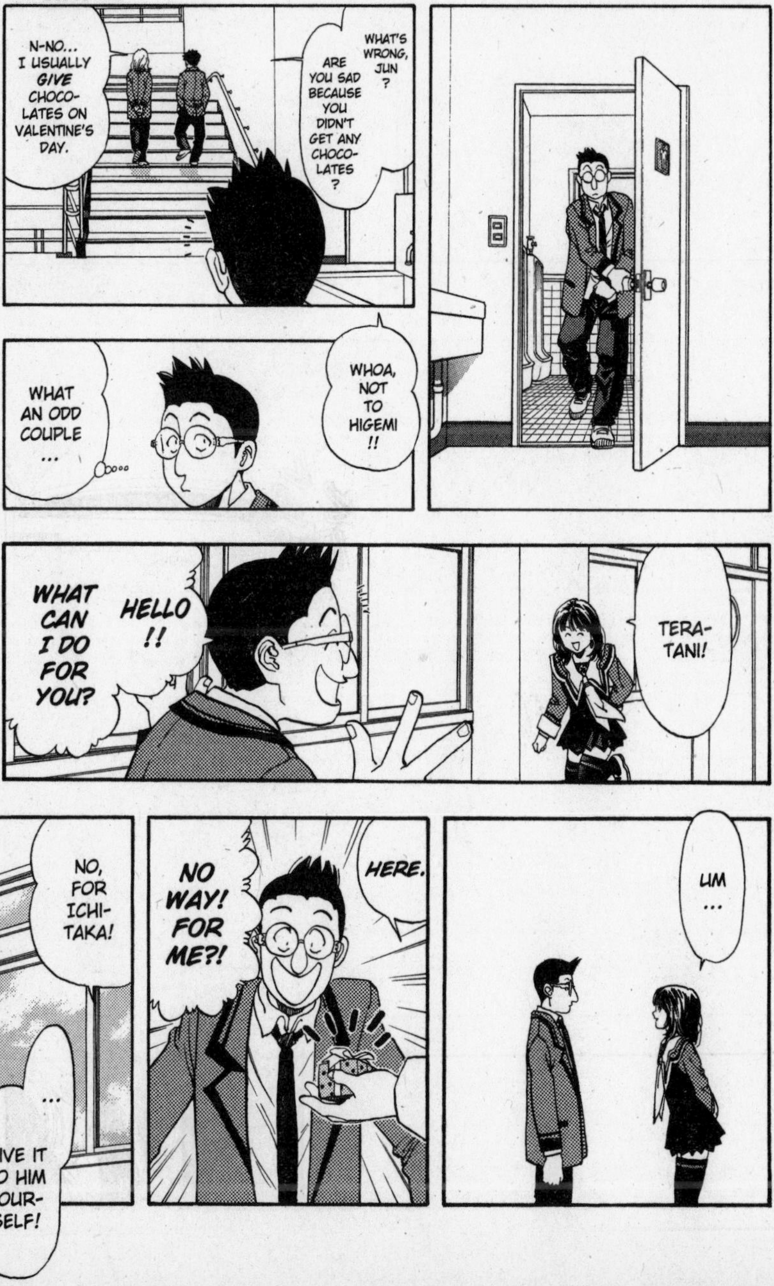
WHAT'S WRONG, JUN?
ARE YOU SAD BECAUSE YOU DIDN'T GET ANY CHOCO-LATES?
N-NO... I USUALLY *GIVE* CHOCO-LATES ON VALENTINE'S DAY.
WHOA, NOT TO HIGEMI!!
WHAT AN ODD COUPLE...
TERA-TANI!
HELLO!!
WHAT CAN I DO FOR YOU?
UM...
HERE.
NO WAY! FOR ME?!
NO, FOR ICHI-TAKA!
... GIVE IT TO HIM YOUR-SELF!

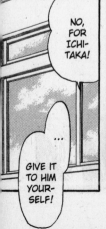

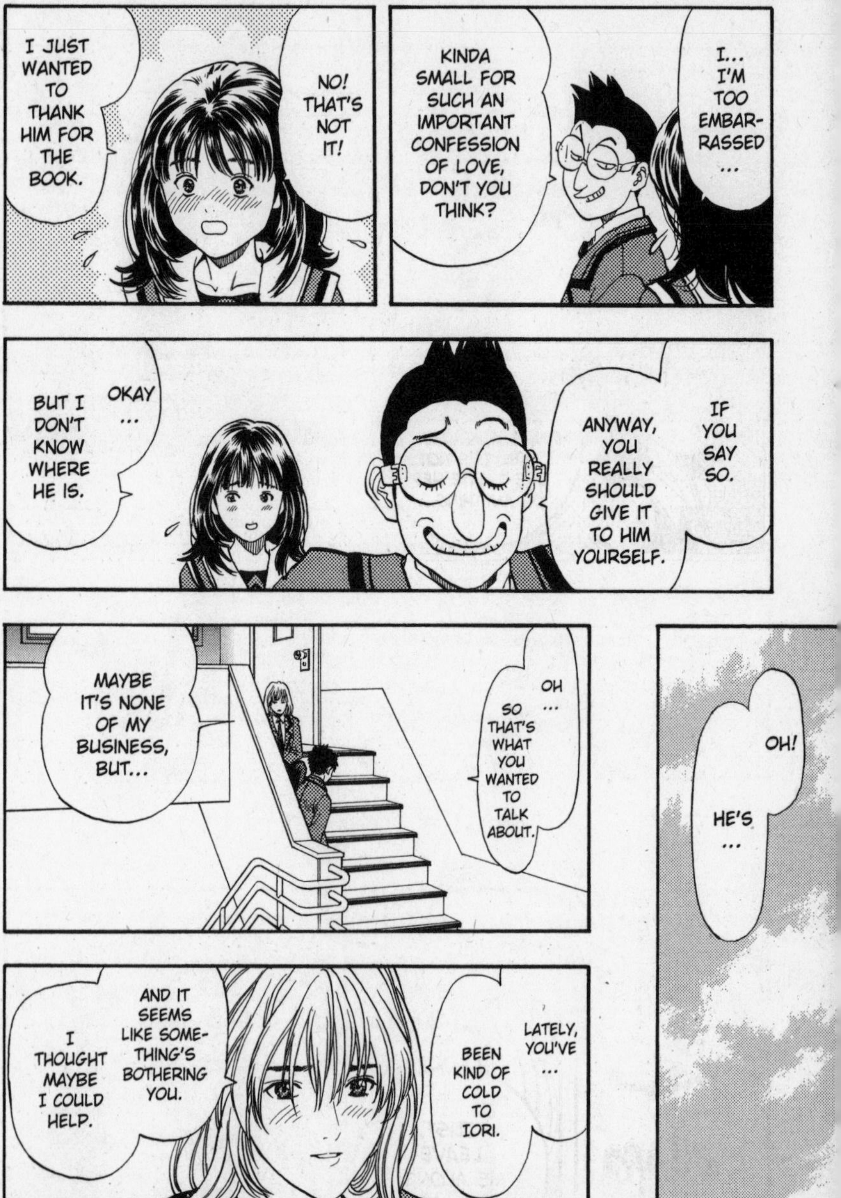
I... I'M TOO EMBARRASSED...
KINDA SMALL FOR SUCH AN IMPORTANT CONFESSION OF LOVE, DON'T YOU THINK?
NO! THAT'S NOT IT!
I JUST WANTED TO THANK HIM FOR THE BOOK.
IF YOU SAY SO.
ANYWAY, YOU REALLY SHOULD GIVE IT TO HIM YOURSELF.
OKAY...
BUT I DON'T KNOW WHERE HE IS.
OH!
HE'S...
OH...
SO THAT'S WHAT YOU WANTED TO TALK ABOUT.
MAYBE IT'S NONE OF MY BUSINESS, BUT...
LATELY, YOU'VE...
BEEN KIND OF COLD TO IORI.
AND IT SEEMS LIKE SOMETHING'S BOTHERING YOU.
I THOUGHT MAYBE I COULD HELP.

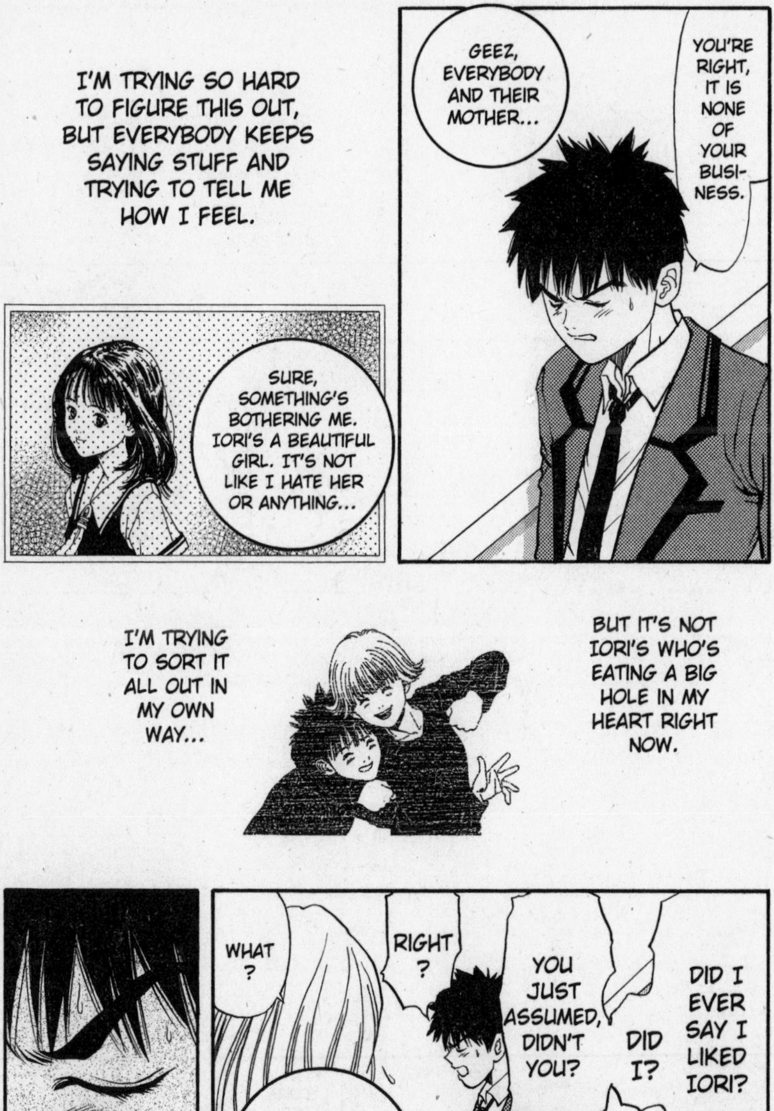

YOU'RE RIGHT, IT IS NONE OF YOUR BUSI-NESS.
GEEZ, EVERYBODY AND THEIR MOTHER...
I'M TRYING SO HARD TO FIGURE THIS OUT, BUT EVERYBODY KEEPS SAYING STUFF AND TRYING TO TELL ME HOW I FEEL.
SURE, SOMETHING'S BOTHERING ME. IORI'S A BEAUTIFUL GIRL. IT'S NOT LIKE I HATE HER OR ANYTHING...
BUT IT'S NOT IORI'S WHO'S EATING A BIG HOLE IN MY HEART RIGHT NOW.
I'M TRYING TO SORT IT ALL OUT IN MY OWN WAY...
DID I EVER SAY I LIKED IORI?
DID I?
YOU JUST ASSUMED, DIDN'T YOU?
RIGHT?
WHAT?
JUST LEAVE ME ALONE! OKAY?!
THROB

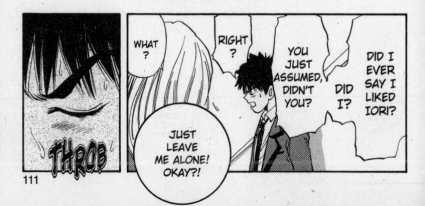

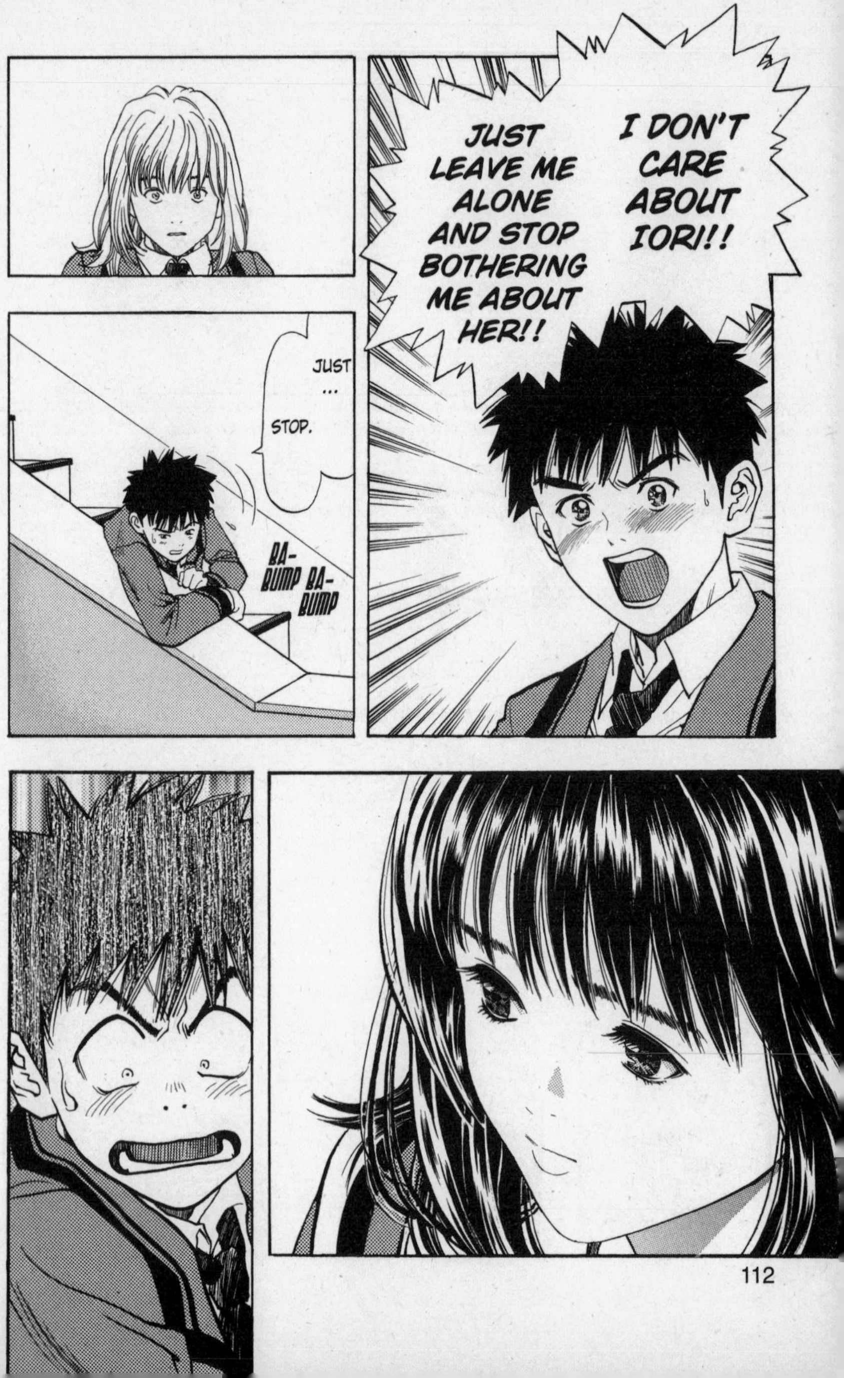
I DON'T CARE ABOUT IORI!!
JUST LEAVE ME ALONE AND STOP BOTHERING ME ABOUT HER!!
JUST ... STOP.
BA-BUMP BA-BUMP

READ THIS WAY

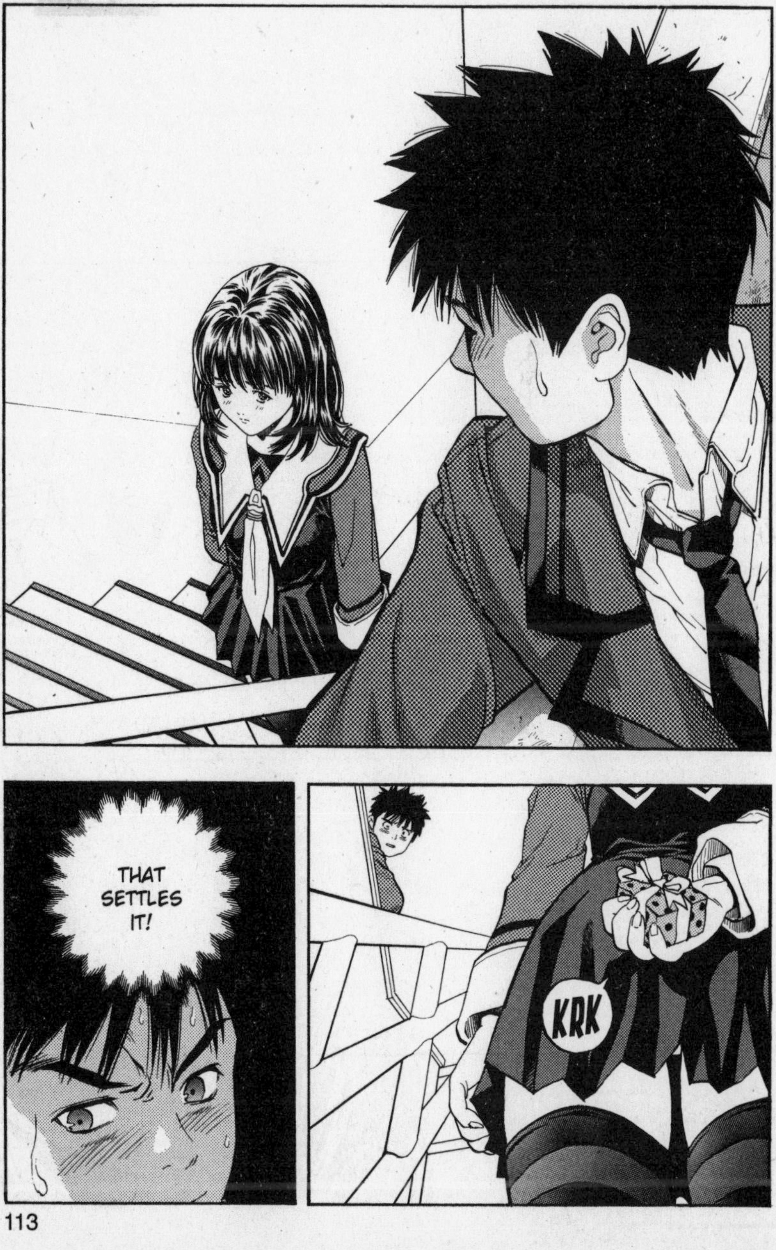
KRK
THAT SETTLES IT!

Chapter 42:
Stop Wavering!

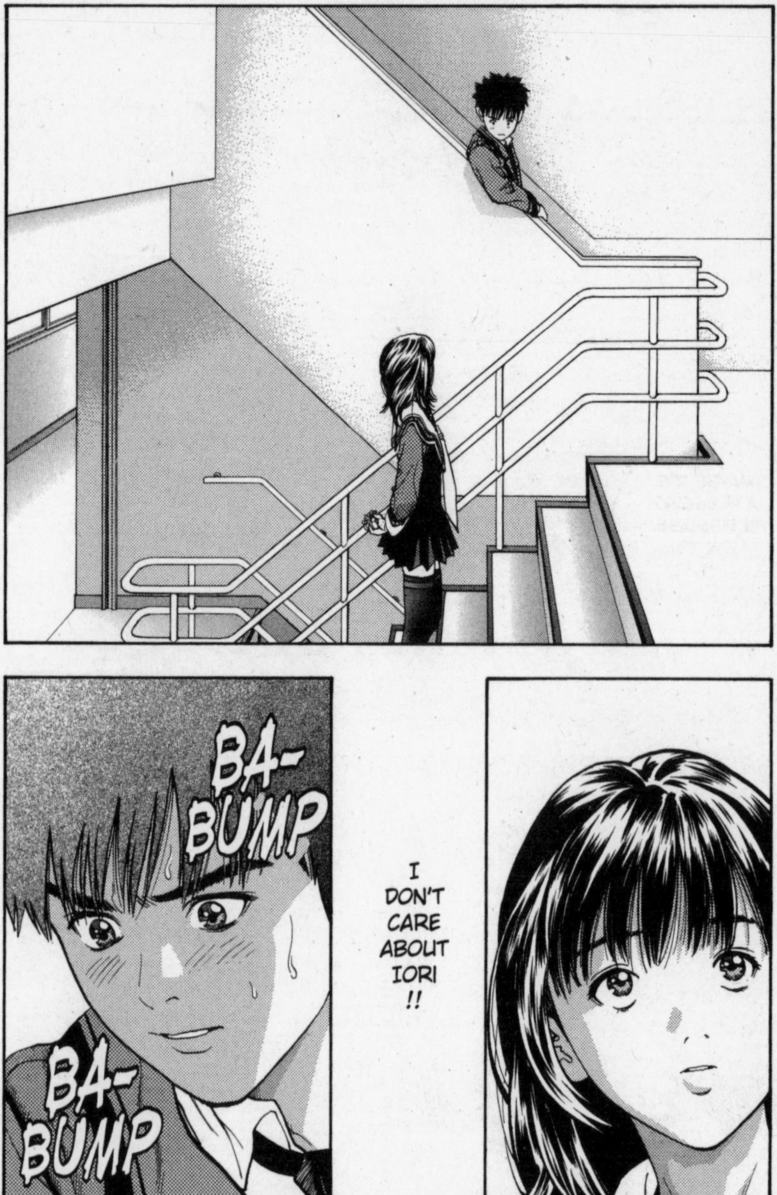
I DON'T CARE ABOUT IORI !!
BA-BUMP
BA-BUMP

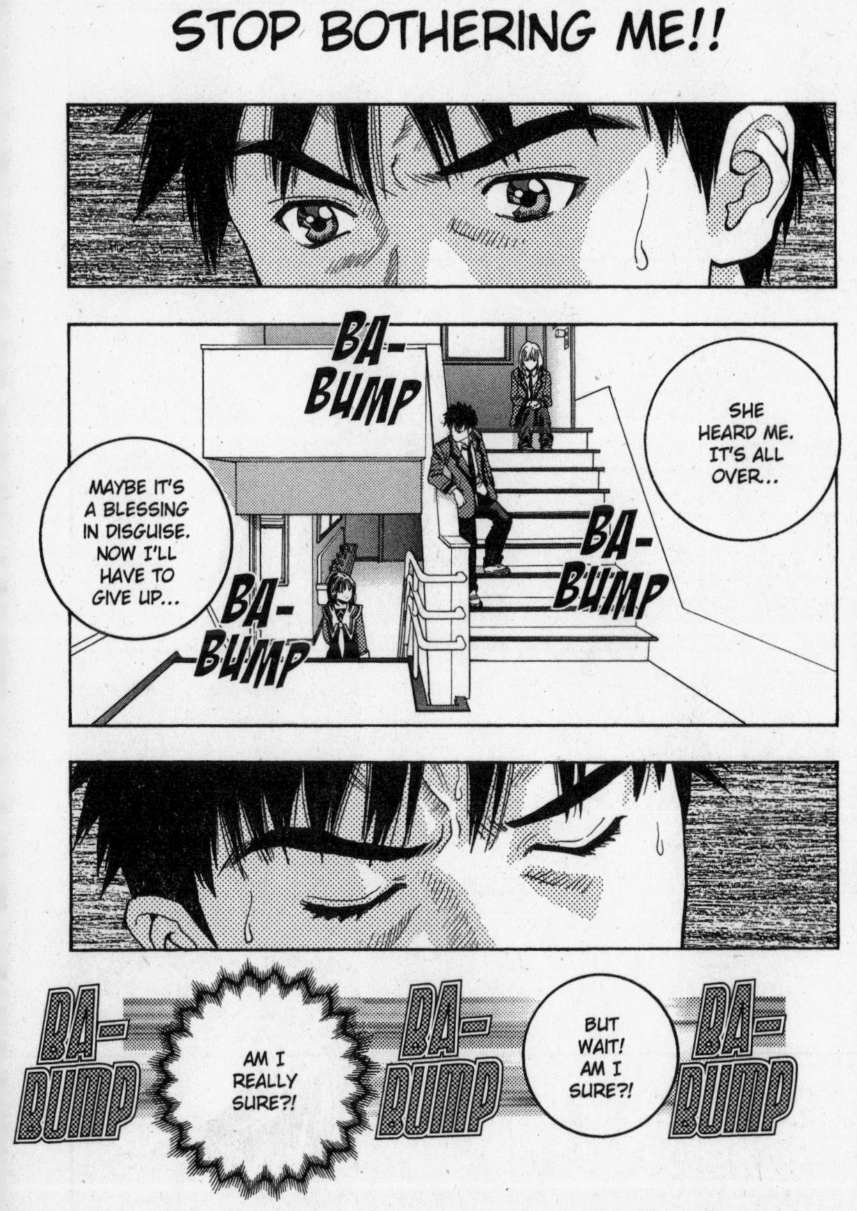
STOP BOTHERING ME!!
BA-BUMP
SHE HEARD ME. IT'S ALL OVER...
BA-BUMP
BA-BUMP
MAYBE IT'S A BLESSING IN DISGUISE. NOW I'LL HAVE TO GIVE UP...
BA-BUMP
BUT WAIT! AM I SURE?!
BA-BUMP
AM I REALLY SURE?!
BA-BUMP

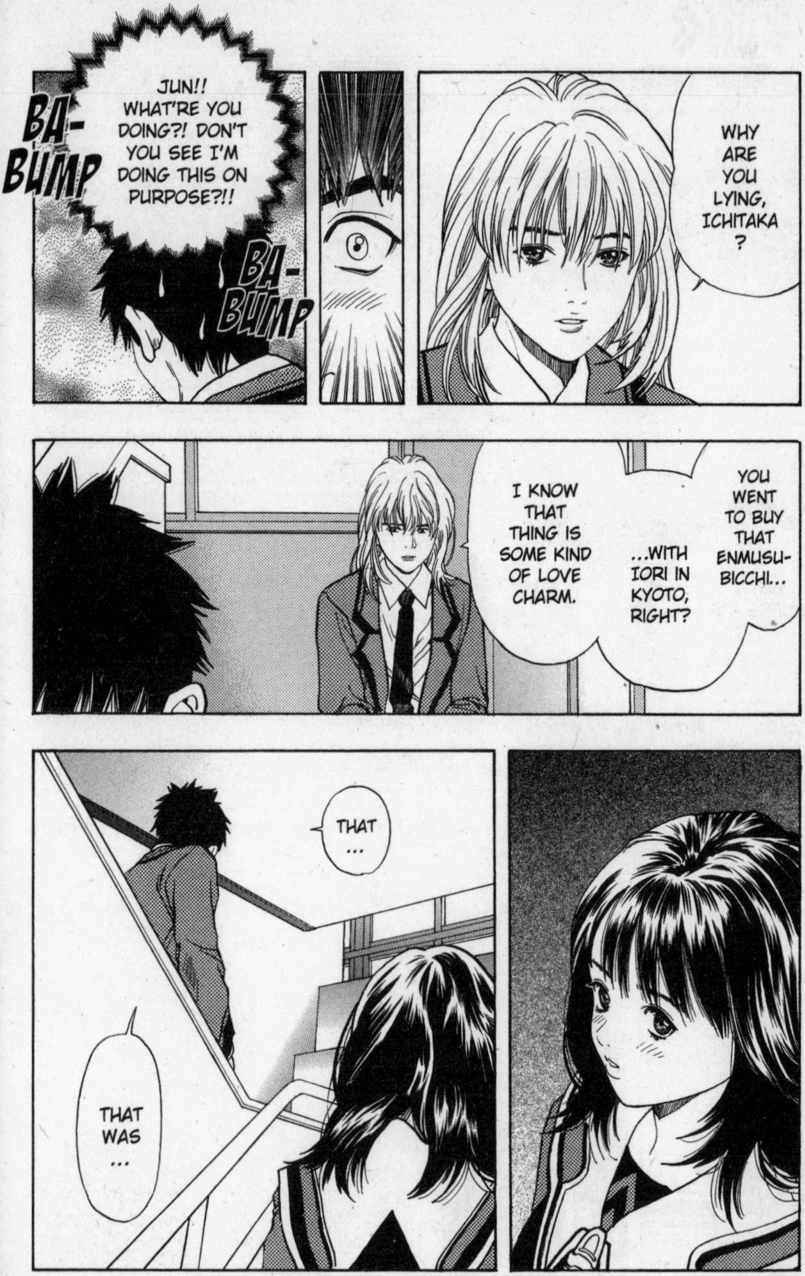
WHY ARE YOU LYING, ICHITAKA?
BA-BUMP
JUN!! WHAT'RE YOU DOING?! DON'T YOU SEE I'M DOING THIS ON PURPOSE?!!
BA-BUMP
YOU WENT TO BUY THAT ENMUSUBICCHI...
...WITH IORI IN KYOTO, RIGHT?
I KNOW THAT THING IS SOME KIND OF LOVE CHARM.
THAT ...
THAT WAS ...

READ THIS WAY

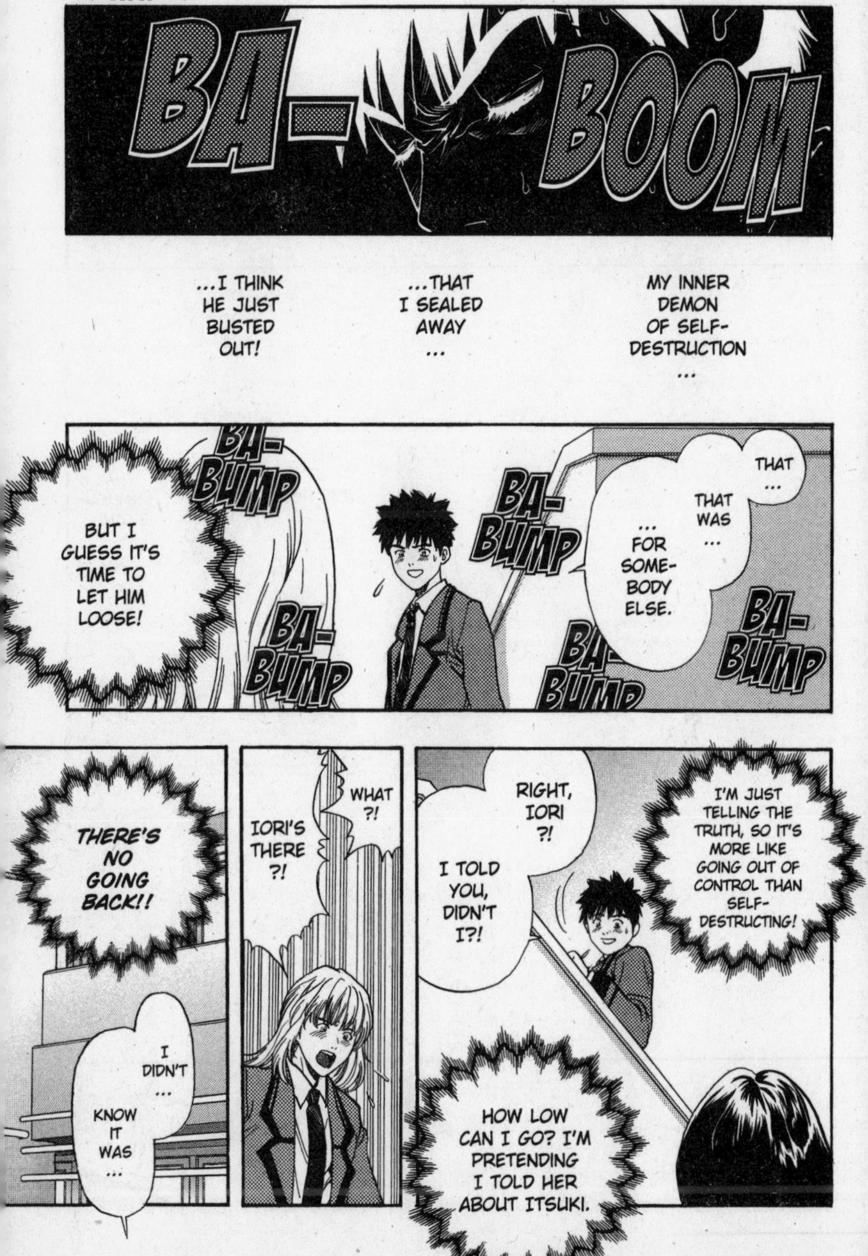
BA-BOOM
MY INNER DEMON OF SELF-DESTRUCTION...
...THAT I SEALED AWAY...
...I THINK HE JUST BUSTED OUT!
BA-BUMP
THAT...
THAT WAS...
...FOR SOMEBODY ELSE.
BA-BUMP
BA-BUMP
BA-BUMP
BUT I GUESS IT'S TIME TO LET HIM LOOSE!
BA-BUMP
I'M JUST TELLING THE TRUTH, SO IT'S MORE LIKE GOING OUT OF CONTROL THAN SELF-DESTRUCTING!
RIGHT, IORI?!
I TOLD YOU, DIDN'T I?!
HOW LOW CAN I GO? I'M PRETENDING I TOLD HER ABOUT ITSUKI.
WHAT?!
IORI'S THERE?!
THERE'S NO GOING BACK!!
I DIDN'T... KNOW IT WAS...

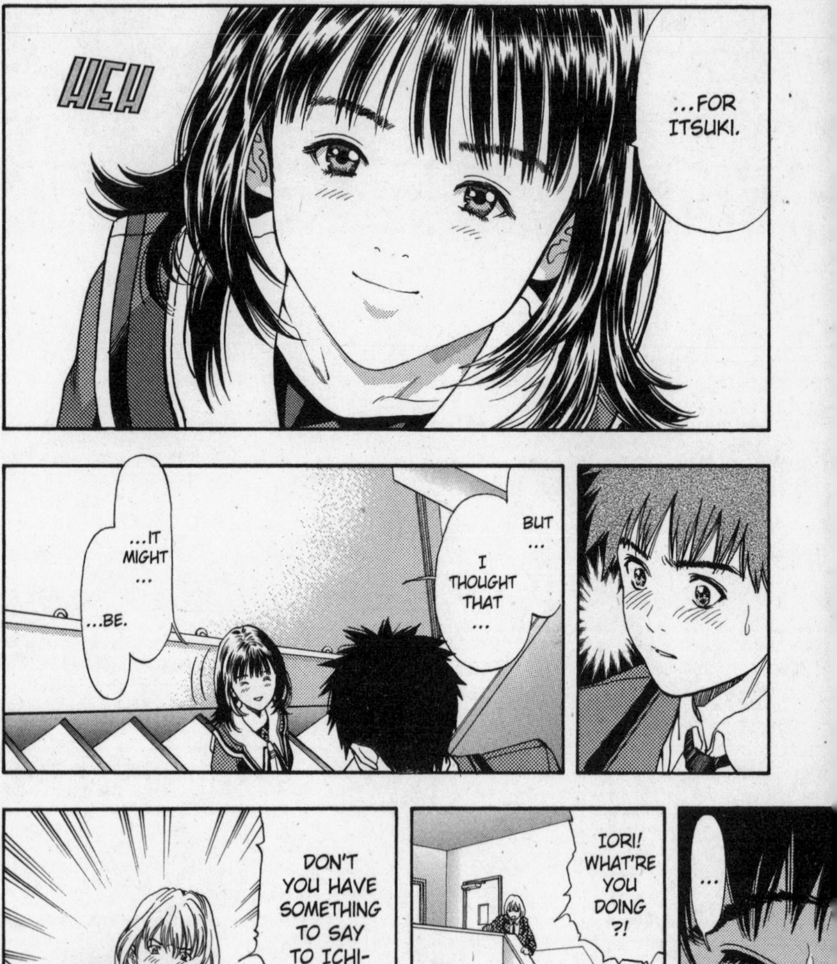
...FOR ITSUKI.
HEH
BUT ... I THOUGHT THAT ...
...IT MIGHT ... ...BE.
...
IORI! WHAT'RE YOU DOING ?!
HUH?
DON'T YOU HAVE SOMETHING TO SAY TO ICHI-TAKA?!

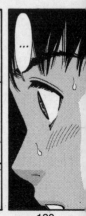

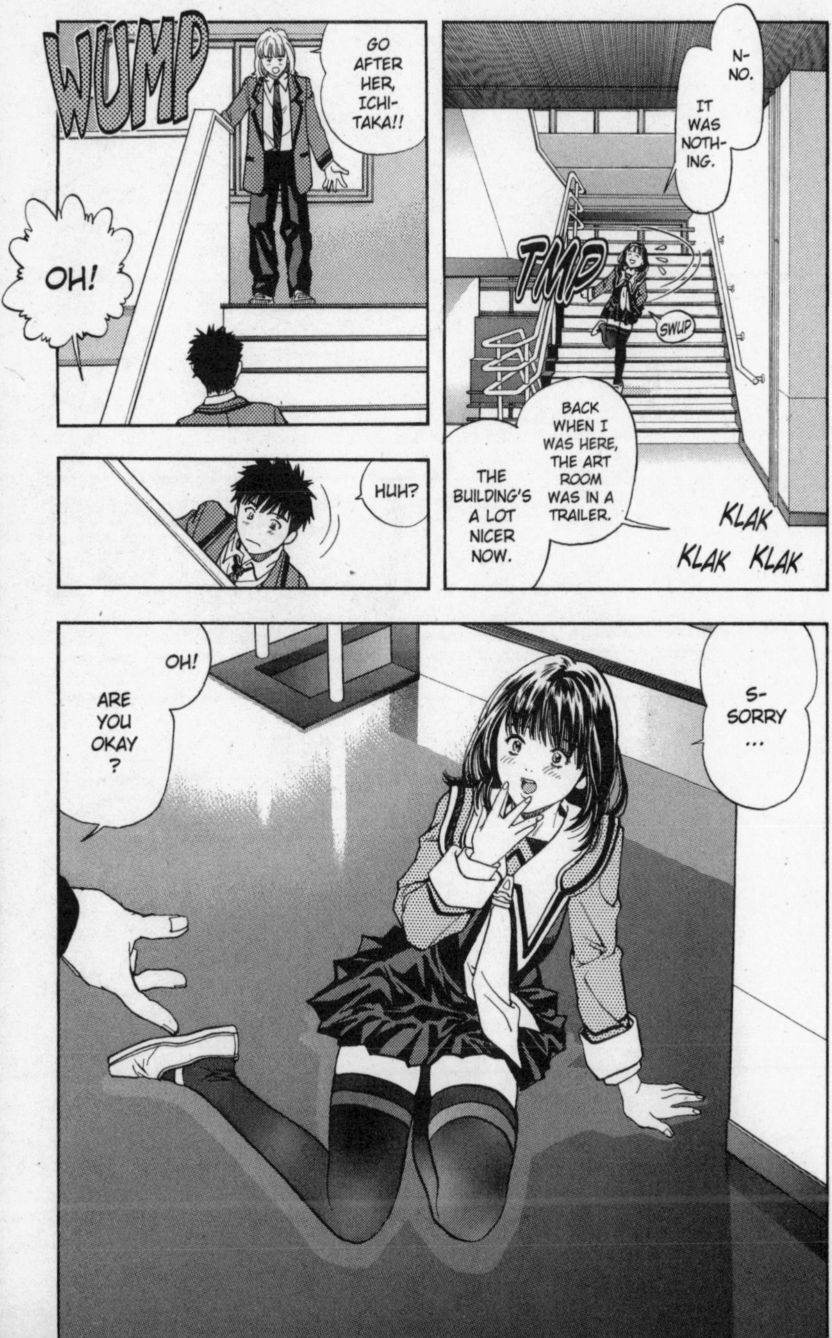
N-NO.
IT WAS NOTHING.
TMP
SWUP
BACK WHEN I WAS HERE, THE ART ROOM WAS IN A TRAILER.
THE BUILDING'S A LOT NICER NOW.
KLAK KLAK KLAK
WUMP
GO AFTER HER, ICHITAKA!!
OH!
HUH?
S-SORRY...
OH!
ARE YOU OKAY?

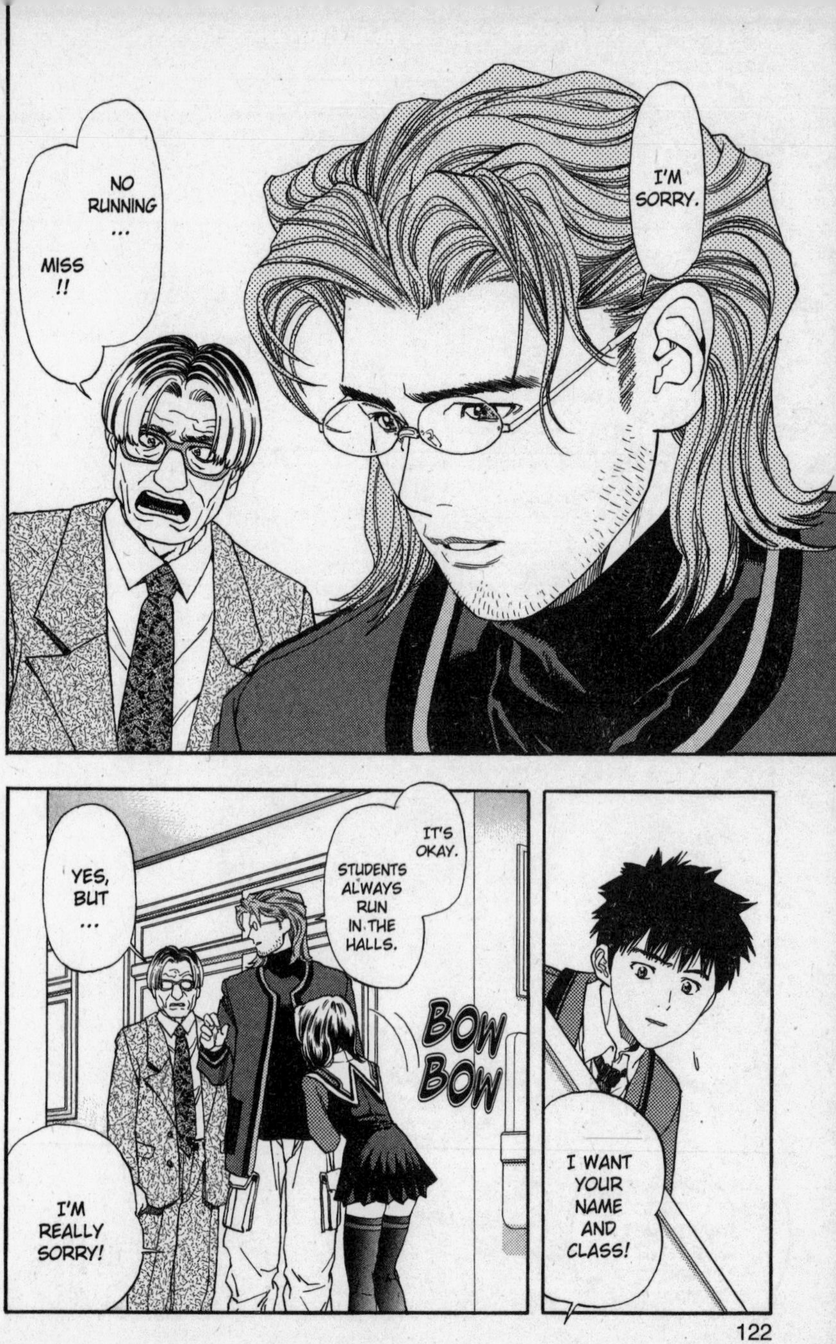
I'M SORRY.
NO RUNNING ... MISS !!
I WANT YOUR NAME AND CLASS!
IT'S OKAY.
STUDENTS ALWAYS RUN IN THE HALLS.
YES, BUT ...
BOW BOW
I'M REALLY SORRY!

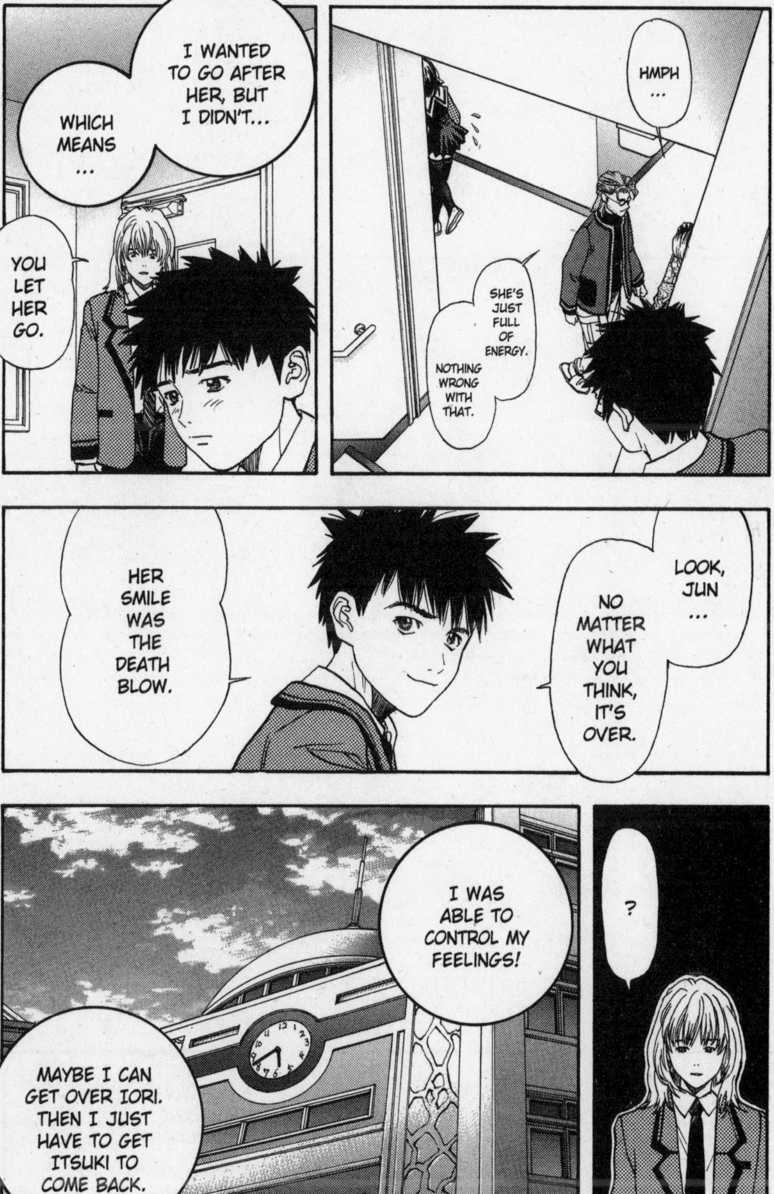
HMPH ...
SHE'S JUST FULL OF ENERGY.
NOTHING WRONG WITH THAT.
I WANTED TO GO AFTER HER, BUT I DIDN'T...
WHICH MEANS ...
YOU LET HER GO.
LOOK, JUN ...
NO MATTER WHAT YOU THINK, IT'S OVER.
HER SMILE WAS THE DEATH BLOW.
?
I WAS ABLE TO CONTROL MY FEELINGS!
MAYBE I CAN GET OVER IORI. THEN I JUST HAVE TO GET ITSUKI TO COME BACK.

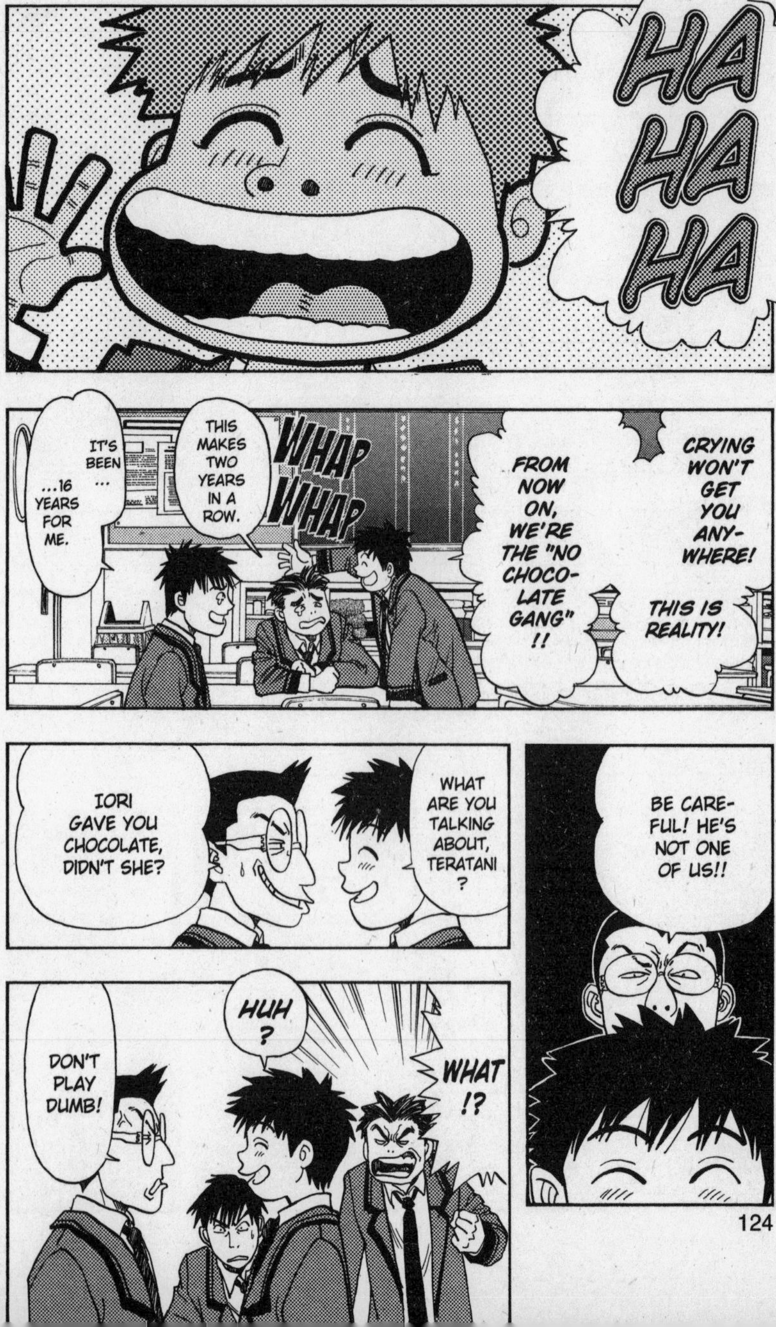
HA HA HA
CRYING WON'T GET YOU ANY-WHERE!
THIS IS REALITY!
FROM NOW ON, WE'RE THE "NO CHOCO-LATE GANG" !!
WHAP WHAP
THIS MAKES TWO YEARS IN A ROW.
IT'S BEEN ...
...16 YEARS FOR ME.
BE CARE-FUL! HE'S NOT ONE OF US!!
WHAT ARE YOU TALKING ABOUT, TERATANI ?
IORI GAVE YOU CHOCOLATE, DIDN'T SHE?
WHAT !?
HUH ?
DON'T PLAY DUMB!

READ THIS WAY

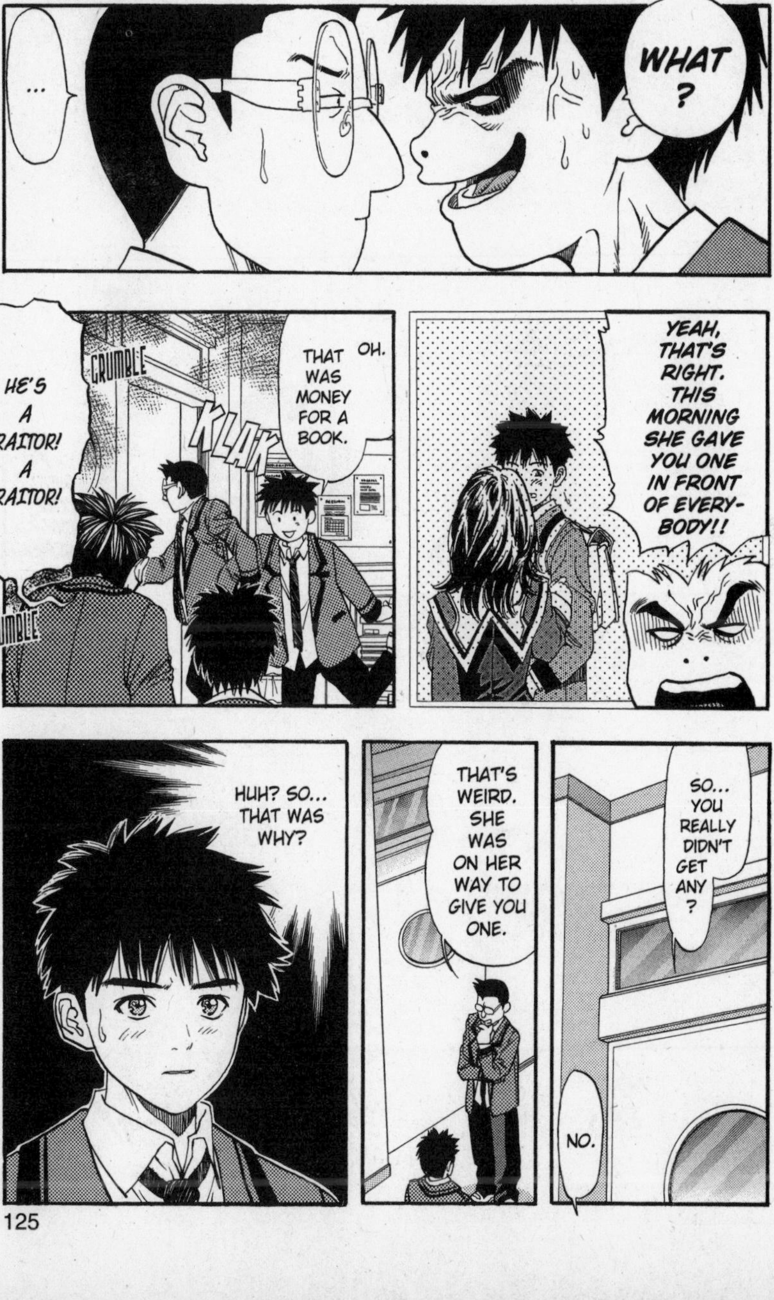

WHAT?
...
YEAH, THAT'S RIGHT. THIS MORNING SHE GAVE YOU ONE IN FRONT OF EVERY-BODY!!
OH.
THAT WAS MONEY FOR A BOOK.
KLAK
GRUMBLE
HE'S A TRAITOR! A TRAITOR!
GRUMBLE
SO... YOU REALLY DIDN'T GET ANY?
NO.
THAT'S WEIRD. SHE WAS ON HER WAY TO GIVE YOU ONE.
HUH? SO... THAT WAS WHY?

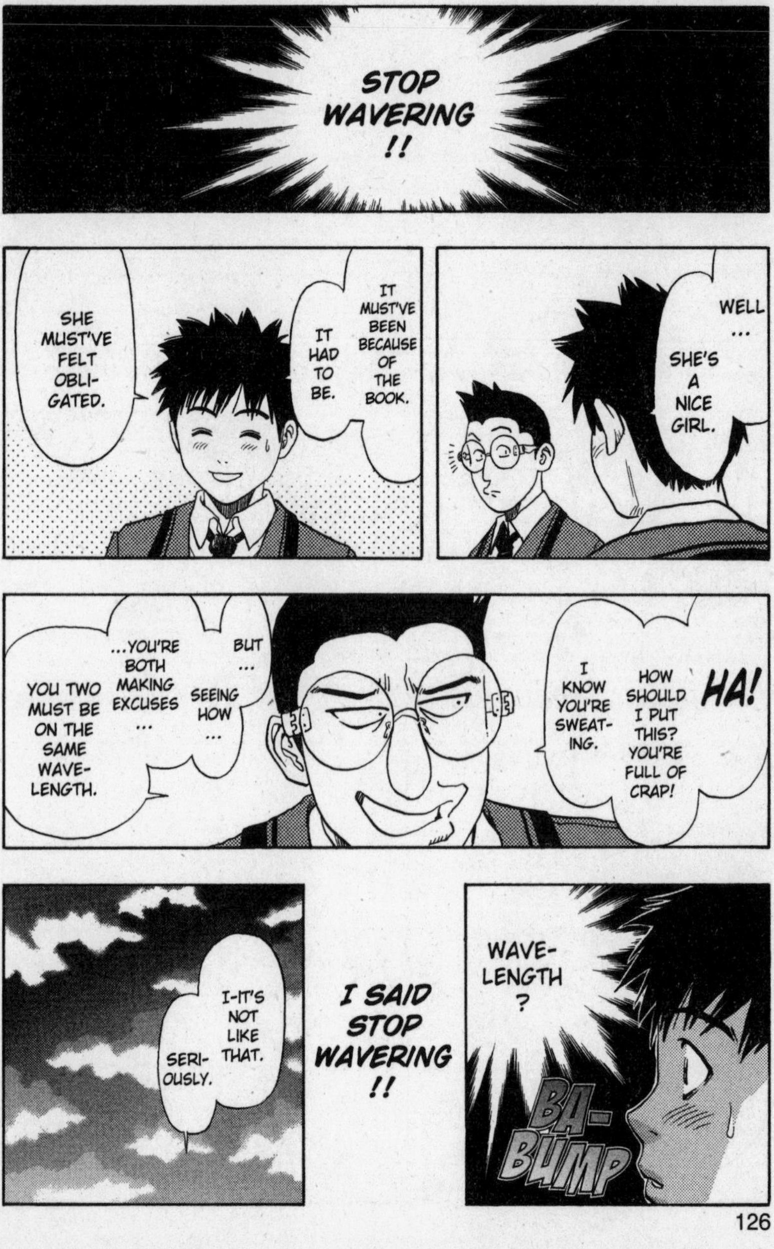
STOP WAVERING !!
WELL ... SHE'S A NICE GIRL.
IT MUST'VE BEEN BECAUSE OF THE BOOK.
IT HAD TO BE.
SHE MUST'VE FELT OBLI-GATED.
HA!
HOW SHOULD I PUT THIS? YOU'RE FULL OF CRAP!
I KNOW YOU'RE SWEAT-ING.
BUT ... SEEING HOW ...
...YOU'RE BOTH MAKING EXCUSES ...
YOU TWO MUST BE ON THE SAME WAVE-LENGTH.
WAVE-LENGTH ?
BA-BUMP
I SAID STOP WAVERING !!
I-IT'S NOT LIKE THAT.
SERI-OUSLY.

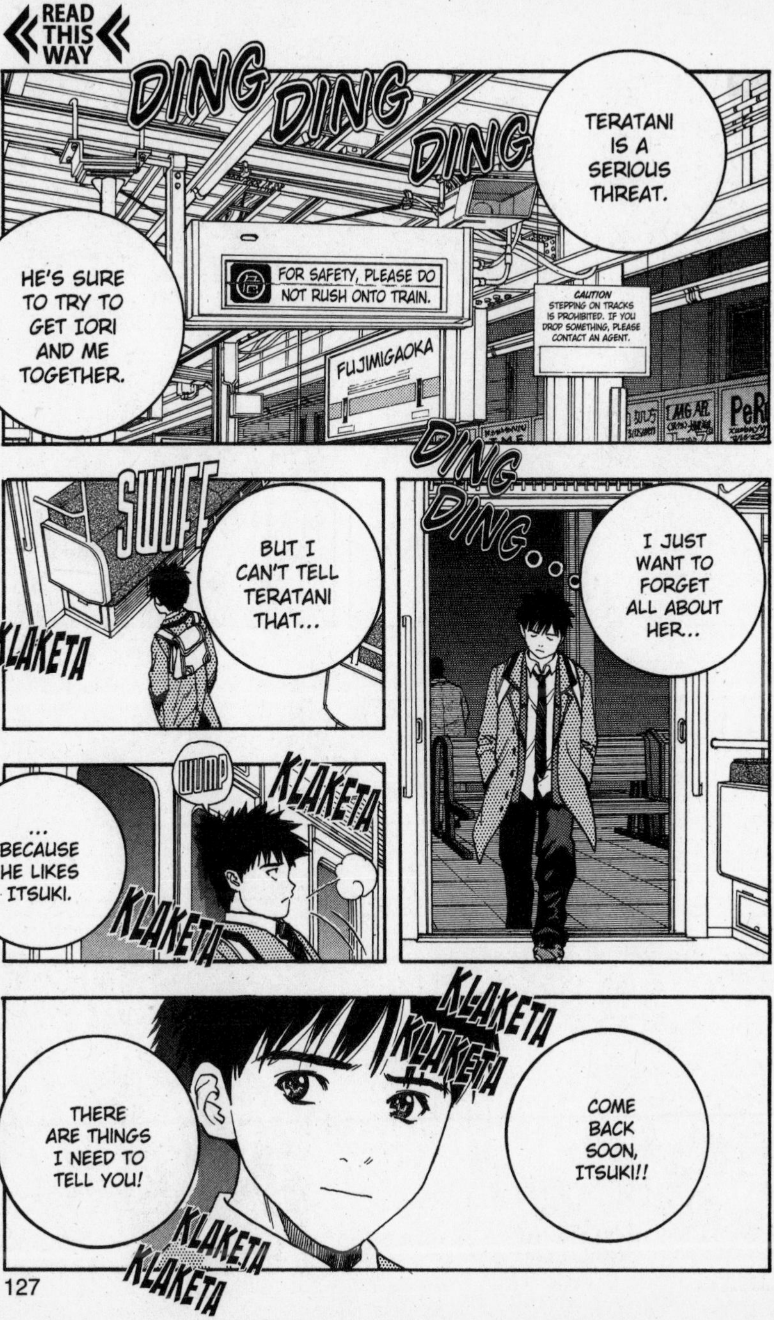
READ THIS WAY
DING DING DING
TERATANI IS A SERIOUS THREAT.
FOR SAFETY, PLEASE DO NOT RUSH ONTO TRAIN.
CAUTION
STEPPING ON TRACKS IS PROHIBITED. IF YOU DROP SOMETHING, PLEASE CONTACT AN AGENT.
FUJIMIGAOKA
HE'S SURE TO TRY TO GET IORI AND ME TOGETHER.
DING DING...
I JUST WANT TO FORGET ALL ABOUT HER...
SWUFF
BUT I CAN'T TELL TERATANI THAT...
KLAKETA
WUMP
KLAKETA
... BECAUSE HE LIKES ITSUKI.
KLAKETA
KLAKETA KLAKETA
COME BACK SOON, ITSUKI!!
THERE ARE THINGS I NEED TO TELL YOU!
KLAKETA KLAKETA

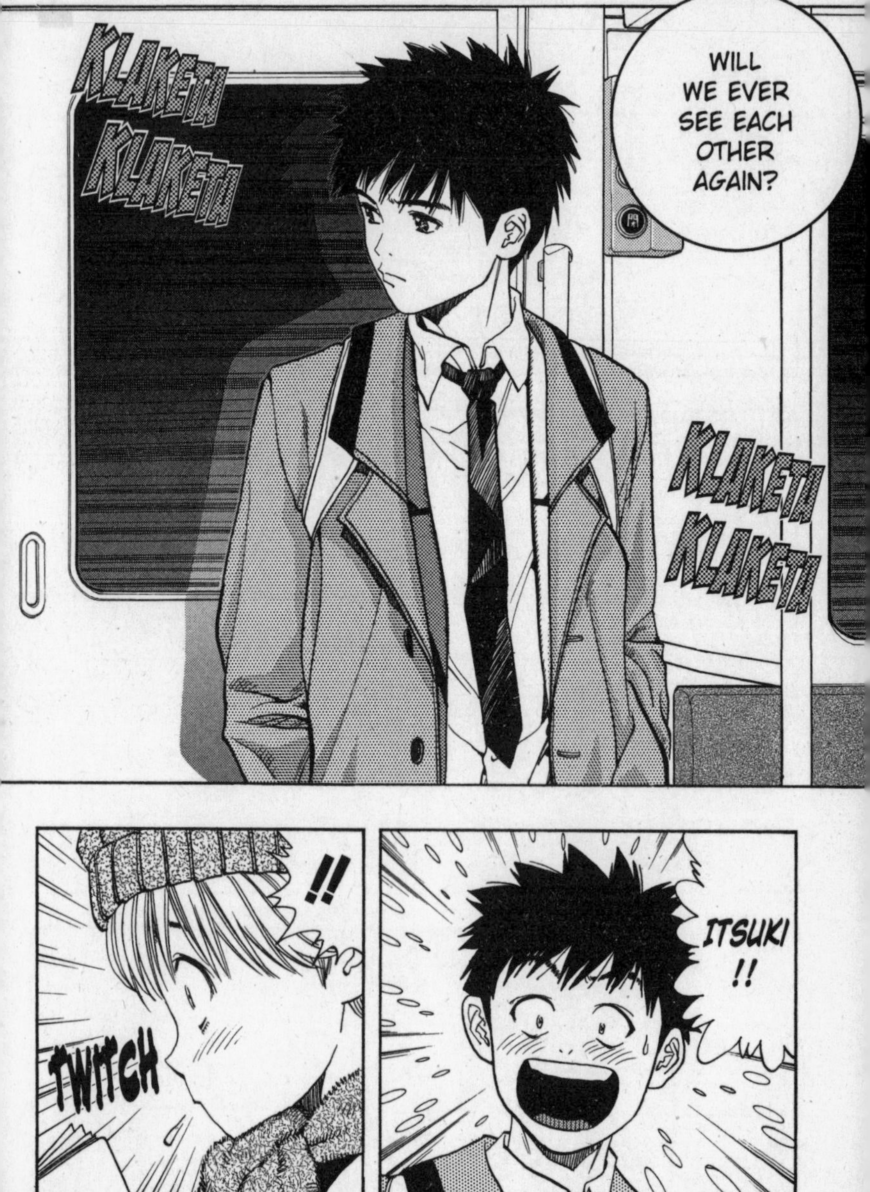
WILL WE EVER SEE EACH OTHER AGAIN?
KLAKETA KLAKETA
KLAKETA KLAKETA
ITSUKI !!
!!
TWITCH

READ THIS WAY

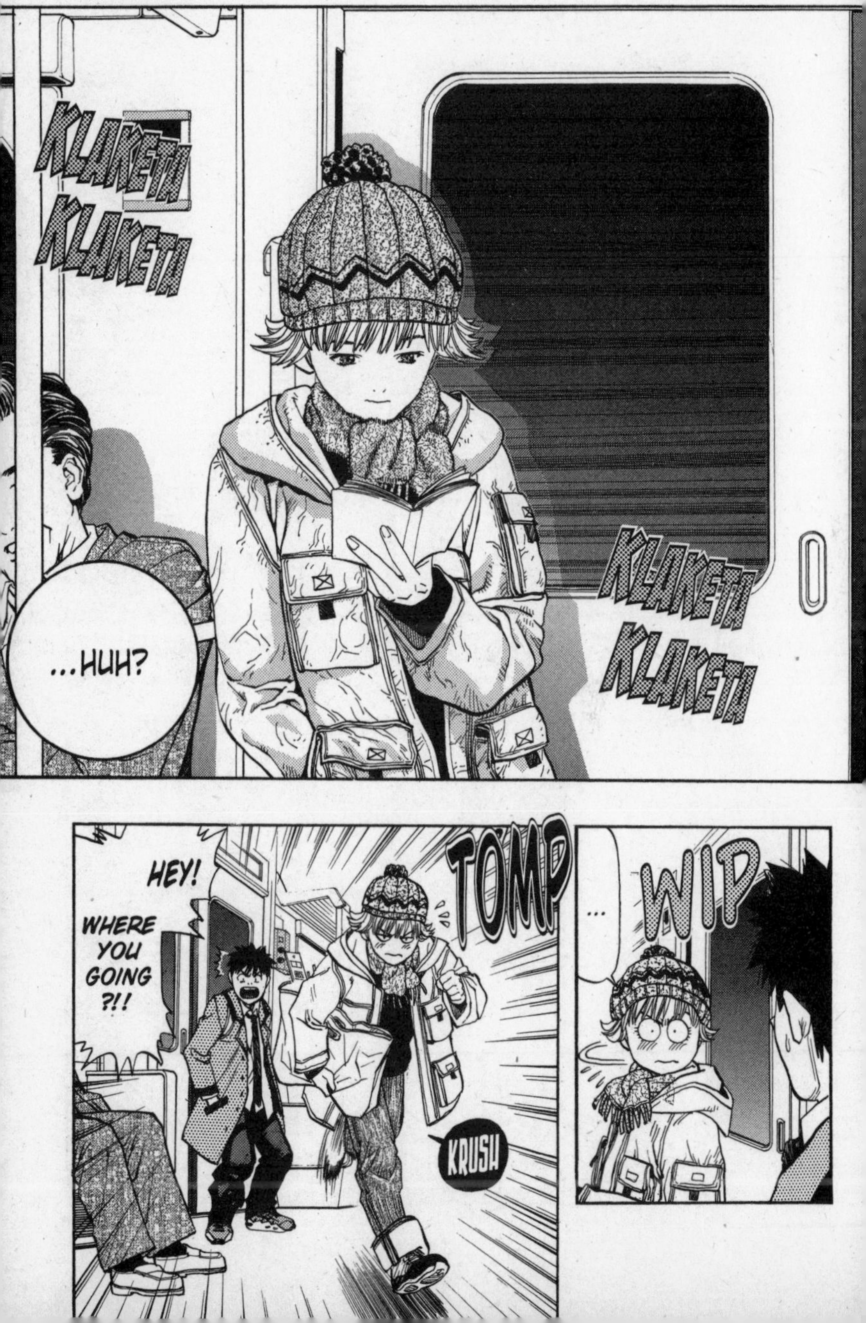
KLAKETA KLAKETA
KLAKETA KLAKETA
...HUH?
...
WIP
TOMP
HEY!
WHERE YOU GOING?!!
KRUSH

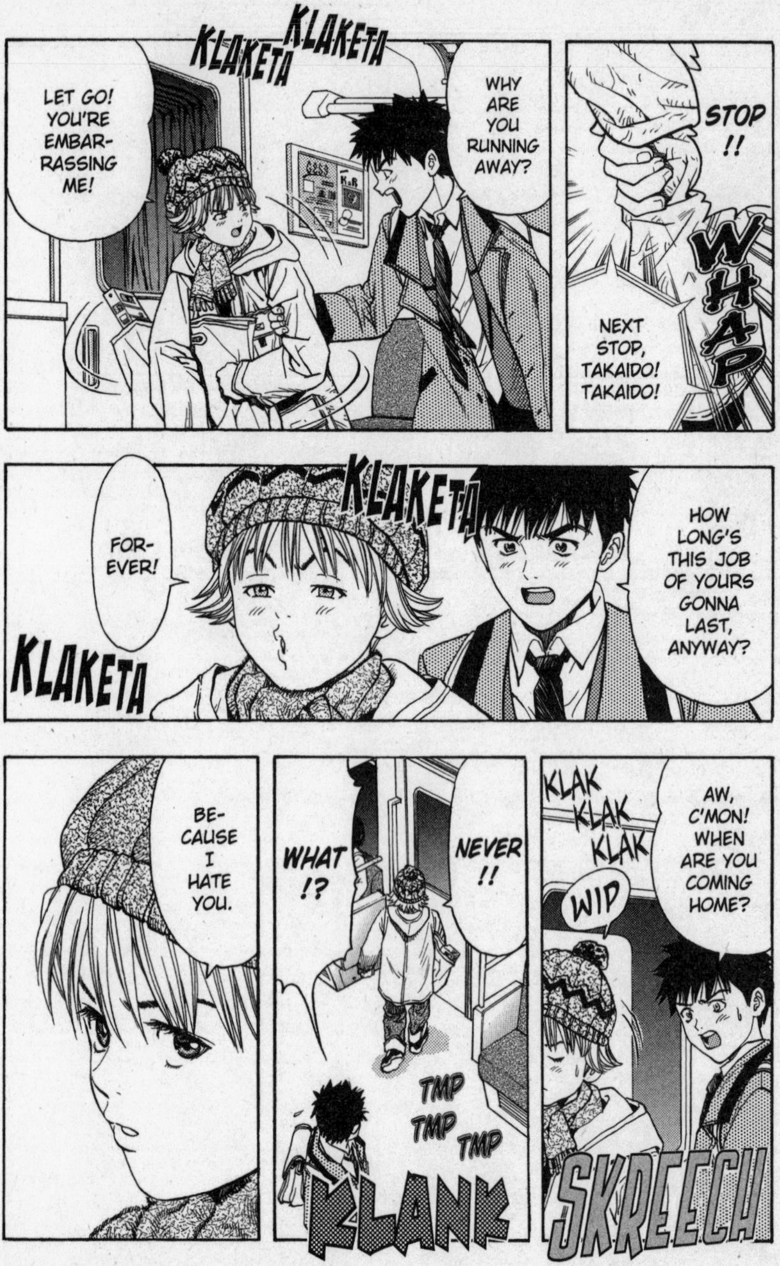
STOP !!
WHAP
NEXT STOP, TAKAIDO! TAKAIDO!
KLAKETA
KLAKETA
WHY ARE YOU RUNNING AWAY?
LET GO! YOU'RE EMBAR-RASSING ME!
KLAKETA
HOW LONG'S THIS JOB OF YOURS GONNA LAST, ANYWAY?
FOR-EVER!
KLAKETA
KLAK KLAK KLAK
AW, C'MON! WHEN ARE YOU COMING HOME?
WIP
SKREECH
NEVER !!
WHAT !?
TMP TMP TMP
KLANK
BE-CAUSE I HATE YOU.

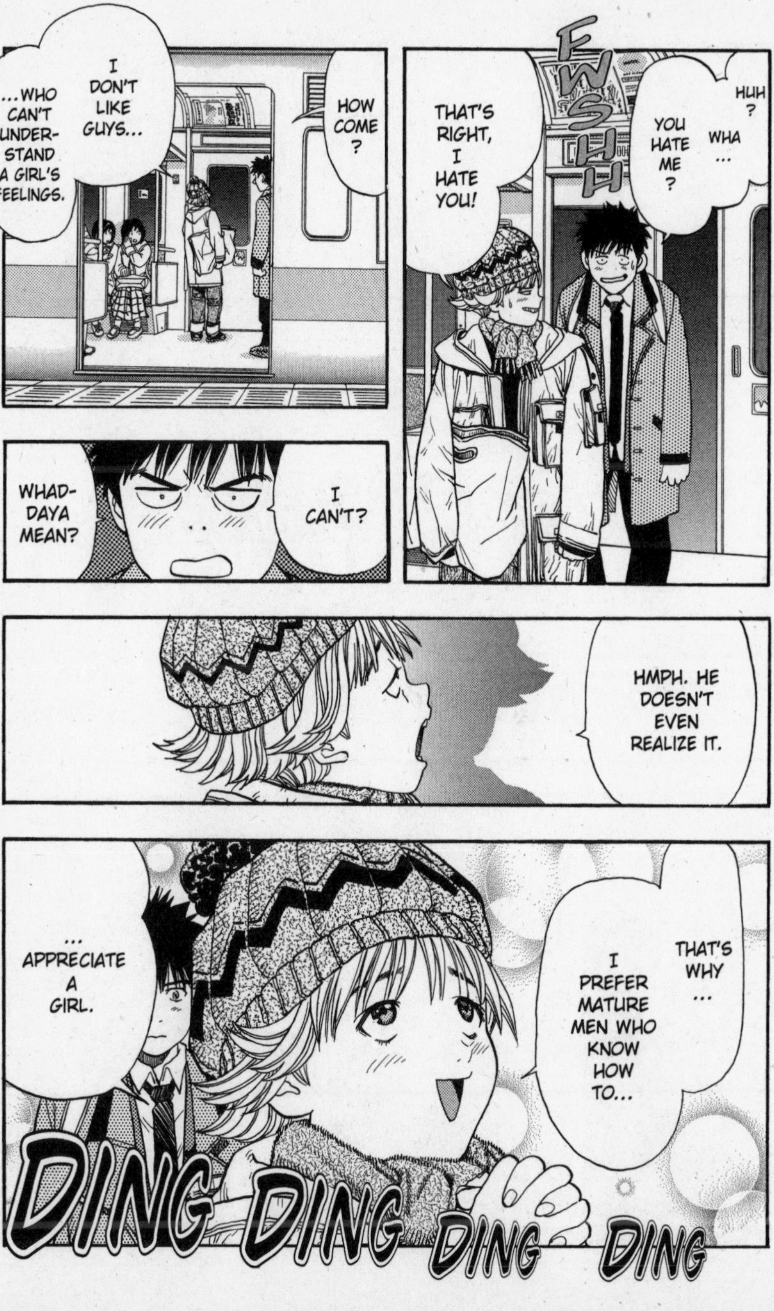
HUH? WHA...
YOU HATE ME?
FWSHH
THAT'S RIGHT, I HATE YOU!
HOW COME?
I DON'T LIKE GUYS...
...WHO CAN'T UNDER-STAND A GIRL'S FEELINGS.
I CAN'T?
WHAD-DAYA MEAN?
HMPH. HE DOESN'T EVEN REALIZE IT.
THAT'S WHY...
I PREFER MATURE MEN WHO KNOW HOW TO...
...APPRECIATE A GIRL.
DING DING DING DING

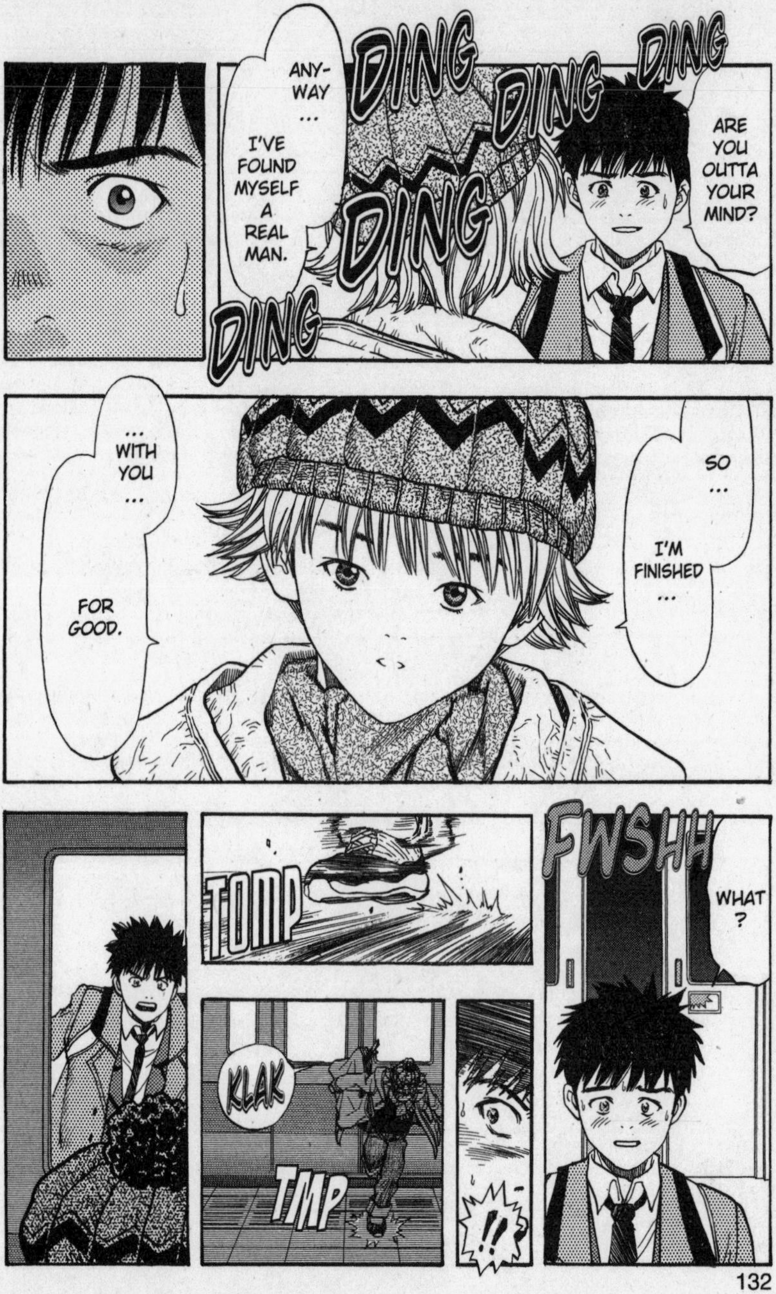
DING
DING
ANY-WAY ... I'VE FOUND MYSELF A REAL MAN.
ARE YOU OUTTA YOUR MIND?
DING
DING
SO ... I'M FINISHED ...
... WITH YOU ... FOR GOOD.
FWSHH
WHAT ?
TOMP
!!
KLAK
TMP

READ THIS WAY

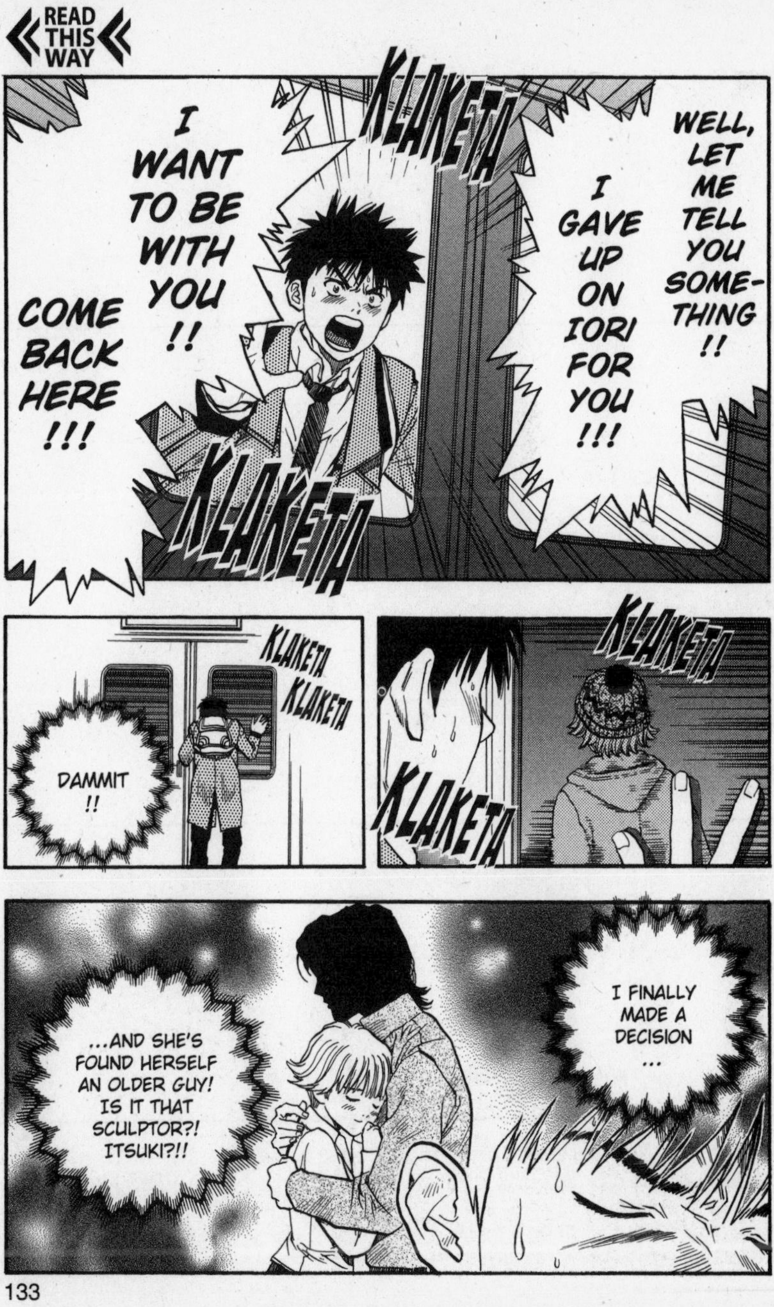

KLAKETA
WELL, LET ME TELL YOU SOMETHING!!
I GAVE UP ON IORI FOR YOU!!!
I WANT TO BE WITH YOU!!
COME BACK HERE!!!
KLAKETA
KLAKETA
KLAKETA
KLAKETA KLAKETA
DAMMIT!!
I FINALLY MADE A DECISION...
...AND SHE'S FOUND HERSELF AN OLDER GUY! IS IT THAT SCULPTOR?! ITSUKI?!!

Chapter 43:
Children's Conversation

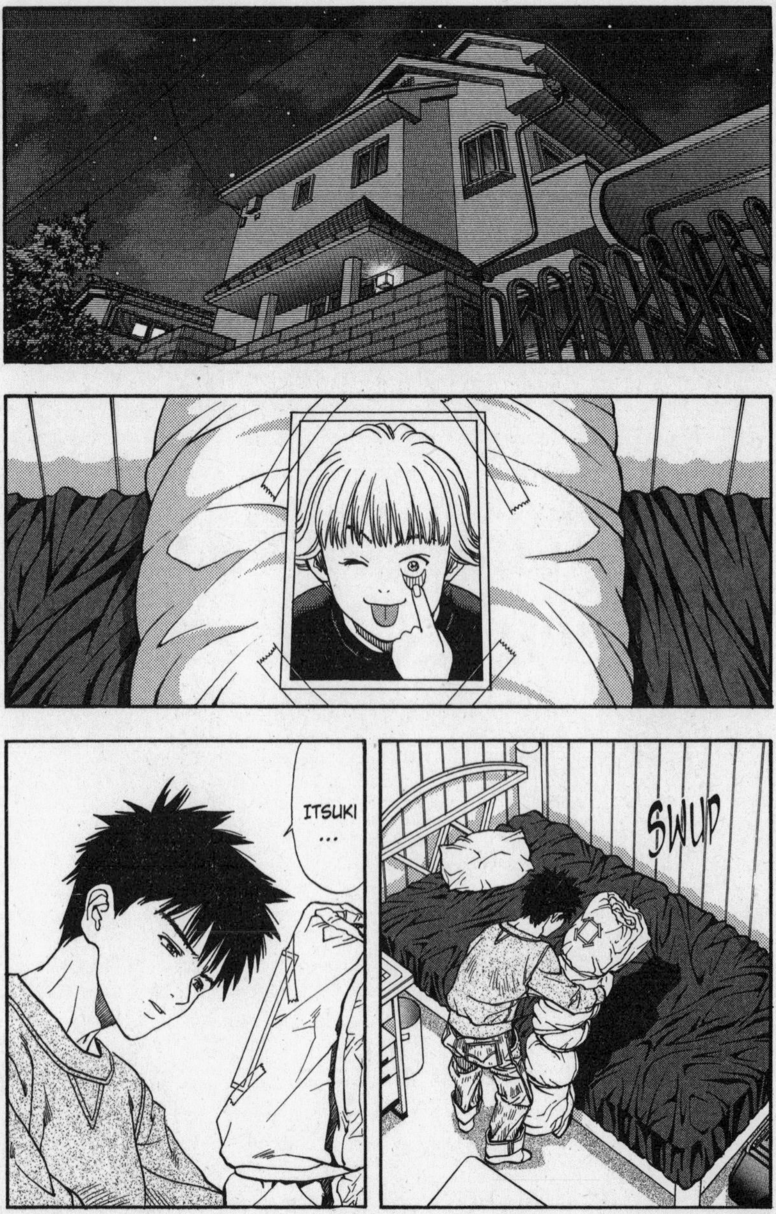
SWUP
ITSUKI
...

READ THIS WAY

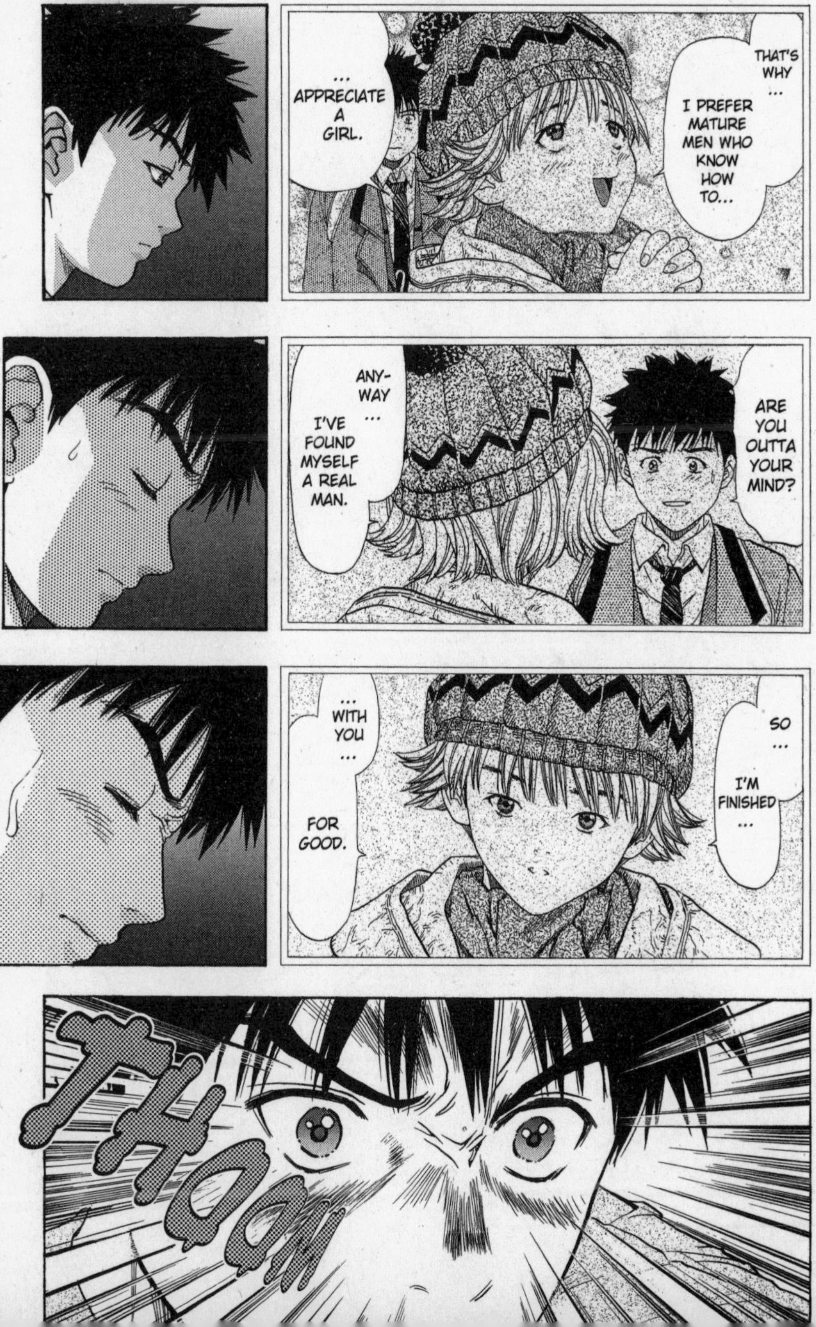
THAT'S WHY ...
I PREFER MATURE MEN WHO KNOW HOW TO...
... APPRECIATE A GIRL.
ARE YOU OUTTA YOUR MIND?
ANY-WAY ...
I'VE FOUND MYSELF A REAL MAN.
SO ...
I'M FINISHED ...
... WITH YOU ...
FOR GOOD.

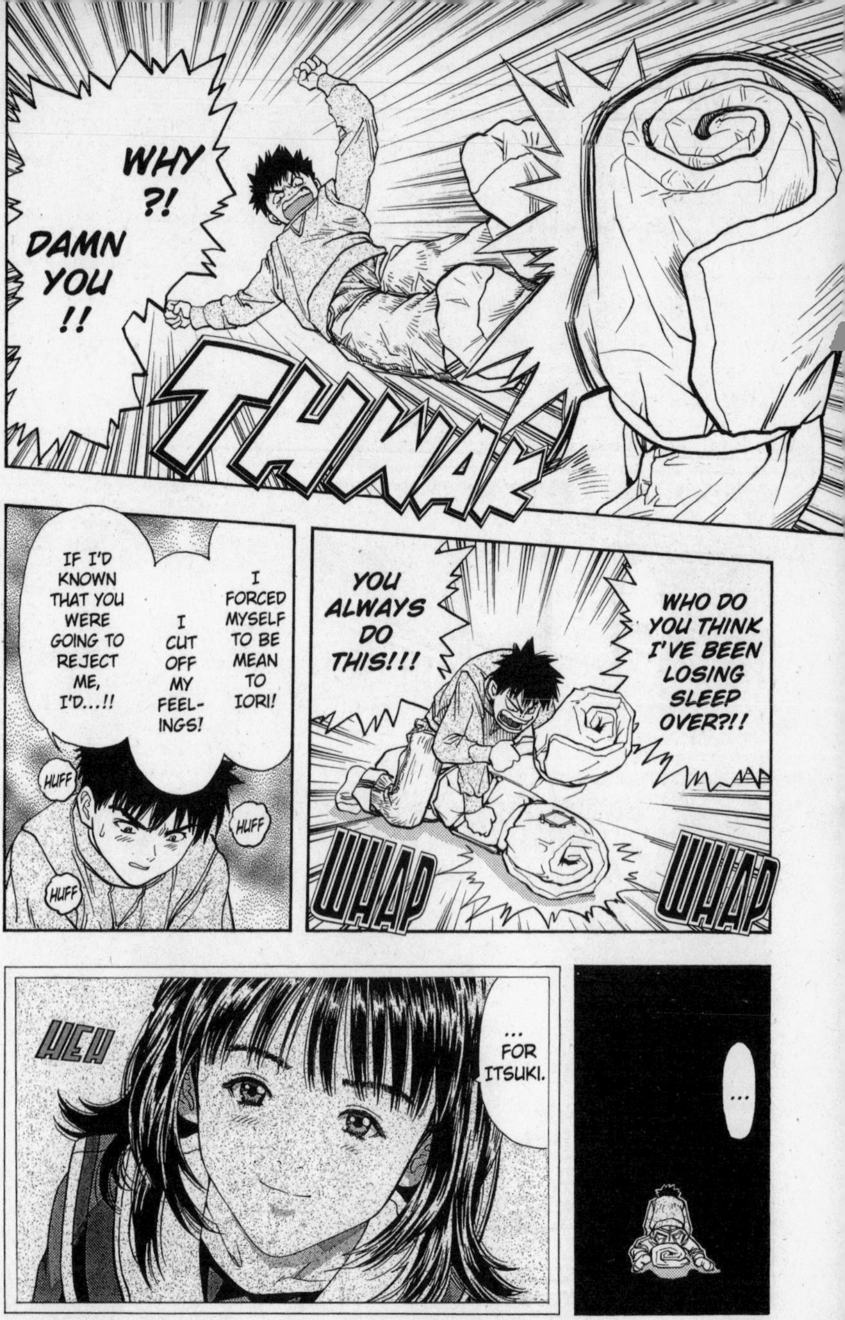
WHY ?!
DAMN YOU !!
THWAK
WHO DO YOU THINK I'VE BEEN LOSING SLEEP OVER?!!
YOU ALWAYS DO THIS!!!
WHAP
WHAP
I FORCED MYSELF TO BE MEAN TO IORI!
I CUT OFF MY FEEL-INGS!
IF I'D KNOWN THAT YOU WERE GOING TO REJECT ME, I'D...!!
HUFF
HUFF
HUFF
...
... FOR ITSUKI.
HEH

READ THIS WAY

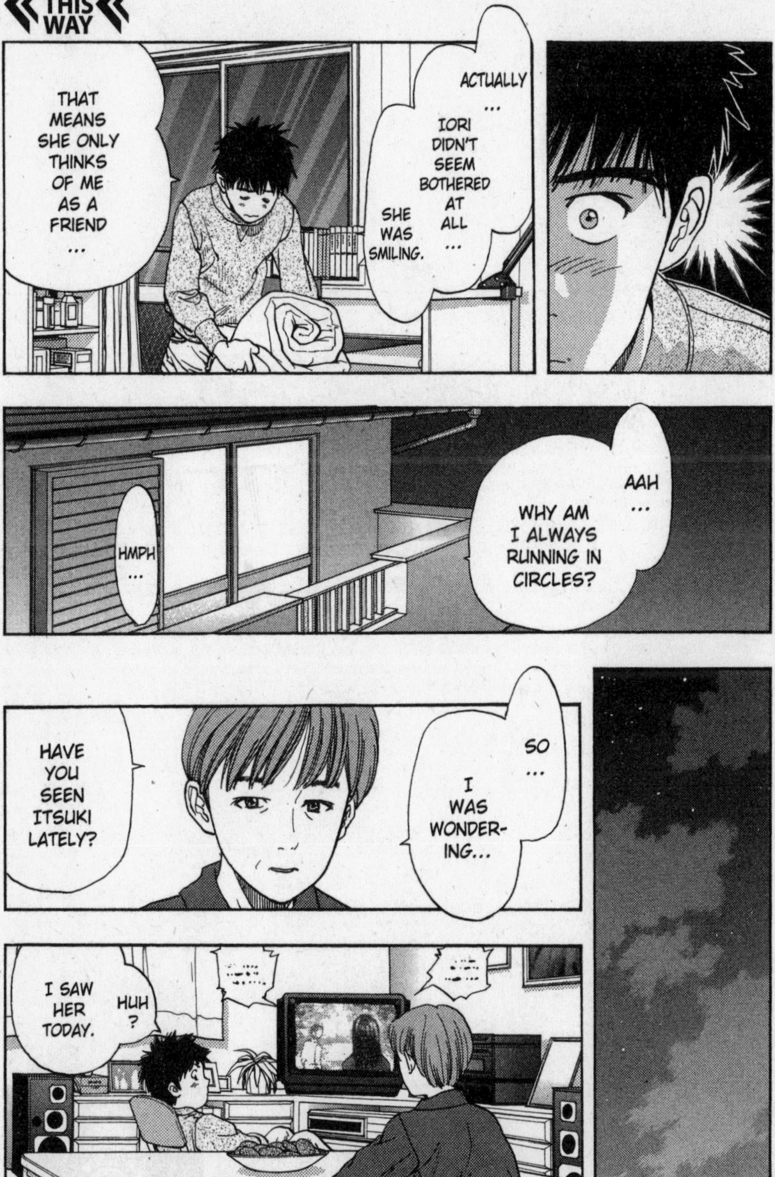
ACTUALLY ... IORI DIDN'T SEEM BOTHERED AT ALL ... SHE WAS SMILING.
THAT MEANS SHE ONLY THINKS OF ME AS A FRIEND ...
AAH ... WHY AM I ALWAYS RUNNING IN CIRCLES?
HMPH ...
SO ... I WAS WONDERING...
HAVE YOU SEEN ITSUKI LATELY?
HUH ?
I SAW HER TODAY.

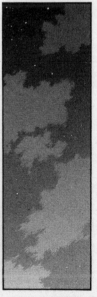

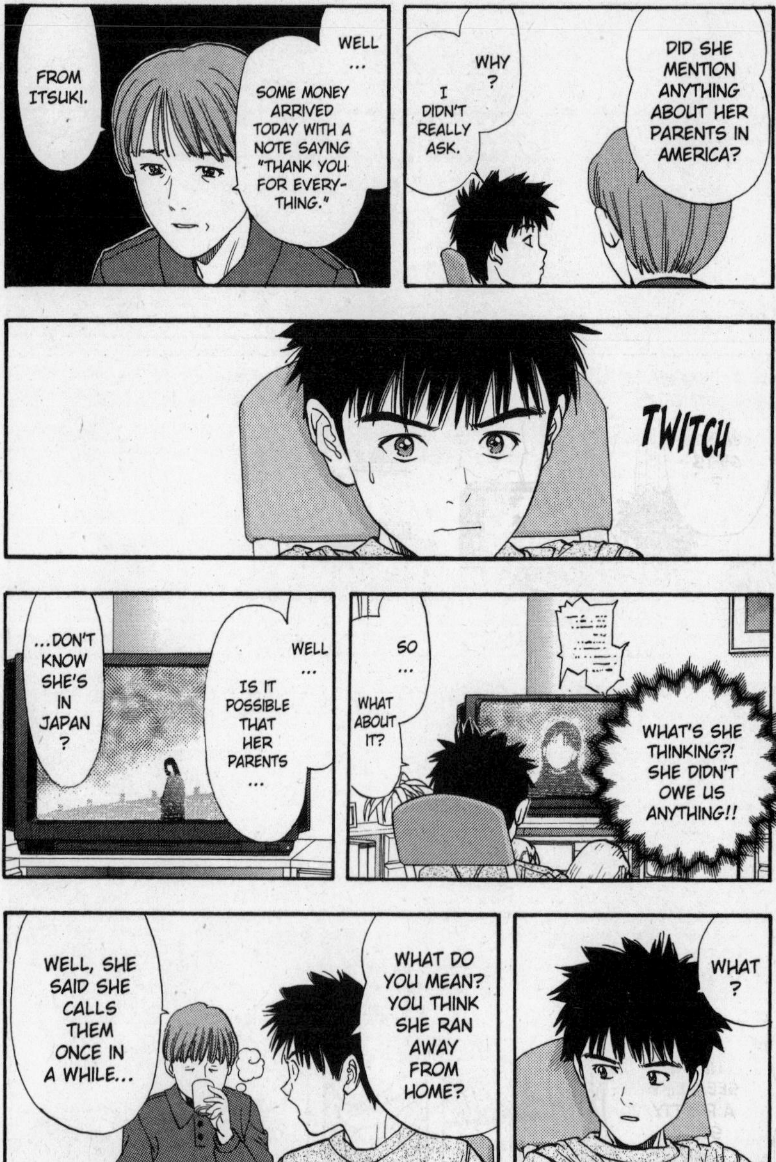
DID SHE MENTION ANYTHING ABOUT HER PARENTS IN AMERICA?
WHY? I DIDN'T REALLY ASK.
WELL ... SOME MONEY ARRIVED TODAY WITH A NOTE SAYING "THANK YOU FOR EVERYTHING."
FROM ITSUKI.
TWITCH
WHAT'S SHE THINKING?! SHE DIDN'T OWE US ANYTHING!!
SO ... WHAT ABOUT IT?
WELL ... IS IT POSSIBLE THAT HER PARENTS ...
...DON'T KNOW SHE'S IN JAPAN?
WHAT?
WHAT DO YOU MEAN? YOU THINK SHE RAN AWAY FROM HOME?
WELL, SHE SAID SHE CALLS THEM ONCE IN A WHILE...

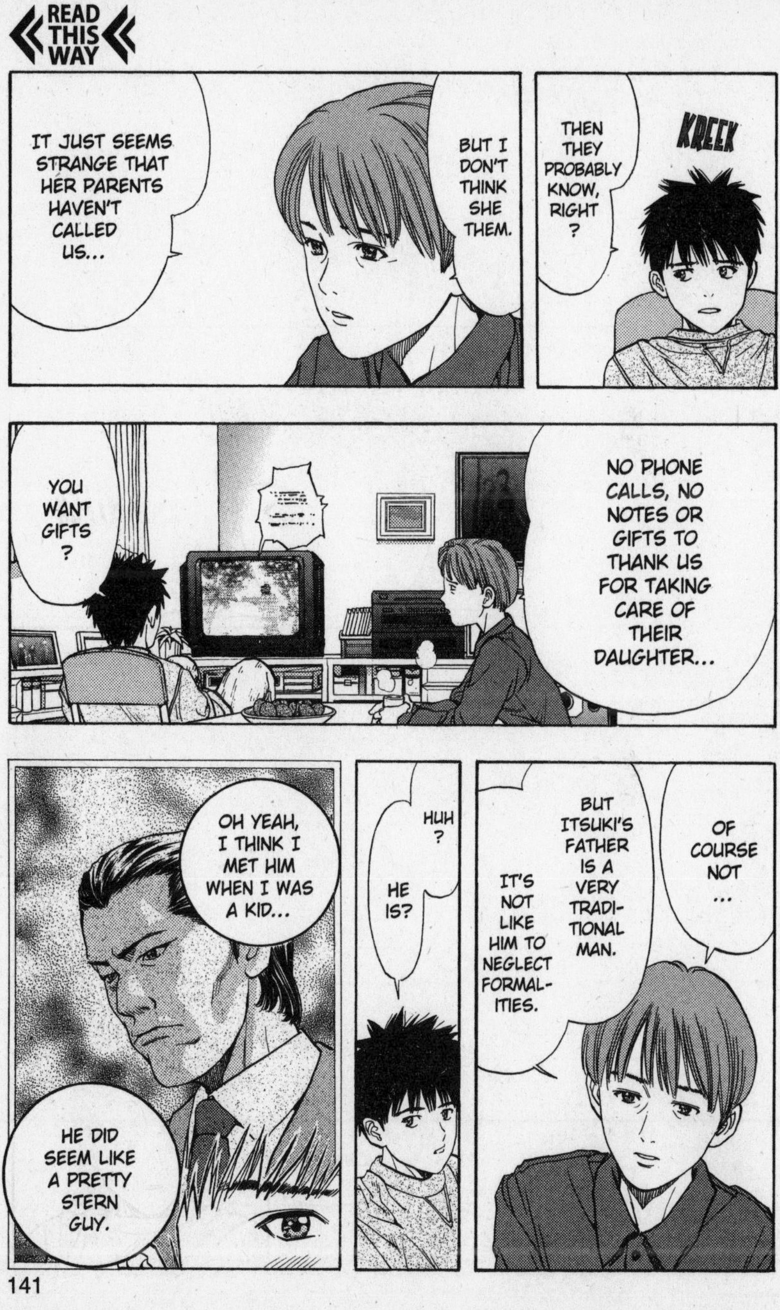
READ THIS WAY
KREEK
THEN THEY PROBABLY KNOW, RIGHT?
BUT I DON'T THINK SHE THEM.
IT JUST SEEMS STRANGE THAT HER PARENTS HAVEN'T CALLED US...
NO PHONE CALLS, NO NOTES OR GIFTS TO THANK US FOR TAKING CARE OF THEIR DAUGHTER...
YOU WANT GIFTS?
OF COURSE NOT...
BUT ITSUKI'S FATHER IS A VERY TRADI-TIONAL MAN.
IT'S NOT LIKE HIM TO NEGLECT FORMAL-ITIES.
HUH?
HE IS?
OH YEAH, I THINK I MET HIM WHEN I WAS A KID...
HE DID SEEM LIKE A PRETTY STERN GUY.

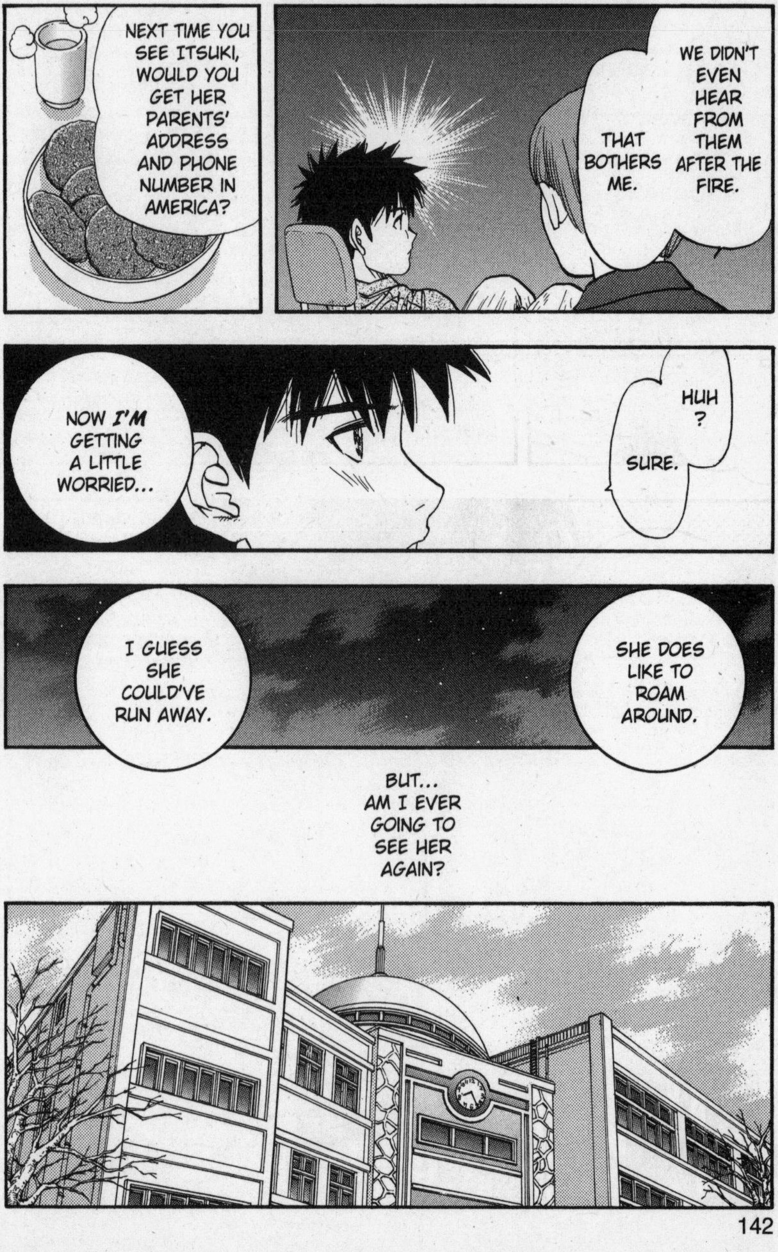
WE DIDN'T EVEN HEAR FROM THEM AFTER THE FIRE.
THAT BOTHERS ME.
NEXT TIME YOU SEE ITSUKI, WOULD YOU GET HER PARENTS' ADDRESS AND PHONE NUMBER IN AMERICA?
HUH?
SURE.
NOW *I'M* GETTING A LITTLE WORRIED...
SHE DOES LIKE TO ROAM AROUND.
I GUESS SHE COULD'VE RUN AWAY.
BUT... AM I EVER GOING TO SEE HER AGAIN?

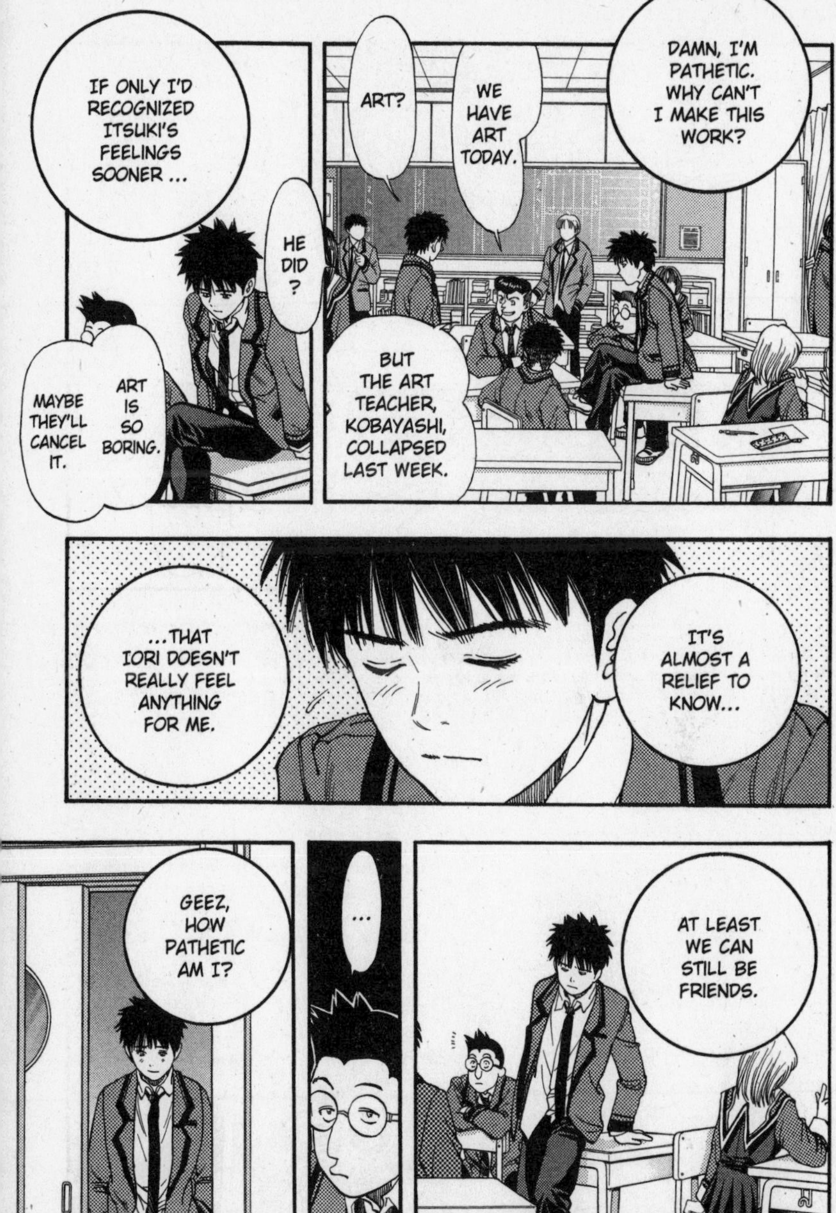
DAMN, I'M PATHETIC. WHY CAN'T I MAKE THIS WORK?
WE HAVE ART TODAY.
ART?
BUT THE ART TEACHER, KOBAYASHI, COLLAPSED LAST WEEK.
HE DID?
IF ONLY I'D RECOGNIZED ITSUKI'S FEELINGS SOONER ...
ART IS SO BORING.
MAYBE THEY'LL CANCEL IT.
IT'S ALMOST A RELIEF TO KNOW...
...THAT IORI DOESN'T REALLY FEEL ANYTHING FOR ME.
AT LEAST WE CAN STILL BE FRIENDS.
...
GEEZ, HOW PATHETIC AM I?

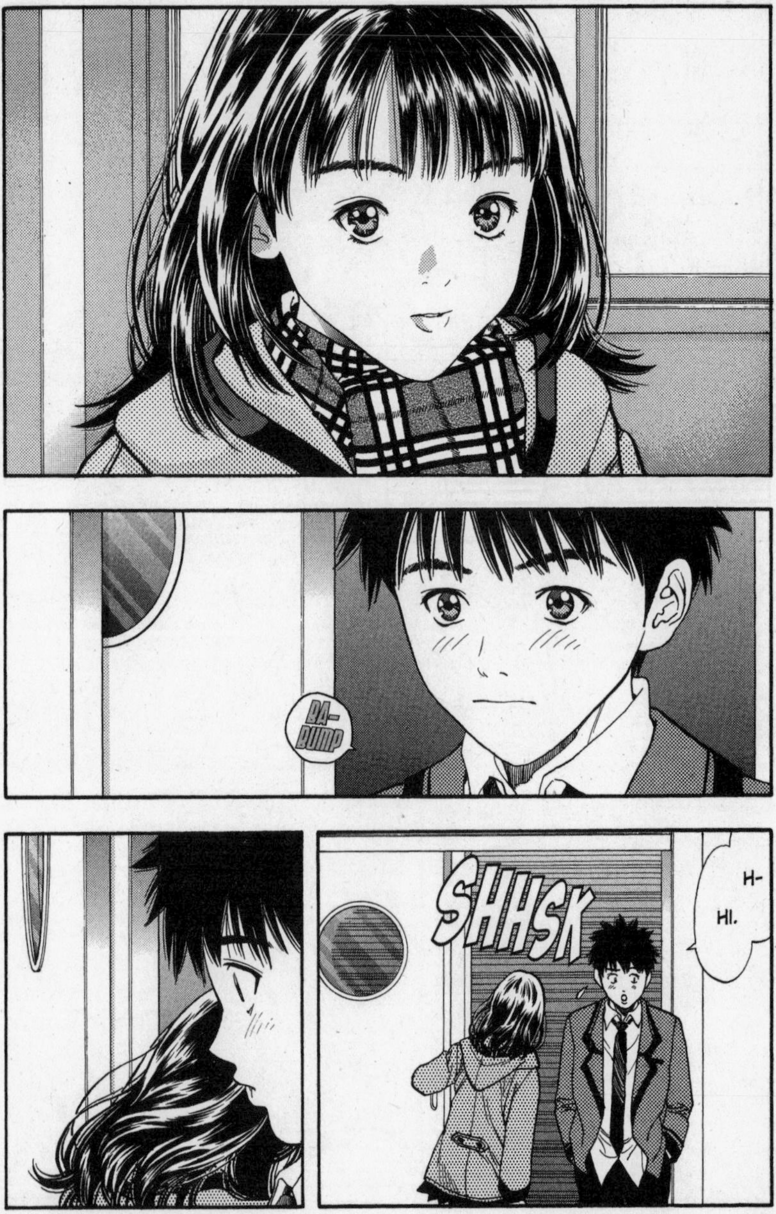
BA-BUMP
H- HI.
SHHSK

READ THIS WAY

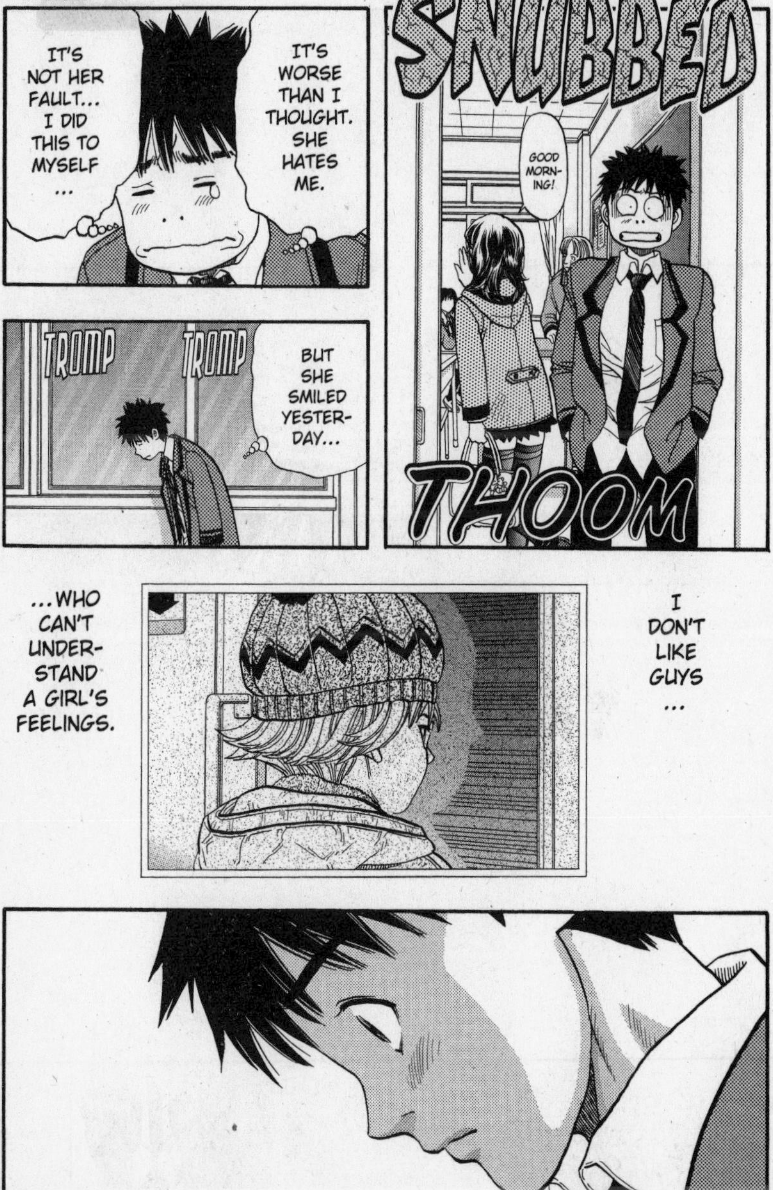
SNUBBED
GOOD MORNING!
THOOM
IT'S WORSE THAN I THOUGHT. SHE HATES ME.
IT'S NOT HER FAULT... I DID THIS TO MYSELF...
TROMP
TROMP
BUT SHE SMILED YESTERDAY...
I DON'T LIKE GUYS...
...WHO CAN'T UNDERSTAND A GIRL'S FEELINGS.

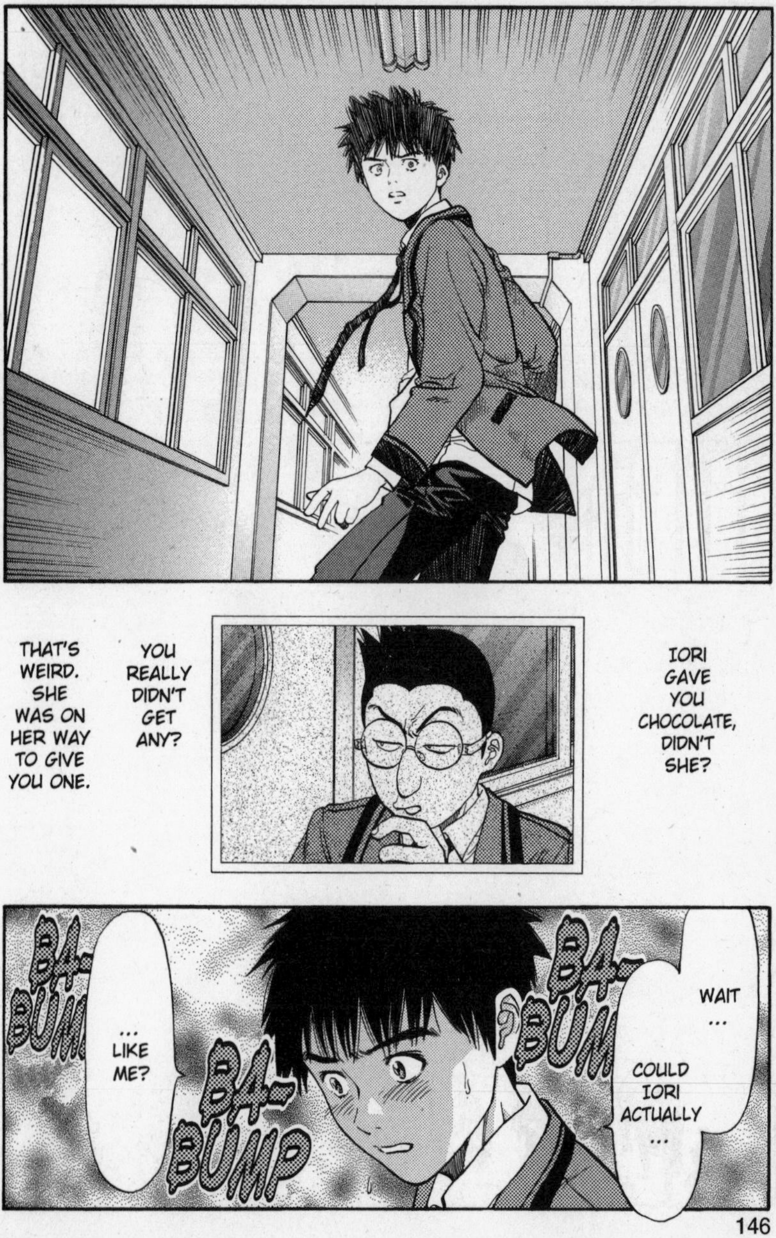
IORI GAVE YOU CHOCOLATE, DIDN'T SHE?
YOU REALLY DIDN'T GET ANY?
THAT'S WEIRD. SHE WAS ON HER WAY TO GIVE YOU ONE.
WAIT ...
COULD IORI ACTUALLY ...
BA-BUMP
... LIKE ME?

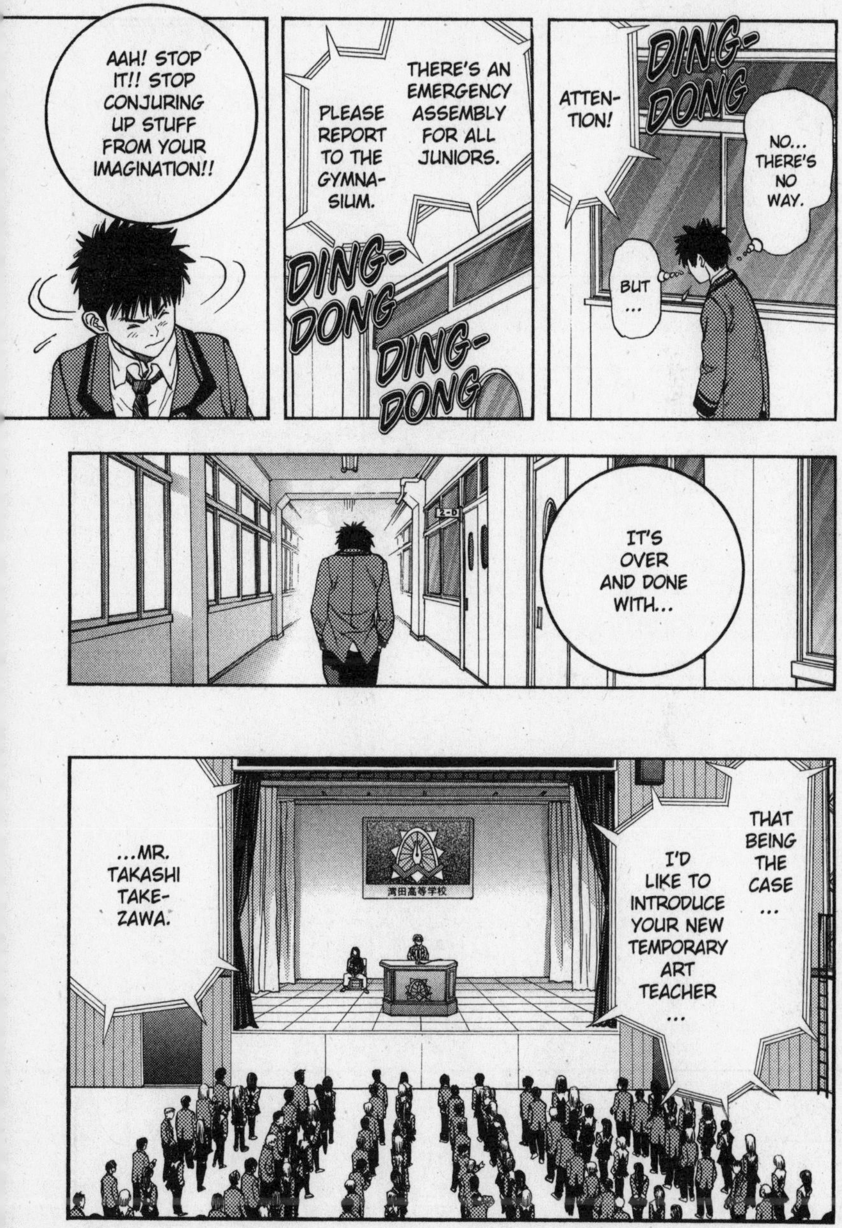
DING-DONG
ATTENTION!
NO... THERE'S NO WAY.
BUT ...
THERE'S AN EMERGENCY ASSEMBLY FOR ALL JUNIORS.
PLEASE REPORT TO THE GYMNASIUM.
DING-DONG
DING-DONG
AAH! STOP IT!! STOP CONJURING UP STUFF FROM YOUR IMAGINATION!!
IT'S OVER AND DONE WITH...
2-D
THAT BEING THE CASE ...
I'D LIKE TO INTRODUCE YOUR NEW TEMPORARY ART TEACHER ...
...MR. TAKASHI TAKE-ZAWA.

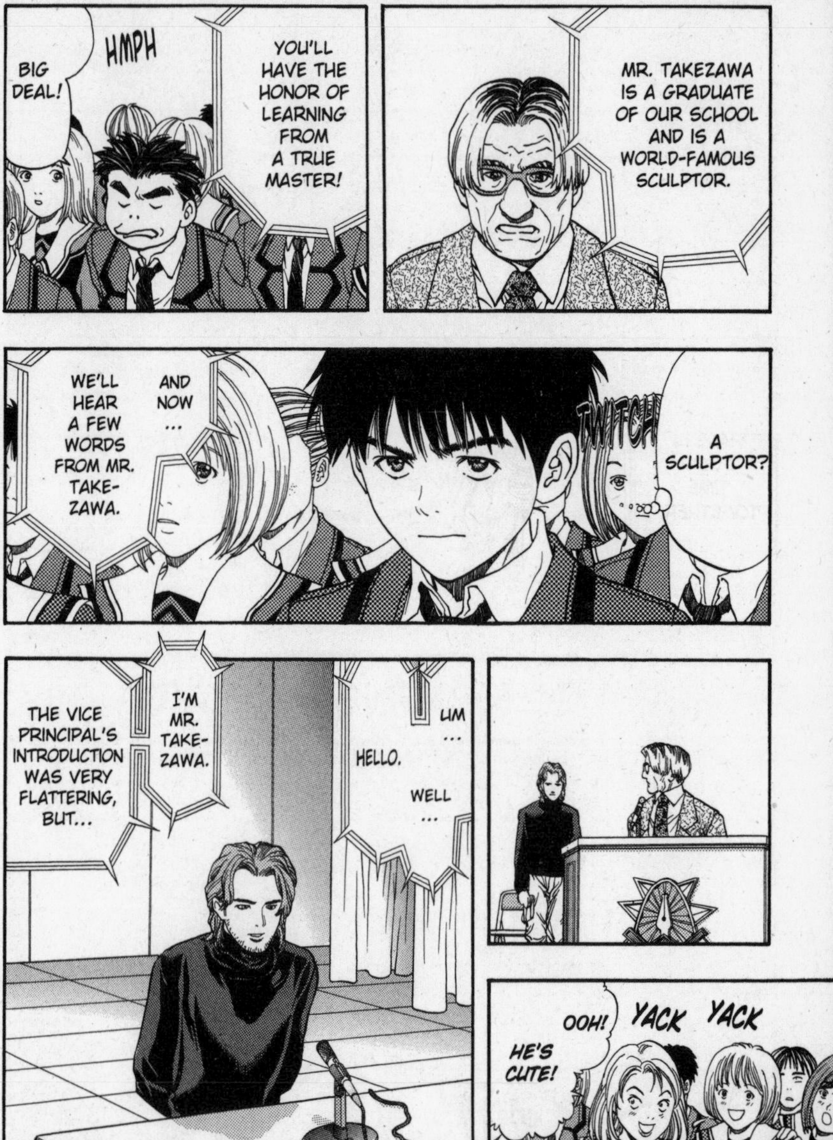
MR. TAKEZAWA IS A GRADUATE OF OUR SCHOOL AND IS A WORLD-FAMOUS SCULPTOR.
YOU'LL HAVE THE HONOR OF LEARNING FROM A TRUE MASTER!
HMPH
BIG DEAL!
TWITCH
A SCULPTOR?
AND NOW ...
WE'LL HEAR A FEW WORDS FROM MR. TAKE-ZAWA.
YACK YACK
OOH!
HE'S CUTE!
UM ...
WELL ...
HELLO.
I'M MR. TAKE-ZAWA.
THE VICE PRINCIPAL'S INTRODUCTION WAS VERY FLATTERING, BUT...

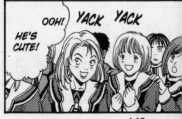

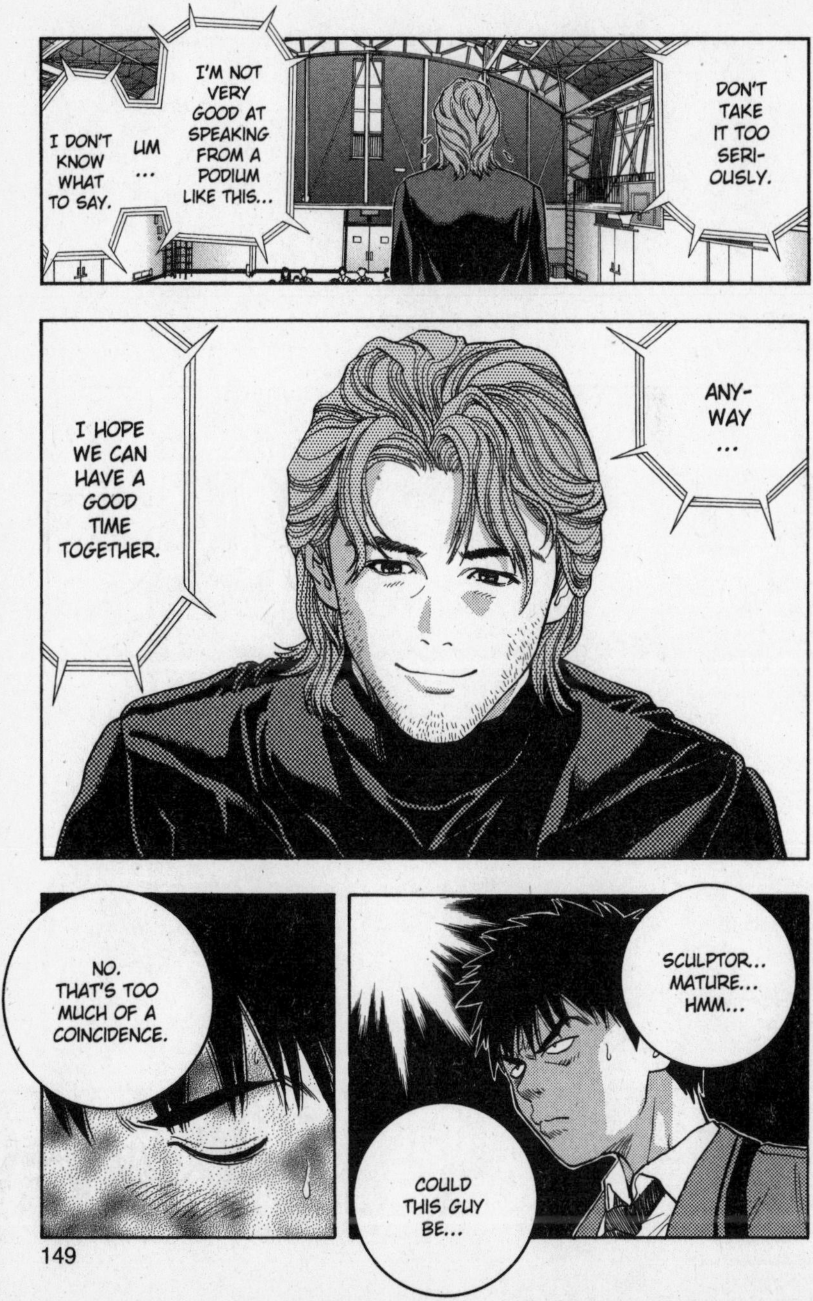
DON'T TAKE IT TOO SERI-OUSLY.
I'M NOT VERY GOOD AT SPEAKING FROM A PODIUM LIKE THIS...
UM ...
I DON'T KNOW WHAT TO SAY.
ANY-WAY ...
I HOPE WE CAN HAVE A GOOD TIME TOGETHER.
SCULPTOR... MATURE... HMM...
COULD THIS GUY BE...
NO. THAT'S TOO MUCH OF A COINCIDENCE.

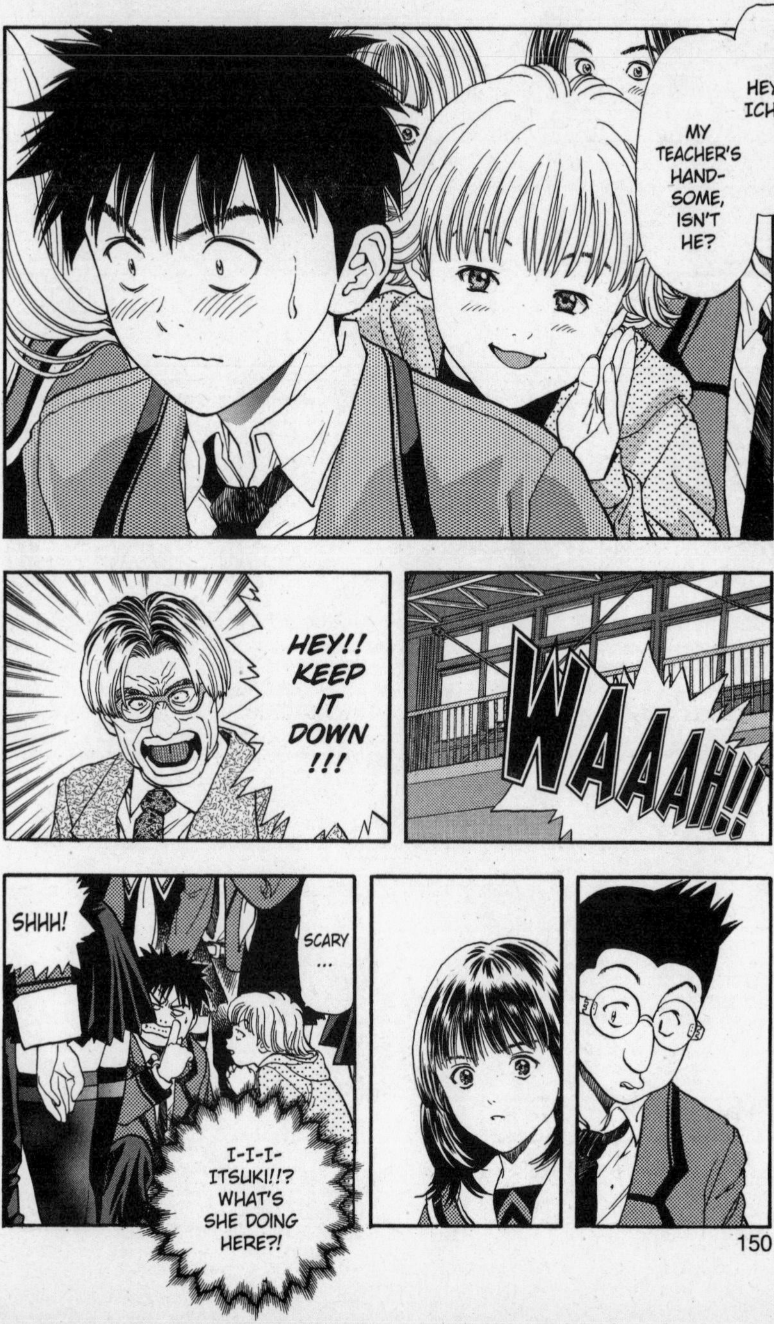
HEY, ICHI.
MY TEACHER'S HAND-SOME, ISN'T HE?
WAAAH!!
HEY!! KEEP IT DOWN!!!
SCARY...
SHHH!
I-I-I-ITSUKI!!? WHAT'S SHE DOING HERE?!

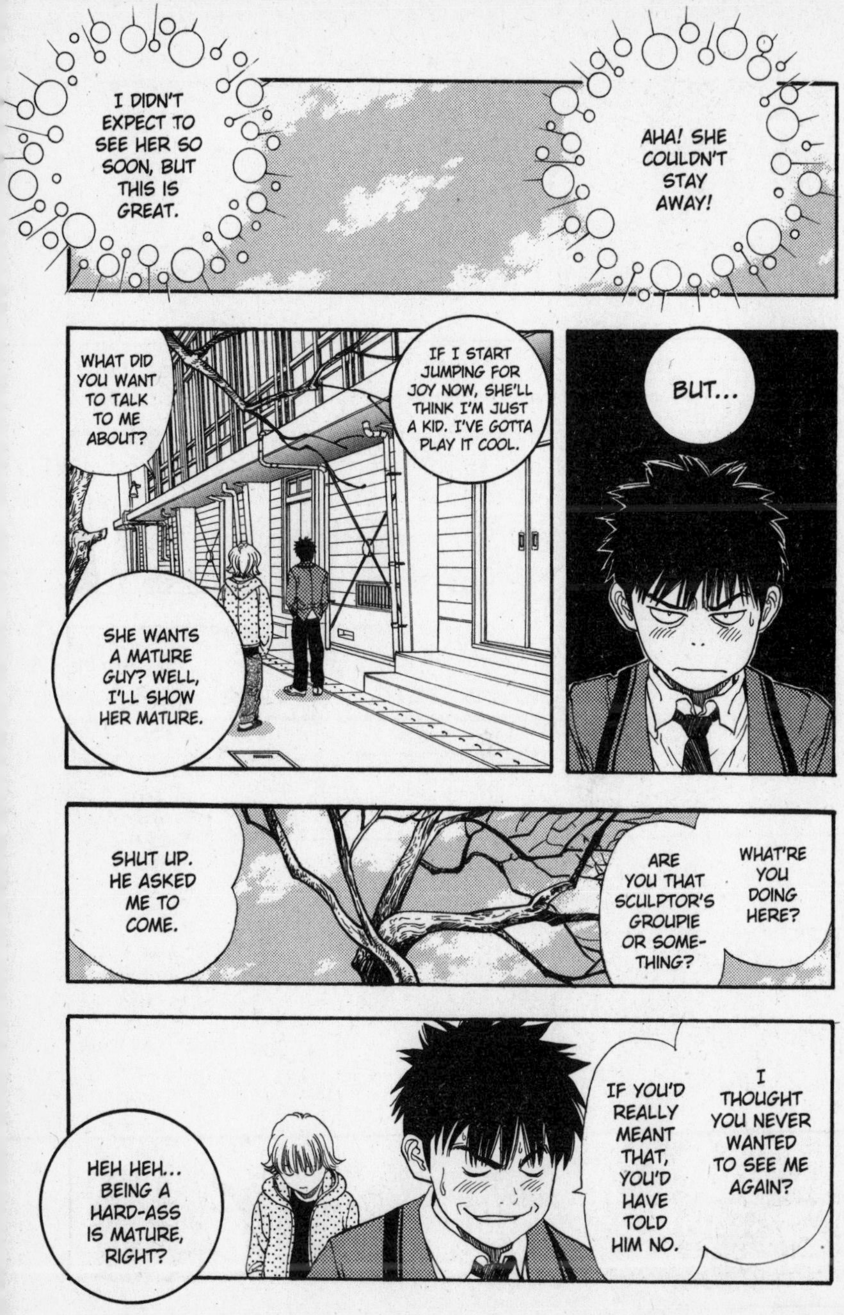
AHA! SHE COULDN'T STAY AWAY!
I DIDN'T EXPECT TO SEE HER SO SOON, BUT THIS IS GREAT.
BUT...
IF I START JUMPING FOR JOY NOW, SHE'LL THINK I'M JUST A KID. I'VE GOTTA PLAY IT COOL.
WHAT DID YOU WANT TO TALK TO ME ABOUT?
SHE WANTS A MATURE GUY? WELL, I'LL SHOW HER MATURE.
WHAT'RE YOU DOING HERE?
ARE YOU THAT SCULPTOR'S GROUPIE OR SOME-THING?
SHUT UP. HE ASKED ME TO COME.
I THOUGHT YOU NEVER WANTED TO SEE ME AGAIN?
IF YOU'D REALLY MEANT THAT, YOU'D HAVE TOLD HIM NO.
HEH HEH... BEING A HARD-ASS IS MATURE, RIGHT?

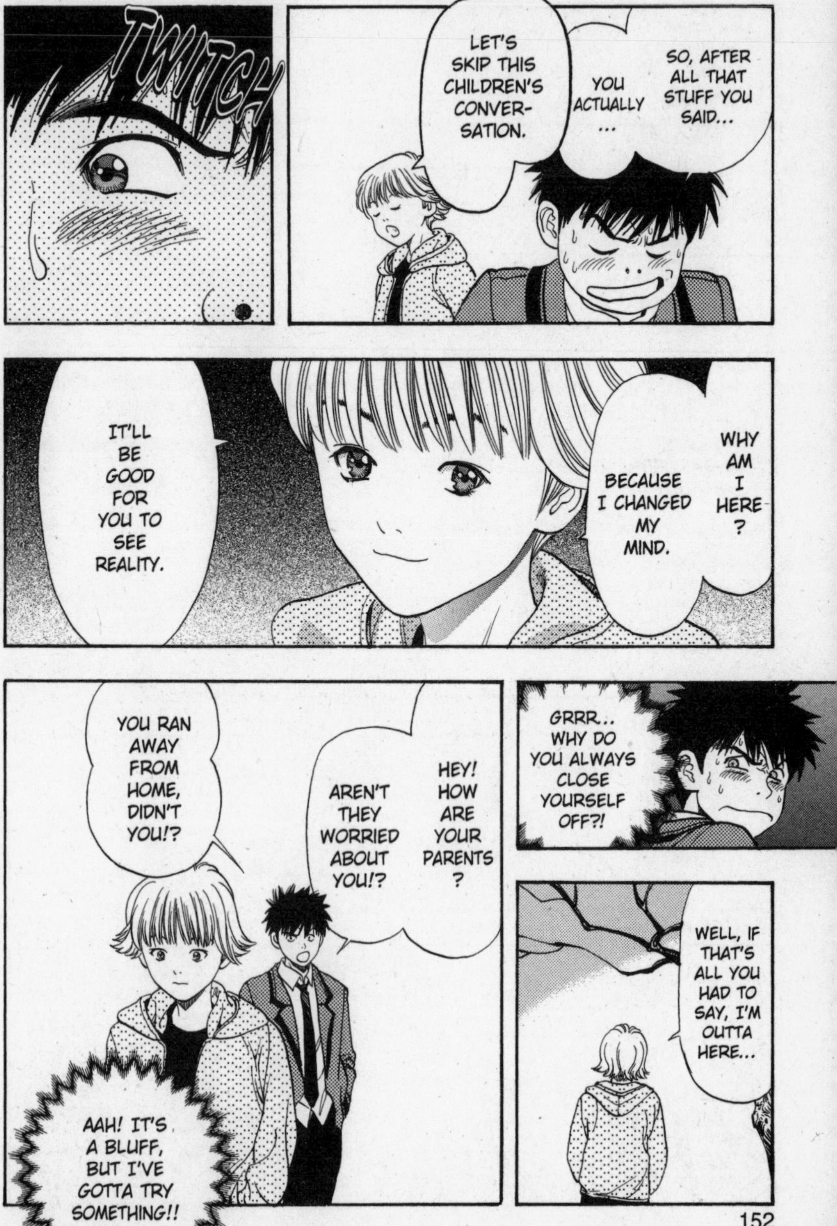
SO, AFTER ALL THAT STUFF YOU SAID...
YOU ACTUALLY ...
LET'S SKIP THIS CHILDREN'S CONVER-SATION.
TWITCH
WHY AM I HERE?
BECAUSE I CHANGED MY MIND.
IT'LL BE GOOD FOR YOU TO SEE REALITY.
GRRR.. WHY DO YOU ALWAYS CLOSE YOURSELF OFF?!
WELL, IF THAT'S ALL YOU HAD TO SAY, I'M OUTTA HERE...
HEY! HOW ARE YOUR PARENTS?
AREN'T THEY WORRIED ABOUT YOU!?
YOU RAN AWAY FROM HOME, DIDN'T YOU!?
AAH! IT'S A BLUFF, BUT I'VE GOTTA TRY SOMETHING!!

READ THIS WAY

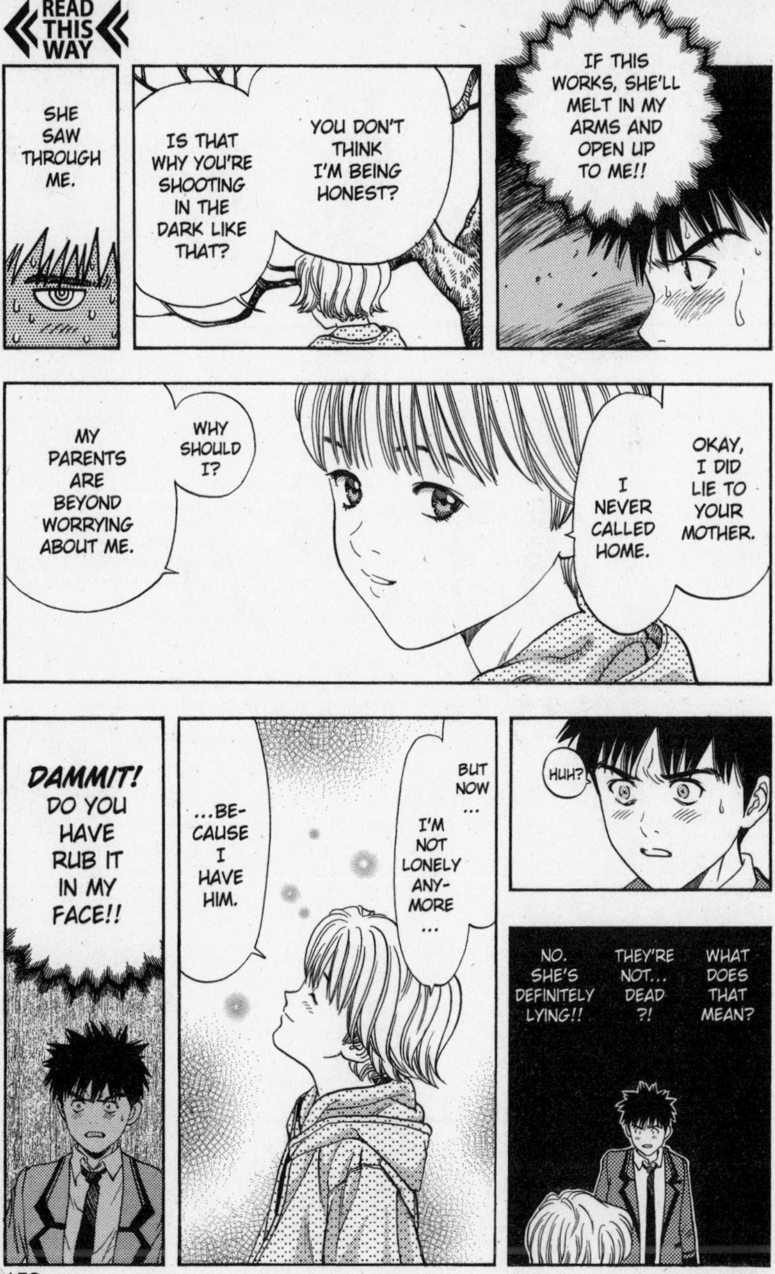
IF THIS WORKS, SHE'LL MELT IN MY ARMS AND OPEN UP TO ME!!
YOU DON'T THINK I'M BEING HONEST?
IS THAT WHY YOU'RE SHOOTING IN THE DARK LIKE THAT?
SHE SAW THROUGH ME.
OKAY, I DID LIE TO YOUR MOTHER.
I NEVER CALLED HOME.
WHY SHOULD I?
MY PARENTS ARE BEYOND WORRYING ABOUT ME.
HUH?
WHAT DOES THAT MEAN?
THEY'RE NOT... DEAD ?!
NO. SHE'S DEFINITELY LYING!!
BUT NOW ...
I'M NOT LONELY ANY-MORE ...
...BE-CAUSE I HAVE HIM.
DAMMIT! DO YOU HAVE RUB IT IN MY FACE!!

I"s
アイズ

Chapter 44: Self-Doubt

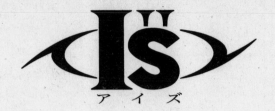

READ THIS WAY

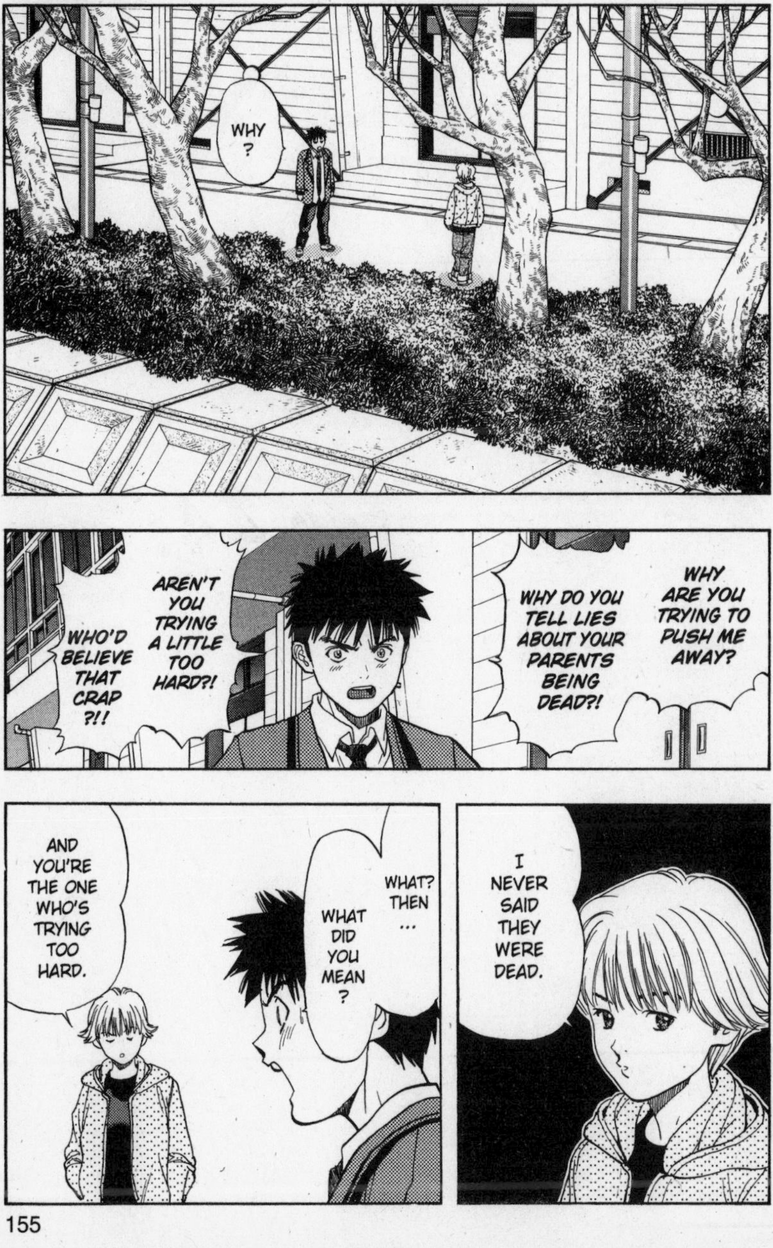
WHY ?
WHY ARE YOU TRYING TO PUSH ME AWAY?
WHY DO YOU TELL LIES ABOUT YOUR PARENTS BEING DEAD?!
AREN'T YOU TRYING A LITTLE TOO HARD?!
WHO'D BELIEVE THAT CRAP ?!!
I NEVER SAID THEY WERE DEAD.
WHAT? THEN ...
WHAT DID YOU MEAN ?
AND YOU'RE THE ONE WHO'S TRYING TOO HARD.

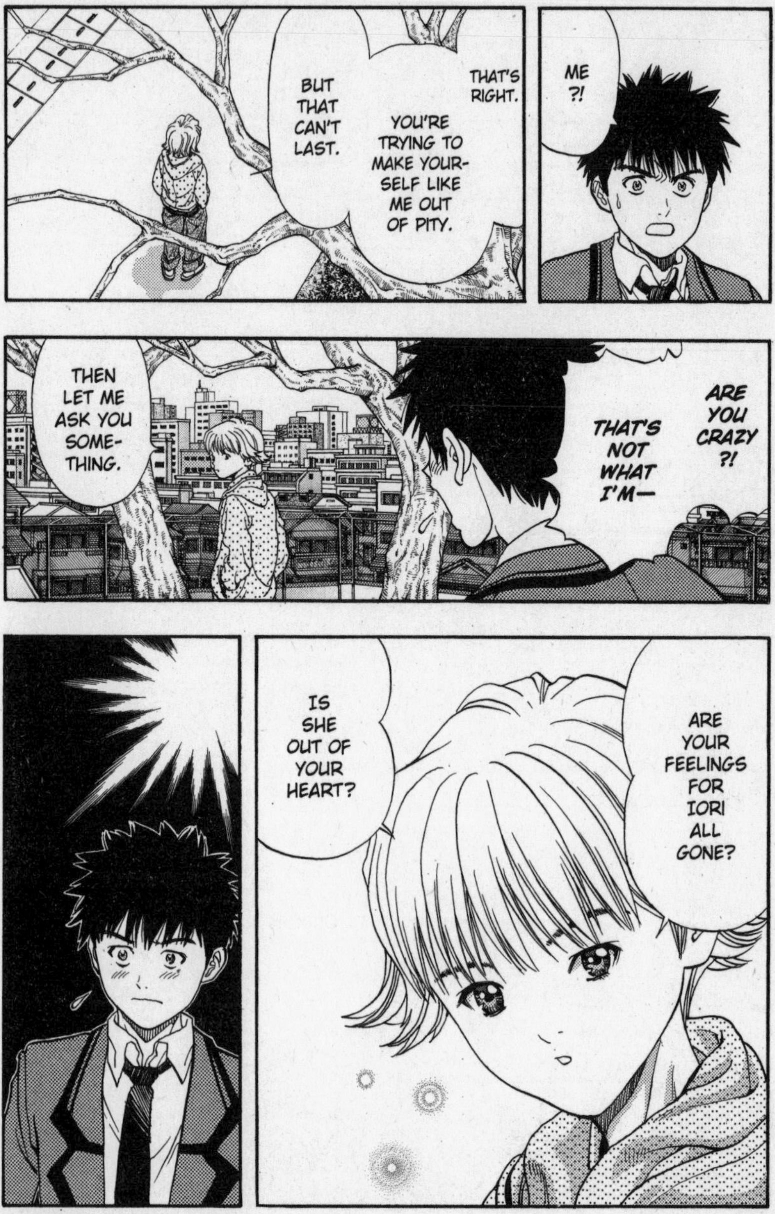
ME ?!
THAT'S RIGHT.
YOU'RE TRYING TO MAKE YOUR-SELF LIKE ME OUT OF PITY.
BUT THAT CAN'T LAST.
ARE YOU CRAZY ?!
THAT'S NOT WHAT I'M—
THEN LET ME ASK YOU SOME-THING.
ARE YOUR FEELINGS FOR IORI ALL GONE?
IS SHE OUT OF YOUR HEART?

READ THIS WAY

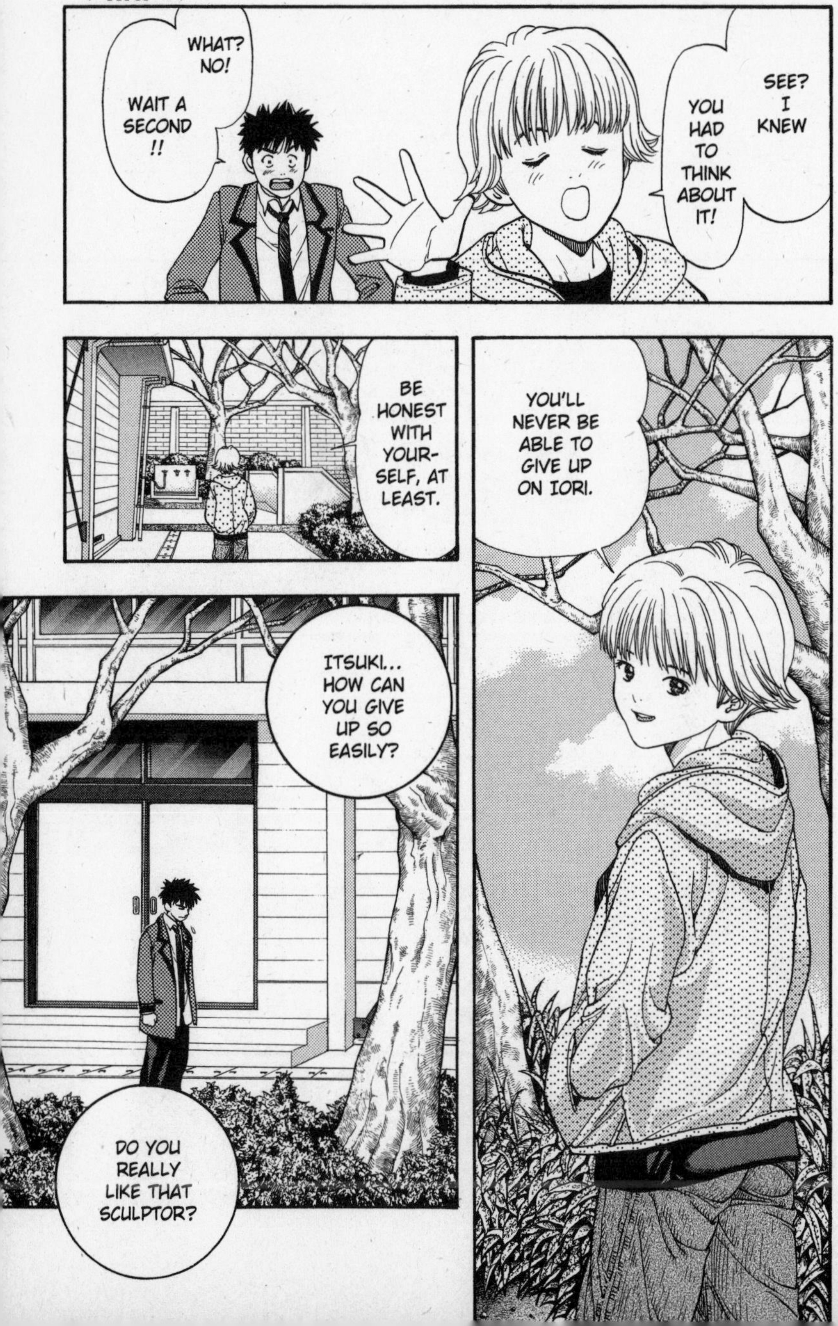
SEE? I KNEW YOU HAD TO THINK ABOUT IT!
WHAT? NO!
WAIT A SECOND!!
YOU'LL NEVER BE ABLE TO GIVE UP ON IORI.
BE HONEST WITH YOURSELF, AT LEAST.
ITSUKI... HOW CAN YOU GIVE UP SO EASILY?
DO YOU REALLY LIKE THAT SCULPTOR?

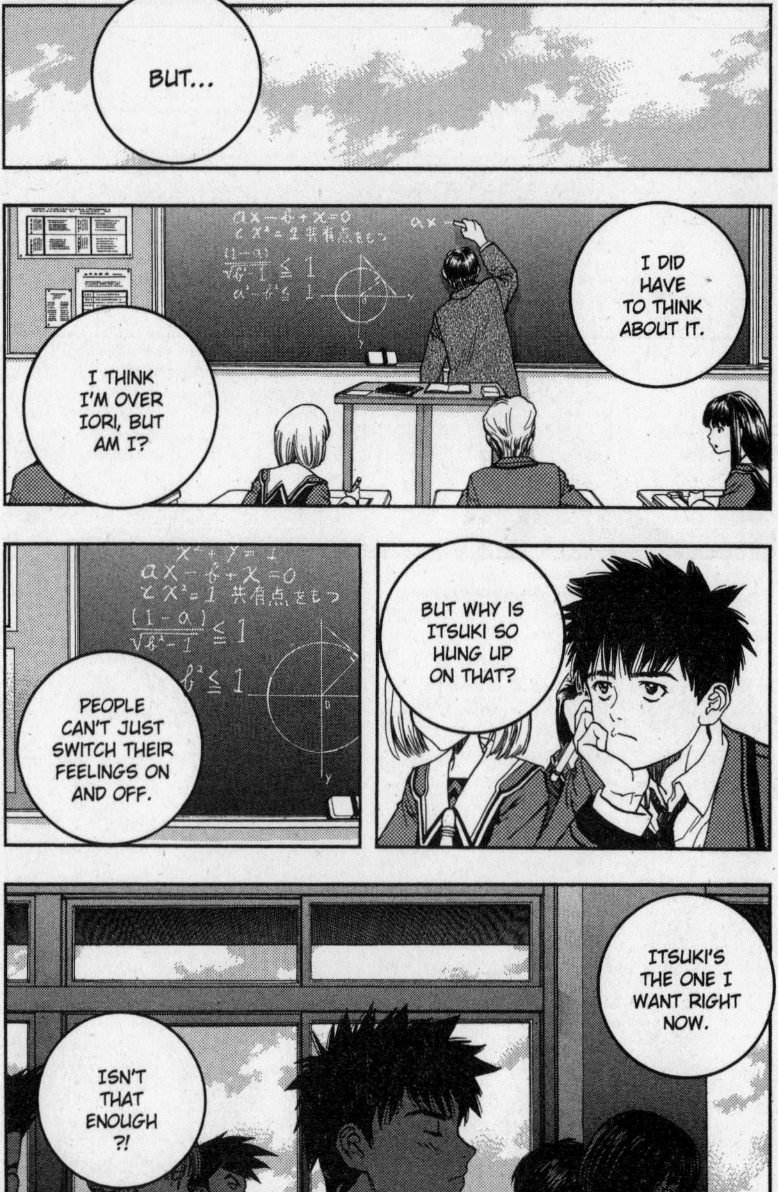
BUT...
I DID HAVE TO THINK ABOUT IT.
I THINK I'M OVER IORI, BUT AM I?
BUT WHY IS ITSUKI SO HUNG UP ON THAT?
PEOPLE CAN'T JUST SWITCH THEIR FEELINGS ON AND OFF.
ITSUKI'S THE ONE I WANT RIGHT NOW.
ISN'T THAT ENOUGH ?!

READ THIS WAY

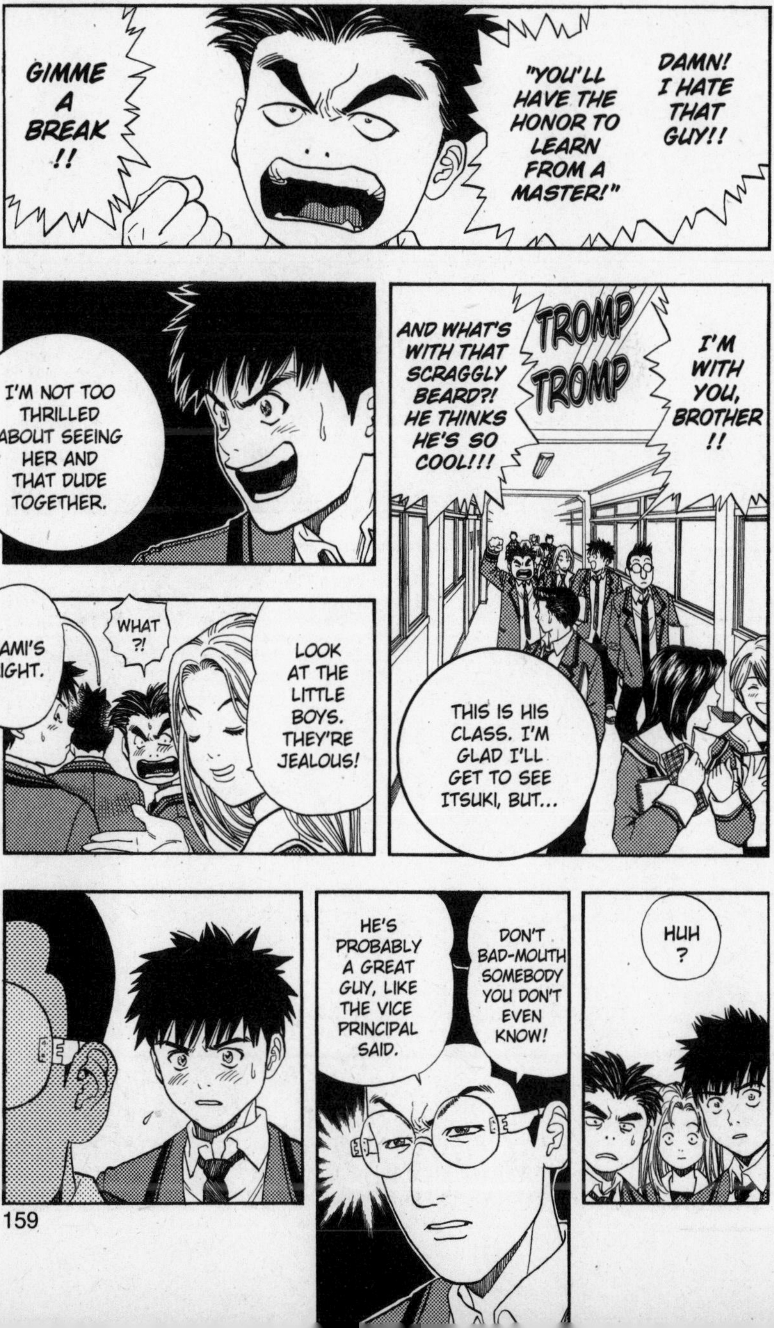
DAMN! I HATE THAT GUY!!
"YOU'LL HAVE THE HONOR TO LEARN FROM A MASTER!"
GIMME A BREAK!!
I'M WITH YOU, BROTHER!!
TROMP TROMP
AND WHAT'S WITH THAT SCRAGGLY BEARD?! HE THINKS HE'S SO COOL!!!
THIS IS HIS CLASS. I'M GLAD I'LL GET TO SEE ITSUKI, BUT...
I'M NOT TOO THRILLED ABOUT SEEING HER AND THAT DUDE TOGETHER.
LOOK AT THE LITTLE BOYS. THEY'RE JEALOUS!
WHAT?!
NAMI'S RIGHT.
HUH?
DON'T BAD-MOUTH SOMEBODY YOU DON'T EVEN KNOW!
HE'S PROBABLY A GREAT GUY, LIKE THE VICE PRINCIPAL SAID.

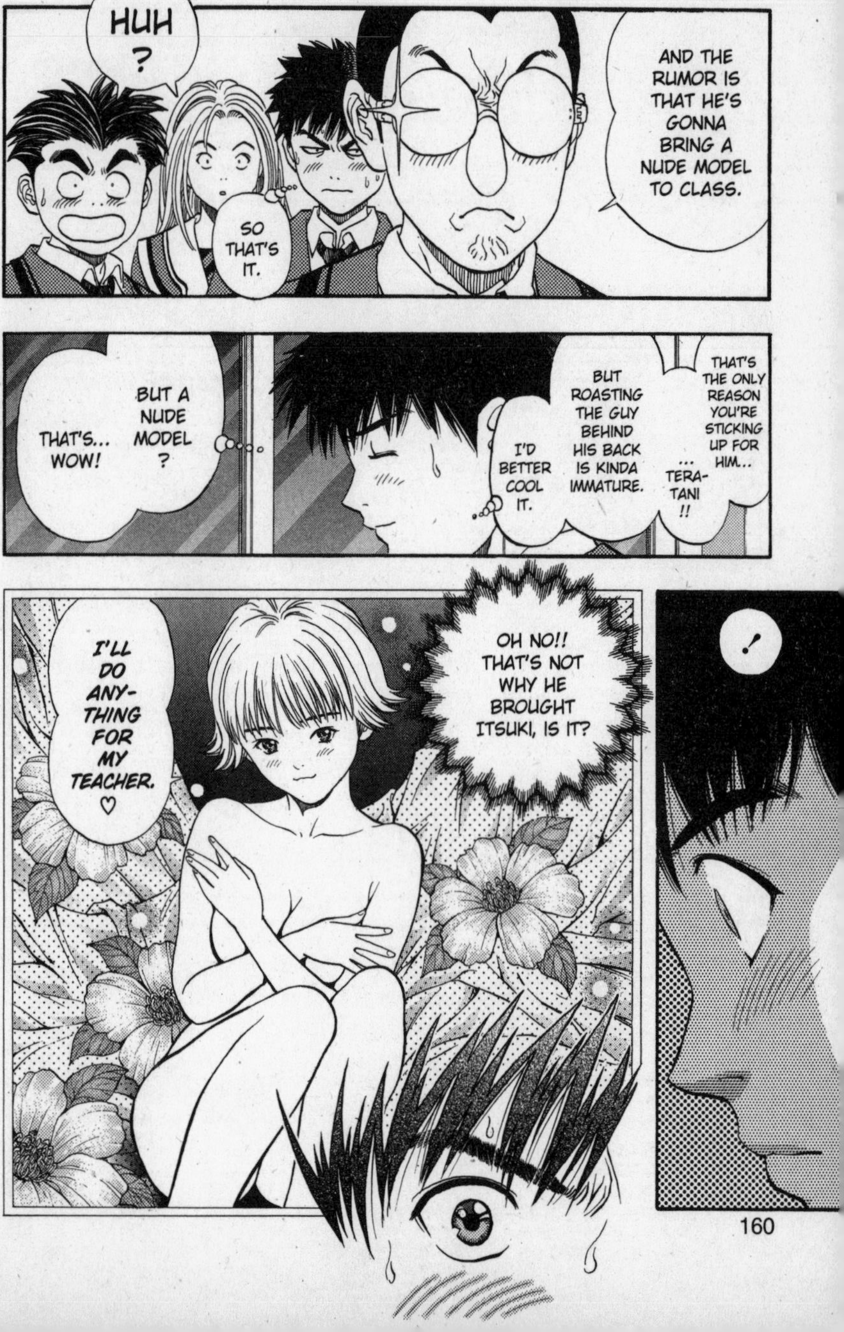
AND THE RUMOR IS THAT HE'S GONNA BRING A NUDE MODEL TO CLASS.
HUH ?
SO THAT'S IT.
THAT'S THE ONLY REASON YOU'RE STICKING UP FOR HIM...
... TERA-TANI !!
BUT ROASTING THE GUY BEHIND HIS BACK IS KINDA IMMATURE.
I'D BETTER COOL IT.
BUT A NUDE MODEL ?
THAT'S... WOW!
!
OH NO!! THAT'S NOT WHY HE BROUGHT ITSUKI, IS IT?
I'LL DO ANY-THING FOR MY TEACHER. ♡

READ THIS WAY

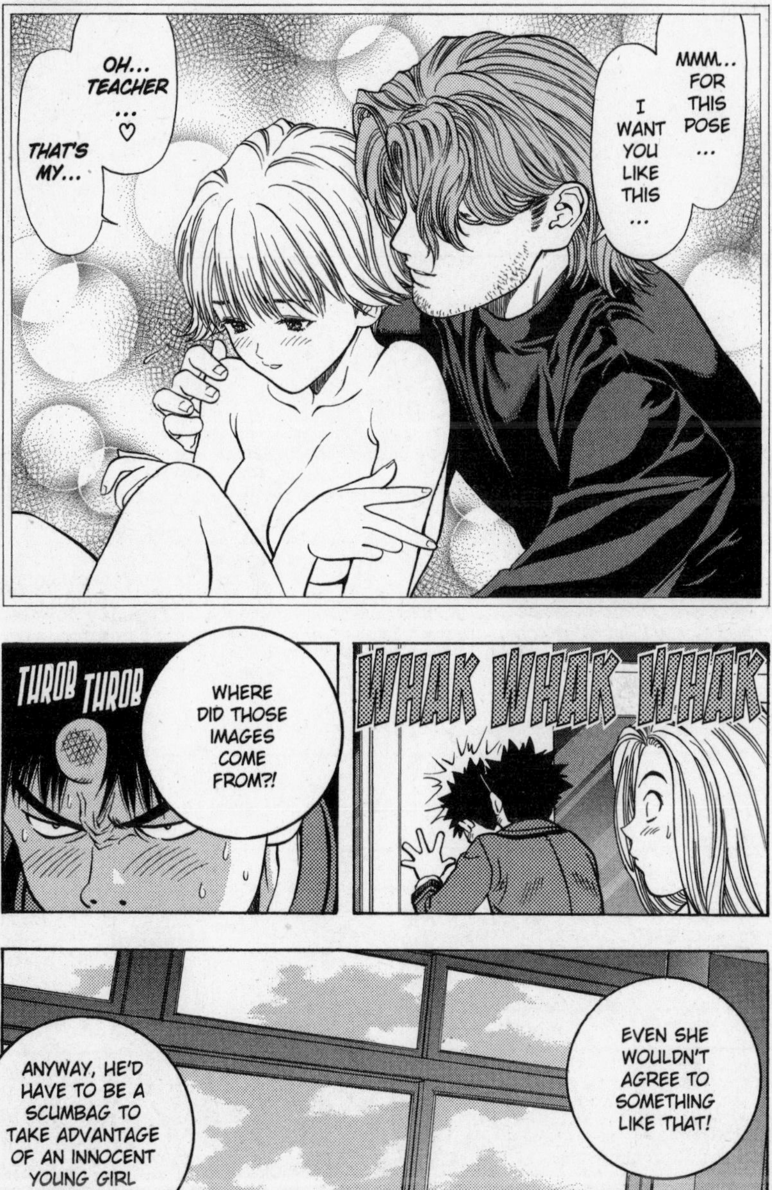
MMM... FOR THIS POSE... I WANT YOU LIKE THIS...
OH... TEACHER... ♡ THAT'S MY...
WHAK WHAK WHAK
THROB THROB
WHERE DID THOSE IMAGES COME FROM?!
EVEN SHE WOULDN'T AGREE TO SOMETHING LIKE THAT!
ANYWAY, HE'D HAVE TO BE A SCUMBAG TO TAKE ADVANTAGE OF AN INNOCENT YOUNG GIRL LIKE THAT!!

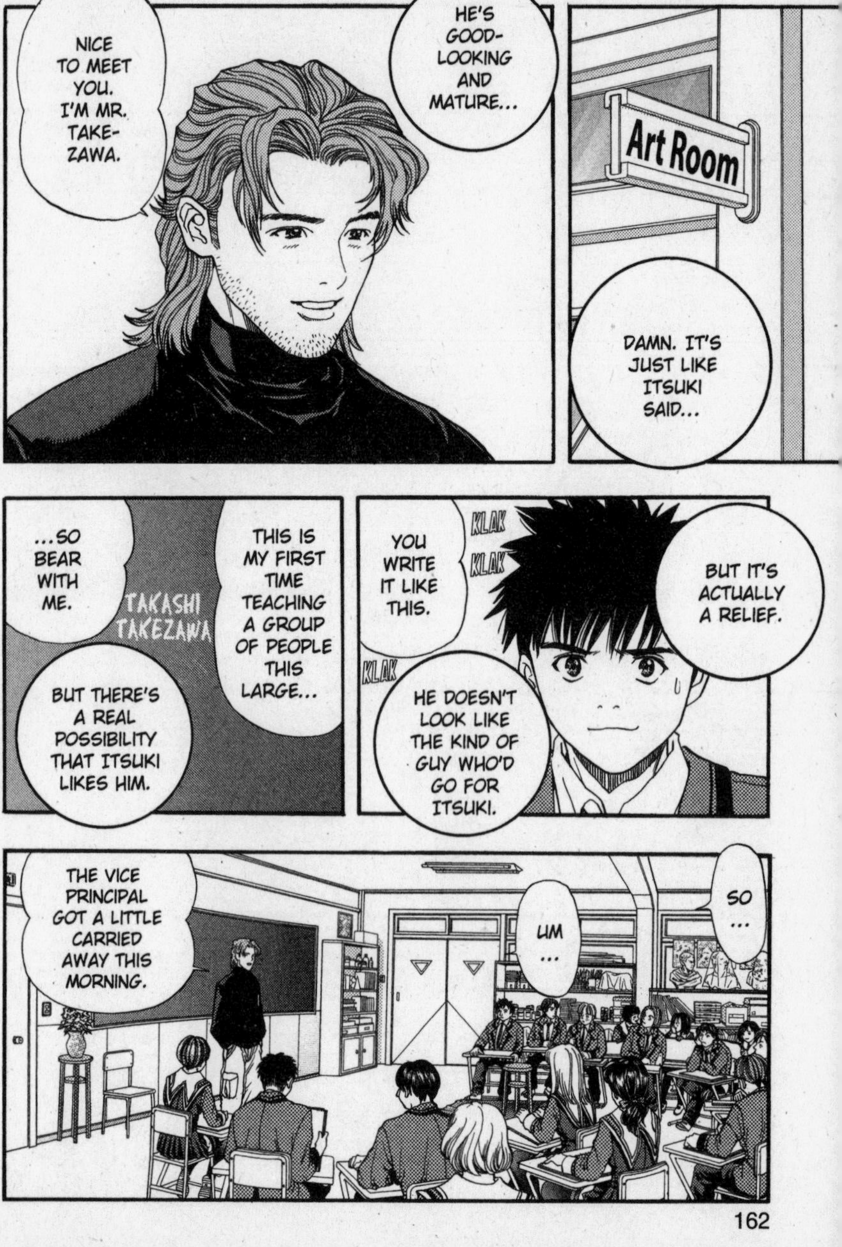
Art Room
DAMN. IT'S JUST LIKE ITSUKI SAID...
HE'S GOOD-LOOKING AND MATURE...
NICE TO MEET YOU. I'M MR. TAKE-ZAWA.
KLAK
KLAK
BUT IT'S ACTUALLY A RELIEF.
YOU WRITE IT LIKE THIS.
KLAK
HE DOESN'T LOOK LIKE THE KIND OF GUY WHO'D GO FOR ITSUKI.
THIS IS MY FIRST TIME TEACHING A GROUP OF PEOPLE THIS LARGE...
...SO BEAR WITH ME.
TAKASHI TAKEZAWA
BUT THERE'S A REAL POSSIBILITY THAT ITSUKI LIKES HIM.
SO ...
UM ...
THE VICE PRINCIPAL GOT A LITTLE CARRIED AWAY THIS MORNING.

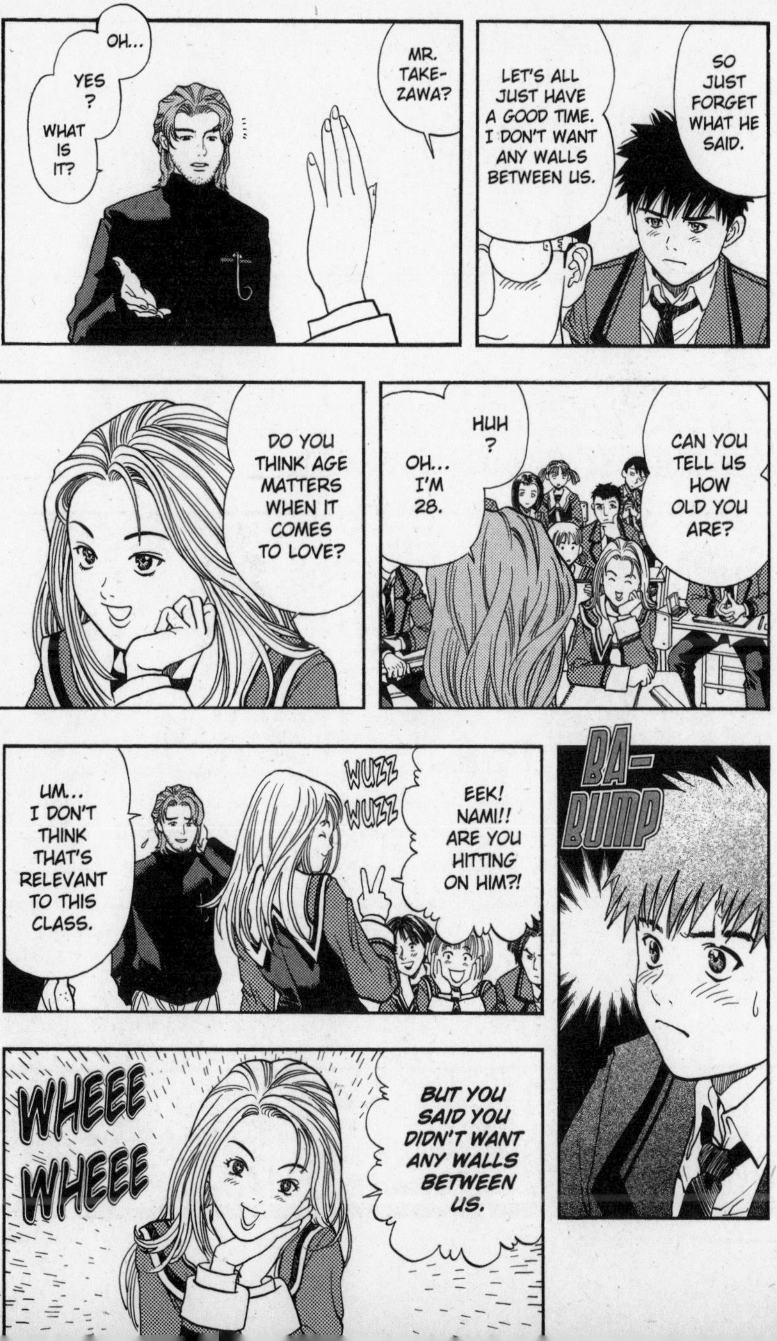
SO JUST FORGET WHAT HE SAID.
LET'S ALL JUST HAVE A GOOD TIME. I DON'T WANT ANY WALLS BETWEEN US.
MR. TAKE-ZAWA?
OH...
YES?
WHAT IS IT?
CAN YOU TELL US HOW OLD YOU ARE?
HUH?
OH... I'M 28.
DO YOU THINK AGE MATTERS WHEN IT COMES TO LOVE?
BA-BUMP
EEK! NAMI!! ARE YOU HITTING ON HIM?!
WUZZ WUZZ
UM... I DON'T THINK THAT'S RELEVANT TO THIS CLASS.
BUT YOU SAID YOU DIDN'T WANT ANY WALLS BETWEEN US.
WHEEE WHEEE

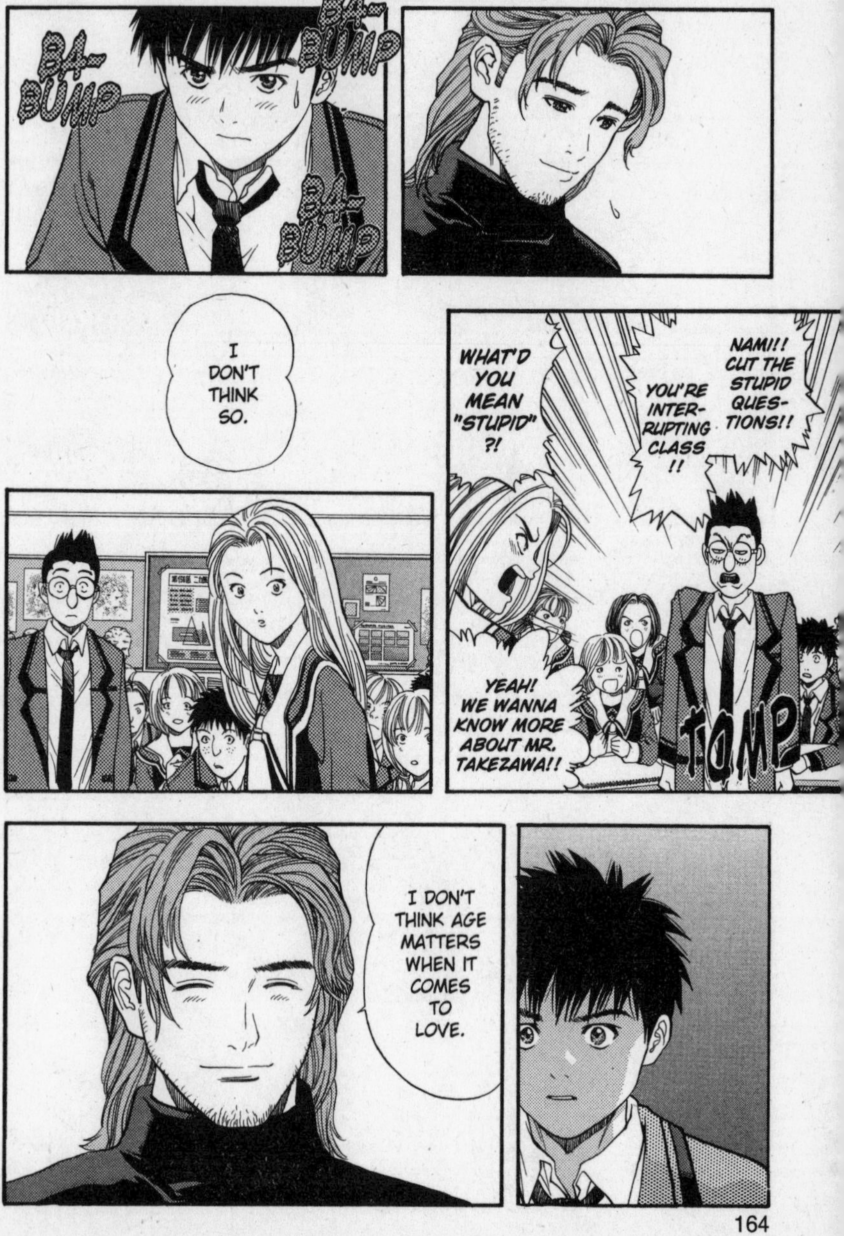
BA-BUMP
BA-BUMP
BA-BUMP
NAMI!! CUT THE STUPID QUES-TIONS!!
YOU'RE INTER-RUPTING CLASS !!
WHAT'D YOU MEAN "STUPID" ?!
TOMP
YEAH! WE WANNA KNOW MORE ABOUT MR. TAKEZAWA!!
I DON'T THINK SO.
I DON'T THINK AGE MATTERS WHEN IT COMES TO LOVE.

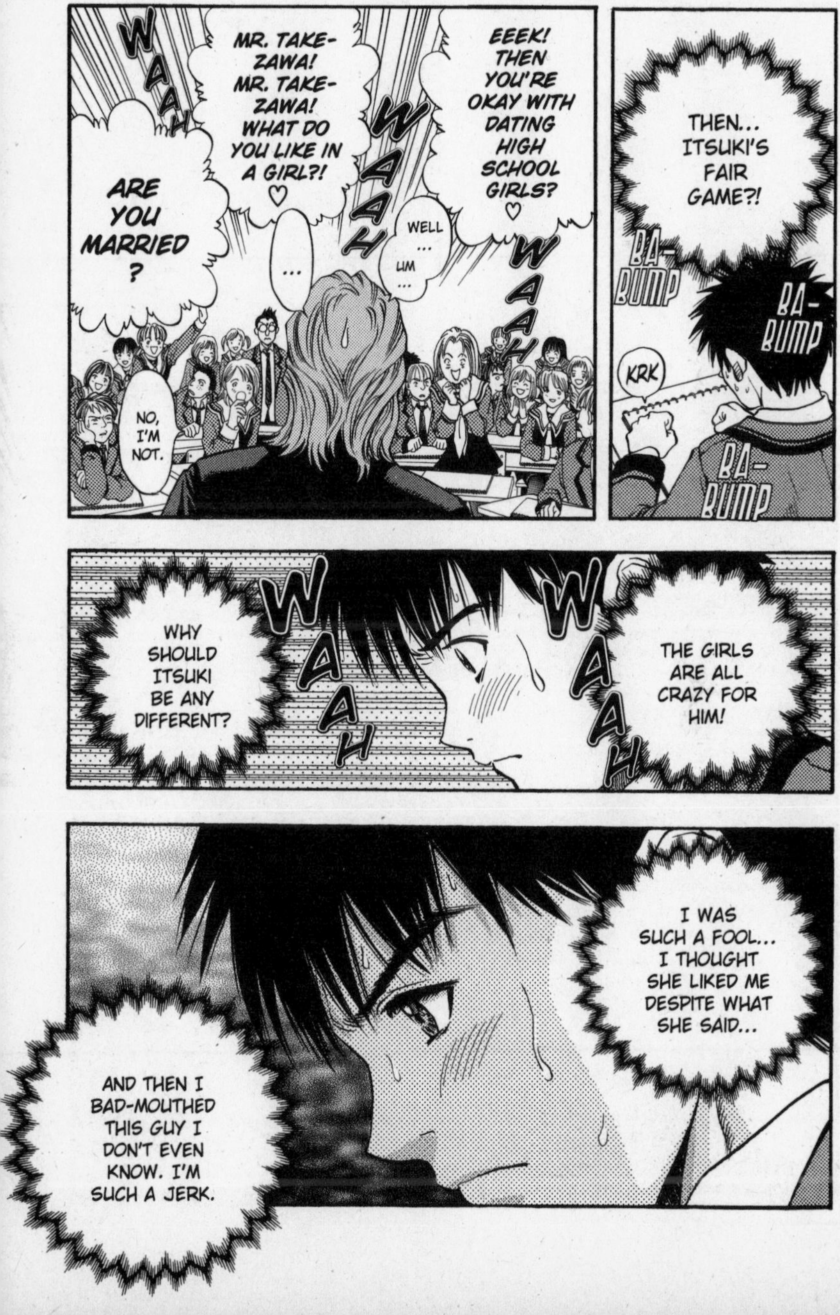
THEN... ITSUKI'S FAIR GAME?!
BA-BUMP
BA-BUMP
KRK
BA-BUMP
EEEK! THEN YOU'RE OKAY WITH DATING HIGH SCHOOL GIRLS? ♡
WAAAH
WELL ... UM ...
MR. TAKE-ZAWA! MR. TAKE-ZAWA! WHAT DO YOU LIKE IN A GIRL?! ♡
WAAAH
...
WAAAH
ARE YOU MARRIED?
NO, I'M NOT.
THE GIRLS ARE ALL CRAZY FOR HIM!
WAAAH
WAAAH
WHY SHOULD ITSUKI BE ANY DIFFERENT?
I WAS SUCH A FOOL... I THOUGHT SHE LIKED ME DESPITE WHAT SHE SAID...
AND THEN I BAD-MOUTHED THIS GUY I DON'T EVEN KNOW. I'M SUCH A JERK.

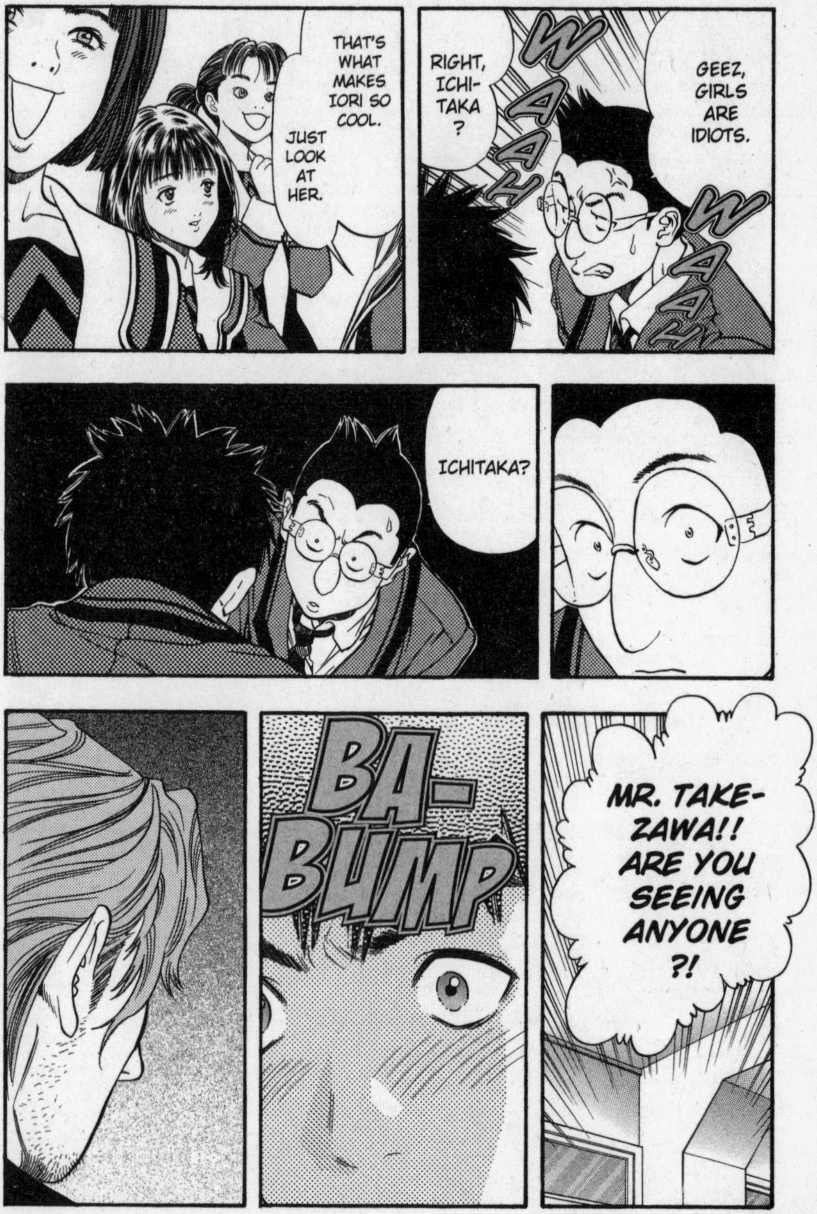
GEEZ, GIRLS ARE IDIOTS.
WAAAH
RIGHT, ICHITAKA?
WAAAH
THAT'S WHAT MAKES IORI SO COOL.
JUST LOOK AT HER.
ICHITAKA?
MR. TAKE-ZAWA!! ARE YOU SEEING ANYONE?!
BA-BUMP

READ THIS WAY

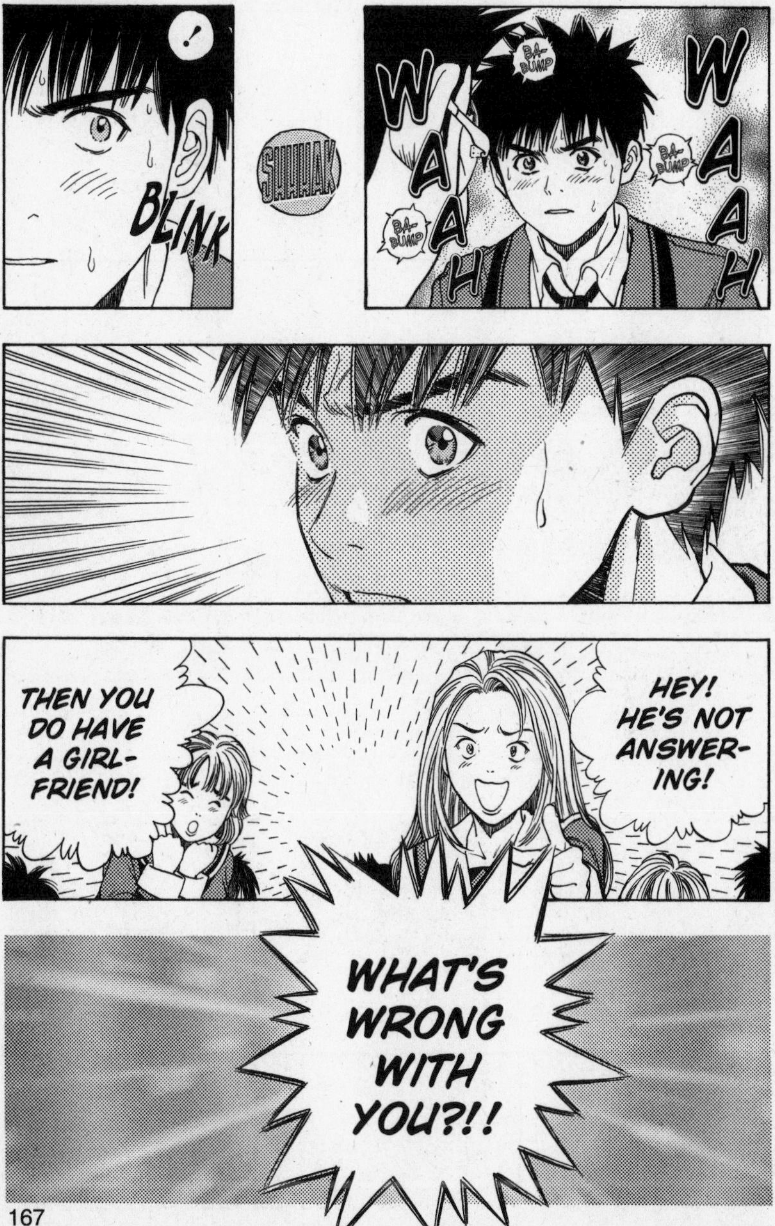

WAAH
BA-BUMP
BA-BUMP
WAAH
BA-BUMP
SHHHAK
!
BLINK
HEY! HE'S NOT ANSWERING!
THEN YOU DO HAVE A GIRLFRIEND!
WHAT'S WRONG WITH YOU?!!

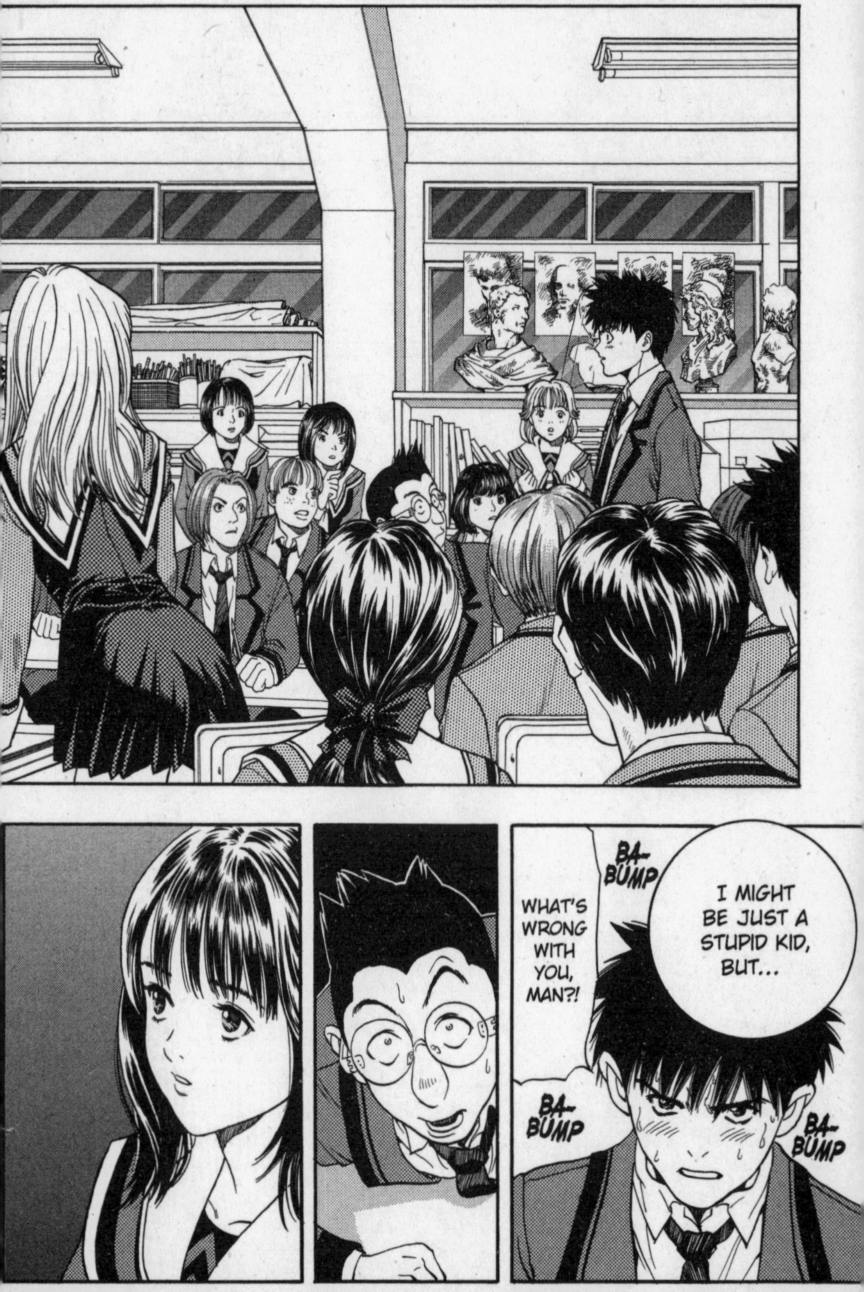
I MIGHT BE JUST A STUPID KID, BUT...
BA-BUMP
WHAT'S WRONG WITH YOU, MAN?!
BA-BUMP
BA-BUMP

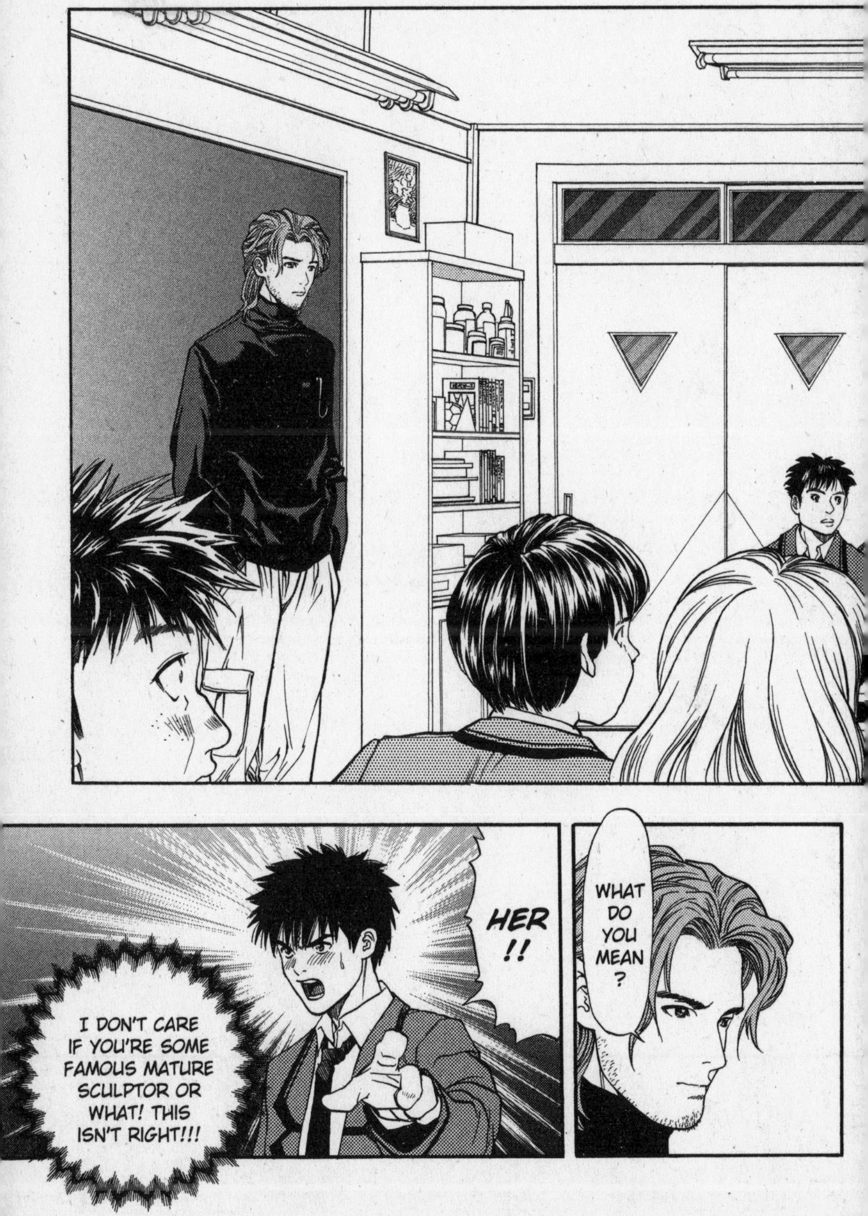
WHAT DO YOU MEAN?
HER!!
I DON'T CARE IF YOU'RE SOME FAMOUS MATURE SCULPTOR OR WHAT! THIS ISN'T RIGHT!!!

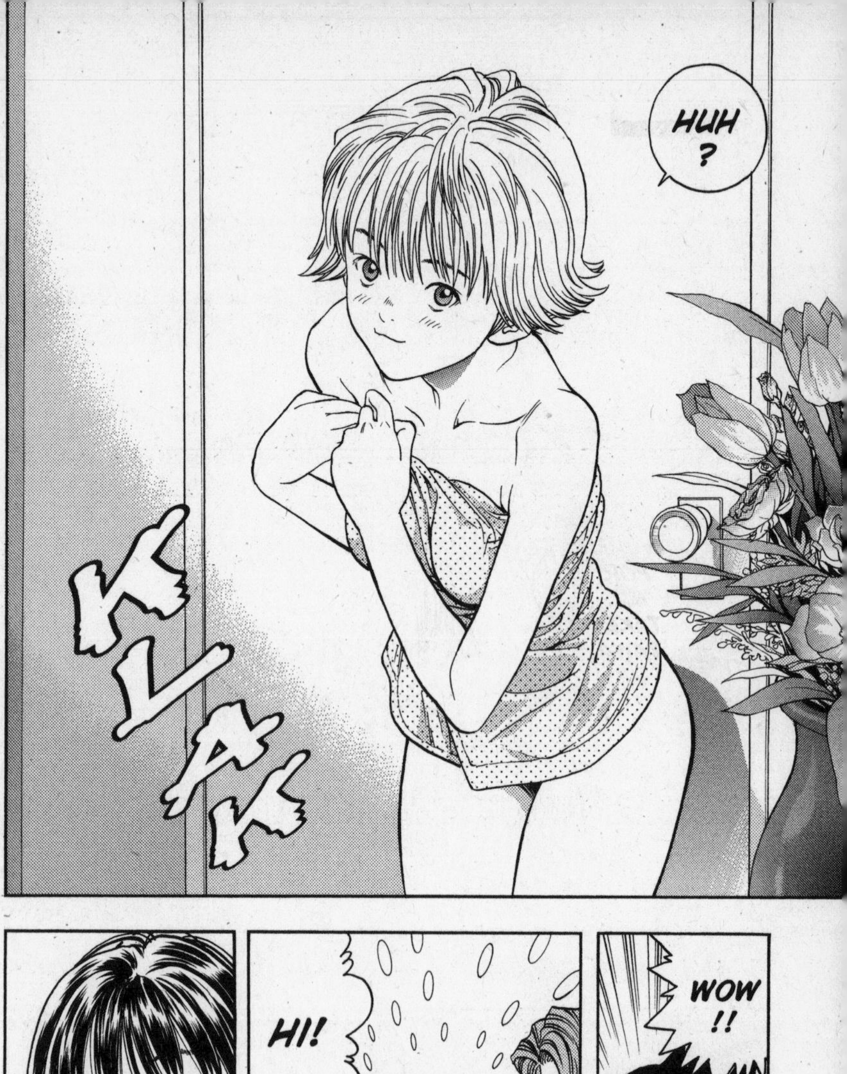
HUH ?
KLAK
WOW !!
HI!

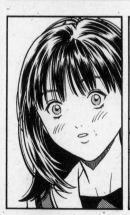

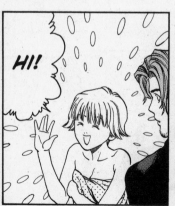

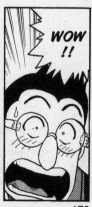

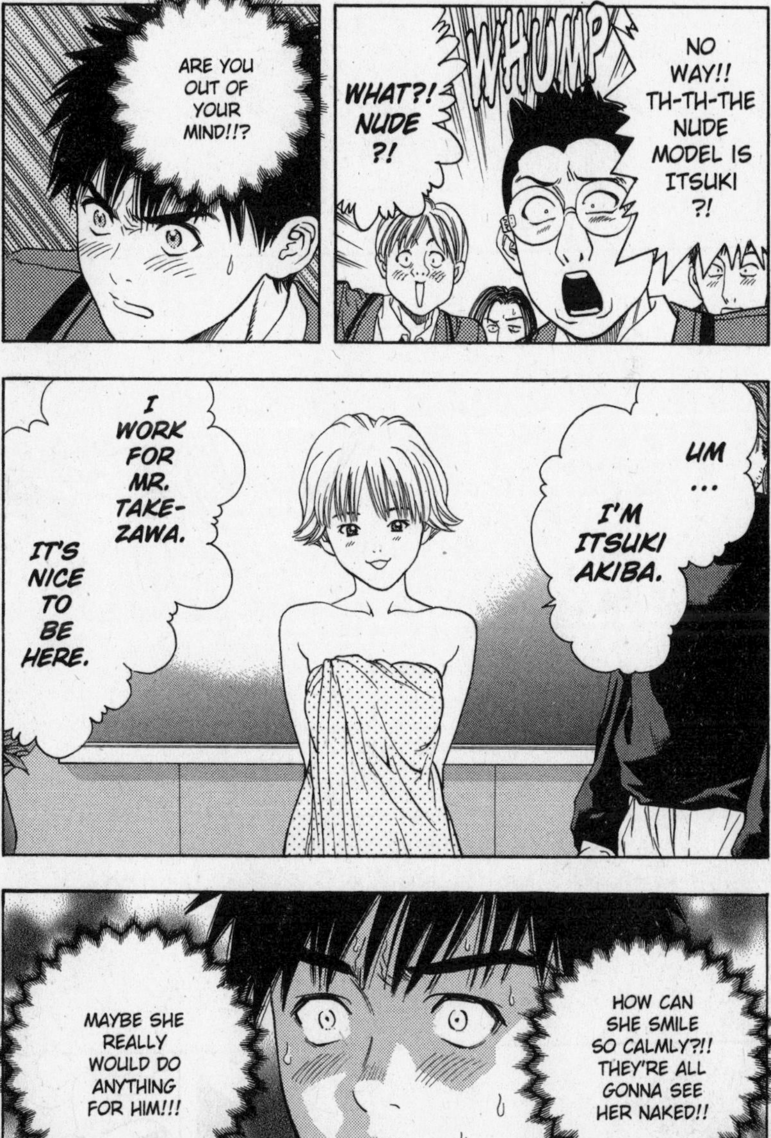
NO WAY!! TH-TH-THE NUDE MODEL IS ITSUKI ?!
WHUMP
WHAT?! NUDE ?!
ARE YOU OUT OF YOUR MIND!!?
UM ... I'M ITSUKI AKIBA.
I WORK FOR MR. TAKE-ZAWA.
IT'S NICE TO BE HERE.
HOW CAN SHE SMILE SO CALMLY?!! THEY'RE ALL GONNA SEE HER NAKED!!
MAYBE SHE REALLY WOULD DO ANYTHING FOR HIM!!!

I"S アイズ

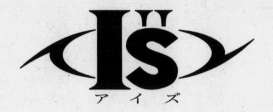

Chapter 45: Unknown World

READ THIS WAY

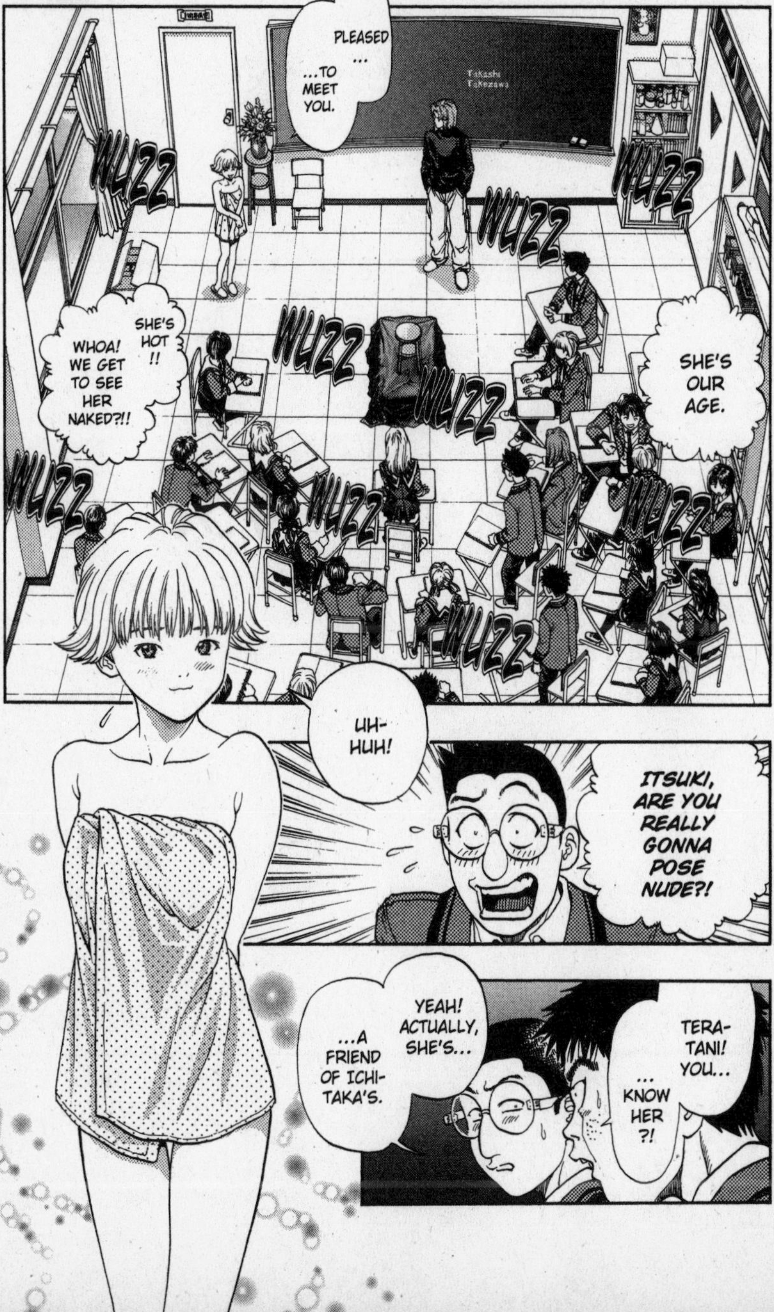
PLEASED ... ...TO MEET YOU.
Takashi Takezawa
WUZZ
SHE'S OUR AGE.
SHE'S HOT!!
WHOA! WE GET TO SEE HER NAKED?!!
ITSUKI, ARE YOU REALLY GONNA POSE NUDE?!
UH-HUH!
TERA-TANI! YOU... ...KNOW HER?!
YEAH! ACTUALLY, SHE'S...
...A FRIEND OF ICHI-TAKA'S.

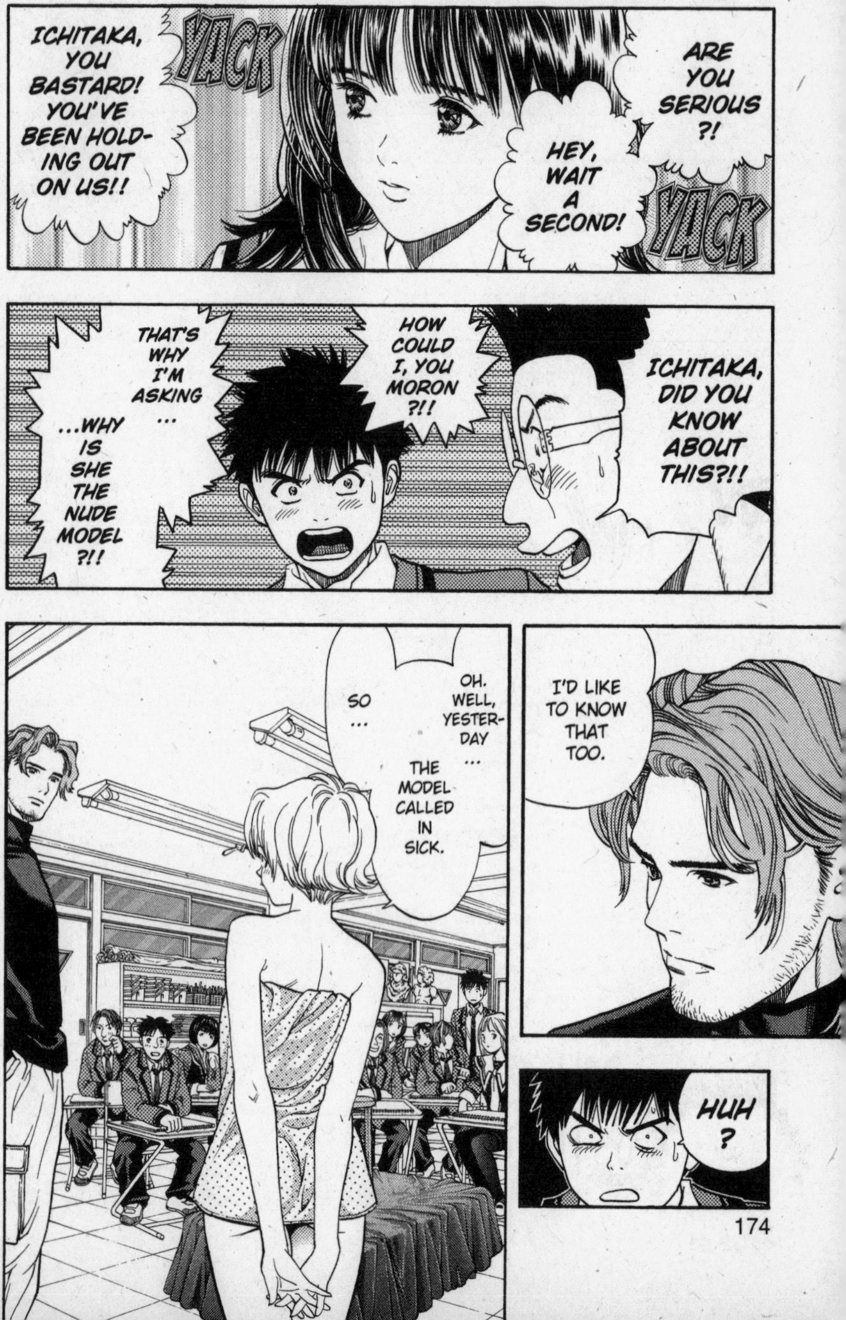
ARE YOU SERIOUS?!
HEY, WAIT A SECOND!
YACK
YACK
ICHITAKA, YOU BASTARD! YOU'VE BEEN HOLDING OUT ON US!!
ICHITAKA, DID YOU KNOW ABOUT THIS?!!
HOW COULD I, YOU MORON?!!
THAT'S WHY I'M ASKING...
...WHY IS SHE THE NUDE MODEL?!!
I'D LIKE TO KNOW THAT TOO.
HUH?
OH. WELL, YESTERDAY...
THE MODEL CALLED IN SICK.
SO...

READ THIS WAY

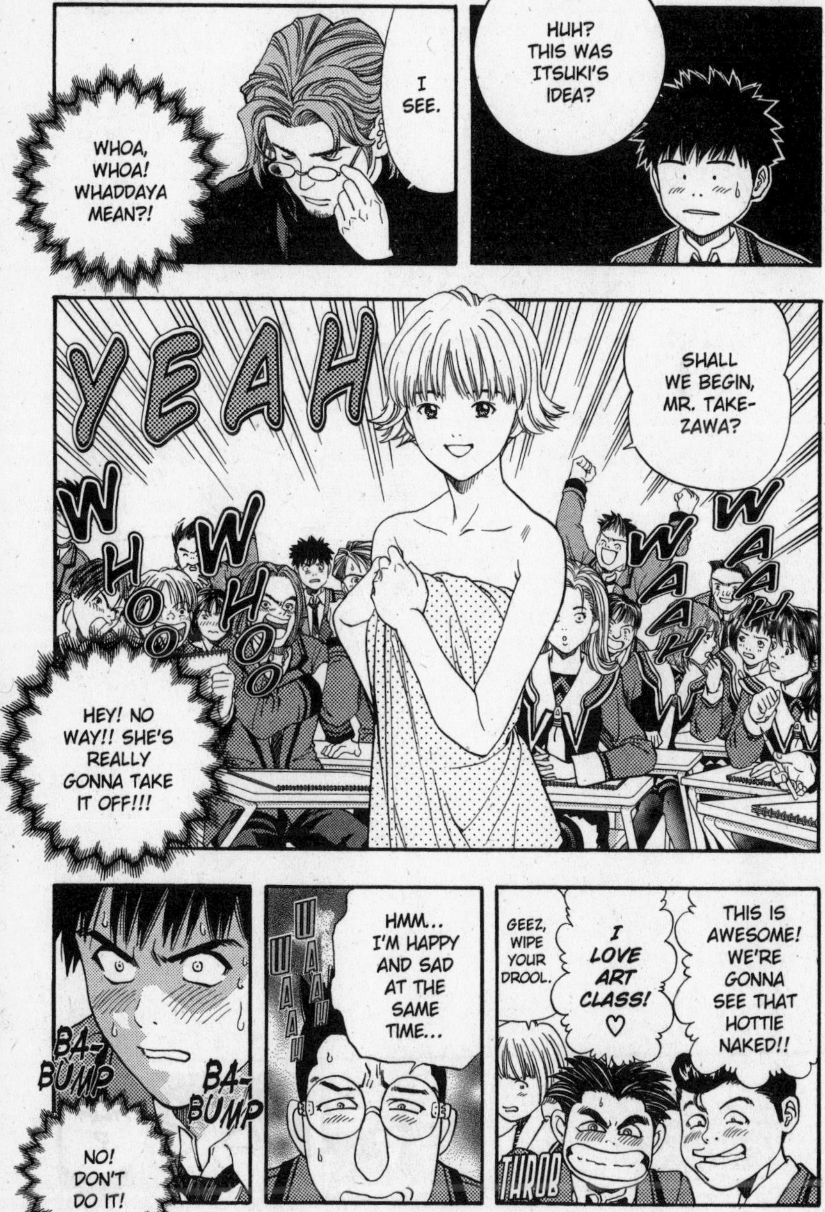
HUH? THIS WAS ITSUKI'S IDEA?
I SEE.
WHOA, WHOA! WHADDAYA MEAN?!
SHALL WE BEGIN, MR. TAKE-ZAWA?
YEAH
WAAAAH
WHOO
WHOOO
HEY! NO WAY!! SHE'S REALLY GONNA TAKE IT OFF!!!
THIS IS AWESOME! WE'RE GONNA SEE THAT HOTTIE NAKED!!
I LOVE ART CLASS! ♡
GEEZ, WIPE YOUR DROOL.
THROB
HMM... I'M HAPPY AND SAD AT THE SAME TIME...
WAAAAH
BA-BUMP
BA-BUMP
NO! DON'T DO IT!

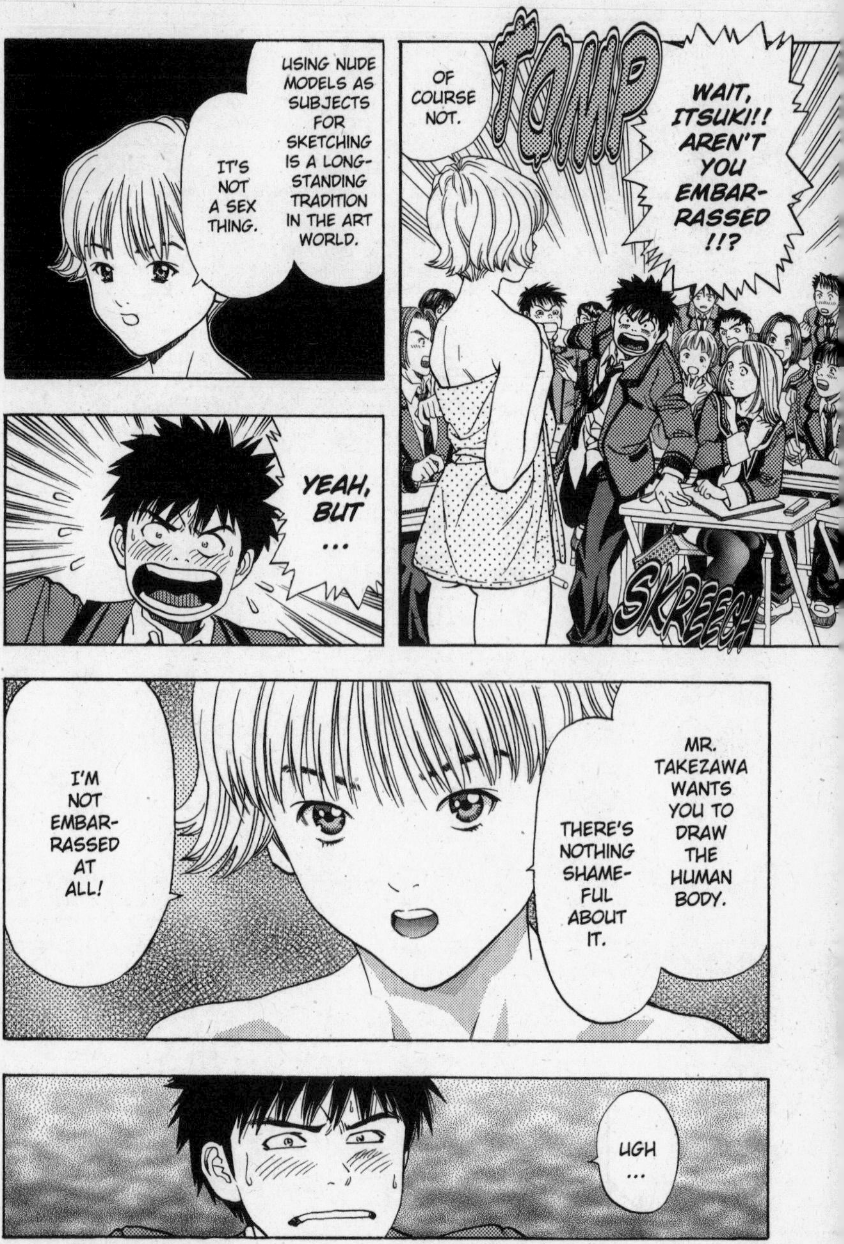
WAIT, ITSUKI!! AREN'T YOU EMBARRASSED!!?
TOMP
OF COURSE NOT.
SKREECH
USING NUDE MODELS AS SUBJECTS FOR SKETCHING IS A LONG-STANDING TRADITION IN THE ART WORLD.
IT'S NOT A SEX THING.
YEAH, BUT ...
MR. TAKEZAWA WANTS YOU TO DRAW THE HUMAN BODY.
THERE'S NOTHING SHAMEFUL ABOUT IT.
I'M NOT EMBARRASSED AT ALL!
UGH ...

READ THIS WAY

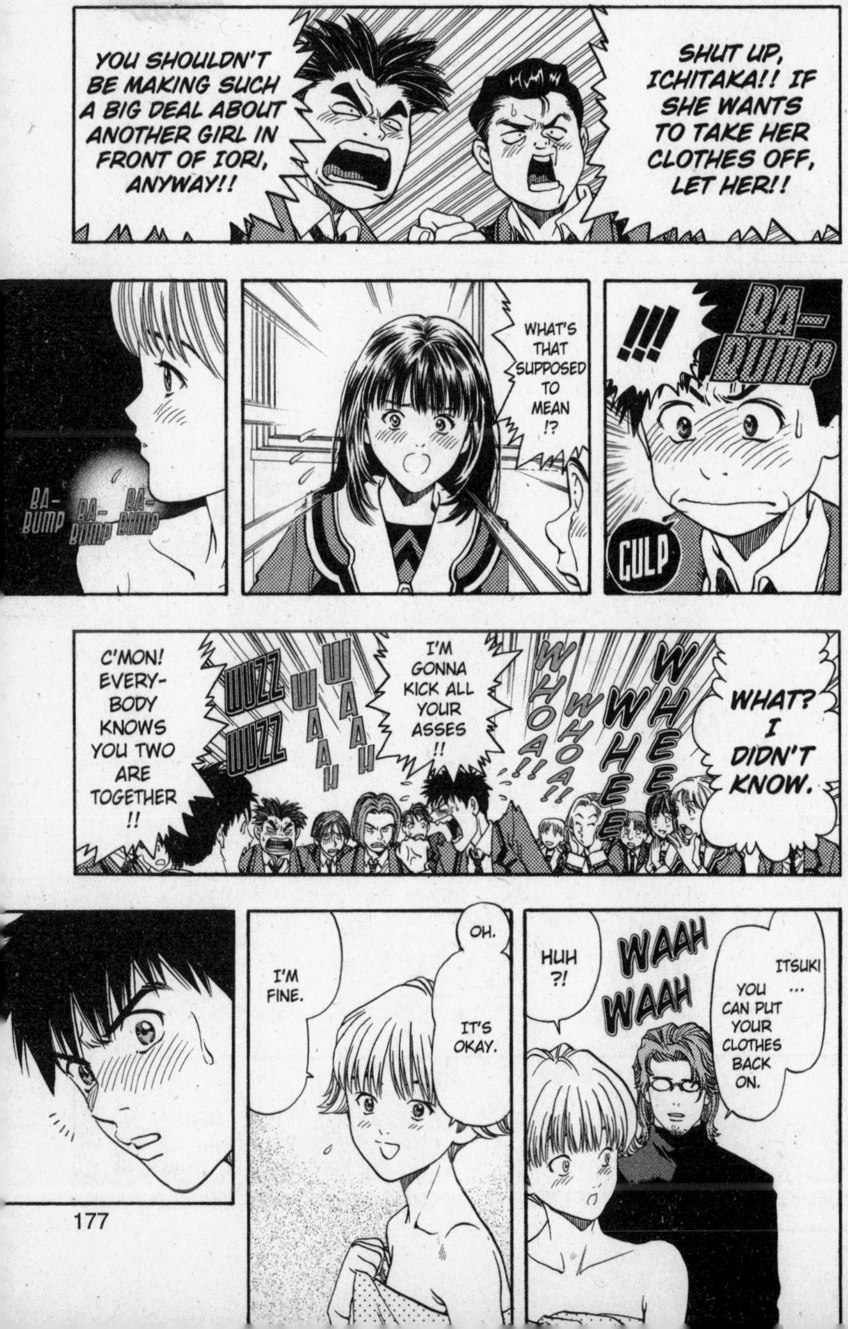
SHUT UP, ICHITAKA!! IF SHE WANTS TO TAKE HER CLOTHES OFF, LET HER!!
YOU SHOULDN'T BE MAKING SUCH A BIG DEAL ABOUT ANOTHER GIRL IN FRONT OF IORI, ANYWAY!!
BA-DUMP
!!!
GULP
WHAT'S THAT SUPPOSED TO MEAN !?
BA-BUMP
BA-BUMP
BA-BUMP
WHAT? I DIDN'T KNOW.
WHEEE
WHEEE
WHOA!!
WHOA!!
I'M GONNA KICK ALL YOUR ASSES !!
WAAAH
WAAAH
WUZZ
WUZZ
C'MON! EVERY-BODY KNOWS YOU TWO ARE TOGETHER !!
ITSUKI ...
YOU CAN PUT YOUR CLOTHES BACK ON.
WAAH WAAH
HUH ?!
OH.
IT'S OKAY.
I'M FINE.

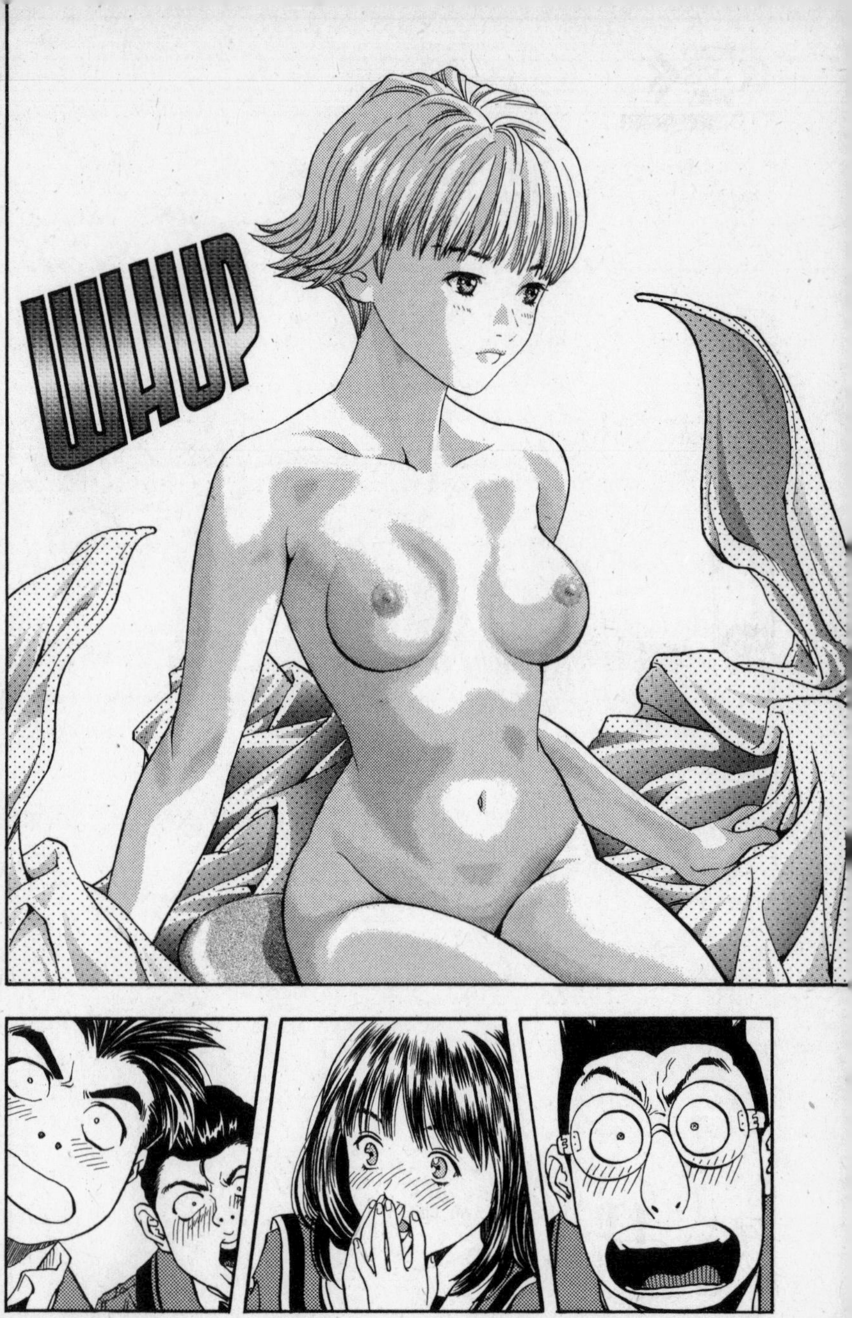
WHUP

READ THIS WAY

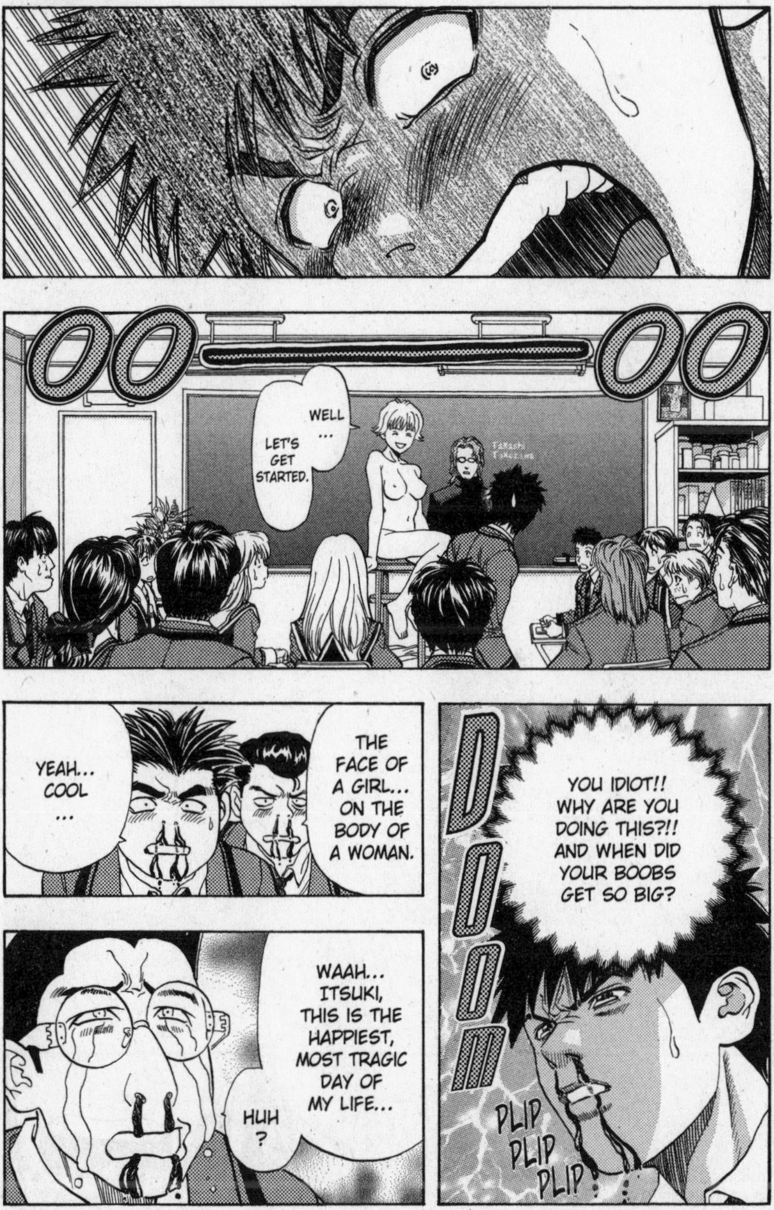
OO—OO
WELL...
LET'S GET STARTED.
DOOM
YOU IDIOT!! WHY ARE YOU DOING THIS?!! AND WHEN DID YOUR BOOBS GET SO BIG?
PLIP PLIP PLIP
THE FACE OF A GIRL... ON THE BODY OF A WOMAN.
YEAH... COOL ...
WAAH... ITSUKI, THIS IS THE HAPPIEST, MOST TRAGIC DAY OF MY LIFE...
HUH ?

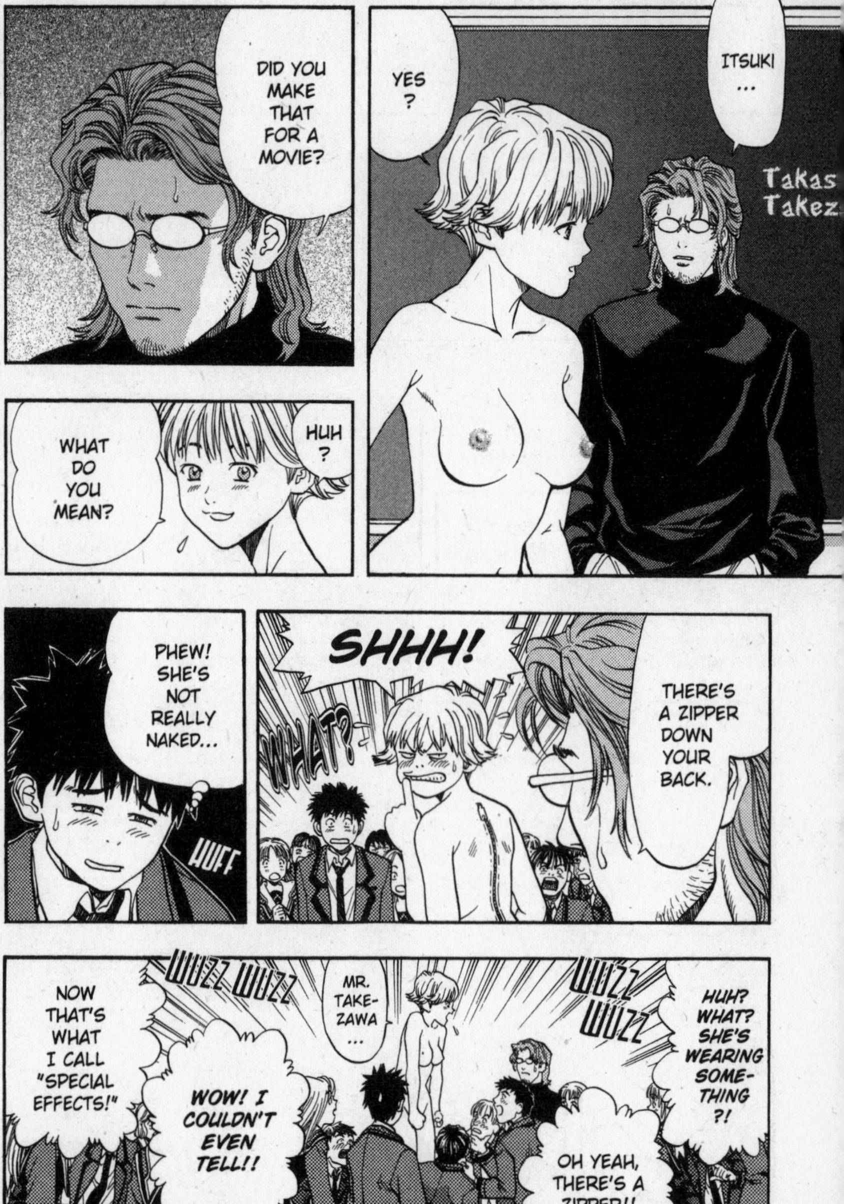
ITSUKI ...
YES ?
Takas
Takez
DID YOU MAKE THAT FOR A MOVIE?
HUH ?
WHAT DO YOU MEAN?
THERE'S A ZIPPER DOWN YOUR BACK.
SHHH!
WHAT?
PHEW! SHE'S NOT REALLY NAKED...
HUFF
HUH? WHAT? SHE'S WEARING SOME-THING ?!
WUZZ WUZZ
OH YEAH, THERE'S A ZIPPER!!
MR. TAKE-ZAWA ...
WUZZ WUZZ
WOW! I COULDN'T EVEN TELL!!
NOW THAT'S WHAT I CALL "SPECIAL EFFECTS!"

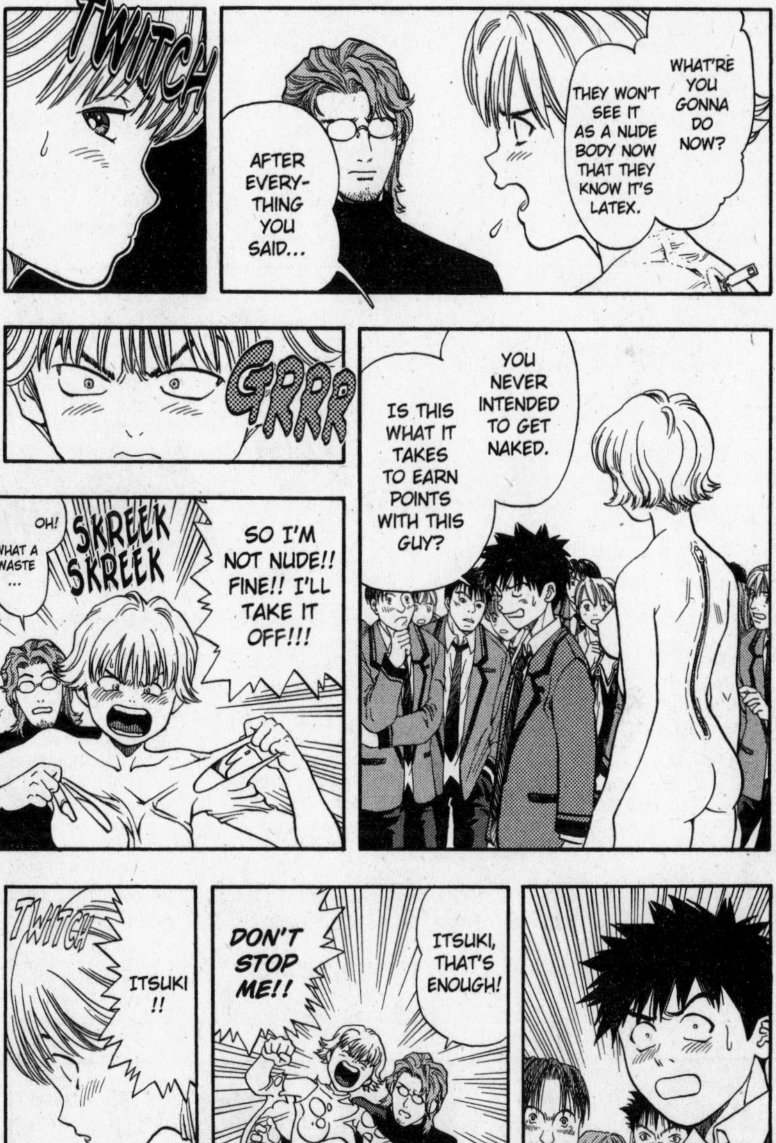
WHAT'RE YOU GONNA DO NOW?
THEY WON'T SEE IT AS A NUDE BODY NOW THAT THEY KNOW IT'S LATEX.
AFTER EVERY-THING YOU SAID...
TWITCH
YOU NEVER INTENDED TO GET NAKED.
IS THIS WHAT IT TAKES TO EARN POINTS WITH THIS GUY?
GRRR
SO I'M NOT NUDE!! FINE!! I'LL TAKE IT OFF!!!
SKREEK SKREEK
OH!
WHAT A WASTE ...
ITSUKI, THAT'S ENOUGH!
DON'T STOP ME!!
ITSUKI !!
TWITCH

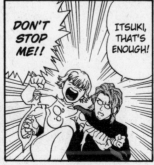

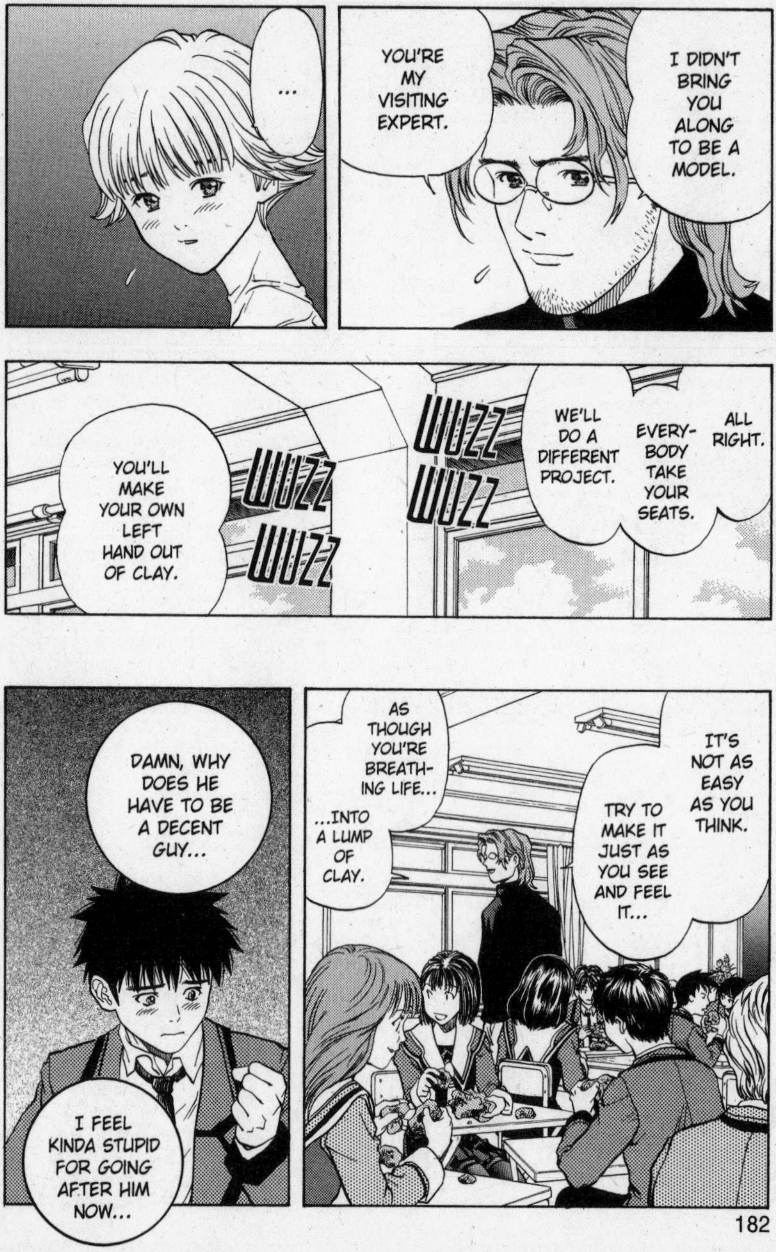
I DIDN'T BRING YOU ALONG TO BE A MODEL.
YOU'RE MY VISITING EXPERT.
...
ALL RIGHT.
EVERY-BODY TAKE YOUR SEATS.
WE'LL DO A DIFFERENT PROJECT.
WUZZ WUZZ
WUZZ WUZZ
YOU'LL MAKE YOUR OWN LEFT HAND OUT OF CLAY.
IT'S NOT AS EASY AS YOU THINK.
TRY TO MAKE IT JUST AS YOU SEE AND FEEL IT...
AS THOUGH YOU'RE BREATHING LIFE...
...INTO A LUMP OF CLAY.
DAMN, WHY DOES HE HAVE TO BE A DECENT GUY...
I FEEL KINDA STUPID FOR GOING AFTER HIM NOW...

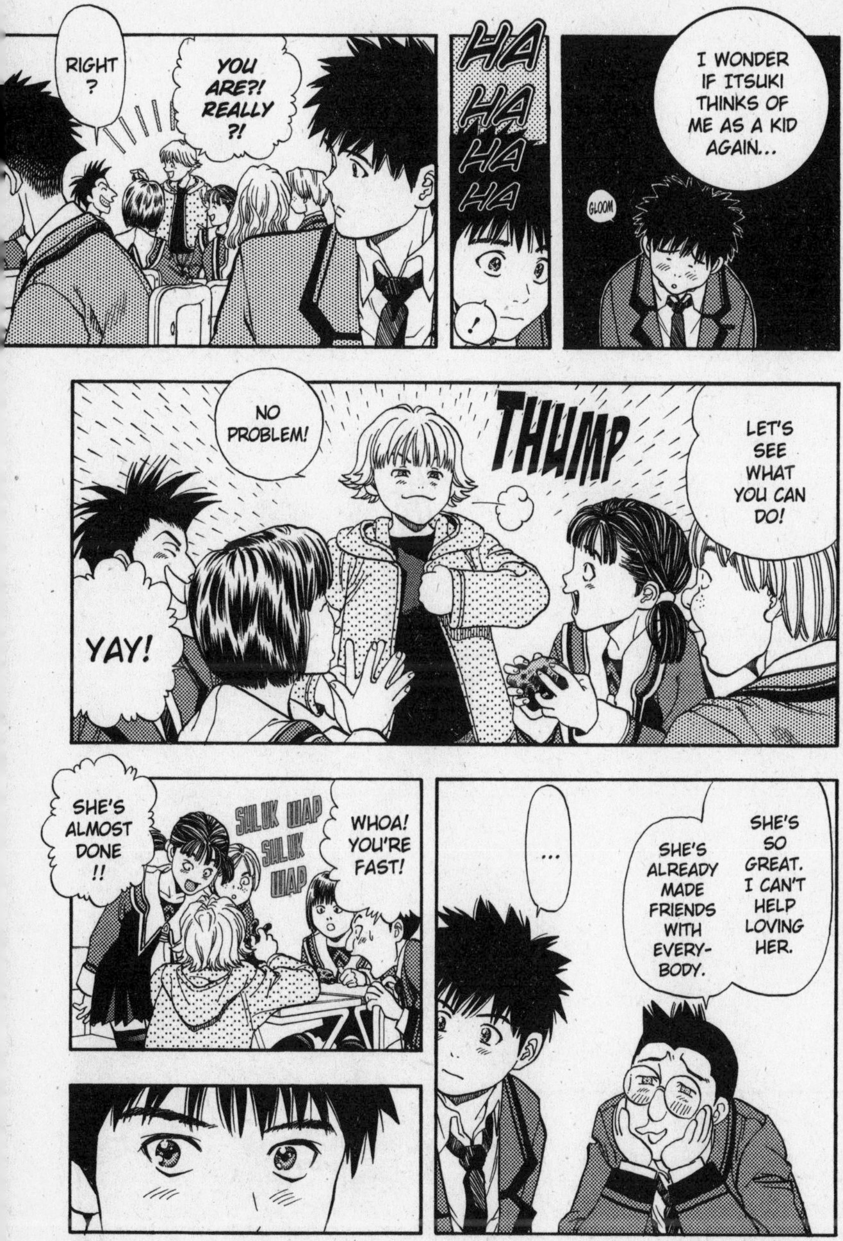
I WONDER IF ITSUKI THINKS OF ME AS A KID AGAIN...
GLOOM
HA HA HA HA
!
YOU ARE?! REALLY ?!
RIGHT ?
LET'S SEE WHAT YOU CAN DO!
THUMP
NO PROBLEM!
YAY!
SHE'S SO GREAT. I CAN'T HELP LOVING HER.
SHE'S ALREADY MADE FRIENDS WITH EVERY-BODY.
...
WHOA! YOU'RE FAST!
SHLUK WAP SHLUK WAP
SHE'S ALMOST DONE !!

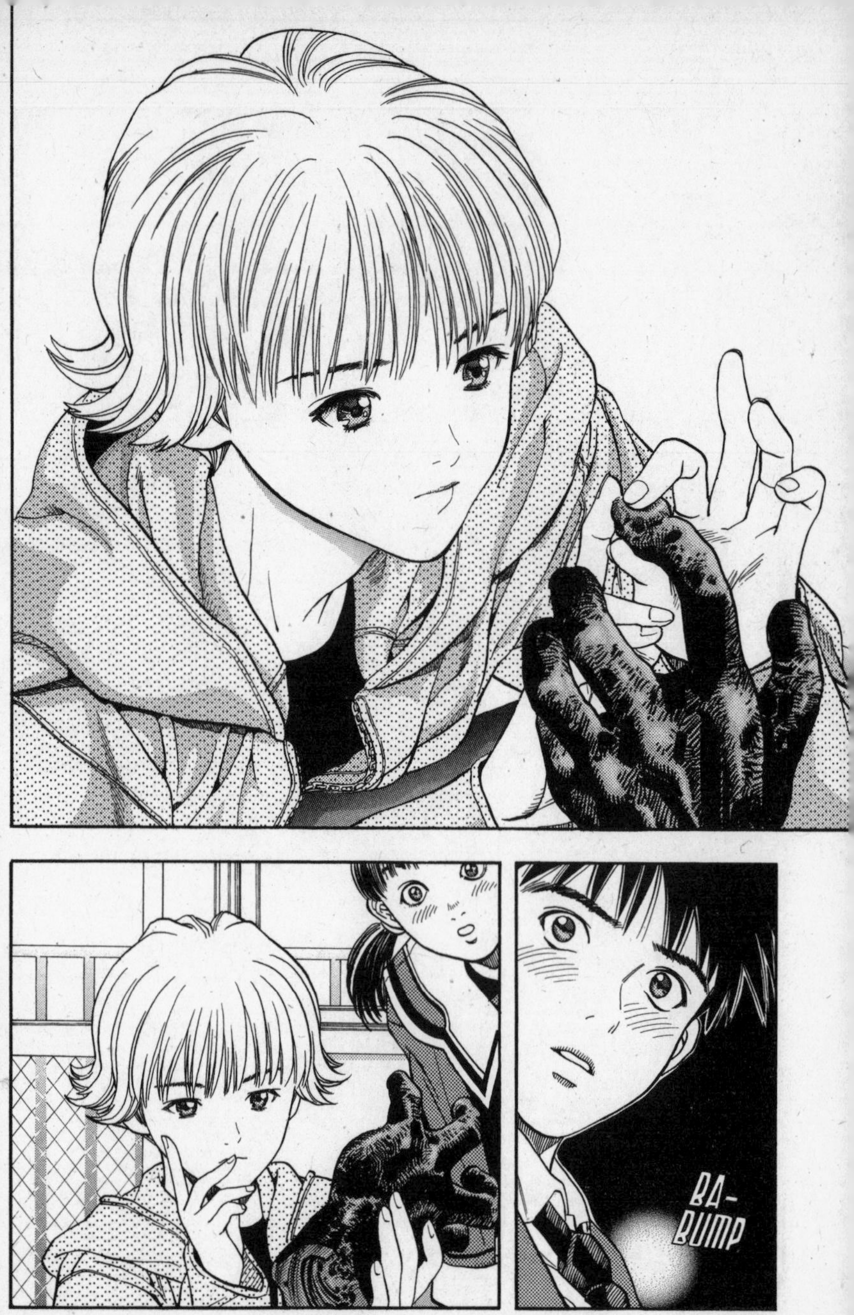
BA-
BUMP

READ THIS WAY

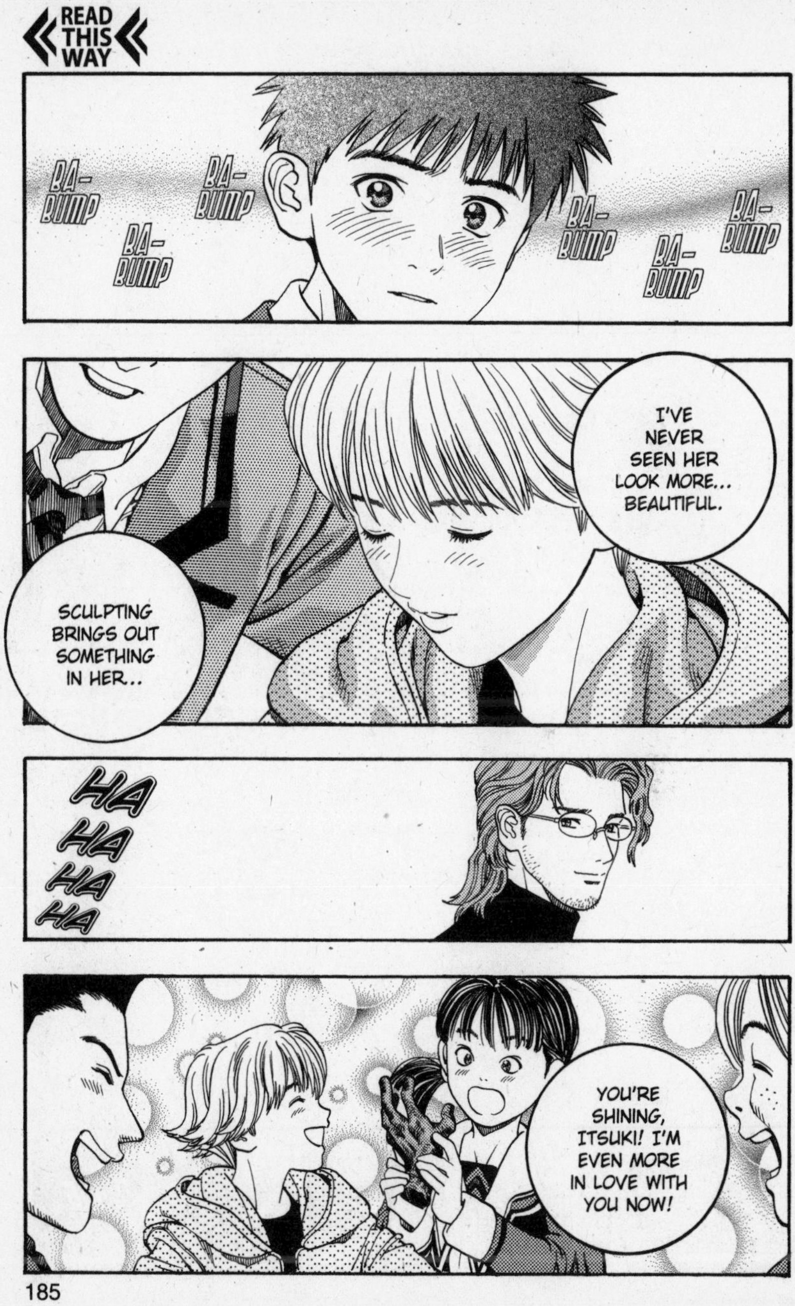
BA-BUMP
BA-BUMP
BA-BUMP
BA-BUMP
BA-BUMP
BA-BUMP
I'VE NEVER SEEN HER LOOK MORE... BEAUTIFUL.
SCULPTING BRINGS OUT SOMETHING IN HER...
HA HA HA HA
YOU'RE SHINING, ITSUKI! I'M EVEN MORE IN LOVE WITH YOU NOW!

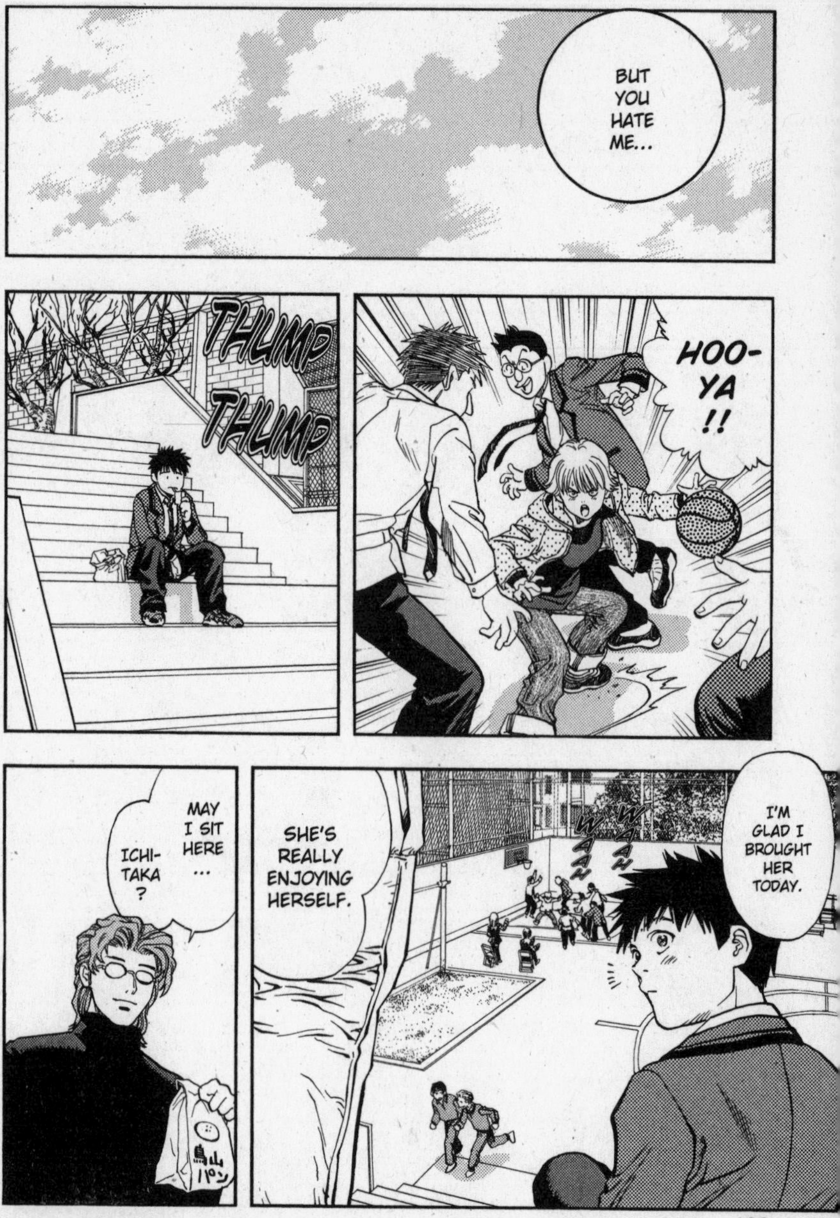
BUT YOU HATE ME...
HOO-YA!!
THUMP THUMP
I'M GLAD I BROUGHT HER TODAY.
WAAAH WAAAH
SHE'S REALLY ENJOYING HERSELF.
MAY I SIT HERE... ICHI-TAKA?

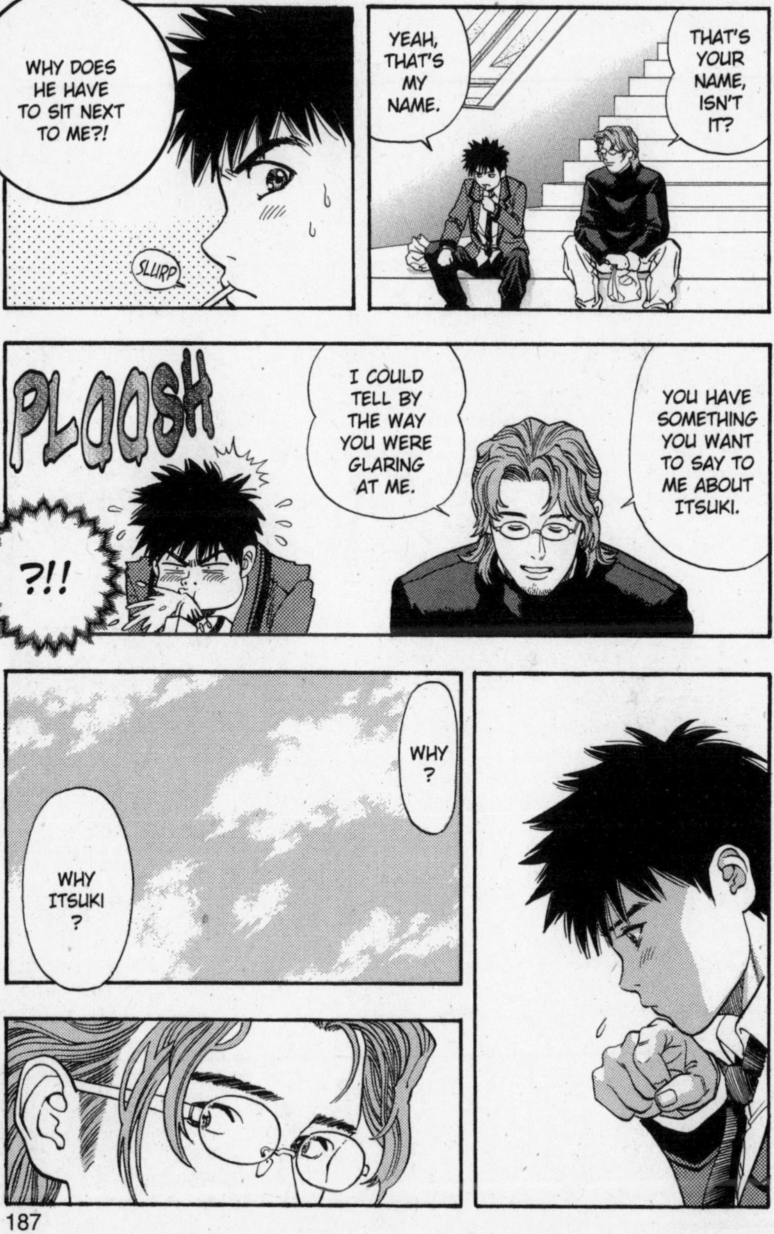
THAT'S YOUR NAME, ISN'T IT?
YEAH, THAT'S MY NAME.
WHY DOES HE HAVE TO SIT NEXT TO ME?!
SLURP
YOU HAVE SOMETHING YOU WANT TO SAY TO ME ABOUT ITSUKI.
I COULD TELL BY THE WAY YOU WERE GLARING AT ME.
PLOOSH
?!!
WHY?
WHY ITSUKI?

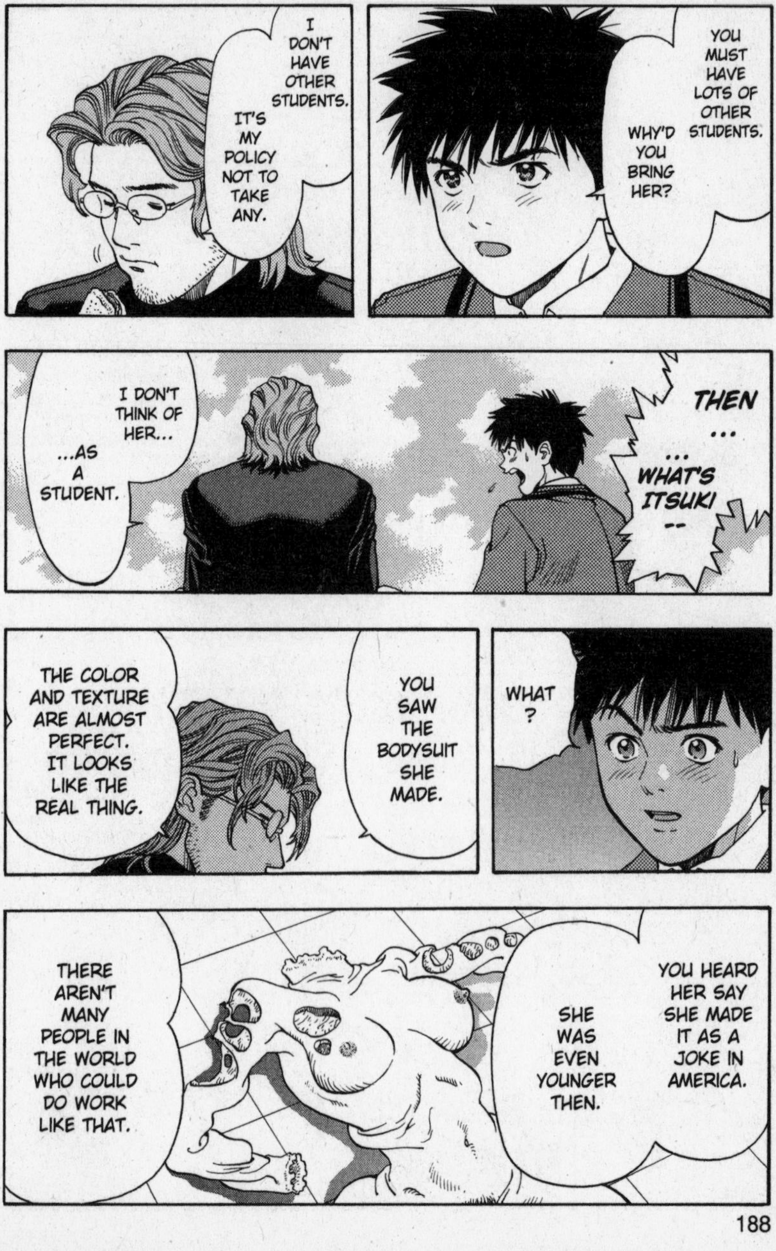
YOU MUST HAVE LOTS OF OTHER STUDENTS.
WHY'D YOU BRING HER?
I DON'T HAVE OTHER STUDENTS.
IT'S MY POLICY NOT TO TAKE ANY.
THEN... ...WHAT'S ITSUKI --
I DON'T THINK OF HER...
...AS A STUDENT.
WHAT?
YOU SAW THE BODYSUIT SHE MADE.
THE COLOR AND TEXTURE ARE ALMOST PERFECT. IT LOOKS LIKE THE REAL THING.
YOU HEARD HER SAY SHE MADE IT AS A JOKE IN AMERICA.
SHE WAS EVEN YOUNGER THEN.
THERE AREN'T MANY PEOPLE IN THE WORLD WHO COULD DO WORK LIKE THAT.

READ THIS WAY

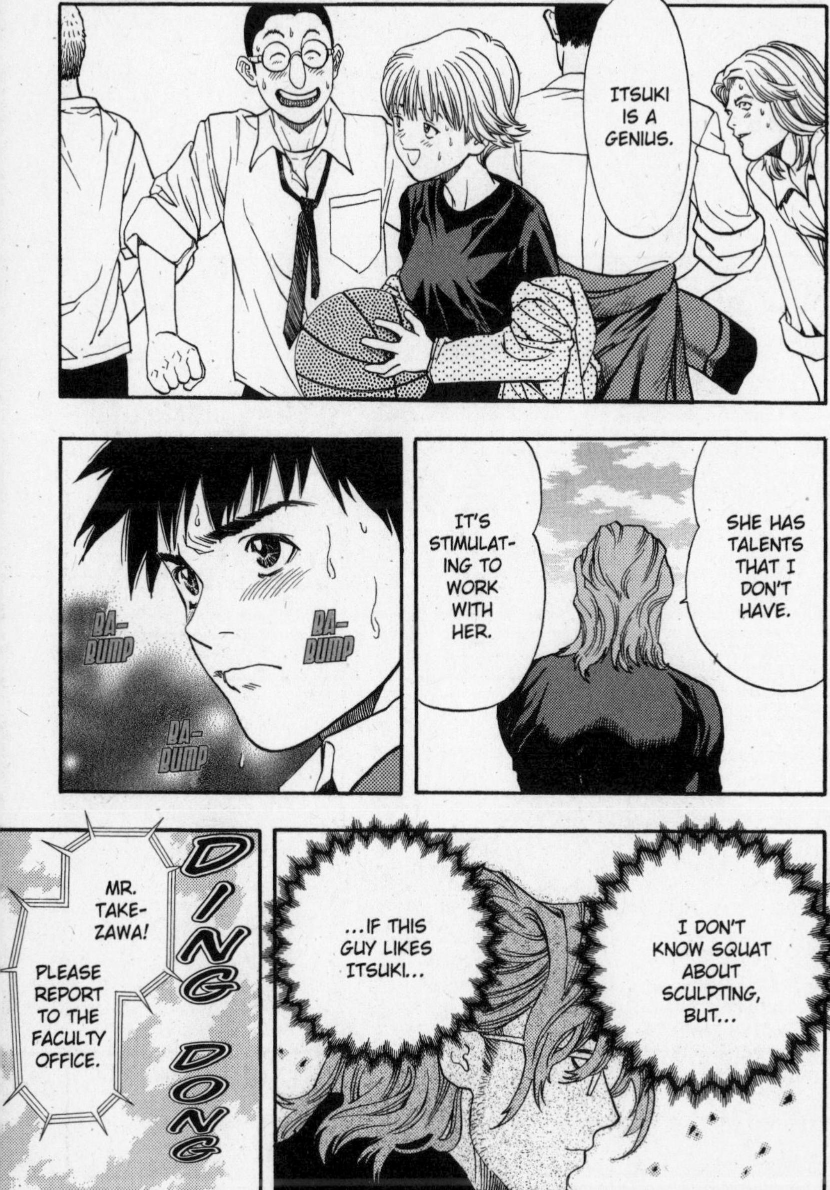
ITSUKI IS A GENIUS.
SHE HAS TALENTS THAT I DON'T HAVE.
IT'S STIMULATING TO WORK WITH HER.
BA-BUMP
BA-BUMP
BA-BUMP
I DON'T KNOW SQUAT ABOUT SCULPTING, BUT...
...IF THIS GUY LIKES ITSUKI...
DING DONG
MR. TAKE-ZAWA!
PLEASE REPORT TO THE FACULTY OFFICE.

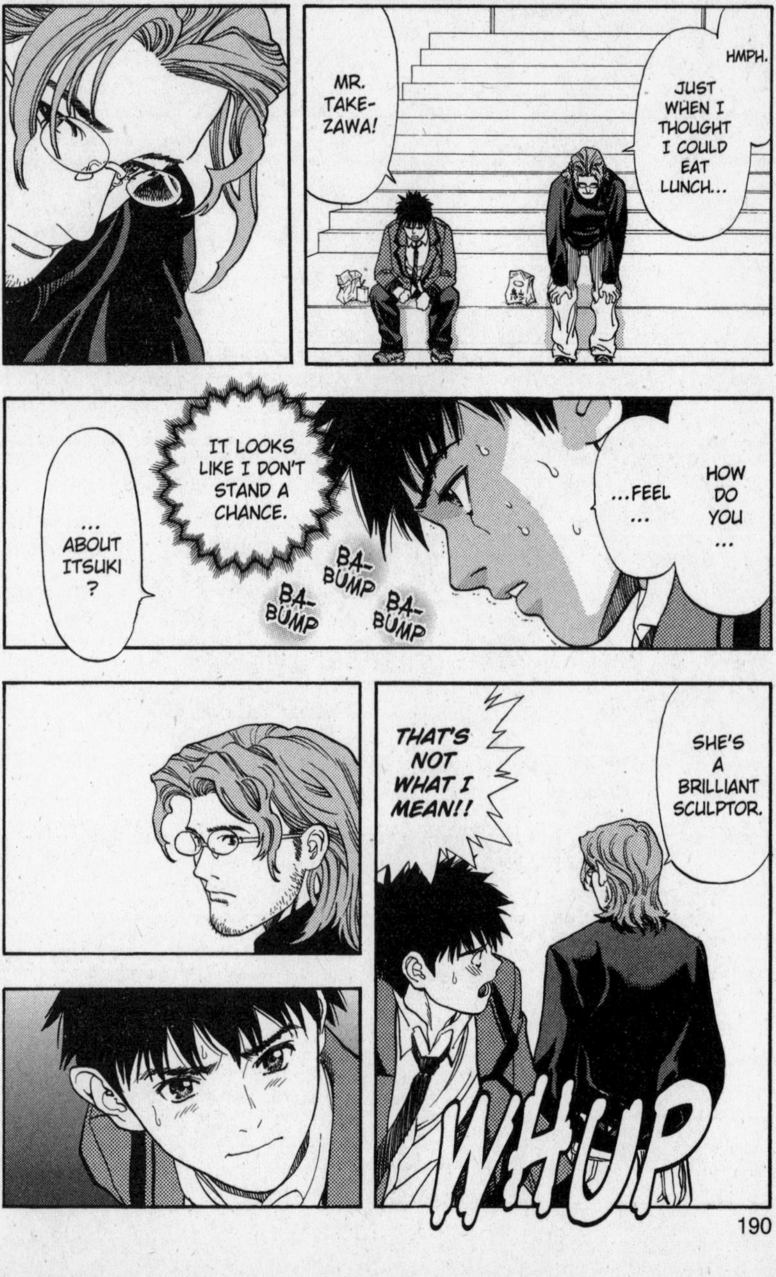
HMPH.
JUST WHEN I THOUGHT I COULD EAT LUNCH...
MR. TAKE-ZAWA!
HOW DO YOU ...
...FEEL ...
IT LOOKS LIKE I DON'T STAND A CHANCE.
BA-BUMP
BA-BUMP
BA-BUMP
... ABOUT ITSUKI ?
SHE'S A BRILLIANT SCULPTOR.
THAT'S NOT WHAT I MEAN!!
WHUP

READ THIS WAY

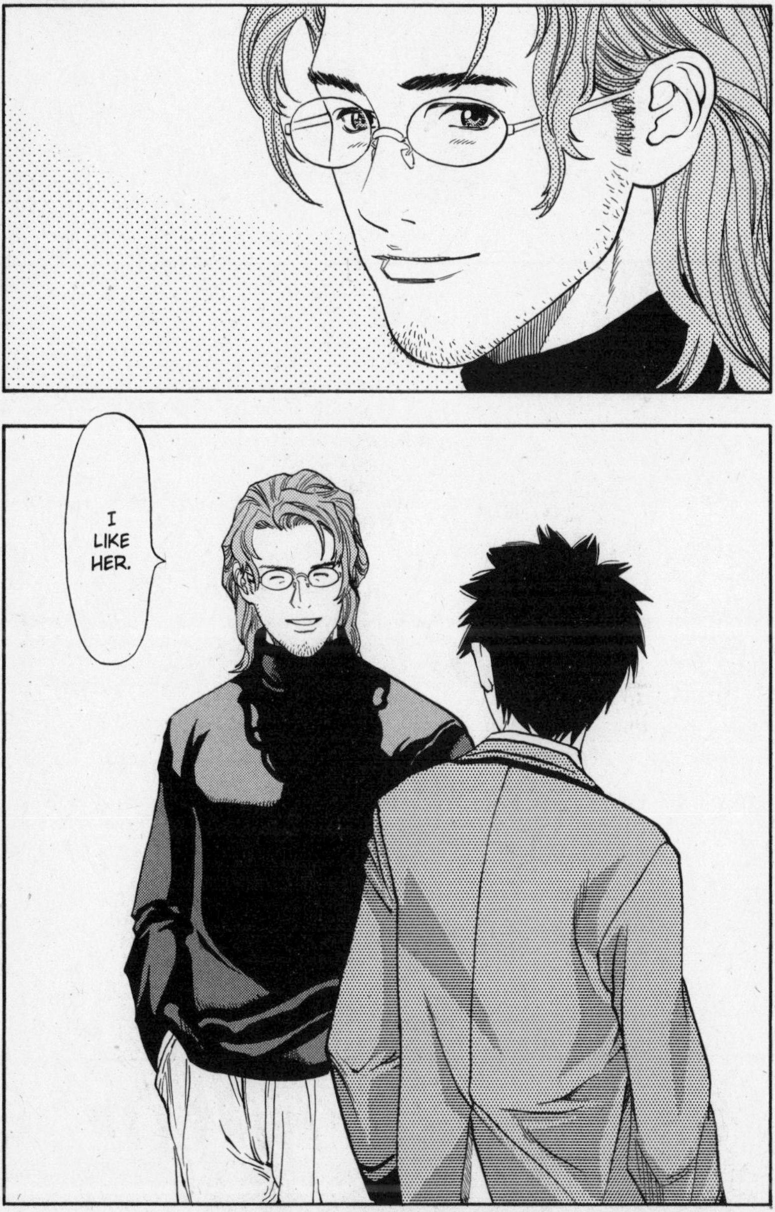
I LIKE HER.

To be continued in Vol. 6!

I"s Illustration Collection

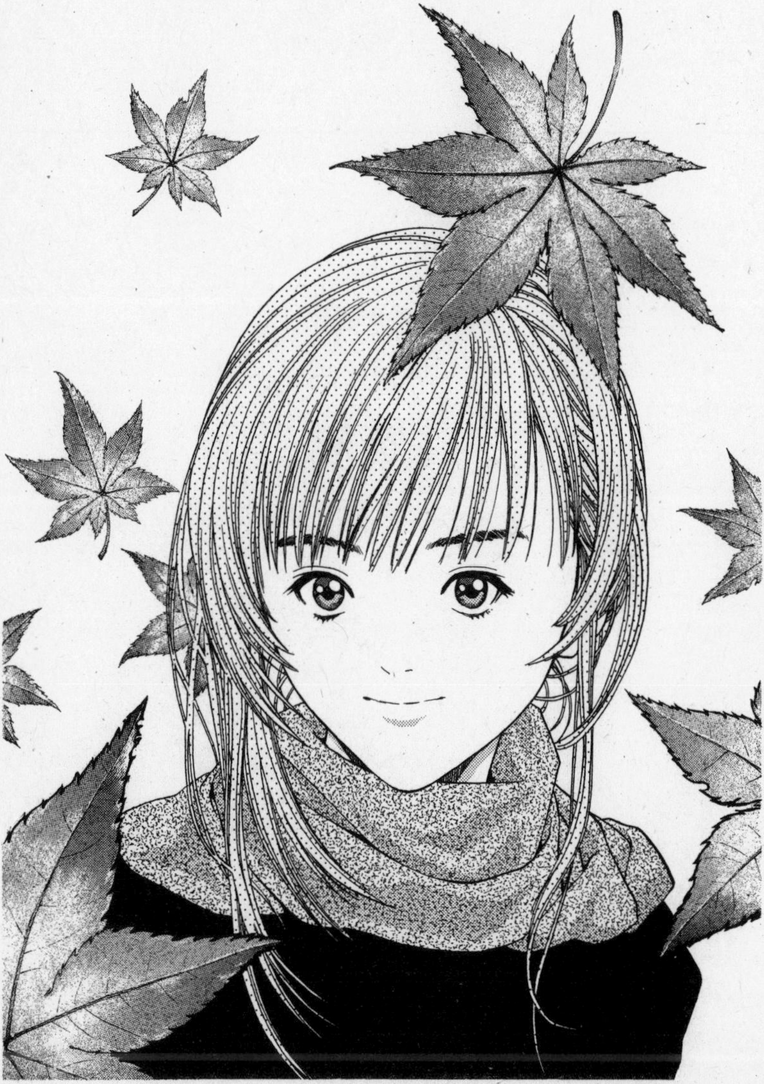

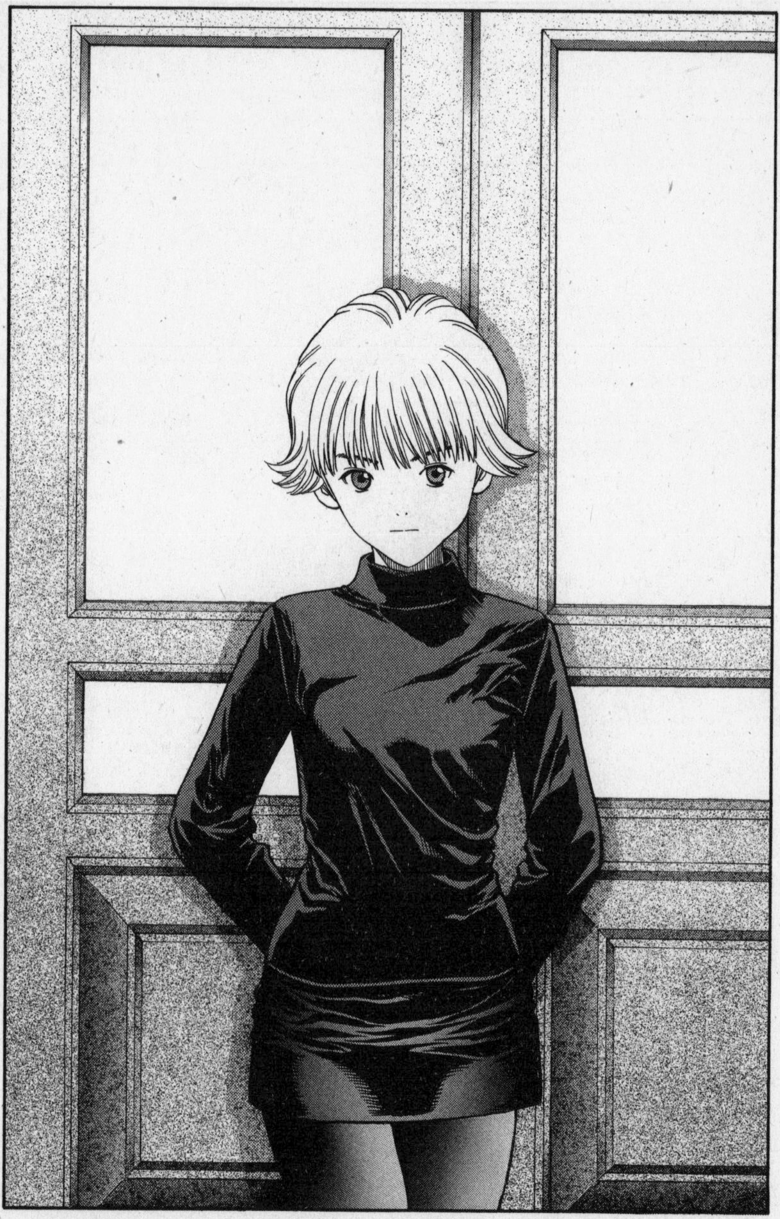

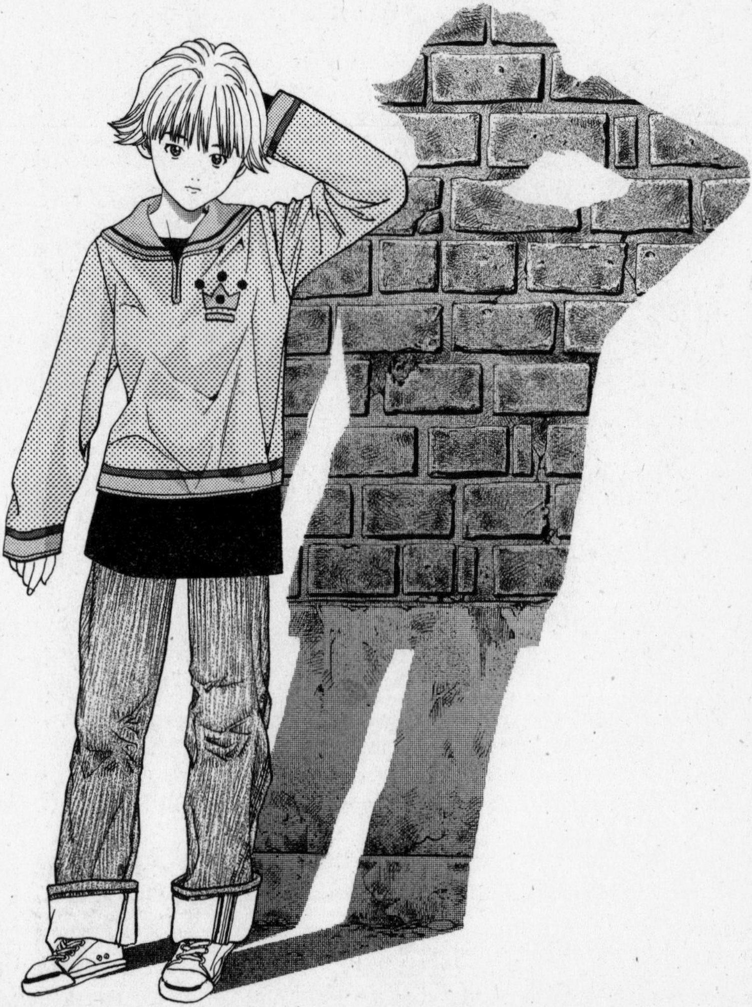

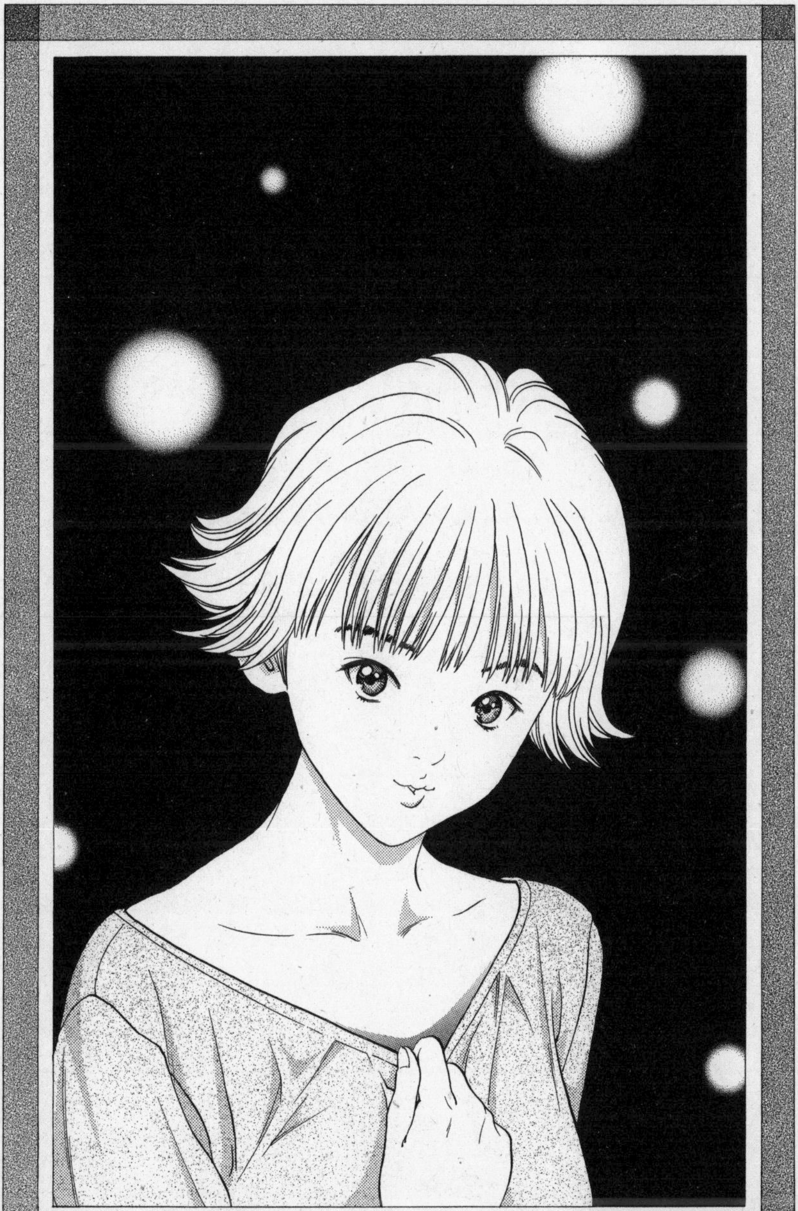

NEXT VOLUME PREVIEW

Ichitaka gets up the guts to ask Itsuki out on a date, and Iori is asked to be in a school newspaper shoot on the same day. Everything would be fine, except the guys photographing Iori turn out to be the jerks who want payback for their foiled attempt at filming the girls changing at school. Will Ichitaka save Iori at the expense of his date with Itsuki?

Available in March 2006

BOBOBO-BO BO-BOBO™

ONLY $7.99

On Sale Now!

BO-BOBO SAYS NO NO NO TO THOSE WHO WOULD HUNT HAIR!

THE WORLD'S MOST CUTTING-EDGE MANGA

SHONEN JUMP ADVANCED

WWW.SHONENJUMP.COM

ON SALE AT:
www.shonenjump.com
Also available at your local bookstore, comic store and Suncoast Motion Picture Company.

RATED T+ FOR OLDER TEEN

ST ADVANCED

VIZ media

BOBOBO-BO BO-BOBO © 2001 by Yoshio Sawai/SHUEISHA Inc.

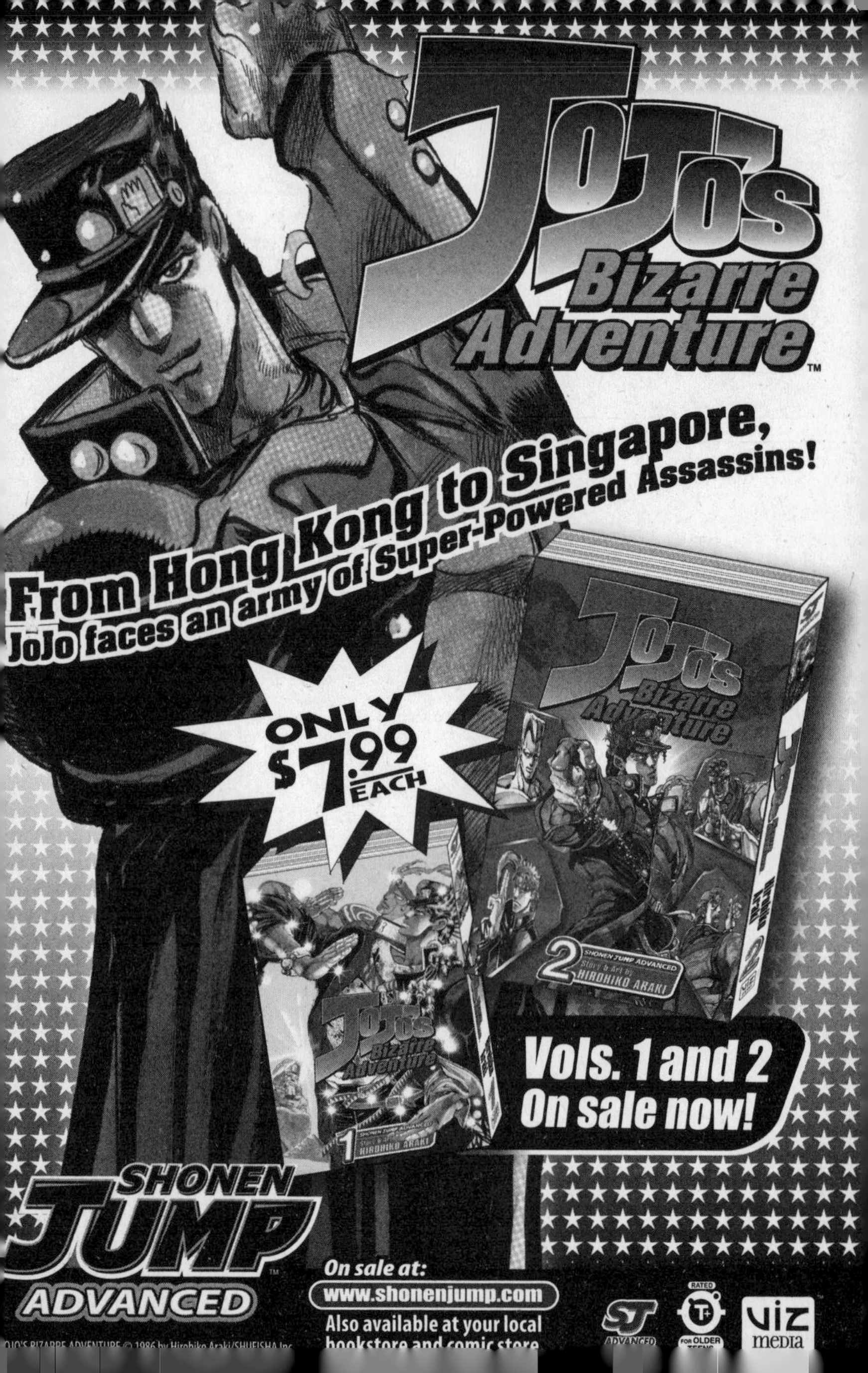

JoJo's Bizarre Adventure™
From Hong Kong to Singapore,
JoJo faces an army of Super-Powered Assassins!
ONLY $7.99 EACH
Vols. 1 and 2
On sale now!
SHONEN JUMP ADVANCED
On sale at:
www.shonenjump.com
Also available at your local
bookstore and comic store
RATED T+ FOR OLDER TEENS
viz media

FREE PREVIEW ISSUE! of SHONEN JUMP Magazine!

THE REAL ACTION STARTS IN... SHONEN JUMP
THE WORLD'S MOST POPULAR MANGA

www.shonenjump.com

SHONEN JUMP Magazine: Contains Yu-Gi-Oh!, One Piece, Naruto, Shaman King, YuYu Hakusho and other HOT manga - STORIES NEVER SEEN IN THE CARTOONS!
Plus, get the latest on what's happening in trading cards, video games, toys and more!

Check out this ultra cool magazine for FREE! Then when you decide you must have SHONE JUMP every month we will send you 11 more issues (12 in all) for only $29.95. A Price so low it's like getting 6 issues FREE!

But that's not all: You'll also become a member of the ST Sub Club wit your paid subscription!

ST SUB CLU Benefits!

Access to exclusive Sub Clu only areas of www.SHONENJUMP.cor

Your Issues Delivered First

Cool Gifts Includ With Some Issue

Get your FREE Preview Issue!

SHONEN JUMP Magazine — the blockbuster English-language version of Japan's #1 action comic book every month features 300+ pages of the hottest manga titles available in the U.S.! Plus the latest on what's happening in cards, and video games, toys and more!

YES! Send me my FREE preview issue of **SHONEN JUMP** Magazine. If I like it I will enjoy 11 more issues (12 in all) for ONLY **$29.95** That's 50% OFF the cover price!

50% OFF the cover price!

THE WORLD'S MOST POPULAR MANGA
SHONEN JUMP
www.shonenjump.com
THE REAL ACTION STARTS IN...

NAME

ADDRESS

CITY   STATE   ZIP

E-MAIL ADDRESS

☐ MY CHECK IS ENCLOSED   ☐ BILL ME LATER

Make checks payable to: SHONEN JUMP. Canada add US $12. No foreign orders. Credit card payments made SECURE & EASY at www.SHONENJUMP.com

Allow 6-8 weeks for delivery.

P5SGN1

YU-GI-OH! © 1996 by Kazuki Takahashi / SHUEISHA Inc.

Check us out
on the web!

www.shonenjump.com

NO POSTAGE
NECESSARY
IF MAILED
IN THE
UNITED STATES

BUSINESS REPLY MAIL
FIRST-CLASS MAIL   PERMIT NO. 113   MT MORRIS IL

POSTAGE WILL BE PAID BY ADDRESSEE

SUBSCRIPTIONS SERVICE DEPT.
PO BOX 509
MT. MORRIS IL 61054-7763